America's Israel

America's Israel

The US Congress and American-Israeli Relations, 1967–1975

Kenneth Kolander

Paperback edition 2022

Scholarly publisher for the Commonwealth,
serving Bellarmine University, Berea College, Centre
College of Kentucky, Eastern Kentucky University,
The Filson Historical Society, Georgetown College,
Kentucky Historical Society, Kentucky State University,
Morehead State University, Murray State University,
Northern Kentucky University, Spalding University,
Transylvania University, University of Kentucky,
University of Louisville, University of Pikeville,
and Western Kentucky University.

Editorial and Sales Offices: The University Press of Kentucky
663 South Limestone Street, Lexington, Kentucky 40508-4008
www.kentuckypress.com

Parts of chapter 2 were originally published as "Phantom Peace: Henry 'Scoop' Jackson, J. William Fulbright, and Military Sales to Israel," *Diplomatic History*, Volume 41, Issue 3, June 2017, p. 567–593.

The Library of Congress has cataloged the hardcover edition as follows:

Names: Kolander, Kenneth, 1981- author.
Title: America's Israel : the U.S. Congress and American-Israeli relations, 1967–1975 / Kenneth Kolander.
Description: Lexington : The University Press of Kentucky, 2020. | Series: Studies in conflict, diplomacy, and peace | Includes bibliographical references and index.
Identifiers: LCCN 2020013204 | ISBN 9780813179476 (hardcover) | ISBN 9780813179490 (pdf) | ISBN 9780813179506 (epub)
Subjects: LCSH: United States—Foreign relations—Israel. | Israel—Foreign relations—United States. | United States. Congress.
Classification: LCC E183.8.I7 K64 2020 | DDC 327.730569409/047—dc23

ISBN 978-0-8131-9592-6 (pbk. : alk. paper)

This book is printed on acid-free paper meeting the requirements of the American National Standard for Permanence in Paper for Printed Library Materials.

Manufactured in the United States of America

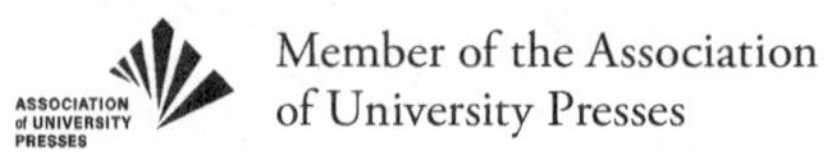

For Mom and Dad

Contents

Introduction 1

1. Johnson, Congress, and the Special Relationship: An American Commitment to the Survival of Israel 23

2. Phantom Peace: Henry "Scoop" Jackson, J. William Fulbright, and Military Sales to Israel 55

3. Stepping Forward? Congress, the Nixon Administration, and Step-by-Step Diplomacy 81

4. The Spirit of the 76: The Israeli Embassy, Congress, and President Ford's Reassessment 116

5. The Sinai II Agreements of 1975: A New Relationship 150

Conclusion: A Separate Peace 176

Acknowledgments 195

Notes 199

Bibliography 241

Index 253

Photos follow page 149

Introduction

The United States and Israel share an uneasy alliance. On the one hand, the two countries need each other. The United States provides Israel with vital military and political protection that ensures its place in the Middle East. Israel serves as a dependable and important ally for the United States in a turbulent region marked by a considerable amount of anti-Westernism. Many Americans feel a cultural connection to Israel and appreciate having a U.S. stronghold in the region. Many Israelis are deeply grateful for American help, especially given Europe's history of anti-Semitism, and dread the thought of ever losing U.S. support.

On the other hand, the two countries have divergent national interests that often lead to conflicts. American officials have criticized Israel for dealing unjustly with Arabs within and beyond its borders, and fear that Israel intends to hold onto substantial tracts of territory it took during the 1967 Arab-Israeli War. These longstanding issues complicate U.S. relations with the Arab world and weaken America's global image. Israeli officials believe that U.S. policymakers are naïve about Arab attitudes toward Israel and fear that U.S. aid and political support can be used to strongarm Israel into accommodating Arab states and nations that are bent on Israel's destruction. Quite certainly, U.S.-Israel relations have an abundance of consensus, conflict, and anxiety.

This uneasy alliance did not happen all at once, but instead grew out of a "special relationship" and a Cold War strategic alliance. The United States formed a special relationship with the State of Israel many years ago, on May 14, 1948, the day of Israel's modern founding. The special relationship, rooted in powerful cultural factors, amounts to an unshakable American commitment to ensure the survival of Israel. After the Holocaust, U.S. policymakers, along with many everyday Americans, felt a moral obligation to protect Israel. The special relationship required American political support and foreign assistance to secure Israel's permanency in the Middle East.

The two countries also developed a strategic alliance during the Cold War. Time and time again, Israeli officials told their American counterparts of Israel's strategic value in the Middle East. They could point to practical results. For example, the Israeli intelligence organization Mossad managed to flip an Iraqi pilot, Munir Redfa, who agreed to fly a Soviet MiG 21 from Iraq to Israel in August 1966. Israel eventually shared that technology with the United States, which helped American military planners, and especially U.S. pilots, to understand the capabilities of the Soviet fighter plane.[1] At the behest of the Richard Nixon administration, Israeli forces mobilized in defense of King Hussein of Jordan during Black September in 1970. Although Israel did not directly intervene in the crisis, which ended in a decisive Jordanian victory over Palestinian and Syrian forces, the move signaled to Moscow that an American ally stood ready to act, if necessary, and also demonstrated to Washington that Israel could be counted on to advance American objectives in the region.

Israeli officials emphasized Israel's strategic utility to justify the acquisition of more weapons from the United States, and to strengthen the bonds between the two countries. Some U.S. policymakers wanted Israel to become an American ally in a crucial region to contain communism, especially given the disastrous war in East Asia, which meant selling more weapons to Israel. U.S. military aid grants to Israel, which in 2019 have come to reach nearly $4 billion annually, grew out of the special relationship and, at times, served American strategic purposes. Yet one has to wonder – at what point does U.S. military aid and political protection for Israel exceed the boundaries of either a special or strategic relationship? At what point does U.S. support for Israel become excessive to the point that it undermines other U.S. interests, as well as the pursuit of peace in the Middle East?

Neither the special relationship nor a strategic alliance properly frames U.S.-Israel relations since the 1970s. Rather, the two countries share an uneasy, yet durable alliance that contains elements of a special relationship and a strategic alliance.

This alliance, which continues into our present time, came into existence between the Six-Day War in June 1967 and the Sinai II Disengagement Agreement in September 1975. A formative moment happened when the Gerald Ford administration agreed to secret executive agreements with Israel, connected to the Sinai II agreement between Israel and Egypt in 1975, which created a new foundation for U.S.-Israel relations moving forward. The United States pledged to provide for Israel's future economic and military needs and, at the same time, agreed to not force Israel to return Arab territories taken in 1967. The administration believed it needed to secure an agreement between Israel and Egypt to keep the peace process alive, to prevent the outbreak of war, and to continue drawing Egypt away from the Soviet Union. Unable to pressure Israel into going along with U.S. foreign policy, the Ford administration instead felt obligated to buy the agreement. With these open-ended and far-reaching commitments, Israel managed to get just what it wanted: virtually unlimited weaponry without American arm-twisting to give back Arab lands. In return, Israeli officials understood that the United States expected Israel's full cooperation with any security issues that might arise in the region. As numerous U.S. legislators noted at the time, these agreements represented a monumental change in U.S.-Israel relations.

A sense of uneasiness persisted between the two countries. This new arrangement severely strained U.S.-Arab relations and diminished the prospect of a regional peace, and U.S. officials continued to stress to Israel the need to address Palestinian grievances and return Arab lands. Israeli officials, for their part, continued to fear the possibility of a Palestinian state—especially one governed by the Palestine Liberation Organization (PLO) —and to worry that U.S. officials would coerce Israel into accepting that reality. These concerns would not abate but, instead, would fester.

The U.S. Congress played a key role in shaping U.S.-Israel relations during this period (as it does today) and, therefore, occupies a central place in this book. Between 1967 and 1975, the United States placed itself in the middle of Arab-Israeli peacemaking and became Israel's closest and most important supporter. Also during this period, congressional power and influence in foreign relations became unusually strong. Yet no study of U.S.-Israel relations focuses primarily on the role of Congress, which can bring together the main factors that scholars use to explain the U.S.-Israel special relationship: national-security concerns, cultural similarities (Judeo-Christian religious tradition, democracy, Western historical experience, and settler colonialism), and the importance of domestic politics, especially the activities of the Israel lobby. Congress, much more than the executive, captures the degree to which many more interests and concerns of Americans can have a voice in foreign policy. In many respects, support for Israel reflected a more democratic foreign policy. By integrating the role of Congress into the historical narrative of U.S.-Israel relations during a crucial period, this work seeks to connect popular affinity for Israel with decidedly pro-Israel positions of the U.S. government.

Traditional approaches to the study of U.S.-Israel relations have emphasized presidential policies.[2] Even in standard textbooks about U.S. foreign relations, the presidential narrative frames the discussion and tends to exclude other perspectives or angles of study.[3] (The State of Israel, by contrast, has been much more interested than scholars in the legislative branch's ability to shape U.S. foreign policy.)

The presidential narrative begins with Harry Truman's recognition of Israel only minutes after the official announcement on May 14, 1948, and scholars like Peter Hahn have pointed out that Truman's presidency, which included an arms embargo to the Middle East, was actually evenhanded, despite the administration's quick recognition of Israel.[4] U.S.-Israel relations during the Eisenhower years were marked by conflict, especially over the Suez Crisis, but as Douglas Little and Abraham Ben-Zvi have noted, a thaw in relations happened toward the end of Eisenhower's presidency.[5] The Kennedy-Johnson years are generally treated as the gradual abandonment of Eisenhower's more evenhanded policy, as two successive Democratic presidencies inched closer and closer to Israel, particularly through modest increases in military aid and weapons sales, as well as political support in the international arena, especially after the 1967 Arab-Israeli War.[6]

Scholars recognize that, in terms of military aid and political support, the 1970s were a crucial period. The Nixon and Ford years witnessed an enormous increase in U.S. military aid to Israel, and Henry Kissinger's shuttle diplomacy, as well as his pro-Israel leanings, have been well documented.[7] The narrative continues with Jimmy Carter's publicized battles with the Israel lobby over weapons sales and peace negotiations, and the peace agreement between Israel and Egypt at Camp David is seen as a watershed event.[8] The United States and Israel moved closer together in the decades that followed. Researchers continue to wait for more declassified records to detail presidential approaches to U.S.-Israel relations after Camp David.

While some scholars have explored the congressional role in U.S. foreign policymaking, particularly in response to the Vietnam War, little attention has been devoted to the Middle East.[9] Robert David Johnson avoids discussion of U.S.–Middle East relations in his outstanding study *Congress and the Cold War*.[10] Books by Mohamed Rabie and Marvin Feuerwerger have shed light on congressional influence on foreign-aid packages for the Middle East, and specifically for Israel.[11] Former State Department Middle East expert Harold Saunders has written a helpful chapter about Congress and U.S.–Middle East policy.[12] No book-length treatment has placed Congress at the center of U.S.-Israel relations, which this work attempts to do.

Basic Argument

The imbalance in the scholarly perspective about U.S.-Israel relations has created a misleading narrative that treats the legislative branch as being incidental to foreign policymaking. But in the years between the 1967 Arab-Israeli War and the 1975 Sinai II agreement, an activist Congress, empowered by the quagmire in Southeast Asia and popular distrust of the presidency, and increasingly influenced by the Israel lobby, played a central role in reworking U.S.-Israel relations, and U.S. relations with the Middle East more generally.

Congress possesses a wealth of tools to influence foreign policy. The U.S. Constitution explicitly protects the president's right to conduct foreign relations. But the Founding Fathers, fearful of the potential excesses of a tyrant, designed Congress to be the much stronger branch. Congress has the power to tax, declare war, make laws, regulate foreign commerce, and pass a yearly federal budget; Congress relies most heavily on the "power of the purse," or its budgetary powers, to influence foreign policy. Following World War II, Congress deferred to the "Imperial Presidency" in order to give the executive branch enough power and flexibility to fight the Cold War.[13] But the war in East Asia emboldened legislators to play a more active role in foreign policy. During the 1970s, Congress chipped away at excessive presidential power in an effort to restore better constitutional balance to foreign policymaking. Congress eventually cut off all funding for the Vietnam War, effectively ending the war, and also passed legislation to restrict executive power, such as the 1973 War Powers Act.

A profound shift happened during the 1970s. After peace negotiations following the 1967 Arab-Israeli War led nowhere, Washington preferred to remain mostly aloof from further peace discussions. Secretary of State William Rogers recognized the dangers of allowing the status quo to remain and tried to initiate peace talks on several occasions. But National Security Advisor Henry Kissinger continually worked to undermine his efforts, and Nixon was much more inclined to deal with Vietnam than the slow-moving peace process. The 1973 Arab-Israeli War (and oil embargo) forced the Nixon administration to play a more active role in facilitating a peace agreement. The Middle

East, largely due to the oil embargo and its effect on Western economies, came to be seen as vital to U.S. security, while East Asia faded in importance. Americans sensed their vulnerability to Middle Eastern oil as they were forced to deal with long gas lines, a recessed economy, and inflated prices on consumer goods. Bruce Schulman, Daniel Sargent, and Salim Yaqub also identify the 1970s as being a crucial period for U.S. foreign policy.[14]

Presidents gradually agreed to provide Israel with weapons so it could protect itself against Arab neighbors that continually pledged to drive it into the sea, and to prevent the spread of communism. Presidents first authorized sales to Israel using military loans, and beginning with Richard Nixon's emergency aid to Israel during the 1973 Arab-Israel War, a combination of loans and grants. Since fiscal year 1985, U.S. military aid to Israel has been exclusively military grants. But presidents also tried to balance U.S.-Israel relations with other interests in the region. The White House recognized that weapons equaled leverage and consistently tried to use the threat of withholding arms from Israel to get it to be more flexible in peace negotiations. Successive presidencies came to recognize that Israel planned to remain in much of the occupied territories and hoped to prevent a fortress mentality from developing in the minds of Israeli leaders. Moreover, the executive branch sought to avoid escalating the arms race in the Middle East and feared that overt support for Israel would compromise other security and economic interests in the region (that is, containing communism and securing access to oil).

But the presidency, crippled by Vietnam and Watergate, was at a low ebb. The United States and Israel developed a much tighter relationship just as congressional involvement in U.S. foreign policymaking reached its highest point in the Cold War.

Congress pushed back when the White House threatened to withhold weapons (or in the minds of some legislators, did not agree to sell enough weapons) and used a combination of policy initiatives and displays of public support for Israel to pressure the president to change course. Like other hotspots during the 1970s—Vietnam, Cyprus, and Angola, for example—Congress took on the White House over U.S. foreign policy in the Middle East and had its way. If the power of the presidency had remained high, the United States might not have developed such a close relationship with Israel.

The weakened White House had to bow to the gathered strength of a decidedly pro-Israel Congress, which helps to explain the sharp rise in U.S. military aid to Israel. Through 1970, annual military aid to Israel had

U.S. Assistance to Israel, FY1949–FY1985 (millions of dollars)

Year	Total	Military Loan	Military Grant	Economic Loan	Economic Grant	FFP Loan	FFP Grant
1949–1961	787	0.9	-	96	279.3	152.3	66
1962	93.4	13.2	-	45	0.4	18.5	6.8
1963	87.9	13.3	-	45	-	12.4	6
1964	37	-	-	20	-	12.2	4.8
1965	65.1	12.9	-	20	-	23.9	4.9
1966	126.8	90	-	10	-	25.9	0.9
1967	23.7	7	-	5.5	-	-	0.6
1968	106.5	25	-	-	-	51.3	0.5
1969	160.3	85	-	-	-	36.1	0.6
1970	93.6	30	-	-	-	40.7	0.4
1971	634.3	545	-	-	-	55.5	0.3
1972	430.9	300	-	-	50	53.8	0.4
1973	492.8	307.5	-	-	50	59.4	0.4
1974	2621.3	982.7	1500	-	50	-	1.5
1975	778	200	100	-	344.5	8.6	-
1976	2337.7	750	750	225	475	14.4	*
TQ	292.5	100	100	25	50	3.6	-
1977	1762.5	500	500	245	490	7	-
1978	1822.6	500	500	260	525	6.8	-
1979	4888	2700	1300	260	525	5.1	-
1980	2121	500	500	260	525	1	-
1981	2413.4	900	500	-	764	-	-
1982	2250.5	850	550	-	806	-	-
1983	2505.6	950	750	-	785	-	-
1984	2631.6	850	850	-	910	-	-
1985	3376.7	-	1400	-	1950	-	-

Table: FFP means Food for Peace. TQ means "Transition Quarter." In 1976, the U.S. federal fiscal calendar changed. Prior to 1976, the fiscal year ended on June 30. But beginning in 1976, the fiscal year ended on September 30. Therefore, TQ refers to the total amount of U.S. aid to Israel between July 1 and September 30, 1976. The amount of the 1976 FFP Grant, represented by *, refers to less than $50,000. There are additional loans and grants that impact the total amount not included in this table: Export-Import Bank Loans, Jewish Refugee Resettlement Grants, American Schools and Hospitals Grants, Cooperative Development Grants, a $20 million grant in 1975 for a seawater desalting plant, and a $17.5 million CCC loan in 1982. (Clyde R. Mark, "Israel: U.S. Foreign Assistance," April 26, 2005, Congressional Research Service, The Library of Congress, *CRS Issue Brief for Congress,* received through the CRS Web, 13.)

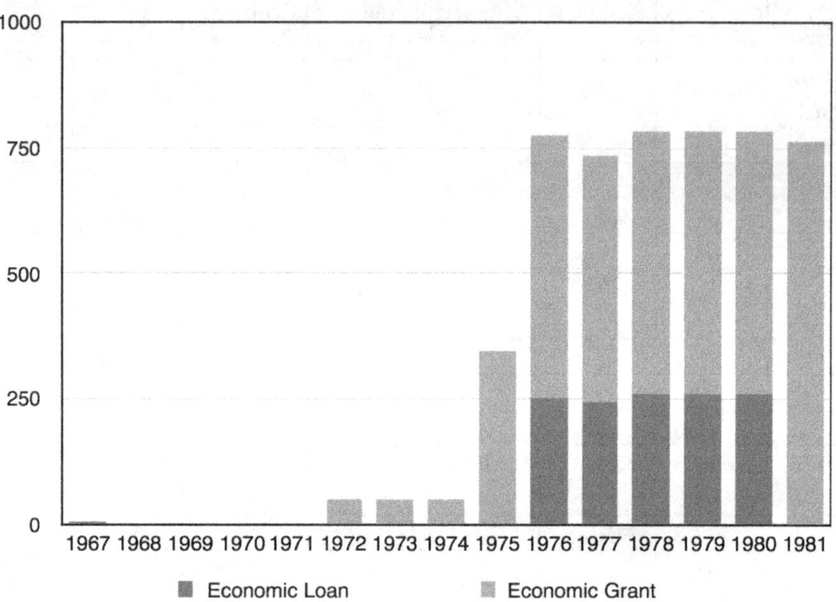

Graph 1: The Sinai II agreement, which included open-ended and far-reaching secret executive agreements between the United States and Israel, led to the establishment of a much higher annual baseline of U.S. economic support, which is reflected in the total for 1976. A transition quarter existed between July 1 and September 30, 1976, when the U.S. government adjusted the fiscal calendar, and that has been added to the total for 1976, which makes the amount seem a bit higher than it actually was since it includes three extra months. The amount of economic assistance for the transition quarter was $25 million in loans and $50 million in grants. (Clyde R. Mark, "Israel: U.S. Foreign Assistance," April 26, 2005, Congressional Research Service, The Library of Congress, *CRS Issue Brief for Congress,* Received through the CRS Web, 13.)

not exceeded $90 million. But in 1971, spurred by Sen. Henry "Scoop" Jackson's amendment to the Defense Procurement Act, the number jumped to $545 million. After the secret executive agreements in 1975, annual military aid to Israel reached $1 billion and has not dipped below that mark ever since. Military aid gradually increased to an annual level of $1.8 billion during the Reagan years and then remained steady through the end of the 1990s. But during the 2000s the number gradually increased again and moved up to $3 billion annually. According to a June 2015 Congressional Research Service report, "Israel is the largest cumulative recipient of U.S. foreign

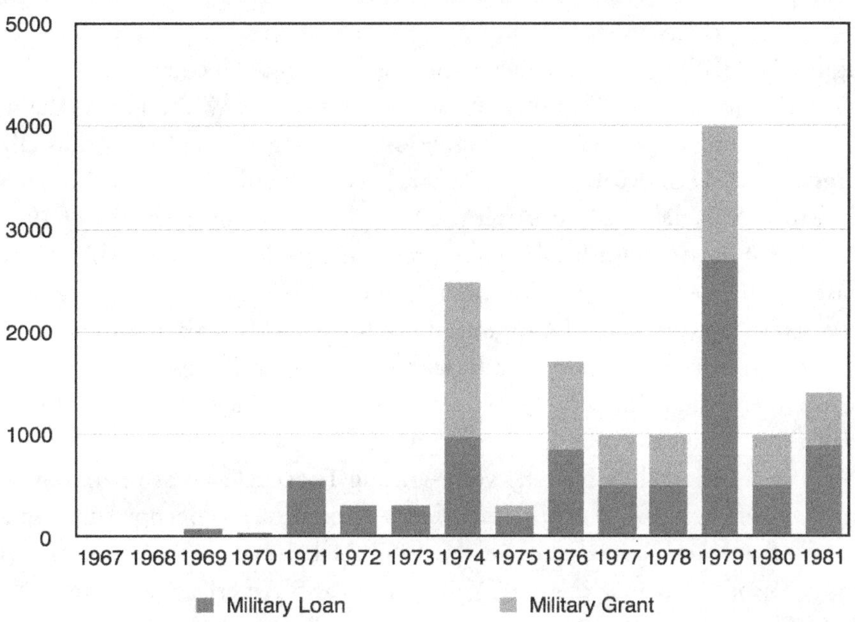

Graph 2: The Sinai II agreement, which included open-ended and far-reaching secret executive agreements between the United States and Israel, led to the establishment of a much higher annual baseline of U.S. military support, which is reflected in the total for 1976. The noticeably larger amounts of military aid were for the 1973 emergency airlift and the Camp David Accords. A transition quarter existed between July 1 and September 30, 1976, when the U.S. government adjusted the fiscal calendar, and that has been added to the total for 1976, which makes the amount seem a bit higher than it actually was since it includes three extra months. The amount of military assistance for the transition quarter was $100 million in loans and $100 million in grants. Since 1976, U.S. military aid to Israel has not dipped below $1 billion annually. (Clyde R. Mark, "Israel: U.S. Foreign Assistance," April 26, 2005, Congressional Research Service, The Library of Congress, *CRS Issue Brief for Congress,* Received through the CRS Web, 13.)

assistance since World War II," with a total that exceeded $125 billion.[15] In September 2016, the United States and Israel agreed to a new ten-year, $38 billion military-aid package, along with an American insistence that Israel use the grants to purchase U.S.-made products and services.[16]

Thus, the present work aims to transform the traditional narrative. Relying on a broad collection of sources, including the *Congressional Record,* presidential libraries, the *Foreign Relations of the United States* (*FRUS*), personal papers of former legislators, the Center for Legislative Archives at the U.S. National Archives, and the Israel State Archives, I argue that U.S. foreign policy with respect to Israel by no means followed a course preferred by successive presidential administrations. An embattled White House due to Watergate and Vietnam created a situation for Congress to play an unusually large role in U.S.–Middle East relations, which resulted in a fundamental shift in U.S.-Israel relations. After the Sinai II agreement in the fall of 1975, the United States committed itself to preserving its dominance in the Middle East at the expense of the Palestinians and other Arab grievances in order to keep Israel powerful and Egypt out of the Soviet orbit. Taking Egypt out of the war with Israel ensured decades of peace between the two countries and further cemented the U.S.-Egypt relationship. But since then, annual military aid to Israel has increased substantially, while peace efforts have ebbed much more than they have flowed. Arming Israel regardless of movement in the peace process has empowered Israel to continue to occupy substantial tracts of the Arab lands taken in the 1967 Arab-Israeli War, which in turn has contributed to an ever-growing amount of anti-Americanism in the Middle East, and other regions as well. The U.S.-Israel relationship that most people recognize today, which includes enormous amounts of U.S. military aid to Israel, a powerful strategic alliance, and an American willingness to acquiesce to Israeli occupation of certain Arab territories taken in 1967, came into existence between 1967 and 1975, particularly with the transformative executive agreements in 1975.

Congress and the Israel Lobby

In the case of Israel, Congress takes on an even more significant role in shaping U.S. policy because of the Israel lobby. John Mearsheimer and Stephen Walt, in *The Israeli Lobby and U.S. Foreign Policy,* describe the Israel lobby as being "a loose coalition of individuals and organizations that actively works to move U.S. foreign policy in a pro-Israel direction."[17] Mearsheimer and Walt argue that the Israel lobby, especially since the end of the Cold War, has been the most important factor influencing U.S.–Middle East policy.[18] Regarding the lobby's influence on U.S. foreign policy, two particular organizations deserve mention. The Conference of Presidents of Major American Jewish Organizations (Conference of Presidents) meets with executive-branch officials and foreign dignitaries to discuss policy issues and put forward a particular position (and had no Arab counterpart until 1972), while the American Israel Public Affairs Committee (AIPAC) primarily lobbies Congress. These two organizations "funnel the bulk of articulate Jewish opinion on policy issues to governmental decision-makers" and thereby influence U.S. foreign policy on a level rivaled by few, if any, countries.[19] While not a monolithic organization, according to Mearsheimer and Walt, the lobby "is simply a powerful interest group, made up of both Jews and gentiles, whose acknowledged purpose is to press Israel's case within the United States and influence American foreign policy in ways that its members believe will benefit the Jewish state."[20] During the 1960s the Israel lobby had already established itself as one of the most powerful lobbying groups in the United States.[21]

The president typically prefers to conduct foreign relations with little input from Congress and out of view of the American public. But the Israel lobby and Israeli officials have convinced many legislators to resist presidential initiatives if they are deemed disadvantageous to Israel. Congressional speeches on the House and Senate floors, statements from congressional offices, and even legislation often bear the imprint of AIPAC. When a U.S. official makes a public statement—regardless of who actually authored the statement—that position becomes legitimized in American political discourse. This dynamic forces the president to publicly contend with an Israeli position effectively channeled through Congress. Moreover, as Steven Spiegel notes, Israel's advocates in the United States can "solicit support in Congress and from friends in the Pentagon appealing directly to the president over the heads of State Department and Defense Department opponents."[22] William Fulbright (D-AR), who served as chair of the Senate Foreign Relations Committee from 1959 to 1975, complained in 1973, "The Israelis can count on 75 to 80 votes 'on anything . . . (they) are interested in in the Senate.'" I. L. "Si" Kenen, then head of AIPAC, confirmed Fulbright's observation: "I rarely go to the Hill. There is so much support for Israel that I don't have to."[23] In addition to contacts with legislators, Kenen admitted that Jewish campaign contributions "play a very real part" in congressional support for Israel.[24]

The American political system is extraordinarily open to influence, and the degree to which it can be penetrated by foreign lobbyists and others representing foreign governments is something that must be understood and not just condemned. Stephen Walt, in an April 2019 article in *Foreign Policy,* makes a similar case. Walt argues "for a more hardheaded, cynical, and realistic approach to the influence that foreigners invariably seek to exercise over U.S. foreign policy. As long as the U.S. political system is so permeable, it behooves Americans to treat foreign efforts to shape their thinking with due discretion."[25] The Israel lobby is strong because for the most part, though not always, it pushes against an open door. There is so much public support and sympathy for Israel that it does not face a great deal of difficulty in convincing legislators to vote its way. While all of the major Arab governments have their lobbyists in Washington, it has taken them a lot longer to learn the game, and they often have a much harder case to sell. However, both Anwar Sadat of Egypt and King Hussein of Jordan proved very effective in generating American sympathy and support. Ultimately, lobbyists and foreign governments recognize that the U.S. Congress can play a very important role in shaping U.S. foreign policy.

Bipartisan Support for Israel

The Israel lobby undoubtedly affects U.S. policy, but overemphasis on the lobby itself can diminish the importance of U.S. popular affinity for Israel. The lobby's ability to influence U.S. policy, to some extent, is rooted in bipartisan American support for Israel. Indeed, any study of Congress's influence on U.S.-Israel relations must recognize overwhelming legislative support for Israel and thereby affirm the solid foundation of the special relationship. While the present book is not about popular support for Israel, it implies that support through an analysis of Congress's influence on U.S. foreign policy.

Many congressional members are happy to boldly, loudly, and publicly back an ally like Israel, and in some cases this support can swing a congressional election. Since many everyday Americans feel a connection to Israel, and for a variety of reasons, it befits legislators to adopt pro-Israel positions, either to represent their constituencies or to have a talking point for the next election, and perhaps both. The U.S. president can serve only two terms, but legislators can serve an unlimited number of terms and generally seek to advance policies that can lead to reelection. For legislators, the line between personal interest and the national interest, unfortunately, does not always appear very clear. It must be noted that legislators use Israel as much as the Israel lobby uses legislators; the political game is played by all parties involved.

In the context of U.S. domestic politics, broadly speaking, Americans more closely identify with Jews and the State of Israel than with Arabs and Arab states and nations in the Middle East. This understandably leads to preferential treatment for Israel vis-à-vis its Arab neighbors. The Israel lobby exerts significant influence on U.S. policy, but its ability to do so stems from popular affinity for Israel and manifests itself in the branch of government meant to represent popular opinion—the legislature. And congressional support for Israel is nothing new. Congress promoted the Zionist movement before Israel's declared statehood. Resolutions in 1922 and 1944 endorsed the Balfour Declaration, while the pro-Zionist American Palestine Committee, founded in 1932 and revived in 1941, included the membership of more than two hundred congresspeople.[26] Many legislators became ardent supporters of Israel after its declared existence in May 1948.

Prior to the Cold War, the United States (similar to Europe) harbored a significant amount of anti-Semitism. But after the horrors of concentration camps became widely known, many Americans reconfigured their ideas about Jews. Cultural representations reflected this evolution of thought. In *Eye on Israel,* Michelle Mart includes a multitude of examples from American newspapers, magazines, fictional stories, and motion pictures to show that by the 1950s, American Jews occupied a much more respectable position than ever before.[27] Rather than depicting Jews as weak victims, cultural products refashioned Jews as masculine and strong. Israelis were also seen as pragmatic and individualistic—characteristics prized by Americans. Images linked Israelis to the pioneers of the American West. They were people who could tame the desert wilderness and transform a backward region into a forward-thinking, modern state. Surrounded by Eastern Arabs, Israel was seen as a "gutsy underdog," like the undersized David slaying the mammoth Goliath.[28] Americans started to see cultural similarities, rather than differences, and even came to admire Israel for its accomplishments, which contributed to acceptance of Israel as an ally. Mart shows that popular culture impacted public opinion and forces one to consider the cultural and intellectual side to U.S.-Israel relations, rather than viewing it as simply a political-strategic relationship.[29]

Many Americans feel a cultural closeness to Israel, and during the Cold War this translated into bipartisan political support for Israel. Beginning with the Truman administration, the Cold War consensus called for both Democrats and Republicans to advance an anti-communist foreign policy. This meant that Israel, a Western, democratic, noncommunist state, received American backing within a region perceived to be Eastern, or Oriental. Gradually, Americans started to view Israel as a crucial ally in the fight against the Soviet Union for global supremacy, and therein culture and Cold War politics overlapped.

The Democratic Party more quickly embraced the State of Israel than the Republican Party, though Republican support for Israel would accelerate during the late 1960s and 1970s. Support for labor, at one point a primary concern of the Democratic Party, inspired some Americans to offer assistance to Israel, which between 1948 and 1977 was governed by a labor-dominated coalition of political parties. Labor leaders emphasized their anti-communist position by arguing that Israel could serve as a Cold War ally, situated to the right of communism but also acceptably to the left of laissez-faire capitalism.

The Democratic Party also promoted civil liberties. Like African Americans, Jewish Americans experienced virulent prejudice from many racist Americans and, following World War II, helped to advance the Civil Rights Movement. (For instance, two Jewish activists and one black activist were murdered in Mississippi during the Freedom Summer of 1964, which formed the basis of the movie *Mississippi Burning*.) However, the relationship soured by the end of the 1960s. The Nation of Islam and the Black Power movement were often very critical of Zionism and what was perceived to be Israeli imperialism during and after the 1967 war, which contributed to a split between the two groups. The New Left in the United States also became critical of Israeli occupation of Palestinian lands and Israeli treatment of Palestinians in occupied territories, despite the presence of many Jewish leaders and rank-and-file members in the movement. Nevertheless, liberal Democratic support for Israel remained strong, and still today, the majority of Jewish Americans lean to the political left.

States with large urban populations have proven to be another Democratic Party ally of Israel. Major American cities, such as New York, Boston, Atlanta, Chicago, Denver, and Los Angeles, contain large numbers of Jewish Americans, with many who vote and actively participate in, and contribute to, political campaigns. Therefore, it behooves legislators from these states to demonstrate that they are responsive to concerns regarding the State of Israel.

Slowly during the Cold War, the interests of Israel and the Republican Party started to align. The Cold War consensus ended with Vietnam, and while liberals tried to reduce defense spending and focus on human rights, some Republicans, conservative Democrats, and Cold War hawks aimed to continue containment. Many conservatives disagreed with détente, which meant a relaxing of tensions with the Soviet Union, and started to view Israel as a powerful ally that could help America continue its global war against communism. Israeli military victories seemed even more impressive (and important) when juxtaposed alongside the quagmire in East Asia.

An emerging neoconservative doctrine added another layer of support for Israel. Some Cold War liberals grew disenchanted with the counterculture of the 1960s and with a liberal foreign policy that was regarded as too willing to give ground to communist forces, especially in light of the perceived weakening of American resolve due to Vietnam. Neoconservatism was driven by the writings of Jewish American intellectuals like Irving Kristol and Norman Podhoretz, and especially by the monthly magazine *Commentary.* Neoconservatives countered the increasingly anti-Israel New Left by pushing for a more assertive foreign policy based on American military might. As some Americans questioned the logic of U.S. internationalism and the employment of force without meaningful diplomacy, neoconservatives feared that liberals were naïve and that the United States might become more isolationist, which would lead to the spread of communism. Neoconservatives, therefore, advocated for a more vigorous defense policy that required a well-armed Israel.

Larger defense contracts for U.S. allies abroad, such as Israel, satisfied the needs of certain constituencies that relied on such contracts for federally subsidized employment. In 1968, Lockheed made 88 percent of its sales to the federal government; McDonnell Douglas, 75 percent; General Dynamics, 67 percent; Grumman, 67 percent; Martin-Marietta, 62 percent; and Boeing, 54 percent.[30] As the U.S. economy faltered in the 1970s, Congress had an incentive to subsidize the weapons industry, since weapons manufacturing was a source of high-paying, skilled-labor jobs in many congressional districts. Even as defense spending dipped in the middle of the 1970s, foreign military sales to the Middle East reached new heights. While many U.S.-made products suffered from international competition, U.S.-made weaponry was generally regarded as the most technologically advanced in the world. Beyond their deadly effectiveness, American weapons represented an important item of trade. U.S.-made weapons found many different homes during the Cold War (and after), with Israel being an important one. The United States has used defense and finance agreements to empower friendly regimes and open the door for more U.S. products and capital, all while providing jobs for Americans. Few countries could absorb and use American weaponry like Israel. Naturally, legislators from states with large defense industries have been some of the most vocal supporters of weapons sales to Israel. Although

Dwight Eisenhower warned against a military-industrial complex, military power was deemed crucial in the fight against communism.

Of all the cultural factors that undergird the U.S.-Israel special relationship, religion is probably the strongest.[31] A reversal of anti-Semitism paved the way for the development of a Judeo-Christian relationship. In Western history, some of the most violent oppressors of Jews have been Christians. But the declaration of the State of Israel inspired many conservative Christians, especially evangelicals and fundamentalists, to advocate for Israel for purely religious reasons. (That support, however, would slowly seep into the political sphere as well.) These Christians emphasized the Judaic foundation of Christianity and rationalized support for Israel based on Genesis 12:3, when GOD told Abraham, "I will bless those who bless you, and whoever curses you I will curse; and all peoples on earth will be blessed through you."[32] For some Christians, literal interpretations of the Word view the modern State of Israel as a necessary precursor to the return of Christ. According to premillennial eschatology, Jews must occupy the Holy Land prior to Christ's return to the Mount of Olives. But with the return of Christ comes the Rapture, a cataclysm for all Jews who will be paid back for their sins against Christ. Thus, Jews must occupy the Holy Land only for Christ to smite the Jews. Despite this dubious reasoning, American Christian Zionist support for Israel has proven to be substantial and impacts the voting behaviors of many Americans.

Christian Zionist sympathies became more pronounced after the 1967 Six-Day War, which enlarged the State of Israel and unified Jerusalem under Jewish control, and found more focused political expression in the late 1970s and early 1980s through the efforts of Ronald Reagan, Jerry Falwell, and Pat Robertson. In the process, evangelicals and fundamentalists started to back hardline positions regarding Israeli occupation of Arab lands, as opposed to Catholics and liberal Protestants, who did not. In that way, political geography took on added importance during the Cold War. As the New Deal coalition dissolved in the midst of the Vietnam War and the Civil Rights Movement, Richard Nixon's "southern strategy" split the South away from the Democratic Party. From 1968 moving forward, many Southerners—including Southern Baptists and other evangelicals—would become allied with the Republican Party. Although in previous years anti-Semitism had found fertile ground in the American South, after the Six-Day War and Nixon's southern strategy, support for Israel gradually became religiously and politically right.

Thus, the U.S.-Israel special relationship is rooted in Western ideals of political liberalism, support for labor (particularly in urban areas), religion and other cultural values, along with defense spending and conservative and neoconservative ideas of projecting power and advancing liberal democracy abroad. Also important, Israeli officials, the Israel lobby, and some religious Jews have worked to cultivate bipartisan support for the State of Israel within the United States. When viewed through this lens, congressional support for Israel, as well as the effectiveness of the Israel lobby, becomes much more understandable.

By contrast, Americans by-and-large do not feel any strong attachment to Arabs. This stems mostly from the absence of such cultural, social, and political factors as undergird Americans' more positive views of Israel. Jewish settlers from Europe (Ashkenazi) laid the foundations of the State of Israel and did so with Western ideas of nationalism, secularism, and social democracy. When Israel emerged as a state in 1948, Arab states were just coming out from under the thumb of European colonialism, in particular, the League of Nations mandate system. Arab societies largely resented the West for denying them basic independence and political liberties and proved reluctant to adopt Western models of political and economic development. Moreover, while Ashkenazi settlers brought with them many centuries of Westernization, no such demographic existed within the Arab world. Simply put, Arab societies lacked a Western tradition while the political body of Israel was steeped in that tradition. When the Cold War divided the globe into West versus East, Israel fit nicely into the American mindset, and Arabs did not.

Many Americans consider Arabs to be the "other," culturally different and unappealing. In *Orientalism,* Edward Said analyzed European othering of the Orient, and while the United States followed a different trajectory than that of Britain or France, Americans still developed similar ideas of cultural difference.[33] Douglas Little, while less interested in the literary and linguistic underpinnings of Orientalism, uses the concept as a way to explain U.S.-Middle East relations since 1945.[34] Melani McAllister devotes more attention to cultural representations and theory when analyzing Americans' distrust of, and dislike for, Arabs.[35]

Demographics naturally favor U.S.-Israel relations more than U.S.-Arab relations. Arab Americans comprise a much smaller percentage of the U.S.

population than Jewish Americans and, therefore, attract much less attention from U.S. politicians. In terms of campaigns and reelections, backing an Arab position vis-à-vis one promoted by American Jews or the State of Israel brings with it very real political risks. Moreover, a sophisticated Arab lobby developed later and more slowly than the Israel lobby, particularly after the formation of the National Association of Arab Americans (NAAA) in 1972 and following the 1973 Arab-Israeli War.[36] In relation to the Israel lobby, the Arab lobby lacked cohesion and organization. By comparison, Arab interests suffered while Jewish interests, persuasively articulated through private meetings with U.S. officials and publications like the *Near East Report,* a lobbying newsletter of AIPAC, gained more traction in American political discourse.

Despite little understanding of the Arab world, as Salim Yaqub notes, during the 1970s "Americans and Arabs came to know each other as never before."[37] Certain events necessitated greater awareness, such as the 1973 oil embargo, U.S. mediation of the Arab-Israeli peace process, expansion of trade with Arab states, international terrorism, an infusion of "petrodollars," and an increase of Arab immigration to the United States.[38] Greater familiarity generated both increased tension and increased understanding. Gradually, due to Arab American activism, an Arab perspective received greater attention in the American media and academia. While many cultural representations "continued to rely on hostile portrayals of the Arab world," this actually encouraged Arab Americans to develop more sophisticated means for challenging such representations, which persuaded some "popular media outlets to soften their anti-Arab caricatures."[39] The events of the 1970s brought "Americans and Arabs into unprecedented proximity with one another. This growing intimacy encouraged attitudes of animosity and acceptance that would characterize U.S.-Arab relations in subsequent decades and, indeed, persist into our own era."[40]

At the same time, Yaqub emphasizes the growing rift in U.S.-Arab foreign relations during the 1970s and cites Henry Kissinger's diplomacy as the main reason for that rift.[41] According to Yaqub, Kissinger's diplomacy after the 1973 war aimed to shield Israel from having to leave the territories taken in 1967, which led to the downfall of the peace process. Yaqub makes a valid point. Kissinger did in fact aim to shield Israel from external pressures. However, while Kissinger tried to protect Israel from being forced to vacate the occupied territories, on numerous occasions he counseled Israeli officials to use the opportunity to secure bilateral peace agreements with Arab states in return for the territories, which would normalize Israel's position in the Middle East. Kissinger, like the presidents between 1967 and 1975, recognized the importance of improved U.S.-Arab foreign relations in order to protect and advance both the American and Israeli national interests. Additionally, while impossible to substantiate using documented evidence, one has to imagine that Henry Kissinger, who prized his Jewish ancestry, hoped to be the diplomat who managed to negotiate lasting peace agreements for Israel. The challenge for Kissinger was in finding a way to secure such agreements without having to force Israel to go along. Kissinger proved unable to do so, and his efforts, like those of the presidents he served, brought him into conflict with Congress and the Israel lobby.

In sum, domestic politics, as much as foreign politics, inspired congressional support for Israel. That support fit within an American cultural preference for Israel, as well as Cold War geopolitics rooted in an us versus them mentality.

Chapter Outline

The present book unfolds in the following manner. Using research from the Lyndon Johnson Presidential Library, *FRUS,* and the *Congressional Record,* the first chapter explores U.S.-Israel relations during Lyndon Johnson's presidency. In 1967, provocative moves made by Egyptian President Gamal Abdel Nasser and an Israeli first strike plunged the region into war. Legislators took to the House and Senate floors to proclaim the essence of the special relationship—an unwavering American commitment to ensure Israel's survival. In the aftermath of the war, the Johnson administration decided to abandon existing U.S. policy regarding territorial integrity in the Middle East and support Israeli occupation of Arab lands in order to pressure Arab states to finally recognize Israel and make peace with it. The Johnson administration, like the administrations before it, could not solve the riddle of Arab-Israeli conflict and regarded the war as an opportunity to pursue a different path. The decision to not push Israel out of the territories, as well as an increase in weapons sales to Israel, were both justified by the American commitment to Israel's survival and had a lasting impact on U.S. relations with the Middle East.

The themes of national security and domestic politics intersect in the second chapter. Based on the papers of Henry "Scoop" Jackson and J. William

Fulbright, the chapter uses the conflict between the two Democratic senators to show how the growing Soviet presence in the Middle East, combined with the deteriorating situation in Southeast Asia in the late 1960s and early 1970s, brought about a major upheaval within the Democratic Party as well as a rise in conservative support for Israel from the halls of Congress. A discussion about the Jackson-Fulbright conflict encourages broader thinking about congressional participation in U.S. foreign policy in the Middle East and also exposes significant political fault lines that would complicate the making of U.S. policy toward Israel for years to come. The United States and Israel developed a strategic alliance during this period, in addition to the special relationship, which involved a sizable increase in weapons sales from the United States to Israel.

The third chapter, based on research from the Richard Nixon Presidential Library, *FRUS,* and the *Congressional Record,* explores congressional reactions to Nixon's request for $2.2 billion in emergency military aid for Israel, as well as U.S. involvement in the peace process. Despite objections from Fulbright and several other legislators, along with the Nixon administration's lack of effort to justify such a massive aid package, Congress passed the emergency aid bill in full. Enough legislators successfully argued that Israel needed the immense amount of aid in order to feel strong enough to take risks in peace negotiations. But by May 1974, fearful that Israel felt too strong, the Nixon administration started to threaten to cut off all military aid to soften Israel's position in peace negotiations. The fall of Nixon due to Watergate sapped the power of the White House at precisely the moment when a strong president was needed to advance such an ambitious program of U.S. peace diplomacy. Also important, Kissinger had to work against pro-Israel elements that sought to scuttle his gradual approach to a comprehensive peace.

The increasing influence of pro-Israel lobbying groups is a central theme of the entire book, and especially the fourth chapter. Research from the Israel State Archives in Jerusalem shows that the Israeli embassy in Washington, D.C. proved very able to influence U.S. policymaking during Ford's reassessment of U.S.–Middle East policy in 1975, which included a freeze on military aid to Israel. In particular, the chapter reveals the efforts made by Israeli officials and pro-Israel lobbyists to secure a Senate letter to President Ford, signed by seventy-six senators in May 1975, that called for the resumption of military aid to Israel; otherwise, the senators insinuated that the upper chamber would kill Ford's upcoming foreign-aid request. In effect, the president could not withhold weapons to pressure Israel into returning territory. Unlike the work by Mearsheimer and Walt, this chapter exhibits the actual dimensions—the extents and limits—of Israeli influence on U.S. foreign policy. The chapter reveals, in full and granular detail, how a foreign government is able to work within the American political system to influence foreign policy. Along with other scholars in the field of U.S.–Middle East relations, like Yaqub, Roham Alvandi, and Paul Chamberlin, this work demonstrates how Middle Eastern nations, in particular Israel, can influence U.S. policy.[42] While these scholars assess influence on the White House and State Department, this book, which is different in detail and evidence, investigates Israeli influence through Congress.

The fifth and final chapter examines the controversial executive agreements connected to Sinai II, concluded in September 1975, in the context of a congressional effort to restrict the broad use of such agreements. In order to make Sinai II acceptable to both Israel and Egypt (and to avoid another war and oil embargo), the United States entered into a series of commitments that signaled a new stage in U.S.-Israel relations. The agreements, made in secret and central to Sinai II, committed the United States to providing for Israel's military and economic security and pledged to not advance any steps in the peace process without Israel's approval. Numerous legislators argued that the secret agreements marked a dramatic and questionable shift in U.S.-Israel relations and that they resembled treaties, which required Senate approval. Based on research from the *Congressional Record,* Center for Legislative Archives at the National Archives in Washington, D.C., and congressional hearing reports, the chapter shows that legislators felt handcuffed by Sinai II. They felt obligated to pass a resolution to allow for U.S. technicians to man an early-warning station in the Sinai Peninsula in order to preserve the agreement between Israel and Egypt and thereby prevent another war. After wars involving Israel and Egypt in 1956, 1967, 1969–1970, and 1973, another war seemed quite possible to U.S. officials. But by passing the resolution, Congress also authorized, by what Senator Joe Biden (D-DE) called "backdoor" approval, the secret agreements that committed the United States to providing for the future economic, military, and energy needs of Israel, regardless of Israel's willingness to adhere to the spirit of U.N. Resolution 242.

The May 1975 Senate letter forced the Ford administration to quit threatening to withhold military aid from Israel and instead buy the Sinai II agreement. But in order to preserve the agreement between Israel and Egypt,

Kissinger's diplomacy, in turn, forced Congress to approve of U.S. technicians and, by extension, of the secret and open-ended executive agreements with Israel. Neither U.S. presidents nor Congress wanted to advance U.S.-Israel relations to such an extreme but did so to prevent another war in the Middle East, which threatened to bring with it another oil embargo and possibly superpower confrontation, and to draw Egypt away from the Soviet Union. The United States developed an uneasy alliance with Israel, not by intent, but out of desperation.

1

Johnson, Congress, and the Special Relationship

An American Commitment to the Survival of Israel

An American commitment to the survival of Israel became evident before and during the Six-Day War in June 1967. For the first time after the Holocaust, Jews in Israel felt genuinely afraid of being overrun.[1] Arab leaders, particularly Egyptian President Gamal Abdel Nasser, refused to recognize Israel and continually threatened to destroy it or to drive it into the sea. Nasser aimed to generate popular support through bombastic rhetoric and likely did not really believe Egypt—or any collection of Arab forces—could, or would, destroy Israel. But threats to exterminate Israel could not be ignored. Israel also contributed to the rising tensions in the region with its attack on Samu, a Jordanian village, in November 1966, and needless provocations with Syria, which led to an air battle in April 1967.

While the threats against Israel added to Nasser's popular appeal in the Arab world, they encouraged American support for Israel just as much. As events moved toward war, U.S. legislators took to the House and Senate floors and collectively declared an uncompromising commitment to protecting Israel. After the war, the United States supported Israel's decision to remain in the occupied territories (Sinai Peninsula, Gaza Strip, West Bank, Golan Heights, and East Jerusalem) until Arab states agreed to make peace with Israel. That decision, which would guide U.S. policy for decades to follow, was originally rooted in an American commitment to securing the safety of Israel.

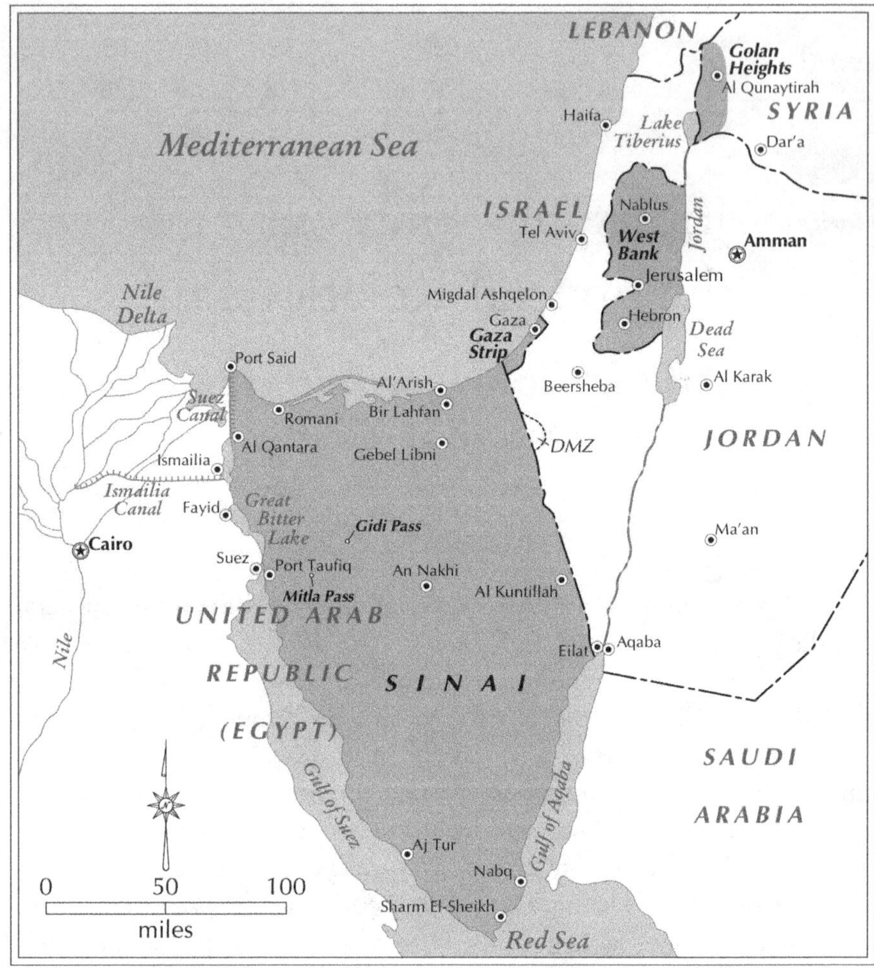

Map: After the Six-Day War, Israel occupied the West Bank, Gaza, Golan Heights, Sinai Peninsula, and East Jerusalem. The Johnson administration initiated land-for-peace diplomacy, whereby Israel would give back Arab lands in return for peace agreements.

Lyndon Johnson felt a strong affection for the State of Israel, but like the presidents before him, he aimed to pursue an evenhanded policy in the Middle East. He often refused Israeli requests for weapons in order to stave off an arms race with the Soviet Union. Unable to prevent an arms race, Johnson tried to avoid selling weapons disproportionally in the region, to support American claims to evenhandedness. Despite his efforts, Johnson became the first U.S. president to sell offensive weapons to Israel. Nevertheless, Johnson's decisions should be considered within the context of a desire to balance weapons sales between Israel and moderate Arab states and to limit such sales altogether. As Zach Levey has argued, Johnson wanted to avoid entering into a strategic relationship with Israel.[2] Israel, for its part, wanted to expand a special relationship into a strategic alliance built on military aid. Walter Hixson has ably demonstrated that the Israel lobby played an important role in pressuring Johnson into adopting a decidedly pro-Israel position.[3]

The U.S. Congress emerged as a vocal branch of dissent to Johnson's foreign policy with Israel and, in particular, to his reluctance to sell weapons to Israel. Legislators forced Johnson to publicly contend with the issue of weapons sales to Israel by using legislation (binding and nonbinding), letters, speeches, and official statements to criticize the president's unwillingness to better arm Israel. These efforts laid a foundation for an ongoing critique of presidential foreign policy in the region that contributed to a dramatic increase of weapons sales. Congress legitimized dissent of presidential foreign policymaking in both East Asia and the Middle East during Johnson's presidency and in that way affected presidential decision-making in both regions.

Several scholars have analyzed U.S.-Israel relations during Johnson's presidency; however, no work situates U.S.-Israel relations within the context of increased congressional activity in foreign policy during the LBJ years in order to explore how a Vietnam War–era Congress impacted the U.S.-Israel special relationship.[4] This chapter attempts to fill that void.

U.S. Weapons Sales to Israel prior to the 1967 War

The persistent instability in the Middle East, which stemmed in part from the ongoing Arab-Israeli conflict, worsened during Lyndon Johnson's presidency and brought about more U.S. involvement in the region. The 1948–1949 Arab-Israeli War was a War for Independence for Jews, who administered the newly declared State of Israel, but a catastrophe (*nakba*) for the stateless Palestinian Arabs, who did not receive the allotment of land designated by the U.N. General Assembly in November 1947. Approximately 700,000 Arabs either fled or were forced from their homes during the 1948–1949 war, which started the Palestinian refugee crisis. Border conflicts persisted throughout the 1950s, and conditions grew worse during the 1960s. Tensions arose between

Syria and Israel over water rights to the headwaters of the Jordan River, with escalations in 1964 and 1965.[5] The Palestine Liberation Organization (PLO), created in 1964, declared its central goal to be the destruction of the State of Israel. Yasser Arafat, the leader of Fatah (the largest and most important member organization of the PLO), continued his instigation of terrorist attacks against Israel.[6] The PLO found more support for a war against Israel after a Syrian revolution brought the Baathist Party to power in 1966, supported by the Soviet Union. Many PLO attacks against Israel came from Syrian territory, with vocal Soviet encouragement for the Arab "progressive revolutionary" front.[7] Terrorist attacks against Israel spiked in 1966 and 1967, and Israel often responded with disproportional force, which created hostile conditions that contributed to the outbreak of war in June 1967.

The Middle East did not figure prominently in Johnson's foreign policy. He was a known "friend of Israel" from his days in the Congress, but the Vietnam War, beyond all other matters, dominated Johnson's presidency. The former Senate majority leader from Texas preferred to focus on domestic issues, and particularly the Great Society, a New Deal–inspired program that aimed to eliminate poverty and promote civil rights. But advancements on the domestic front were undercut by the worsening war in East Asia. To make matters worse, the combination of a costly war with an overly ambitious domestic reform project, along with the end of the postwar boom in the United States and a consistent unwillingness to raise taxes, altogether created an economic malaise. Economic problems were compounded by social divisiveness, as the Civil Rights Movement and anti-war protests divided the nation. The beleaguered Johnson was so embattled he did not even run for reelection in 1968. After a poor showing in the New Hampshire primary in March 1968 (which he actually won), Johnson withdrew his candidacy.

Like many Americans, LBJ felt a cultural affinity for the people of Israel.[8] He told a B'nai B'rith meeting in 1968, "Most, if not all of you, have very deep ties with the land and with the people of Israel, as I do, for my Christian faith sprang from yours."[9] While he regarded Israelis as tough pioneers, he regarded Arabs as "culturally different" with experiences "alien to his own."[10] As Spiegel notes, "Johnson tended to see the Israelis fighting the Arabs as a modern-day version of the Texans struggling with the Mexicans. The analogy between the Alamo and Masada was not far below the surface."[11] Cultural factors certainly undergirded Johnson's perspective; however, as president—entrusted with executing the foreign relations of the United States—the Cold War and domestic politics weighed much more heavily on his thinking regarding weapons sales to Israel.

As more and more Soviet weaponry made its way to client states in the region, Israel requested weaponry from the United States. According to Levey, between 1955 and 1965, the Soviet Union sold Egypt, Syria, Iraq, and the People's Democratic Republic of Yemen approximately $2 billion worth of weaponry. Egypt was the main recipient. By the beginning of 1965, Egypt had 300 combat planes, including MiG jet interceptors and Tupelov bombers; by comparison, Israel had 250 warplanes, but no bombers. In terms of tanks, Egypt enjoyed a qualitative advantage over Israel. At the beginning of 1964, Israel had 798 tanks, compared with Egypt's 739, but 300 of Israel's tanks were obsolete M-4 Shermans, and only 150 British-made Centurions were of relatively recent manufacture.[12]

The United States preferred that Israel purchase its weapons from Western Europe. France had served as Israel's primary weapons supplier. Like Israel, France resented Nasser's influence in the region. But the Israel-France relationship cooled after the French exit from Algeria, and Western Europe proved reluctant to provide Israel with more weapons.[13]

U.S. weapons sales to Israel had grown from virtually nonexistent in the 1950s to several select packages in the 1960s. During 1962, John Kennedy authorized the first sale of U.S. weaponry to Israel—the defensive HAWK antiaircraft missile systems. But Kennedy refused to sell offensive weapons, in part because of Israel's controversial nuclear weapons program, and also to limit American involvement in the Arab-Israeli conflict. In early 1964, Israel requested to purchase five hundred tanks from the United States to offset Soviet tanks sold to Egypt. Both the State Department and the Defense Department recognized the validity of Israel's arms request but also warned of the political cost to U.S. relations with Arab states. Johnson agreed with the assessment and offered to help Israel "behind the scenes" to find alternate sources. Soon thereafter, Israel quietly signed agreements with Britain and West Germany for tank purchases.[14]

In the summer of 1964, the Kingdom of Jordan informed U.S. policymakers that unless it could purchase fighter jets from the United States, Jordan would buy MiG fighters from the Soviet Union. Naturally, Johnson did not want Jordan to develop closer relations with Moscow. And while he wanted to bolster King Hussein's government, he did not want to furnish Jordan with weapons that could potentially be used against Israel. Hixson details how the Israel lobby worked hard to scuttle the deal, and then decided to support it so long as Israel could acquire more sophisticated weaponry from the United States.[15] Thus, the arms race would accelerate because Israel would undoubtedly demand a similar deal, and Soviet client states would demand more weapons, too. Johnson promised to sell Jordan twenty F-104 jets in February 1965.

The promise of more U.S. weapons to Jordan amplified Israel's request for weapons. To make matters worse, West Germany decided to abandon its agreement with Israel after delivering less than half of the number of promised tanks.[16] Still reluctant to sell weapons to Israel directly, Johnson sent National Security Council staffer Robert Komer and Undersecretary of State for Political Affairs W. Averell Harriman to Israel to stress that the Jordanian package was simply to prevent a similar deal with the Soviets, and that Israel should expect no weapons sales from the United States. But the Harriman-Komer mission failed to get Israel on board with a U.S.-Jordan weapons agreement without, at least, a similar agreement with Israel.[17]

Cold War politics made an arms race in the Middle East unavoidable, which positioned the United States closer to Israel. To pacify the Israelis, Johnson agreed to sell the tanks promised from West Germany, which marked the first time that a U.S. president agreed to sell offensive weapons to the State of Israel. However, Israeli officials balked at this proposal, too, for being insufficient. Johnson then agreed to supply Israel with arms comparable to those it sold to Jordan, but with an understanding that it was a one-time deal; in other words, Johnson emphasized that such a sale would not set a precedent.[18] Although Israeli officials continued to push for a decisive military advantage over Arab states, Johnson wanted to "turn talks away from an open-ended arms commitment."[19] Johnson agreed to supply Israel with ninety tanks by 1966, along with another one hundred tanks of superior quality to those sold to Jordan, and the promise to sell Israel twenty-four aircraft if it could not find a supplier in Western Europe.[20] Selling more weapons to Israel threatened to undermine U.S. claims to evenhandedness in the Middle East, but American officials were in a bind given Soviet involvement in the region.

Johnson and Congress

Johnson initially enjoyed overwhelming support from the legislative branch (and the American people) for his foreign policies. Congress had deferred to the president during the early years of the Cold War to give him enough freedom to effectively fight the Soviet Union, a dynamic often called the Imperial Presidency.[21] But beginning in early 1966, Sen. J. William Fulbright (D-AR), chair of the Foreign Relations Committee, started to publicly question American involvement in Vietnam. Fulbright's efforts would eventually lead to a full congressional assault on presidential foreign policy during the Nixon and Ford years. According to Robert David Johnson, "By the middle of 1968, a majority of Senate Democrats and a growing number of GOP senators, while not willing to advocate withdrawal from Vietnam, were sufficiently radicalized by the war to reverse their previous support for a weak legislative role in international affairs."[22]

The Johnson administration tried to limit congressional pressure. In August 1965, Komer and National Security Advisor McGeorge Bundy met with eleven Jewish members of the House of Representatives to offer what the administration called "an insider's view," in order "to reassure our Hill friends by appearing to lift the veil on our Israeli affairs *on a confidential* basis." The key was secrecy. Bundy and Komer informed the congressmembers that U.S. aid to Israel, primarily economic to that point, totaled more than $1 billion and noted that "we want to convince them that we are really going all out to support Israel, so long as we can do it quietly." The message from Bundy and Komer was this: "the more quiet . . . the more we can do."[23]

As with East Asia, Congress proved to be a thorn in Johnson's side about foreign policy in the Middle East. Pressure mounted on Johnson to sell Skyhawk jets to Israel. On February 1, 1966, more than seventy-five representatives wrote Secretary of State Dean Rusk to communicate their displeasure for an impending deal with Jordan without a corresponding deal for Israel.[24] It was no secret to the administration that Israel possessed a great deal of influence over members of Congress through lobbyists, and Komer pressed Johnson to "cope with this problem *by requiring the Israelis themselves quietly to warn off their Hill lobbyists.*"[25] Johnson finally agreed to sell Skyhawk bomber jets to Israel that February, and Secretary of Defense Robert McNamara insisted that the Israelis agree to "sew up everyone in Congress to keep quiet."[26]

Just like the deal on tanks, President Johnson and his administration made it clear to Israeli officials that the sale of the Skyhawks was an exceptional case and constituted no change in the U.S.-Israel relationship. American officials informed the Israelis "not to bother us on planes for the next several years."[27] Secretary McNamara also wanted Congress to understand that the Skyhawks sale signaled no change in U.S. arms-sales policies, and in May 1966, when speaking to the Senate Foreign Relations Committee, he emphasized that the Skyhawk sale was "very restrictive."[28]

A few members of Congress started to press Johnson to sell weapons to Israel in order to contain communism. In September 1966, Rep. Seymour Halpern (R-NY) explained to the House floor that the PLO was amassing weapons for a war against Israel, and they had been "earmarked" by "Chinese Communists" to be "an effective instrument for revolutionary activity in this region." Halpern submitted to the Record a letter from Congressman Glenn Cunningham (R-NE), which referenced the representatives' letter from February 1966 that recommended strengthening Israel's defenses, and further argued that recent developments required a reexamination of the U.S.-Israel relationship.[29] Rep. Lester Wolff (D-NY) spoke about tension on the Israel-Syria border and called for Americans to reaffirm their support for Israel, due largely to cultural ties between the United States and Israel, and especially because Israel was the only democracy in the Middle East.[30]

The sale of the Skyhawks did not prevent the United States from voting to censure Israel in the U.N. Security Council in November 1966. The censure came in response to Israeli military attacks on Jordan due to an increase in terrorism along the Israel-Jordan border. On November 13, an Israeli raid leveled the Jordanian border settlement of Samu, which resulted in the deaths of fifteen Jordanian soldiers, ten Israeli soldiers, and an Israeli commander; three villagers also died, along with nearly one hundred wounded. Syria had been behind the terrorist attacks, and Israel knew it. But Israel feared to attack Syria since it had just signed a defense pact with Egypt. The move against Jordan alienated King Hussein, who had been secretly collaborating with Israel, and convinced Hussein to move closer to Nasser, which he wanted to avoid.[31]

As U.S. forces were bogged down in East Asia, the Middle East appeared to be heading to another war. Terrorist border attacks on Israel, many by the Palestinian organization Fatah, with Syrian support, had significantly increased since 1965. The Israeli response was often disproportional, such as at Samu, and Israel proved to be equally responsible for the outbreak of war.[32] U.S. officials believed Israel to have a decisive military advantage vis-à-vis its Arab neighbors. In April 1967, McNamara related to Johnson that, according to the Joint Chiefs of Staff, "Israel will be militarily unchallengeable by any combination of Arab states at least during the next five years."[33] Undersecretary of State Nicholas Katzenbach reiterated this point to President Johnson in a May 1 memo, about five weeks before the outbreak of war.[34] Nevertheless, in May, the Johnson administration completed negotiations with Israel for one hundred armored personnel carriers (APCs), military spare parts, and other assistance that totaled $72 million.[35] The U.S. assessments were on point as Israel would soon demonstrate in a lightning-quick defeat of Arab militaries.

The 1967 War and the Congressional Response

The June 1967 Arab-Israeli War and political aftermath proved to be one of the most significant events in modern Middle East history. Nasser did not want war with Israel. In fact, prior to the 1967 war, Israel was not a central concern of the Arab world; instead, inter-Arab politics, Arab nationalism, anticolonialism, and revolutionary socialism dominated Arab politics.[36] Arab states pursued their own national goals, and there was no monolithic or coordinated Arab strategy vis-à-vis Israel. But the Egyptian president made provocative moves against Israel, short of outright aggression, that led to an Israeli first strike and the outbreak of war. In response to a false report from Moscow about Israeli troop movements on the Syrian border, Nasser asked U.N. Secretary General U Thant to remove the U.N. Emergency Force (UNEF) in the Sinai Peninsula that had been deployed there in the aftermath of the 1956–1957 Suez Crisis. To the surprise of many, U Thant quickly agreed to Nasser's request, which removed the stabilizing force that had acted as a buffer between the two states. On May 22, Nasser also ordered a naval blockade against Israeli shipping through the Straits of Tiran, which violated the agreement reached in 1957.

Perhaps most important for American legislators, some Arab leaders—and Nasser in particular—made inflammatory comments about destroying Israel. Ernest Gruening (D-AK), for example, referenced "repeated threats by Egypt, in which it was joined by some of the Arab countries, that its intention was the liquidation of the tiny nation of Israel."[37] James Scheuer (D-NY) added that Nasser "encourages Arab refugees to believe that they will destroy Israel and he arms them."[38] In all likelihood, Nasser's rhetoric aimed to generate popular support for his leadership in the Arab world and did not accurately reflect Egyptian goals. Thomas Pelly (R-WA) made a perceptive remark on May 23 when he said, "I do not know if President Nasser is engaging in psychological semantics or if his war threats to Israel are serious, but there is no doubt that his words are like striking a match on a powder keg."[39]

Sincere or not, Nasser's declarations reminded many of the Holocaust and brought about legislative expressions of support for Israel. Sen. Joseph Montoya (D-NM) wondered, "Are there not some of us here who remember the death camps. . . . I ask any humane and fairminded man here—have the Jews not paid out enough in the blood and agony of their people?"[40] Rep. Claude Pepper (D-NY) called Nasser "Little Hitler," and Halpern warned against a "Munich-type sellout of Israel."[41]

Many members of Congress spoke of the American commitment to ensure Israel's survival dating back to Harry Truman's administration. In separate speeches on May 23, Senators Walter Mondale (D-MN) and Edward "Ted" Kennedy (D-MA) reminded their colleagues of the U.S. commitment to preserve the boundaries of Israel and the adjacent Arab states and to oppose the use of force in the Middle East, in line with the Tripartite Declaration of 1950, a joint declaration of the United States, Britain, and France.[42] Wayne Morse (D-OR), for his part, added that in the Tripartite Declaration, the three major powers pledged to "come to the assistance of the party against whom aggression had been committed."[43] More often than not, legislators referenced only an American commitment to the territorial integrity of Israel.

The United States, true to its special relationship with Israel, would not allow Israel to be destroyed. Sen. Joseph Clark (D-PA) spoke "to anybody in the Soviet Union . . . do not think that the United States of America is going to permit the Arab nations to overrun Israel."[44] A few days later, Rep. Jack Brinkley (D-GA) extolled the historical virtues of the Hebrew people and echoed Clark: "We cannot permit Israel to be overrun."[45] Sen. Jacob Javits (R-NY) argued that the United States had a "clear obligation and responsibility and a vital national interest in the area and in Israel." He cited John Foster Dulles's statement that "it is U.S. policy that the preservation of the State of Israel is a fundamental tenet of U.S. foreign policy."[46] Rep. Wayne Hayes (D-OH), aware of the divisive Vietnam War, observed that an Egyptian attack on Israel would turn "a lot of the doves in this country into hawks immediately."[47] Hayes returned to the same theme the next day and mentioned that Representatives Sidney Yates (D-IL) and Jonathan Bingham (D-NY)—two doves on Vietnam—had explained to him that one can "be a hawk with Israel and a dove with Vietnam."[48] Gruening and Pepper each suggested a mutual-defense pact with Israel.[49] Numerous additional legislators rose in vocal support of an American commitment to ensure Israel's survival.

Israel chose war on the morning of June 5. According to William Quandt, who served in the National Security Council for Richard Nixon and Jimmy Carter, the Johnson administration changed its "red light" to a "yellow light," which meant the administration would not protest an Israeli first strike.[50] In addition to the exit of UNEF and the blockade in the Straits of Tiran, Israel felt hemmed in by a collection of Arab states that called for its destruction. Also, Jordan signed a defense treaty with Egypt on the eve of war in 1967, which heightened Israel's fears. Within hours of the first morning, the Israeli Air Force had destroyed approximately 90 percent of the Egyptian Air Force. In control of the skies, Israel proceeded to decimate the Arab armies in six days. The war ended with a cease-fire after Moscow threatened military intervention to save its allies, especially the shaky Syrian government, as Israeli forces seemed poised to strike Damascus.

The outbreak of war intensified legislative voices of support for Israel. On June 5, Rep. William Ryan (D-NY) called on the United States "to do whatever is necessary to protect Israel in this hour of crisis."[51] Fellow congressman Leonard Farbstein (D-NY) followed by arguing that "Israel represents the American presence in the Middle East."[52] Rep. Silvio Conte (R-MA) stated, "The commitments of the United States to uphold and safeguard the national and territorial integrity of Israel are clear. We are the moral and legal ally of Israel in defense against territorial aggressors. We must and do stand ready with unilateral military assistance in behalf of the Israelis."[53] Rep. John Conyers (D-MI), among other legislators, claimed that the United States had a moral and legal obligation to defend Israel.[54] Bingham encouraged other legislators to follow his lead in giving blood to support Israel.[55] Regarding an Israeli first strike, which started the war, Javits assured the Senate and the American people, "Israel's Prime Minister has declared that his nation has no territorial ambitions. He did not have to make that declaration. We all know that."[56] This would become a debatable point in years to come.

President Johnson felt heavy domestic pressure to back Israel. As Hixson has argued, the Israel lobby undertook intensive efforts to elicit U.S. support from the legislative and executive branches for Israel against Nasser.[57] Prior to the war, hoping to persuade the Johnson administration to support an Israeli first strike, the Israeli government instructed its ambassador in Washington to "create a public atmosphere that will constitute pressure on the [Johnson] administration . . . without it being explicitly clear that we are behind this public campaign."[58] The effort aimed to get sympathetic Americans to write letters, editorials, telegrams, and public statements to "strengthen our friends within the administration." The pressure was so bothersome that the White House requested that the Israelis shut it down, although the Israeli ambassador reported back, "Of course we are continuing it."[59]

To the dismay of Israeli officials and Israel's supporters in the United States, the Johnson administration tried to maintain an evenhanded position. On the first day of the war, State Department spokesman Robert McCloskey communicated to the press, "We have tried to steer an even-handed course. . . . Our position is neutral in thought, word and deed."[60] McCloskey's statement drew the ire of many Jewish Americans.[61] Later that day, Special Assistant to the President Joseph Califano phoned Secretary of State Rusk to say that McCloskey's statement was "killing us with the Jews in this country" and asked Rusk to issue a more pro-Israel statement. Rusk released a statement that blandly reaffirmed Johnson's position of independence and territorial integrity in the Middle East.[62] Two days later, American Jewish Zionists communicated their "sharp disillusion and dismay" to the White House.[63] David Ginsburg, the long-time advocate for American Jewish Zionists, pressured U.S. officials to not force an Israeli withdrawal, which Eisenhower had done during the Suez Crisis. He wrote in a memo to Vice President Hubert Humphrey, "Here I'll add a word of my own: what was done particularly in 1956 and 1957 but since then as well, from the viewpoint of U.S. interests alone, was appalling." Ginsburg also warned the White House, "What the Administration is saying and doing now is being watched carefully not only by the Jewish community, but by others who should be and have been close to the Administration and whose support—and advice—we need, have had, and should have again."[64]

Legislators took aim at McCloskey's statement of neutrality and denounced it on the floors of the House and the Senate. Rep. William Scott (R-VA) stated, "The people of this country are not neutral in thought and word. Everything I hear, every expression of opinion from people in all walks of life, shows a deep concern for the preservation of the State of Israel."[65] Senator Clark remarked, "Morally and legally we are an ally of Israel. Their cause is our cause. We are not neutral in thought, word, or deed. I am distressed by our Government's ambiguous declaration of neutrality."[66] Rep. Louis Wyman (R-NH) derided the Johnson administration for "flubbing the ball just at the wrong time" and for giving "the impression to the world that we are pussyfooting. . . . We cannot possibly be neutral in the situation of Nasser versus Israel."[67] Representative Ryan called the neutrality declaration "grotesque" and insisted that "the United States has never been 'neutral in thought, word, and deed' on the matter of Israel's right to exist."[68] For Rep. Margaret Heckler (R-MA), "Historically, we have had a close and special relationship with the State of Israel from the time of its inception. Consequently, I rise to protest against the administration's declaration of 'neutrality' in this great crisis."[69]

Several legislators used a familial analogy, of an American mother to an Israeli child, to describe U.S.-Israel relations. Rep. Jacob Gilbert (D-NY), for one, regarded Israel as "the child of Western humanitarianism and U. N. diplomacy."[70] According Rep. Joseph Addabbo (D-NY), "Since its inception in 1948, Israel has been a stepchild of the United States. . . . If necessary, this country must defend Israel's territorial integrity."[71] Benjamin Blackburn (R-GA) claimed that the United States "served as midwife during the birth of Israel as a free and independent nation" and, therefore, "now has a moral responsibility to protect her rights as such."[72] Not long after the war, Sen. Frank Church (D-ID) similarly stated that "the United States was the midwife at the birth of Israel, and the Arab countries have been determined, ever since, to kill the child."[73]

Some State Department officials stressed the need to continue an evenhanded position and not appear biased by Israeli sympathies. Benjamin Read, the executive secretary for Rusk, informed Bundy that it was in "our national interest" to maintain "reasonably friendly relations with both Israel and the Arab states" in order to "preserve some continuing role in the development of petroleum and other resources." Read argued that "we must avoid full commitment to either side or to any party. . . . Our influence is greatest if we serve as a balance, not a partisan."[74] Zbigniew Brzezinski, a member of the State Department's policy planning staff and future National Security Advisor for Jimmy Carter, recommended that the best path would probably be "publicly defining a U.S. position that is reasonable, fair and constructive, even if initially not satisfactory to any of the belligerents." The United States had to keep in mind "the long-range interests of the region" and not become "identified with one side alone." Brzezinski realized, "Some Israeli resentment of the above posture is to be expected, but that is unavoidable unless the United States wishes to become fully identified with it."[75]

The war severely strained U.S.-Arab relations. During the course of the war several Arab countries—including Egypt, Syria, and Iraq—broke diplomatic relations with the United States, and Arab oil-producing states unsheathed the "oil weapon" against the United States and Britain. Although the uncoordinated attempt failed to influence either American or British policy, the effort provided the groundwork for a future oil embargo, with much greater impact, in 1973. According to an intelligence memorandum, "the course of the present Arab-Israeli crisis has already done considerable damage to the U.S. position in the Arab world. Most Arabs believe the U.S. is the staunch ally of Israel and can in effect control its actions."[76] Even further, "the damage to the U.S. position in the area already appears serious."[77]

Not even an Israeli attack on the USS *Liberty,* an American spy ship in the Mediterranean, lessened support for Israel. On June 8, Israeli aircraft struck the *Liberty* with rockets and napalm, followed by boat-launched torpedoes, which killed 34 crewmembers and wounded 171. Israeli officials insisted the attack was a result of mistaken identity, believing the ship to be Egyptian. But *Liberty* crewmen had notified Israeli forces that they were Americans, and Israel Defense Forces (IDF) headquarters had identified the *Liberty* only several hours before. Many Americans never accepted the Israeli explanation and felt the attack was a deliberate attempt to prevent American monitoring of a potential Israeli attack on Syria or Israeli executions of Egyptian captives, or to keep the *Liberty* from jamming Israeli communications.[78]

Little was said on the House and Senate floors about the controversial attack. Rep. Roman Pucinski (D-IL) and Sen. Robert Kennedy (D-NY) both called the attack on the *Liberty* a "tragic mistake," and Pucinski and Senator Javits noted that Israel had already apologized for the attack.[79] Javits excused the apparent mishap: "I have heard Senator after Senator say that while they were terribly dismayed and saddened by this accident, they understood how it could take place under the terrible stress which the forces of Israel have been under in these last few weeks."[80] Almost two months later, John Tower (R-TX) submitted a resolution from the American Legion Post 52 of Houston that denounced the "unprovoked attack" and aimed "to see that those Israel officials or personnel who were responsible for the attacks be punished in keeping with their participation and in keeping with the enormity of their criminal acts."[81] Israel paid millions of dollars in compensation, but no Israeli was ever blamed or punished.[82] Rep. Harold Royce (H. R.) Gross (R-IA) wondered, based on reports that the U.S. government had made $27 million available to Israel for food and other supplies, if the United States was subsidizing Israel's "payment of full compensation for the lives that were destroyed, the suffering of the wounded, and the damage from this wanton attack."[83]

Legislators broadly supported Israeli occupation of Arab lands taken during the war. Representative Pucinski, with the aftermath of the 1956 war in mind, did not want to "again rob Israel of the gains she has won on the hard-fought fields of battle."[84] Rep. Robert Sikes (D-FL) went further than Pucinski. Sikes suggested that Israel "simply annex" the West Bank and the Sinai Peninsula "and eliminate future problems." For Sikes, the move would have biblical implications as Israel "would then control, essentially, the Jewish homeland." Sikes closed with a contestable point: "Had we and our allies kept hands off in 1956, the situation could have been solved permanently at that time."[85] Rep. Donald Clausen (R-CA), who also used a religious allusion, believed "Israel was 'sinned' against . . . and is entitled to retain whatever gains she has made in the interim."[86] Rep. Alphonzo Bell (R-CA) supported Israeli occupation and predicted that Israel "will prove herself to be a magnanimous victor, but this magnanimity must be allowed to be voluntary."[87] Representatives Ogden Reid (R-NY) and Floyd Hicks (D-WA) stressed the need to not repeat the perceived mistake of 1956–1957.[88]

Some legislators made the specific connection between Israeli occupation of Arab lands and a diplomatic plan to secure a lasting peace in the region. A poll conducted by the Associated Press revealed that 365 out of 438 responses from legislators "were opposed to withdrawal without peace."[89] Rep. Thomas Morris (D-NM) wanted Israel to keep the territories to secure its "right to live in peace with her neighbors."[90] Halpern followed, "If the Arabs expect Israel to leave the territory she has won, then Israel is entitled to a treaty of peace, signed by the Arabs."[91] Rep. James Corman (D-CA) argued, "The Arab world must accept the permanency of the State of Israel," and therefore he wanted "no attempt" by the United Nations or the United States to force an Israeli withdrawal.[92] Senator Mondale stressed that "there must be no return to a quasi-permanent supervised military standoff between Israel and the Arab nations. . . . We must reinforce our historic commitment to the existence and permanence of the State of Israel."[93] Rep. William Widnall (R-NJ) called for U.S. support "of the present lines" until Israel received recognition and peace.[94] Halpern reiterated his earlier point: "No withdrawal can be expected of Israel without . . . peace and stability." He also mocked the State Department's neutrality statement and wondered, "Is our Government going to heed our voices, the voices of the vast majority of the

American people? Or are we going to crawl back into the State Department shells and let the striped-pants boys continue to guide U.S. policy."[95] Indeed, Congress stood solidly behind Israel's occupation of Arab lands until its neighbors offered recognition and peace.

But Israel wanted land more than it wanted peace. According to Avi Raz, Israel did not genuinely seek peace with its Arab neighbors after the war. The Israeli cabinet developed a June 19 peace plan that would have returned the Golan Heights and Sinai Peninsula in return for peace agreements with Syria and Egypt. But the "generous peace offer" was never communicated to the Arab states. Instead, Israeli officials, particularly Foreign Minister Abba Eban, perpetuated the myth of such an offer to secure U.S. support against a Soviet measure at the United Nations that called for an immediate Israeli withdrawal.[96] According to Shaiel Ben-Ephraim, in the wake of the war, Israel started to construct settlements in the occupied territories, which Israeli officials claimed were reversible military outposts and not civilian in nature. This deception aimed to provide cover from international pressure during a vulnerable period of civilian settlement construction. The Johnson administration, distracted by the Vietnam War, failed to offer any substantial resistance to the settlement construction and missed an early opportunity to shut down Israel's efforts to create "facts on the ground." Israel would continue to build more and more settlements in the occupied territories in the years and decades to follow, which added a major obstacle to peace efforts and fulfillment of a two-state solution.[97]

Legislators did not demand the return of Arab territory; however, a few voices cautioned against indefinite Israeli occupation. On the second day of the war, Representative Hayes reasoned that "if we are going to maintain the territorial integrity of all the states out there in the Middle East, we will possibly have to get in against Israel."[98] After the war, Rep. Jim Wright (D-TX) pointed out that "Israel has every right to demand security, no right to demand spoils."[99] Representatives Pucinski and Ray Madden (D-IN) both criticized the Soviet Union for demanding an Israeli withdrawal, given its occupation of Eastern Europe.[100]

Numerous legislators stressed the need to address the grievances of Palestinian refugees. On June 8, Sen. Robert Byrd (D-WV) hoped that "some headway can be made in the Arab refugee problems, which have long been the source of deep irritation." Senator Javits, known for his pro-Israel orientation, followed by agreeing with his colleague. According to Javits, an acceptable settlement "includes the Palestinian and Arab refugees. . . . Israel is not going to like this. We know that. There are some things that Israel may have to do which it finds especially distasteful, especially after such an enormous victory at arms. We must, however, bring about an end to this situation."[101] Sen. Edward Brooke (R-MA) called for "Israel and Arab nations" to "be more flexible in their refugee resettlement policies."[102] According to Sen. Claiborne Pell (D-RI), "The refugee shame must be liquidated once and for all. It is a crime against humanity to incarcerate a million people for 20 years simply as pawns in an international political disagreement." Pell, however, failed to mention Israel's role in the ongoing refugee crisis and placed the onus of responsibility squarely on Arab states, saying, "I believe this problem could have been resolved by the Arab nations if they had really desired to do so."[103] Several other legislators agreed with the need to address Palestinian grievances, such as Senator Mondale and Representatives Wright, Ryan, and Paul Fino (R-NY).

Legislators felt far less sympathy for Egypt or Jordan, and some questioned the U.S. policy of trying to remain friendly with Arab states that threatened to destroy Israel. In a lengthy speech on June 26, Senator Church called Johnson's "arsenal diplomacy" in the Middle East a "failure." He noted that Jordanian arms from the United States had been used in a war against Israel and questioned the "policy which assumes that we can exercise a restraining influence by judicious distribution of our weapons." For Church, the June war demonstrated that the "misguided attempt to prevent 'polarization' of western arms in Israel against Soviet arms in Arab hands, and still keep on friendly terms with both sides, called for omniscient qualities of judgment which our Defense officials, or indeed any mortals, do not possess."[104] Senator Gruening picked up where Church left off. He questioned the broader American policy of pressing "our aid on nations whose policies were antagonistic to ours," which he called "an extremely shortsighted policy. . . . In all history no nation has ever squandered so much on so many." He also noted that U.S. arms to Jordan "got there just in time to enable Jordan to embrace Nasser."[105] Gruening continued his attack on U.S. foreign policy in the Middle East the following day in an even longer speech. Comparing the situation to Munich, he said, "The United States sought to appease those nations bent on the destruction of Israel. The policy of appeasement failed."[106] Johnson's efforts to balance weapons sales and still protect Israel, or to avoid an arms race in the Middle East altogether, had both foundered, which must have made it easier for the president to support Israeli occupation of Arab lands.

The Johnson administration determined, in opposition to Eisenhower's policy in 1957, that Israel did not need to vacate the occupied territories. In 1957, numerous legislators (most notably, then-Senate Majority Leader Lyndon Johnson) disagreed with Eisenhower's decision to push Israel out of the Sinai Peninsula and Gaza Strip. Ten years later, the Johnson administration encouraged a land-for-peace arrangement, whereby Arab states would make peace with Israel in exchange for the return of Arab territories. The move received overwhelming approval from Congress.

The land-for-peace formula signaled a major transformation of U.S. policy. Rather than pressure Israel to withdraw from the occupied territories, Johnson released his "Five Principles" for peace on June 19: the right to national life, justice for the refugees, free maritime passage, limits on the arms race, and political independence and territorial integrity for all. Despite Johnson's fifth principle, the administration did not honor its pledge to protect the territorial integrity of Arab states. Rather than preserve existing boundaries in line with the Tripartite Declaration, Johnson decided to support altered boundaries in order to pressure Arab states to make peace with Israel. The reasoning was simple. The armistice agreements of 1949 failed to bring about peace, and so did Eisenhower's policy of forced Israeli removal. The volatile region seemed combustible, and the situation demanded a new approach that could lead to a lasting peace. Otherwise, another war could lead to superpower confrontation, maybe even nuclear warfare, and perhaps the annihilation of Jews in the Middle East. But by tying land to peace, Johnson also tied an American special commitment to ensure Israel's survival to support of Israeli occupation of Arab lands until peace could be achieved. From that point, the two became inseparable.

The war demonstrated that Israel could effectively employ military force against its neighbors, which supported the conclusion that, with ample weaponry, Israel could defend itself until the Arab states agreed to make peace. But additional U.S. military sales to Israel did not happen immediately after the war. President Johnson had ordered an embargo on new U.S. arms shipments to the Middle East once the fighting started. He hoped the Soviets would reciprocate, but Washington again found Moscow uninterested in arms restraint.[107] French President Charles de Gaulle ordered an embargo on weapons sales to Israel after its preemptive strike, which ended the Israel-

France weapons arrangement and left Israel without a major supplier of weaponry.

Congress pushed for more weapons sales to Israel. On August 1, Representative Sikes claimed that "efforts to put a brake on the sale of American military equipment abroad" negatively impacted Israel. Referring to Israel as "the only friend we have left in the Middle East," Sikes called on the United States to fill the void left by France to challenge "Arab forces" that were "being resupplied rapidly by the Russians."[108] Senator Tower also argued for selling more weapons to Israel. He wondered, "Mr. President are we to leave Israel to the tender mercies of the dictatorial designs of Nasser over all the Middle East as a pawn of the Soviet Union?" He added that the Soviet Union was "dumping arms back into the United Arab Republic just as fast as they can. Already they have replaced half the equipment the Arab States lost in the Arab-Israel war."[109]

Congress debated restricting arms sales, especially to Arab states, in order to prevent a global arms race. Legislators considered an amendment to limit the credit resources of the U.S. Export-Import Bank, which could be used by less developed countries to finance arms sales, including certain Arab states, such as Jordan. (The purpose of the credit financing was to assist in economic development, but it was also used for military purchases.) Sen. Daniel Brewster (D-MD) "was shocked to learn that almost 36 percent of all Export-Import loans this year went for the purchase of American armaments." He also added that credit financing helped Jordan to "wage war on her declared enemy, Israel."[110] Henry "Scoop" Jackson (D-WA), who supported large defense contracts to create jobs for Boeing in his home state, urged rejection of the amendment, which, he said, "would unduly and dangerously tie the hands of the President . . . in the conduct of foreign policy." He recognized that the amendment would not deny Israel assistance in the future but that it may be in the "national interest" of both the United States and Israel "that certain assistance be given to certain developing countries in the Middle East."[111] Rep. Joshua Eilberg (D-PA) supported an amendment to restrict the training of certain foreign nationals and wondered why the United States trained pilots and military personnel from Arab states that severed relations and aimed to destroy Israel. Representative Ryan sought to eliminate all assistance to Egypt and "other Arab nations which have waged war against Israel." He supported a different amendment to enable "Congress to end this bankrupt policy which is so detrimental to peace in the Middle East."[112]

Some legislators wanted to prevent a global arms race but also wanted to provide for Israel's defense. Gruening called on "the United States to take leadership in the world in stopping the arms race." Although U.S. officials aimed to use weapons sales to contain communism, Gruening pointed out that U.S. tanks to Jordan, justified by containment, were used against Israel, a noncommunist country.[113] Representative Sikes pushed for more weapons for Israel and warned that limiting arms sales to foreign countries would potentially hurt "the best friend we have in the Middle East." He believed Israel to be "seriously, almost desperately, in need of aircraft and spares." He also noted that airpower had been the decisive factor in the recent war and argued in support of more aircraft for Israel.[114] Emmanuel Celler (D-NY), in his twenty-third term and the most senior member of the House (Dean of the House), worried that an existing amendment to eliminate a proposed program that would have granted new authority to the president to finance arms sales might "militate against our desire to supply Israel properly with arms. . . . it would be tragic indeed if Israel could not forfend against her Arab neighbors who are bent upon plunging her into the sea."[115] Representatives Bingham, Ryan, and John Dow (D-NY) all assured Celler that Israel would not be affected. Bingham said, "There are plenty of ways for us to supply Israel with all necessary arms," and Ryan added that he wanted to eliminate a "new blank check authority" that "may be used to arm Israel's eternal enemies." The House passed the amendment.[116]

As Congress encouraged a one-sided U.S. policy in the Middle East, the prospect for peace seemed to take a negative turn. On September 1, the heads of thirteen Arab states released the Khartoum Declaration, which famously declared the three "No's"—no peace with Israel, no recognition of Israel, and no negotiations with Israel. The declaration came about six weeks after Arab states refused to accept a joint U.S.-Soviet draft resolution that called for Israel to withdraw "without delay" in return for nonbelligerency. The Arab states, according to Spiegel, "flatly rejected it," and Quandt explains that "radical Arab objections to provisions calling for an end of war with Israel" led to the rejection.[117] Israel also opposed the U.S.-Soviet resolution because it did not call for direct negotiations, did not mention Israel by name, and included only vague arrangements for peace.[118] Israel was determined not to withdraw to previous lines without guarantees of peace—precisely what had happened with the Suez Crisis only ten years before. U.S. policy had already evolved to a point that peace with Israel must happen before the return of Arab territories; therefore, the Khartoum Declaration, which denied both formal recognition and a peace treaty, portended even worse U.S.-Arab relations.

Similar to Nasser's saber-rattling before the war, the Khartoum Declaration should not be taken at face value. According to Avi Shlaim, the Arab heads of state were prepared to recognize Israel as a state, though short of legal *de jure* recognition; were willing to negotiate with Israel through a third party, though not directly; and were willing to move to a state of peace short of a formal peace treaty. According to King Hussein of Jordan, Nasser encouraged him to "speak of a comprehensive solution to the problem and a comprehensive peace and go and do anything you can short of signing a peace." Shlaim notes that Khartoum was a victory for moderate Arabs who wanted a political rather than military solution, and that the meeting marked "a real turning point in Nasser's attitude to Israel."[119] Israeli leaders intentionally misrepresented Khartoum in order to justify their own hard line.[120]

According to U.S. documents, U.S. and Israeli officials clearly recognized the apparent moderation of Khartoum but doubted the sincerity of an Arab change of heart. On September 25, Johnson sent a letter to King Faisal of Saudi Arabia that stated, "I agree that the recent Khartoum conference marked notable progress for the forces of Arab moderation." But Johnson also added that the Arab position "states what the Arabs will not do but, except by indirection, is silent on what the Arabs may be willing to do." He welcomed the decision to move from a military to a political solution but questioned the Arab insistence on belligerency if they really hoped for a peaceful resolution.[121] The State Department reiterated Johnson's position on Khartoum in a telegram to Jordan a few days later.[122] Lucius Battle, Assistant Secretary of State for Near East Affairs, told Adan Pachachi, Iraqi Minister of Foreign Affairs, "that it was difficult indeed for us to encourage the Israelis or anyone else to believe the Arabs wanted a political settlement when statements continued to emanate from Arab countries indicating the war would go on."[123] Battle told Israeli Ambassador Abraham Harman that "reports of growing moderateness after Khartoum have so far not been borne out by any concrete Arab steps."[124]

As Arab states searched for some way to secure a political agreement, Israeli flexibility diminished. Arthur Goldberg, U.S. ambassador to the United Nations, told President Johnson that there were "some signs of moderation in the Arab camp, and some signs of hardening in the Israeli camp." Goldberg cited "serious internal problems" in Israel, likely meaning a euphoric public mood following the dramatic victory, which made it "difficult for any Israeli spokesman to be 'sweetly reasonable.'"[125] Eugene Rostow noted that "accepted wisdom" held that "the Israeli position is 'hardening.'"[126] Battle questioned Harman about the announced establishment of Israeli settlements in the West Bank and on the Syrian border. He advised the Israeli ambassador to "not provide ammunition for those at U.N. who would interpret" the Israeli "position as hardening in direction of territorial acquisition rather than negotiated settlement."[127] Secretary of State Rusk, when talking about territorial withdrawal in the Middle East, told Johnson, "In my opinion we are going to have to wrestle with Israel."[128]

The Johnson administration could not mesh a commitment to territorial integrity for all states in the Middle East with a policy of protecting Israeli occupation until Arab states made peace. In response to Arab ambassadors' questions about territorial integrity, National Security Advisor Walt Rostow wrote Johnson, "Our best answer is that we stand by that pledge, but the only way to make good on it is to have a genuine peace." But even with "an honest peace settlement," Rostow recognized that pushing "Israel back to 4 June borders . . . could lead to a tangle with the Israelis."[129] King Hussein sent President Johnson a letter in early October, which noted that Khartoum reflected Arab flexibility, and that even Israeli navigation through the Suez Canal was possible if Israel would redress wrongs done to Palestinians since 1948. Hussein expressed his "deep hurt" by what he regarded as a "basic pro-Israel position" of the United States. He lamented the "double standard" applied to Arabs and Israelis regarding territorial integrity.[130] The Jordanian ambassador, Abdul-Hamid Sharaf, also communicated to Johnson an Arab frustration with an American double standard regarding territorial integrity. According to Harold Saunders's notes from the meeting, "The Arab governments feel they have a right to expect the Government of the United States to honor that pledge. They have been deeply hurt that we have not." Johnson responded that "we continue to support strongly the principle of territorial integrity but that the problem of putting that support in practice was a difficult one which we had not yet solved."[131] Also in the spirit of compromise, Egyptian Foreign Minister Mahmoud Riad admitted to U.S. officials that Egypt's calls for the destruction of Israel had been a "mistake" and that Egypt did not challenge "Israel's right to exist." Rather, the main problem was refugees.[132]

The administration's perception of the U.S.-Israel relationship continued to evolve. According to Saunders's notes of a conversation with Israeli diplomat Ephraim Evron, Israel wanted new weapons sales connected to a strategic alliance. Evron asked that the Johnson administration treat Israelis "as close friends . . . rather than treating them like bazaar hagglers." Evron recommended that the administration not try to exact any conditions for the sale of additional aircraft but to instead tell Israel through an informal channel "that we were doing this at some political cost and would therefore expect something from them in return." By implication, Evron suggested the United States and Israel develop a strategic alliance in addition to a special relationship. Saunders made an insightful remark: "This strikes once again at the heart of our relationship with Israel. The Israelis always tried to get close to us and to build the kind of relationship we have with the British. We have—at least at the professional level of our government—kept them at arms length, and they have been deeply hurt. Evron and I have discussed this aspect of our relationship before, and it's no surprise that he sees here a chance for a new start." Saunders added that before the June war, the argument against more arms deals with Israel had nothing to do with dollars or armored personnel carriers—"the real argument was over what kind of relationship we should have with Israel." Saunders added, "I'm tempted to take the risk Evron suggests . . . the real leverage we have is not a specific number of aircraft but our total relationship."[133]

As the administration considered the next step in U.S.-Israel relations, a few legislators challenged Johnson's arms embargo that held up the delivery of the Skyhawks purchased in 1966. On September 21, Donald Rumsfeld, a Republican representative from Illinois and future Secretary of Defense for Gerald Ford and George W. Bush, cautioned the administration against putting pressure on Israel by threatening to withhold arms. He noted that the Soviets had already resupplied their client states and that France refused to sell more aircraft to Israel. Rumsfeld was worried "that the U.S. position might be based on a desire to exert pressure on the Israelis to withdraw," which Rumsfeld called "most unwise." He further argued that it was "imprudent" to put "pressure on Israel by denying her the needed capability to deter further aggression."[134] Rep. Charles H. Wilson (D-CA) reminded his colleagues that Congress is "charged with the responsibility for overseeing our foreign policy," and he blasted the administration for providing disproportionate arms sales to Arab states. He noted with disdain McCloskey's June 5 statement that the United States was "neutral in thought, word, and deed." Wilson wanted to "junk our policy of restricting arms sales to Israel" and to immediately approve the delivery of Skyhawks.[135] Congressman Joel Broyhill (R-VA), similar to Rumsfeld, worried "that the planes are being withheld to obtain bargaining leverage to force Israeli concessions." In his speech to a Virginia Lodge of B'nai B'rith, Broyhill vowed to "urge, with every bit of persuasion at my command, that these planes be released."[136] Representative Halpern called for the delivery of the Skyhawks and complained that "the Department of State is using the Congress as an excuse" for not honoring the sale of Skyhawks to Israel. (He pointed out that congressional concern had been about the financing of arms sales to Arabs and in no way meant "to obstruct the arming of Israel.")[137]

Johnson wanted to release the Skyhawks to Israel, but he also wanted to resume arms shipments to moderate Arab states. On October 9, Walt Rostow informed Johnson that Israeli officials were "deeply suspicious—despite our contrary assurances—that our freezing past aid means we're going to use it as leverage to force them to terms with Arabs. They well remember 1956–57 when we froze their assets here and then forced them back to the armistice lines." Secretary of Defense McNamara wanted to continue the freeze, not to pressure Israel, but to avoid upsetting legislators on the issue of military credit sales.[138] However, as noted above, Representative Halpern obviously disagreed with the administration's position on the matter. By October 12, the administration had determined to resume shipments to Israel and planned for the delivery of the Skyhawks to begin in December; McNamara sent a letter to Israeli Foreign Minister Abba Eban to that effect.[139] But the administration also indicated that arms shipments would resume to moderate Arab states. Walt Rostow told Evron "that it would be impossible for the U.S. to have an Israel policy without a Middle East policy." Evron agreed and added, "If we are to work together, as we must, on issues like Middle East arms supply, we ought to try to work out a more lucid common strategy for the whole region."[140] Here again, Evron pushed for a stronger strategic relationship between the two countries. But for domestic political reasons, Israeli officials could not formally approve of the U.S. decision to resume arms shipments to Arab states. Therefore, on October 18, McNamara decided with Israeli ambassador Harman that Israel would not respond to McNamara's letter to Eban, and instead, the two sides informally agreed to the arrangement.[141]

Before the administration formally announced its decision to lift the arms embargo, another violent event in the Middle East hastened congressional calls for more arms to Israel. On October 21, Egypt sank the Israeli destroyer *Eilat*. An Egyptian boat within the harbor at Port Said, armed with Soviet missiles, fired upon and ultimately sank the *Eilat,* which had been in international waters approximately ten miles from the harbor. The attack was in response to a July attack by the *Eilat* on Egyptian boats that happened within Egyptian waters. Several Republican representatives voiced their Cold War concerns about Soviet activity in the Middle East. Bob Wilson (R-CA) believed the Soviets were testing the United States, since they had rearmed their Arab allies "without the United States keeping its commitment to sell a limited number of military jets to Israel."[142] Like Wilson, Edward Gurney (R-FL) was disturbed by the use of sophisticated Soviet weaponry as the sinking of the *Eilat* was "the first time in history that this type of radar missile has been used to sink a ship of any flag." Gurney found it "inconceivable" that the Johnson administration "is reneging on its commitment to Israel. . . . By withholding this sale of jets to Israel . . . we are encouraging further Communist Russia intervention into the Middle East."[143] By October 25, the administration had announced the lifting of the arms embargo, which pleased Bingham, who added his satisfaction for the administration's decision during his denunciation of the *Eilat* attack.[144] James Fulton (R-PA) went even further. In addition to delivery of Skyhawks, he called on the U.S. Congress to pass a resolution to give "Israel at once, a late series destroyer to replace the Israel destroyer."[145] Representative Farbstein, a New York Democrat, echoed the call for a replacement of the *Eilat.*[146] Surprisingly, perhaps, representatives and senators voiced more concern on the House and Senate floors with Egypt's attack on the Israeli *Eilat* than with Israel's attack on the USS *Liberty.*

While Soviet weapons threatened Israel in the Middle East, reports surfaced that Moscow had taken measures to oppress Jews living in the Soviet Union by placing restrictions on emigration. Speaker of the House John McCormack (D-MA) reported that Soviet treatment of Jews worsened after the June war, and that in August "the Soviet government barred the emigration of some 6,000 Soviet Jews to Israel." McCormack added that "Soviet authorities" were pressuring "Soviet satellite countries in Europe to do likewise."[147] (In the years to follow, the Soviet Union would place greater restrictions on emigration, which prompted further congressional action—the Jackson-Vanik Amendment to the 1974 Trade Act.)

Finally, in November, after months of negotiations, the U.N. Security Council agreed to Resolution 242, which called on Israel to withdraw from territories occupied in the conflict in return for peace agreements. The resolution formalized the land-for-peace framework as the basis for the Arab-Israeli peace process. However, the resolution failed to mention the Palestinians by name, and unfortunately their plight would often be overlooked in the peace process. At the time, no serious discussion was devoted to a two-state solution. Moreover, Israel fought hard to remove the word "the" from the phrase: "Withdrawal of Israel armed forces from [the] territories occupied in the recent conflict." In doing so, the resolution failed to firmly articulate which territories should be evacuated by Israel's forces. The Israeli interpretation held that Israel did not have to leave all of the territories, and that the ambiguity of 242 provided room for negotiations; the Arab interpretation held that Israel had to leave all of the territories, not just some of them, which made negotiations much less essential to the process. Thus Gunnar Jarring, the diplomat appointed by the United Nations to facilitate peace negotiations, faced the unenviable task of trying to build agreements on an intentionally vague resolution. All the while, the United States and the Soviet Union sent more weapons to the region for purposes of the Cold War.

Phantom Feud

Johnson's foreign and domestic problems came to a head in 1968, and an increasingly assertive Congress pushed Johnson to move closer to Israel with another major weapons sale—Phantom jets. After the weapons embargo was lifted, Israel requested twenty-seven more Skyhawks and fifty Phantom jets.[148] With supersonic speed, radar-guided missiles, and the potential to deliver a nuclear weapon, the Phantoms were far more sophisticated than the Skyhawks. The State Department opposed the sale in the hopes of advancing arms-limitation agreements and repairing the damage done to U.S.-Arab relations during the recent war. The Joint Chiefs opposed the sale because, according to analyses, Israel did not need the Phantoms. The Defense Department did not necessarily oppose the sale, as long as moderate Arab regimes also received arms.[149] Johnson again proved reluctant to sell weapons to Israel. He hoped to avoid a strategic alliance with Israel, and selling Phantoms would further alienate Arab states. Johnson also wanted to support the efforts of Jarring, and selling the Phantoms would undercut his peace efforts. As Bard notes, "No decision was reached during the remainder of the year [1967], despite a deluge of letters from congressmen urging the president to sell airplanes to Israel."[150]

Johnson met with Israeli Prime Minister Levi Eshkol at his Texas ranch in January 1968 to discuss U.S.-Israel relations. Johnson insisted that Israel enjoyed a position of strength and would be wise to pursue a peace program with its neighbors, rather than an arms program with the United States. Johnson told Eshkol bluntly, "Phantoms won't determine security. Planes won't change things that basically. The big problem is how 2–1/2 million Jews can live in a sea of Arabs."[151] Johnson also mentioned the stiff congressional resistance to recent military-assistance programs due to Vietnam, suggesting that if Israel hoped to get the Phantoms, Israelis needed to cultivate congressional support.[152] The following day Johnson reiterated that the pursuit of peace, not weapons sales, would drive U.S. policymaking. He wanted to provide the Israeli Air Force with necessary equipment but stressed the importance of Jarring's efforts to negotiate peace agreements, along with the need to reach an agreement with the Soviets on the arms race.[153] Selling Phantoms would hinder, rather than advance, both of those goals. The Johnson administration hoped to use the Phantoms as leverage to ensure Israel's best efforts to reach peace agreements.[154] Nevertheless, Johnson agreed to put fifty planes in the production line in case an arms agreement with Moscow could not be reached.[155]

For Johnson, the decision to sell Phantoms to Israel had much more to do with a moral commitment to ensure Israel's survival than with any strategic alliance between the two countries. On March 24, Johnson intimated to Arthur Goldberg that he felt compelled to sell the Phantoms because the Soviets would not agree to arms control. Johnson worried that Israel would be crushed by Soviet weaponry without American military assistance. He told Goldberg, "They don't know when they're going to be run over; they don't know when they're going to die; they don't know when those goddamn Russians are going to come in there. They don't know anything."[156] A week later, overwhelmed by the Vietnam War and domestic divisiveness, the embattled Johnson became a "lame duck" president as he declared he would not seek reelection.

Administration officials stressed the need to link weapons sales to peace talks and nuclear nonproliferation. According to Quandt, "some" administration officials "felt that Israel should be asked to agree to the principle of full withdrawal in the context of peace in exchange for the jets. Others, fearful of Israeli nuclear development, argued that Israel should be required to sign the Nuclear Nonproliferation Treaty (NPT) before receiving U.S. arms."

Although Israel would not publicly acknowledge possessing any nuclear weapons, Israeli representatives assured U.S. officials that Israel would not be the first Middle East country to "introduce" nuclear weapons into the region. The United States never reached a quid pro quo with Israel regarding nuclear nonproliferation and weapons sales.[157]

Congress offered solid backing for the sale of Phantoms to Israel, hopefully (though not necessarily) in the context of peace agreements in the Middle East. During an election year, some Republicans challenged Democrats over their pro-Israel credentials. Representative Widnall pointed out several times in a speech to the House floor, "It was not a Republican administration" that withheld jet sales to Israel to counterbalance Soviet MiGs going to Egypt, or provided secret arms financing to Arab states, or sent fighter jets to Jordan.[158] Rep. S. Fletcher Thompson (R-GA) called the U.S. policy of providing jets to Jordan "idiotic" and insisted on more weapons sales to Israel, particularly fighter jets.[159] Democratic representative Farbstein noted the ever-increasing numbers of Soviet weapons being sent to Egypt, including ground-to-ground missiles, and urged the government to sell Israel enough planes "to deter the Arab States and their Russian masters from starting hostilities."[160]

The State of Israel and pro-Israel forces in the United States undertook efforts to pressure Johnson into selling the Phantoms. Israel sent Yitzhak Rabin, former chief of staff (and future prime minister), as ambassador to Washington to advance the Israeli position with American officials. According to Spiegel, "In the Jewish community, every major organization stressed the importance of the jets in its political or educational activities (depending on the nature of the group)."[161] Non-Jewish organizations, like the AFL-CIO, Democratic Action, and the American Legion, also endorsed the sale.[162] But according to Bard, Johnson was especially irritated by pro-Israel lobbyists who pushed for weapons sales to Israel but failed to support the administration on Vietnam, which made him less inclined to sell the Phantoms.[163]

Congress tried to force the sale of Phantoms through legislation. In April, Rep. Bertram Podell (D-NY), in coordination with AIPAC, introduced a "sense of the House" resolution favoring the sale.[164] While not a binding piece of legislation, a sense of the House seeks to demonstrate general support for a certain measure. Ultimately, more than one hundred representatives and a few senators either signed or voiced support for the resolution.[165] In June, Sen. Stuart Symington (D-MO) "threatened to kill the military sales bill if the president did not deliver the Phantoms," though

Symington's motivation for the sale was likely due to the fact that they would be built in his home state.[166] The following month, Representative Wolff offered an amendment to the Foreign Assistance Act of 1968 that ordered the president to sell fifty Phantoms to Israel and replace losses suffered in the 1967 war. The Wolff amendment, after numerous representatives rose in support, cleared the House as part of the Foreign Aid Bill of 1968.[167]

Unlike Podell's resolution from April, Wolff's amendment did not have the backing of AIPAC because the legislation would have intruded too much on the president's right to conduct foreign relations. I. L. Kenen, head of AIPAC, informed the Senate Foreign Relations Committee that a resolution like Podell's that expressed the "sense of the Congress" would be sufficient.[168] According to John Mearsheimer and Stephen Walt, "AIPAC generally followed 'Kenen's Rules' to advance Israel's cause. Rule No. 1 was: 'Get behind legislation; don't step out in front of it (that is, keep a low profile).'"[169] Senator Church offered a substitute amendment to the Foreign Aid Bill that indicated congressional support for sale of the Phantoms, which passed the Senate on July 31.[170] Senator Javits urged President Johnson to take note of the section of the bill that called for immediate negotiations for the sale of supersonic jets to Israel as a deterrent force against future aggression.[171]

The Phantoms became an issue leading up to the 1968 presidential election. AIPAC, more commonly associated with lobbying the legislative branch than the executive branch, secured statements of support for the sale from the major presidential candidates and worked to get favorable planks at each party convention in 1968.[172] Presidential hopefuls Richard Nixon and Hubert Humphrey trumpeted their support for the sale while speaking at the B'nai B'rith convention in Washington on September 8. President Johnson spoke after the two candidates and shifted the discussion to the need for an arms-limitation agreement with the Soviet Union. The next day both Nixon and Humphrey reasserted their positions, and Humphrey claimed the sale of Phantoms was "now a necessity."[173]

Congress displayed strong, bipartisan support for the sale.[174] After rumor spread that the administration was leaning against it, Hugh Scott (R-PA) read on the Senate floor part of a letter he had just sent President Johnson that restated his repeated calls for the sale of the Phantoms. Scott also suggested his close relationship with AIPAC when he claimed to be "responsible in large measure for the language in the 1968 Republican platform which urged that the United States provide supersonic jets to Israel."[175] Rep. Jacob

Gilbert (D-NY) called for the sale of fifty Phantoms to Israel to restore the balance of power; Rep. Ovie Clark "O. C." Fisher (D-TX) wanted the U.S. government "to provide Israel with the arms that it needs for its own defense"; and Representative Blackburn went so far as to write a letter to Johnson to explain that even though he voted against the Foreign Assistance Act of 1968, he still wanted Johnson to sell the planes to Israel.[176] Representative Podell criticized the State Department for not recommending the sale and pointed out, "Both Houses of Congress believe that Phantom jets should be sold to Israel. The major party candidates for President are in full agreement on this policy. The failure to agree to this sale brings joy only to the Arab States and to the Soviet Union."[177] Additional remarks in support of the bill came from Representatives Pelly, Bell Jr., Richard McCarthy (D-NY), and Senator Javits.[178]

Opposition to the sale from within the administration started to soften due to Soviet aggression and congressional assertiveness. Previously, bureaucratic officials believed that Israel's forces were already superior; that selling the Phantoms would harm diplomatic relations with Arab states; that the sale would undermine Jarring's peace efforts; and that Israel should agree to nuclear nonproliferation as a precondition.[179] But ongoing efforts to reach an arms-control agreement with Moscow again came to naught.[180] The Soviet invasion of Czechoslovakia in August signaled Moscow's willingness to employ its military power, and the failure to reach an arms agreement in the Middle East compounded American concerns about Soviet machinations. Secretary of State Rusk ultimately concluded that the Phantom deal "is the most we can get away with in the light of the action of the Congress."[181]

The congressional message to the president was received. When Johnson signed the Foreign Assistance Act in October, he "announced that he had taken note of the section concerning the sale of airplanes to Israel, and was asking the Secretary of State to initiate negotiations with Israel."[182] Legislators happily noted the cooperation of the two branches in foreign policy decision-making. Sen. Clifford Case (R-NJ) applauded Johnson's "prompt response to the request by Congress," while Rep. Bill Roth (R-DE) noted with satisfaction how the president had responded to "Congress' mandate" and started negotiations with Israel. Farbstein congratulated the president and stated his belief that "the action of the Congress in recommending the sale of Phantom jets to Israel carried great weight with President Johnson in coming to his conclusion."[183] While congressional insistence likely influenced the president's decision to agree to the sale, Johnson, a consummate politician, undoubtedly recognized that the announcement of the sale of Phantoms would help Vice President Humphrey in the upcoming presidential election.[184]

Johnson agreed to sell fifty Phantoms in December 1968, with sixteen to be delivered in late 1969 and another thirty-four in 1970.[185] President-elect Nixon was left with the task of delivering the Phantoms to Israel, as well as dealing with more Israeli requests for additional weapons sales, supported by an increasingly combative Congress. Assistant Secretary of Defense Paul Warnke observed, "We will henceforth become the principal arms supplier to Israel, involving us even more intimately with Israel's security situation and involving more directly the security of the United States."[186] After the Phantom sale, the Soviet Union began delivering two hundred MiG 23s to Egypt, which escalated the arms race in the Middle East.[187]

Conclusion

The June war concretized the U.S.-Israel special relationship, strained American relations with the Arab world, and redefined the nature of the conflict and peace process. Johnson felt a strong cultural connection to Israel, but he did not want to develop a strategic partnership with Israel, either. As in later years, congressional insistence on weapons sales to Israel beyond the desires of the president worked to undercut peace initiatives by placing the United States more squarely on the side of Israel, and by empowering Israel to the point at which there was less incentive to compromise in peace negotiations. While Jarring's efforts to reach peace probably would have failed regardless of U.S. arms to Israel, the sale of the sophisticated Phantoms only further militarized the region. Over time, Israel developed such a military advantage, thanks largely to the United States, that it severely hampered the peace process. The United States shifted its policy from territorial integrity in the Middle East to support for Israeli occupation in order to force Arab states to make peace. That would remain U.S. policy, presumably, until peace was achieved by the warring parties.

The Vietnam War opened the door for more congressional involvement in foreign policy, and even though concerns about Vietnam would continue, the Middle East would gradually become more important in the minds of Americans and U.S. policymakers, and much more so after the 1973 oil embargo. Moving forward, between the Vietnam War and Nixon's Watergate fiasco, as Johnson notes, "Congress was situated to assume a degree of control over U.S. foreign policy unmatched since before World War II."[188] The Vietnam War also created enough distraction for the Johnson administration to fail to check Israel's ambition to construct civilian settlements and hold onto the territories taken during the war.

Congressional activity pointed to shifting support for Israel that increasingly reflected conservative political priorities and, overall, reflected a bipartisan consensus. Traditionally, U.S. political support for Israel came from the Democratic Party. But the political left had fragmented: support for labor declined, the Civil Rights Movement alienated Southern Democrats, and the Vietnam War and antiwar protesters furthered the split of the Democratic Party. Liberal support for Israel would continue to remain strong, but the New Left started to support Arab states against Israel's perceived imperialism. At the same time, the political right started to warm up to Israel.[189] Israel demonstrated military might at a time when the left started to crack, and when the right longed for a reliable partner in the Cold War. The swift Israeli victory in June 1967 stood in stark contrast to the quagmire in East Asia. Israel exhibited traits prized by Americans—"self-reliance, democracy, anti-communism, successful pragmatism, idealism."[190] The split in the Democratic Party over U.S.-Israel relations could be seen very clearly through the perspectives of William Fulbright and Henry "Scoop" Jackson, two leading Senate Democrats, to whom the story now turns.

2

Phantom Peace

Henry "Scoop" Jackson, J. William Fulbright, and Military Sales to Israel

When Richard Nixon assumed the presidency in 1969, despite Johnson's decision to sell offensive weapons, the future of U.S.-Israel relations remained uncertain. While Democratic presidents (Harry Truman, John Kennedy, and Lyndon Johnson) maintained generally positive relations with Israel, the Republican Dwight Eisenhower did not.[1] As former vice president for Eisenhower, President Nixon did not want to get too close to Israel, a position that can also be gleaned from his anti-Semitic comments recorded on Oval Office tapes and his many outbursts about Israel during the course of his one and one-half terms.[2] However, Nixon regarded Israel as an important friend in the Cold War, and he admired Israeli toughness and, therefore, sought a closer strategic alliance with Israel. But much like his predecessors, regardless of party affiliation, he actually pursued an evenhanded position in the Arab-Israeli conflict. Congress and the Cold War, along with Nixon's weakened position due to Watergate and Vietnam, reworked Nixon's policy aims in the Middle East.

During Nixon's first term as president, Congress played an influential role in securing larger military-aid packages for Israel, especially F-4 Phantom jets. Johnson agreed to sell fifty Phantoms in his last month in office, and Israeli officials hoped to persuade Nixon to sell more. The Phantoms promised to swing the balance of power in the Middle East even further in Israel's direction. Israeli airpower proved decisive in the 1967 Arab-Israeli War, and the War of Attrition between Israel and Egypt, which followed the 1967 war and ended in August 1970, showed the necessity of the sophisticated Phantoms to combat Soviet-supplied, Egyptian artillery along the Suez Canal Zone.[3] Nixon's first term witnessed a significant increase in military assistance to Israel that cannot be understood without looking at congressional—and, in particular, Senate—politics.

This chapter focuses on the battle between Henry "Scoop" Jackson (D-WA) and J. William Fulbright (D-AR) over U.S. foreign policy in the Middle East and, specifically, about military sales to Israel.[4] Jackson, who ran for president in 1972 and 1976, and Fulbright, the longest-tenured chair of the Senate Foreign Relations Committee, staked out very different positions for the proper relationship between the United States and Israel. Jackson viewed the Arab-Israeli conflict through the lens of the Cold War and wanted the president to authorize more military credit sales to Israel to match the growing Soviet presence in the region. Jackson planned to challenge détente, bolster his conservative position in foreign policy, and generate goodwill in the American Jewish community to support his upcoming bid for president. In doing so, he demonstrated that a senator can be just as apt to use the State of Israel to his advantage as the Israel lobby is to use a congressional official, which is a counterpoint to the argument made by Mearsheimer and Walt regarding the Israel lobby.[5] Fulbright, on the other hand, advocated for more cooperation with the Soviet Union in the hopes of facilitating a comprehensive peace agreement through the United Nations. He regarded increased military sales as a threat to a potential peace agreement.

Instead of looking at the Arab-Israeli peace process through the executive branch, as other scholars have done, this chapter views the issue of military sales seen primarily through the legislative branch, using the often-overlooked collections of important congressmembers to make its case.[6] That does not mean to suggest, however, that military sales and peace discussions existed in separate vacuums. Rather, the two have shared something of a symbiotic relationship, with each impacting discussions about the other. One reason Nixon sought to limit military sales was his fear that if Israel were too strong it would resist peace negotiations. Yet Israel fit perfectly into the Nixon Doctrine, which, in light of Vietnam, prescribed sending arms and providing a nuclear umbrella for regional allies in lieu of sending U.S. combat troops abroad. Therefore, the two discussions speak well to each other.

The debates about military aid for Israel revealed a developing alliance between U.S. conservatives and the State of Israel that would continue to impact U.S. foreign policy for decades to follow, in particular with regard to the peace process.[7] As shown in the Johnson years, support for Israel started to come from both liberals and conservatives, and increasingly from the latter. This dynamic accelerated during the Nixon years. Conservatives and Cold War hawks like Jackson advanced the congressional critique of Nixon's foreign policy, putting both Nixon and some liberals on the defensive. They disagreed with détente and aimed to continue the global war against communism, which included substantial military-aid packages, while liberals became more interested in human rights, nuclear nonproliferation, and reduced defense spending.

The perceived interests of U.S. conservatives and the State of Israel started to align. Both sides argued that a strong Israel was important for reasons of Cold War national security, and to achieve a lasting peace in the Middle East required large-scale military sales to Israel, including more Phantoms. For Israel, the United States could replace France as its primary weapons supplier, and for U.S. conservatives, especially in the context of the Vietnam War, Israel could become the new centerpiece of U.S. Cold War foreign policy. As the Cold War consensus fell apart, and as South Vietnam's position became increasingly untenable, conservative members of Congress shifted more of their focus from East Asia to the Middle East, where they joined many liberals in a revamped, bipartisan support for Israel that resulted in a powerful strategic alliance.

More Phantoms?

Unsatisfied with the status quo, Nasser declared a "War of Attrition" against Israel beginning in March 1969. Using Soviet weaponry, Egyptian forces began a heavy bombardment of Israeli forces along the Suez Canal Zone.[8] Israel was largely successful in repelling attacks and offered some of its own, conducting deep raids into Egyptian territory during the first few months of 1970, thanks to U.S.-made Phantoms.[9] The first delivery of Phantoms, which arrived in September 1969, extended Israel's strategic reach and abruptly changed the balance of power. Previously, Israel had launched only a few commando raids into Egypt. But by January 1970 the Phantoms allowed Israel to fly deep bombing raids into Egyptian territory, including the Cairo area. Egypt responded by asking Moscow for greater Soviet involvement, which in turn increased U.S. concern.[10]

Secretary of State William Rogers tried to assist U.N. special envoy Gunnar Jarring and restart the stalled peace process by offering his own plan. The

Rogers Plan, which was announced on December 9, 1969, focused on an Israel-Egypt agreement as a first step in the peace process. Israel was to withdraw from Egyptian territory occupied in 1967, in return for a peace agreement with Egypt that included safe passage of Israeli shipping through the Suez Canal.[11] However, the Rogers Plan met a strong refusal. National Security Advisor Henry Kissinger opposed the plan, and Nixon demonstrated ambivalence, not support. As William Quandt writes in *Peace Process,* "The Israeli and Soviet rejections of the Rogers Plan, and Egypt's nonacceptance, put a sudden end to the first Middle East initiative of the Nixon administration."[12]

The War of Attrition entered a new phase in early 1970 when the Soviet Union secretly increased its military involvement in Egypt with Operation *Kavkas.*[13] In response to Israeli air raids, and using the situation to its geopolitical advantage, the Kremlin substantially increased its military presence in Egypt by sending more than ten thousand "instructors" and "advisers," along with numerous SA-3 surface-to-air missile systems, which were quietly installed along the Suez Canal. The Soviet Navy strengthened its presence in the Mediterranean, and Soviet pilots became actively engaged in Egyptian air defense.[14] Soviet involvement reached a new level on April 18, when Soviet pilots chased down two Israeli jets that had been conducting reconnaissance inside Egypt. The Israeli jets were not attacked, but the Soviet willingness to directly challenge Israeli planes—and by extension the United States—brought with it the possibility for superpower confrontation in the Middle East.

Israel sought to advance its strategic alliance with the United States, but President Nixon responded coolly. Israeli officials asked to purchase an additional 125 planes (one hundred Skyhawks and twenty-five Phantoms) in September 1969. But Nixon declined to meet the new request. Nixon declined the same request again in March 1970, even after it became known that Moscow had increased its military involvement in Egypt. Nixon and Rogers believed that the existing order of fifty Phantoms was enough to keep the military balance of power in Israel's favor; however, the administration reserved the right to sell new aircraft if the situation changed significantly.[15] The administration viewed the Soviet weaponry as defensive in nature and wanted to avoid a further escalation unless it appeared that offensive weapons were being employed.[16]

Nixon declined to sell additional Phantoms to Israel for several reasons. For one, he believed that U.S. foreign policy in the region had been too biased in favor of Israel. He told Rogers, "I believe that an even-handed policy is, on balance, the best one for us to pursue as far as our own interests are concerned."[17] Second, Nixon recognized that Israel had secretly become a nuclear power and did not want to provide a vehicle to deliver such weapons. Third, he resented the influence of pro-Israel forces in Washington and was determined to conduct U.S. foreign policy apart from domestic influences. Fourth, he hoped peace discussions in the Middle East could advance détente with the Soviet Union.[18] Finally, Nixon feared that if Israel had a steady supply of Phantom jets, it would be even less inclined to work with Jarring to implement Resolution 242. In short, by denying further Phantom sales to Israel, Nixon hoped to cultivate better relations with the USSR and Arab states while maintaining leverage with Israel. Therefore, Nixon was unreceptive to repeated calls for the sale of additional F-4s to Israel. But as it had for Johnson, the decision to withhold Phantom sales to Israel put Nixon on a collision course with Congress.

Henry "Scoop" Jackson and William Fulbright

The Democratic Party started to fracture on Israel, and an emerging conservative bloc in Congress, which included hawkish Democrats and some Republicans, proved able to redraw the contours of U.S.-Israel relations. That split was best exemplified by the contentious relations between Henry "Scoop" Jackson and James William Fulbright.

Jackson and Fulbright were senatorial colleagues, but the two were not friends. "Indeed," says Jackson biographer Robert Kaufman, "the two men detested one another."[19] According to Helen Jackson, Henry's wife, "The only thing that Scoop and Senator Fulbright agreed on was where to buy wing-tip shoes in London."[20] Fulbright referred to Jackson as "the congressional spokesman for the military-industrial complex," while Jackson regarded Fulbright as "arrogant and a hypocrite"—someone who claimed to have sympathies for people abroad who were hurt by the "arrogance of American power, yet voted for the Southern Manifesto of 1956 and against every major piece of civil rights legislation that came before the Senate."[21] After Fulbright lost the Arkansas Democratic primary to Dale Bumpers in 1974, Jackson and his staff celebrated with a case of whiskey.[22]

In terms of U.S. foreign policy, Jackson and Fulbright represented the different ends of the political spectrum in the Democratic Party. Jackson was a realist and Cold War liberal who wanted nothing to do with détente and insisted on using military power to challenge the evil designs of the Soviet Union. Fulbright, on the other hand, was an idealist in the Wilsonian tradition who advocated a "new internationalism"—rooted in educational and cultural programs, reduced military spending, détente with the Soviet Union, and a more activist United Nations—to facilitate increased international understanding and a stronger position abroad. Fulbright hoped that a settlement to the Arab-Israeli crisis could be completed through the United Nations, which he explained in a speech on "A New Internationalism" to Yale University on April 4, 1971, as well as in his book about U.S. foreign policy, *The Crippled Giant*.[23]

The two had very different ideas about military sales and the Vietnam War. Jackson had long supported federal spending (especially defense spending) as a way to both contain communism and fuel the U.S. economy. Some officials, like Robert McNamara, labeled Jackson "the Senator from Boeing" for his efforts to secure defense contracts for the giant aviation company from his home state.[24] Sen. George Aiken (R-VT) once remarked that "other areas benefit from government contracts, too, but not all their elected members of Congress are as ardent in their endeavors as Scoop Jackson is."[25] Jackson supported U.S. involvement in the Vietnam War until very late and sought to counterbalance the influence of the New Left by supporting federal defense spending in order to challenge communist aggression abroad.

While Jackson sought to expand defense spending and supported U.S. military involvement in East Asia, Fulbright took the opposite position. Although he actually sponsored the Tonkin Gulf Resolution that granted President Johnson virtually unlimited powers to wage a war in Vietnam, Fulbright soon withdrew his support and eventually emerged as one of the leading voices against U.S. military involvement in East Asia.[26] Because he was head of the powerful Senate Foreign Relations Committee, the Johnson administration much disliked Fulbright's opposition to Vietnam.

Perhaps the greatest source of conflict between Jackson and Fulbright was about U.S. involvement in the Arab-Israeli conflict. Jackson was one of the loudest and strongest senatorial voices in support of a pro-Israel policy. He regarded Israel as a strategic asset that could protect U.S. interests in the region and prevent, or at least limit, Soviet involvement in the Middle East. Although Fulbright continually stressed his support for Israel, he sought a more evenhanded policy in which Israel would not be given much preferential treatment. He viewed U.S. support for Israel as a liability because it soured relations with Arab states and could potentially undermine efforts to work constructively with the Soviet Union.

Jackson had supported the State of Israel from his childhood years. He recalled that his mother first instilled in him a desire to defend Jewish people. He described her as "a Christian who believed in a strong Judaism. She taught me to respect the Jews, help the Jews! It was a lesson I never forgot."[27] In May 1944, Jackson publicly pledged: "If in any way, through my offices as a Congressman, I can forward the work of making the dream of a Jewish Homeland in Palestine come true, my most earnest efforts in this great humanitarian cause can be counted on."[28] While a congressman in 1945, Jackson and seven fellow congressmen traveled to the Buchenwald concentration camp in Germany upon invitation from Dwight Eisenhower to see firsthand the horrors of Nazi atrocities. According to Kaufman, this experience, along with Jackson's philo-Semitism, help to explain the senator's strong support for the Jewish state.[29] Naturally, Jackson supported Harry Truman's decision to immediately recognize the State of Israel in May 1948, and even before the Suez Crisis in the fall of 1956, provoked in part by Egyptian acceptance of a Soviet aid package, Jackson argued that the Soviet Union was "stirring a witches' brew for the Free World in the Middle East."[30]

Fulbright supported the State of Israel but also wanted U.S. foreign policy to reflect a balanced desire to help both Israelis and Arabs. His position reflected the Eisenhower policy toward the Middle East; however, Fulbright later parted ways with Eisenhower. He objected to the Eisenhower Doctrine, which promised military or economic aid to any Middle Eastern country to resist the spread of communism, and instead offered a substitute resolution that called for freedom of navigation through the Suez Canal, a comprehensive settlement to the Arab-Israeli conflict, and a reaffirmation of America's right to participate in regional collective security under Article 51 of the U.N. Charter.[31]

Fulbright often found himself at odds with pro-Israel lobbying groups. When JFK was considering Fulbright for Secretary of State, "American Jews and officials of the Israeli embassy bombarded members of Kennedy's entourage with entreaties to pick anybody but Fulbright."[32] During the early 1960s, Fulbright worked with the Senate Foreign Relations Committee to investigate unregistered agents for foreign governments. The investigation, which ultimately led to major revisions to the 1938 Foreign Agents Registration Act, put Fulbright at odds with pro-Israel supporters in the United States.[33] According to Woods, the animosity created by this investigation ran deep, and "the Israeli government and American Zionists would neither forget nor forgive Fulbright."[34]

The different positions of Jackson and Fulbright became more pronounced following the 1967 Arab-Israeli War. Jackson supported the Johnson administration's strong backing of Israel.[35] He viewed the Arab-Israeli conflict through the prism of the Cold War; the main problem in the region was the same problem elsewhere—the Soviet Union. Fulbright, on the other hand, believed that more superpower cooperation, conducted through the United Nations, could diffuse the situation by guaranteeing Israeli shipping through the Gulf of Aqaba, combined with an Israeli withdrawal from the territories occupied in the recent war. In return for an Israeli withdrawal, the Soviet Union could potentially use its influence with North Vietnam to help end the fighting in East Asia.[36] But Fulbright recognized the challenges in such a course because the U.S. "role in that area has indeed been complicated by the unbalanced policy we have followed there. The truth is that the dominant influence in our domestic-political scene of the Zionist organization makes it very difficult for any Administration to be objective about the Middle East."[37] The influence of pro-Israel lobbyists would continue to play a central role in Fulbright's critique of U.S. foreign policy in the region.

Although Fulbright took on the Nixon administration over Vietnam, he emerged as the Senate's strongest supporter of Nixon and Rogers in the Middle East. He recognized that the administration, to his liking, sought to pursue an evenhanded approach. He supported the Rogers Plan but bemoaned "the enormous influence of the Zionists in this country," which made the administration's task much more difficult.[38] Moreover, Fulbright resented the way "the subject of peace in the Middle East is one upon which American citizens are not viewed as either patriotic or unbiased unless they endorse and even embrace the policies of a single foreign government."[39] Although he hoped to "contribute to the improvement of relations in the Middle East," Fulbright recognized that "I am, after all, a legislator, and it is not my responsibility to supplant the Ambassadors or other representatives of the Executive Branch" in matters of foreign policy.[40] He similarly downplayed the legislative role to a constituent, explaining that a solution to the Arab-Israeli conflict was "not a legislative matter, but an executive matter."[41] In the Middle East,

Fulbright desired greater presidential assertiveness coupled with congressional acquiescence, likely because he agreed with Nixon's policy aims in that region.

Jackson regarded U.S. foreign policy in the Middle East as fundamentally flawed because it failed to recognize that the Soviet Union was trying to take over the region through its regional ally, Egypt. Operation *Kavkas* and the substantial increase in the Soviet presence in 1970 seemed to validate, to some extent, Jackson's argument. He viewed the situation as a continuation of the historical Russian drive for domination of the region for a warm-water port, and for the more recent discovery of oil supplies. Especially affected by the Cuban Missile Crisis, Jackson considered the Soviet buildup of arms in Egypt to be another attempt to undermine U.S. interests, or at least to create leverage for more favorable negotiations. Kissinger, too, considered the Soviet tactics to be similar to those employed in Cuba.[42]

Jackson argued that the best way to achieve a settlement to the Arab-Israeli conflict required substantially increasing military aid to Israel. Such a move would deter Soviet meddling and allow Israel "to take risks at the negotiating table."[43] Military aid promised to play an important role in the Arab-Israeli peace process.

The Jackson Amendment, or Section 501 of the Defense Procurement Act

The positions of Jackson and Fulbright diverged even further in the spring of 1970. In light of revelations of increased Soviet activity in Egypt, and as Nixon widened the Vietnam War by invading Cambodia, Israeli ambassador Yitzhak Rabin stirred up congressional opposition to the administration's unwillingness to sell more Phantoms to Israel. The Nixon administration hoped to parlay a hold on Phantom sales to Israel into closer relations with Egypt and movement forward in the peace process. Therefore, Nixon sent Joseph Sisco to Cairo to meet with Nasser in mid-April. Nasser had little reason to believe that U.S.-Egypt negotiations could lead to a peace agreement with Israel, but he also realized that the appearance of movement toward peace could prevent new shipments of Phantoms to Israel. In a May 1 speech, Nasser invited the United States to advance a new political initiative. The following month Secretary of State Rogers responded with a "second" Rogers Plan, which called on Egypt and Israel to accept a cease-fire and end the War of Attrition.[44]

The White House wanted to restrict weapons to Israel to force it to compromise, but Congress wanted to increase weapons to Israel so it would feel strong enough to make concessions. Legislators occasionally used open letters to the executive branch in an effort to influence policy, as in February 1966, when more than seventy-five representatives wrote to Secretary of State Rusk to call for more weapons sales to Israel; or in the fall of 1968, when seventy senators signed a letter to LBJ, asking that he sell Phantom jets to Israel.[45] On May 26, 1970, Jackson joined with seventy-two other senators in signing a letter to Secretary of State Rogers that asked the administration to authorize the sale of 125 warplanes to Israel, the same request made in September 1969, in order to restore the military balance in Israel's favor.[46] Invited by Sen. Abe Ribicoff (D-CT) to sign the letter, Fulbright declined.[47] On June 4, the House of Representatives forwarded a similar letter with ninety signatures.[48] Never one to be pressured by either Congress or pro-Israel lobbyists, Nixon again refused to meet the request.

Jackson responded by using his position within the Senate Armed Services Committee to sponsor an amendment to give the president broad powers to supply Israel with military arms. The Jackson amendment, otherwise known as Section 501 of the Defense Procurement Act, linked a strong Israel to Cold War geopolitics: "The Congress views with grave concern the deepening involvement of the Soviet Union in the Middle East. . . . In order to restore and maintain the military balance in the Middle East, by furnishing to Israel the means of providing for its own security, the President is authorized to transfer to Israel, by sale, credit sale or guaranty, such aircraft, and equipment appropriate to use, maintain and protect such aircraft."[49] Jackson included the phrase "grave concern" to reference a February 18 speech by Nixon, in which the president noted that the United States would view with "grave concern" any Soviet efforts to seek predomination in the Middle East. Jackson explained in a statement that the committee wanted "the Soviet Union to understand that its effort to achieve dominance in the Middle East by tipping the military balance cannot be ignored by the United States."[50] Although Phantoms were not specifically mentioned by name, the implication was obvious. The Armed Services Committee passed the Jackson amendment on June 17, 1970.

Amos Eiran, who served as Israel's liaison to Congress from 1966 to 1972, played an integral role in the formulation and passage of the Jackson amendment. In an interview, Eiran offered an insider's account and admitted, "I was behind that from A to Z."[51] Eiran explained that he did not personally know Scoop Jackson before June 1970, so he phoned Jackson's office in order to arrange a meeting with the senator to discuss the Phantoms. He spoke with Jackson's longtime assistant, Dorothy Fosdick, who Eiran remembered "was very helpful from the beginning." Jackson's schedule did not allow for any meetings during the day, so Fosdick suggested that Eiran wait for Jackson at the senators' breakfast room at 8:00 a.m. the next morning. Eiran followed Fosdick's advice, and the two men had breakfast and discussed the possibility of an amendment to finance Phantom jets for Israel. During their talk, Jackson mentioned that the Foreign Relations Committee, chaired by Fulbright, wanted to include an amendment to the Foreign Military Sales Act, proposed by John Sherman Cooper (R-KY) and Frank Church (D-ID), which aimed to cut off all funding for ground troops and military advisers to Cambodia and Laos. Therefore, Jackson said an amendment to the Defense Procurement Act by way of the Armed Services Committee made more sense.[52]

In order to bypass Foreign Relations and Fulbright (whom some Israelis jokingly called "Half-bright"), Jackson told Eiran that he needed to secure the support of Stuart Symington. Symington, a Democrat from Missouri, served on both Senate committees—Foreign Relations and Armed Services. Eiran recalled, "Jackson said, 'If Symington will support you, he can come and say that also the Foreign Relations committee is present in some way or another.'" Eiran met with Symington and explained the situation. "And Symington was keen and supported this all because of the employment in his state."[53] The Phantom planes sought by Israel and Eiran were made by McDonnell Douglas, near St. Louis, Missouri.

Even with the support of Symington and Jackson, Eiran still had to navigate an odd and humorous situation in order to get the amendment through Armed Services. Jackson told Eiran he would propose the amendment at the next committee meeting, but he needed Symington to second the amendment. Symington agreed. But on the day Jackson planned to bring the motion, Symington was absent. Jackson sent Eiran a note from the meeting: "Amos, you have let me down. Symington didn't even show up!" Eiran raced to Symington's office and asked, "What happened to the Senator? He is supposed to be in a meeting!" Symington's assistant responded, "Don't ask, don't ask—terrible teeth pain!" So Eiran quickly sent a note to Jackson: "Listen, Symington went to the dentist and that's why he didn't show up. He didn't notify because he was in terrible pain." Jackson decided, "If that's the case, I will not propose. I will wait until another meeting on Thursday and make sure!" The committee met again on that Thursday, with Symington present, and the Jackson amendment cleared the committee.[54]

Eiran realized that the amendment represented a major achievement for Israel in its efforts to become a strategic partner of the United States during the Cold War. He acknowledged that the Israeli "goal was to convince the U.S. administration, whether its executive or legislative, that Israel is a strategic venue. And we were convinced that they were never exactly convinced." The 1967 war, which led to a marked increase in Soviet involvement in Egypt and Syria, made his job easier. Eiran wanted "to inform, convince if possible, all those legislators that Israel's role in the Middle East is a part of the world picture of the Cold War at that time." To that end, "We made a great effort to convince, on the legislative side, to convince all the senators and congressmen as well as the public opinion . . . the columnists, the major columnists." He called the Jackson amendment a "major breakthrough. For the first time, that particular defense act for domestic purposes, related to U.S. forces, was used to finance planes for Israel." Eiran suggested that Israel needed only $270 million, but Jackson said, "We are not dealing in those amounts. Let's make it $500 million." Eiran rightly noted that "it was not just important for the sum of money, but it was important strategically. . . . Israel became a part of the American defense budget . . . like it had never been before."[55] Also important, the language of the Jackson amendment specifically cited Soviet involvement in the Middle East as the primary justification for empowering the president to sell more planes to Israel. With the Jackson amendment, the United States and Israel solidified a formal strategic relationship.

Jackson, like Eiran, understood that the amendment signaled that a dramatic transformation of the U.S.-Israel relationship was in the making. He recognized that the amendment would be "the first time a military assistance commitment to Israel has become the law of the land."[56] The amendment indicated that any weaponry to "maintain and protect such aircraft" could be sold to Israel, which opened the door to a broad interpretation. And within six months, the U.S. Congress would authorize the president to sell to Israel, by the most favorable credit terms available, virtually any piece of nonnuclear military hardware. However, time would tell that Nixon had reservations about sending more and more sophisticated arms to Israel.

Fulbright opposed the Jackson amendment for two reasons. First, he believed that U.S. foreign policy needed to become more evenhanded in the Middle East, and the amendment clearly positioned the United States on the side of Israel. Second, Fulbright argued that Jackson was exceeding his legislative authority. Jackson intentionally circumvented the Foreign Relations Committee because he understood that the Fulbright-chaired committee would never approve such an amendment. So Fulbright tried to persuade Armed Services chairman John C. Stennis (D-MN) to let Foreign Relations take the lead on the issue, arguing that the subject was "within the jurisdiction of the Foreign Relations Committee on the grounds that the amendment relates to 'foreign loans,' 'relations . . . with foreign nations generally,' or 'commercial intercourse with foreign nations.'"[57] Fulbright also pointed out that the Senate was already considering an amendment to the Foreign Military Sales Act that addressed the issue of "cash and credit sales of military equipment to foreign nations," including Israel.[58] Although the Jackson amendment passed the committee level, Stennis reportedly had "misgivings."[59]

In the specific case of Israel, the Senate sought to broaden the president's authority to furnish weapons. Considering the unpopularity of the Vietnam War (the invasion of Cambodia and shootings at Kent State had just happened that spring), and with congressional efforts to rein in executive power (the Senate repealed the Tonkin Gulf Resolution on June 24 and passed Cooper-Church on June 30), the Jackson amendment went against the grain of recent developments. According to Robert David Johnson, "In 1969, legislators cut the administration's requested defense budget by more than $8 billion, the largest such reduction, in percentage terms, since the first post-Korean War budget. In 1970, the pattern continued, with Congress ultimately appropriating $66.6 billion in defense funds, 6.3 percent below the administration's request."[60]

Another pivotal air battle in the Middle East took place on July 29, which led to acceptance of the cease-fire that eventually ended the War of Attrition.[61] The Nixon administration, undoubtedly displeased that U.S.-made Phantoms participated in the conflict, pressed Golda Meir's cabinet to accept the cease-fire proposed by Rogers. Just a week before the air battle, in order to soften the Israeli position, Nixon gave Meir his word that when peace talks began, the United States would not pressure Israel to accept the Arab interpretation of U.N. Resolution 242. While pleased with the idea, Meir also reportedly expected "additional compensation" in terms of military and economic aid.[62]

Ultimately, the Meir cabinet voted to approve the cease-fire on July 31, and the War of Attrition ended on August 7.

Some congressional members, especially in the Senate, continued to push the president to increase military sales to Israel. On July 30, the day after the air battle, Nixon received a letter from seventy-two senators, echoing the message sent eight weeks earlier to Rogers, to pursue peace in the Middle East based on U.S. military might offered to Israel.[63] The next day, on the Senate floor, Joseph Tydings (D-MD) called the administration's unwillingness to sell Phantoms "a tragic mistake."[64] On August 7, Bob Dole (R-KS) and Birch Bayh (D-IN) both voiced their support for selling Phantoms to Israel.[65] In the House, Rep. Graham Purcell (D-TX) submitted to the *Record* a resolution from the Texas Department of the American Legion that urged the U.S. government "to allow Israel to obtain F-4 Phantom jet fighter aircraft, Skyhawk fighter-bombers, and other sophisticated equipment it has requested or may need in order to insure its own defense."[66] Rep. Michael Harrington (D-MA) reminded his constituents in his personal newsletter, which he submitted to the *Record* on August 10, that he "joined with 221 colleagues in the House in writing the President on June 10 urging that the U.S. provide Israel with additional supersonic jet aircraft."[67]

However, a few senators, in light of the July 30 cease-fire, did not call for weapons sales and instead urged negotiations that aimed to implement U.N. Resolution 242. On August 3, Senate Majority Leader Mike Mansfield (D-MT), Minority Leader Hugh Scott (R-PA), and Henry Bellmon (R-OK) all commended Nixon and Rogers for pursuing a policy of peace.[68] Neither Mansfield nor Bellmon signed the May letter to Rogers or the July letter to Nixon; Scott signed both.

Egyptian violations of the cease-fire encouraged more senators to vocalize their support for Phantom sales to Israel. Soviet surface-to-air missile sites had been advanced along the Suez Canal, along with the construction of new missile sites, to strengthen Egypt's position; Israel, however, did not violate the cease-fire.[69] On August 20, Senator Javits called on Nixon to supply "Israel with the military equipment, including aircraft, parts, electronic, and so forth, which it needs in order to maintain its balance of force, which the president himself spoke about on July 1."[70] Sen. Charles Percy (R-IL) commended Javits and added that there were "very few controversial matters where greater unanimity of accord has been reached in the Senate than in this matter."[71] Ribicoff soon followed with a longer, more impassioned plea on behalf of weapons sales to Israel. He communicated being "saddened and perplexed by our Government's treatment of a staunch and trustworthy ally—Israel"—and called specifically "for the extension of the Nixon doctrine to the Middle East." He reminded the Senate (and Nixon) that Israel "does not need American troops—nor does she want them. . . . But Israel does need our help and support now—not against her Arab foes—but against the Soviet Union."[72] The following day, Richard Schweiker (R-PA) noted that the situation created "a marked deterioration in Israel's strategic position" and criticized the State Department for being "strangely silent" about the cease-fire violations, despite the fact that it "does not deny that the movement of missiles took place or that this constitutes a breach of the cease-fire."[73]

For his part, Fulbright thought long-term peace in the region could be secured only by limiting U.S. aircraft sales to Israel. He floated the possibility of a treaty with Israel in a lengthy speech on the Senate floor on August 24. He urged Israel to agree to a peace settlement that included withdrawal from the occupied territories and a just settlement for the refugee problem.[74] In return, Fulbright proposed a "treaty of guarantee" with Israel that included a U.S. commitment to protect, militarily if necessary, "the territory and independence of Israel within the borders of 1967." But Israel rejected the proposal immediately, arguing such assurances were no substitute for bilateral peace agreements with Arab states. The Nixon administration, too, backed away from the proposal.[75]

Unable to find support for his treaty plan, Fulbright offered his own amendment on August 30, hoping to outmaneuver Jackson. Fulbright's proposal sought to link the president's authority to extend credits to Israel to enactment of the Foreign Military Sales Act, rather than the Defense Procurement Act, thereby nullifying the Jackson amendment. The Fulbright amendment did, however, contain a safeguard—if the Foreign Military Sales Act failed to be passed, which would have deprived Israel of arms, then the Jackson amendment would automatically be enacted. Jackson, of course, opposed the amendment and included for the *Record* the names of eighty-one senators who, in support of more military aid for Israel, had "expressed themselves in letters to the President or the Secretary of State."[76] John Tower (R-TX), member of the Armed Services Committee, claimed that Section 501 did not aim "to usurp the jurisdiction of any other committee" but was approved to provide the president with "sufficient flexibility to meet its Mideast commitments."[77] Fulbright pleaded with the Senate. He noted that the

Nixon administration had not asked for the authority provided for in Section 501 and that Stennis, the chair of Armed Services, opposed it, too.[78]

But Fulbright's efforts came to naught. The Senate overwhelmingly rejected his measure by a landslide vote (87–7) on September 1, and congressional support for Israel reached a new high point. Situated somewhere between Jackson and Fulbright were many of the Senate doves who supported Israel but also wanted to curb the White House's ability to sell weapons to foreign nations. Many of these doves supported section 501. Jackson's committee—Armed Services—was generally a hawkish group of senators who, in the summer of 1970, supported the war in East Asia as well as military sales for Israel.[79] Yet an alliance between hawks and doves in the Senate in support of a dramatic increase of military weapons sales to Israel muted the few calls for a more balanced policy in the region. Later in September the Senate passed the $19.2 billion Defense Procurement Act by a vote of 84–3.[80]

Nixon finally agreed to sell more Phantoms to Israel on the same day that section 501 cleared the Senate; however, he agreed to sell only eighteen Phantoms, rather than the more ambitious Israeli request for one hundred Skyhawks and twenty-five Phantoms. The administration informed Cairo that the violations of the August cease-fire freed it from a June 19 pledge made to Egypt that the United States would not sell further Phantoms to Israel.[81] Thus, Nixon was prepared to arm Israel if he felt Egypt and the Soviet Union, not Israel, threatened to undermine peace efforts.

The reaction to the cease-fire violations revealed the tension between Secretary of State Rogers and National Security Advisor Kissinger. Rogers argued that the violations did not represent a "major change" in the military situation, and he accused Kissinger of trying to "foment a crisis by being so insistent on ceasefire violations."[82] Kissinger pushed so hard for more Phantoms to Israel that Nixon told Chief of Staff H. R. Haldeman to "get K[issinger] off of the Middle East."[83] For the time being (but not for long), Rogers remained in charge of U.S. foreign policy in the Middle East.

Soon after the Senate passed the Defense Procurement Act, the Jackson amendment was broadened to allow for the sale of nearly any weaponry to Israel. Although the initial proposal was "already one of the most generous arms transfer measures ever written by Congress," according to a report written by Senate and House negotiators, Israel would be able to purchase, on credit, "ground weapons, such as missiles, tanks, howitzers, armored personnel carriers, ordnance, etc. as well as aircraft."[84]

After working to secure massive military sales for Israel, Jackson was invited to visit Israel as a guest of the Israeli government in November 1970.[85] While in Israel he met with Prime Minister Golda Meir and Defense Minister Moshe Dayan, Chief of Staff of the Armed Forces General Haim Bar-Lev, and Chief of Intelligence General Aharon Yariv; he also visited the Golan Heights and Israeli settlements.[86] His strong popularity in Israel was confirmed by Hannah Zemer, "the blond beauty" who was editor-in-chief of *Davar,* a Tel Aviv daily publication. Referring to Jackson's landslide reelection victory in his home state of Washington in 1970 (winning with a whopping 84 percent), Zemer commented on an Israeli television program, "You are as popular in Israel as you proved to be in your state of Washington which re-elected you. If you moved to Israel and ran for the Knesset I think you would win by as big a margin as you did in Washington."[87]

As he neared the end of his trip, Jackson had time to reflect on his amendment. According to Jackson, section 501 "gave the President very, very broad authority to make available military equipment, virtually of all kinds, on long term and favorable credit arrangements." Jackson indicated that the next step was to wait for Nixon to submit a supplemental budget request that utilized the powers given to the president. Jackson expected the administration to request $500 million, although he admitted, "I have no official knowledge as to what the Administration, meaning the President, will request of the Congress."[88] But he urged "the Nixon administration to tell the Soviet Union that unless those surface-to-air missiles are removed from the Suez Canal zone, Israel will get all the American-made weapons she needs to defend herself."[89] When Nixon submitted the supplemental budget request, he asked for the $500 million already authorized by Congress through the Jackson amendment. Among the items promised to Israel were 180 modern tanks (a combination of M-60 main battle tanks and M-48 Patton tanks), as well as eighteen more Skyhawks and the eighteen Phantoms agreed to in September.[90]

While the scope and extent of the military hardware far exceeded what any previous arrangement had allowed, Nixon did not open up the entire U.S. arsenal. Not until the airlift during the 1973 Arab-Israeli War, after significant and surprising Israeli losses, did Nixon agree to provide Israel with more advanced transport planes and helicopters, as well as an assortment of missiles, such as Chaparral surface-to-air missiles, Maverick and Shrike air-to-ground missiles, LAW anti-tank missiles, and TOW missile launchers.[91]

After returning from Israel, Jackson submitted a report to his committee, which argued that the best path to peace lay with arming Israel. He cited Soviet troublemaking as the primary problem in the region. "If there were no Arab-Israeli conflict," wrote Jackson, "the Soviets would invent one."[92] Jackson argued, "The central problem in the Middle East is the Soviet drive for hegemony."[93] The solution, according to Jackson, required military support for Israel in order to convince the Soviet Union that diplomacy was the only real option. By arming Israel, the United States could further the cause of peace by "discouraging radical Arab hopes for the eventual military defeat of Israel—hopes that lead to a menacing and destabilizing alliance with the Soviet Union and that deepen Soviet influence in the region as a whole."[94] Jackson recommended abandoning Rogers's insistence on "insubstantial alterations" to Israeli borders; instead, he called for "defensible borders" and "concrete, physical arrangements to assure Israel's security which, if imperiled, merely invites Soviet exploitation and plants the seed of future war."[95] Until then, Jackson believed it was "unwise to return to the Jarring talks."[96]

But Nixon continued to fear Israeli intransigence due to military strength. Turning the tables on Jackson, Nixon actually declined to use the broad powers authorized to the president via the Jackson amendment during the next fiscal year. Instead, when Nixon submitted the new budget in early 1971, he included Israel within the more general request through the Foreign Military Sales Act, rather than the Defense Procurement Act. Instead of authorizing $500 million of military sales to Israel through the Jackson amendment, the administration requested $582 million for fifteen countries, of which Israel would receive a large share.[97] The move demonstrated the alliance of Rogers and Fulbright, as Foreign Relations, rather than Armed Services, would handle the request. Jackson was "dismayed by the failure of the Administration's new budget to use the broad authority to extend military credits to Israel that was overwhelmingly voted by the last Congress." Calling the Middle East "the cockpit of the cold war," Jackson noted that Moscow might interpret the budget request "as an indication of the indecision and ambivalence at precisely the time when firmness and resolve are needed."[98]

Speaking at the B'nai B'rith Inaugural Israel Bond Dinner in Los Angeles on February 7, Jackson made an obvious point. "The truth is that the strongest U.S. policy statement in support of Israel's security has come not from the White House or the State Department," said Jackson, "but from the Congress by adoption of my amendment to the Defense Procurement Act of

1970."[99] Rowland Evans and Robert Novak, writing for the *Washington Post,* recognized that Jackson was "attracting wide political support from the American Jewish community" as he prepared to run for president in 1972.[100]

Privately, Fulbright expressed his concerns about Senate support for Israel. He wrote to David Nes, a diplomat and old friend, "I am unable to find any substantial support in the Senate for a balanced attitude toward the two contending forces in the Middle East." He blamed, in part, an alliance between Zionists and "our own military establishment."[101] In a letter to West German ambassador M. Kamel, Fulbright bemoaned the influence of the Senate. "In this instance," wrote Fulbright, "I really believe that the President and the Secretary of State have desired to follow a more even-handed and balanced policy, but that the Congress, especially such members as Senator Jackson, have undermined the Administration's policy."[102]

Another Failed Initiative

The battle between the executive and legislative branches about U.S. foreign policy in the Middle East extended beyond military sales. In early 1971, the Senate took on Secretary Rogers and his newest idea for the Arab-Israeli peace process.

As in the previous spring, Nixon hoped to withhold Phantom sales to better U.S.-Egypt relations and advance peace negotiations through Jarring. After Nasser suffered a fatal heart attack during the Black September crisis in Jordan, he was replaced by Vice President Anwar Sadat. Sadat proved more willing than Nasser to warm relations with the United States and search for a peace arrangement with Israel. In early November he extended the cease-fire by three months, and a November 23 letter from Sadat to Nixon indicated that Egypt was prepared to engage Jarring in further peace discussions. On December 28, Meir announced that Israel would participate in the talks as well.[103]

The peace process seemed to get a boost in early February when Sadat extended the Egyptian-Israeli cease-fire another thirty days and declared that he intended to reopen the Suez Canal to Israeli shipping in return for an Israeli withdrawal from the Canal Zone. Shortly after, Sadat informed Jarring that Egypt was ready to "terminate all states of claims of belligerency with Israel, as well as respect Israel's 'right to live within secure and recognized boundaries.'"[104] Jarring sent Israel an appealing proposal—Israel was to withdraw to the international boundary in return for Egypt's terminating all states of belligerency and opening the Suez Canal and Straits of Tiran to international shipping.[105] But the Israelis balked at the proposal and chose not to engage Jarring in further discussions.

Rogers and Nixon were infuriated by the Israelis. Rogers had a heated meeting with Israeli ambassador Yitzhak Rabin on February 24, while Nixon openly questioned sending arms to Israel when they refused to negotiate. During a March 9 meeting, Rogers informed Kissinger, CIA Director Richard Helms, and Defense Secretary Melvin Laird "that he intended to push the Israelis hard over the coming weeks so that they would be more forthcoming in working with Sadat." Rogers intended to offer military sales and financial aid for refugee resettlement and other issues, and in return Israel would withdraw to roughly the 1967 borders. Kissinger warned him that meant a "total confrontation" with Israel, but Rogers was determined. That evening he declared to the Public Broadcasting Service that the United States was willing to contribute military forces to an international peacekeeping force in the area, presumably with a Soviet troop commitment, in order to provide heightened security.[106]

The Senate critics sparred with Fulbright over Rogers's new proposal. Jackson called it "the stupidest thing. It is hard to imagine a more shortsighted and dangerous arrangement for the Middle East than the one that forces Israel back to indefensible borders and then installs Russian troops along those borders."[107] Both Jackson and Jacob Javits delivered speeches on the Senate floor that took aim at Rogers and his proposal, and they were joined in their support by Ribicoff and other influential senators, like Hugh Scott, Hubert Humphrey (D-MN), and Joseph Montoya (D-NM); Rep. Bill Frenzel (R-MN) voiced his opposition in the House.[108] Fulbright again came to the defense of the administration. He agreed with Rogers in that a negotiated settlement, rather than "geography and the force of arms," was in the interest of Israel. Furthermore, Fulbright feared that Israel was "giving notice that they do not intend to withdraw from the territories that they took" during the 1967 war.[109]

The Senate uproar convinced Rogers to take an unprecedented step. "For the first time in the nation's history," according to a March 25 article in the *Houston Chronicle,* "a secretary of state will meet with the entire Senate today for an interchange devoted exclusively to the Middle East."[110] Rogers volunteered to appear in a closed-door session after Senate leadership requested a briefing by "some Middle East policymaker."[111] But the decision by Rogers to be *that* policymaker was surprising and indicated the administration's hope to rally Senate support for an initiative that could restart the peace process. Rogers felt inclined to address the Senate after Israeli Foreign Minister Abba Eban presented the Israeli position at a recent breakfast with forty senators.[112] At the same time, the appearance by Rogers would work to offset mounting criticisms that the president did not consult enough with Congress about foreign-policy matters.

The meeting revealed the strength of Senate opposition. Rogers had been pushing for Israel to agree in principle to withdrawal as a precondition for peace agreements, but when meeting with the senators he backed off that idea. Instead, he shifted the emphasis to "demilitarization of the Sinai Peninsula and an as yet undefined security arrangement for Sharm El-Sheikh that is satisfactory to Israel." According to Jackson, "Rogers promised that if an American military role in the Middle East with the Russians ever was contemplated again, the administration would seek Senate approval."[113] Perhaps most importantly, as Javits reported after the meeting, the Rogers proposal meant that "no settlement would be imposed" on Israel.[114] After Rogers met with Sadat in Cairo that May, Senator Bayh expressed his concern over reports that Rogers had promised Sadat that the United States would demand "no further compromises" from Egypt. Bayh hoped that such reports were false, and Ribicoff reminded his colleagues that Rogers had assured the Senate in March that Israel would not be pressured at all to remove from the occupied territories.[115] In combination with determined support for an enormous increase in military sales to Israel, the Senate emerged as a formidable challenge to the Nixon administration's handling of the peace process and its attempts to chart an evenhanded course.

Conservative Support for Israel

Liberal support for Israel was ebbing, and conservative support was rapidly increasing. A March 29 article in *The Christian Science Monitor* stated, "A rift has begun to open in the hitherto almost solid support of the American political Left in Washington for Israel's bargaining position in the Middle East conflict." The article explained that Nixon and Rogers enjoyed "somewhat more support from Democratic and Republican liberal sources," and that two left-leaning newspapers, the *New York Times* and the *Washington Post,* "both ran editorials calling on Israel to end its categorical demands for territory."[116] At the American Zionist Federation's celebration of Israel's independence on April 28, Jackson and Sen. James L. Buckley (R-NY) each spoke out against the administration's policies.[117] During a two-day luncheon for Congress hosted by AIPAC, Senate Minority Leader Scott spoke about a "genuine convergence of interest" between Israel and the United States. He added that providing arms to Israel "must and will continue . . . and frankly, it will continue under any administration in this country." During the House luncheon, Michigan Republican Rep. Gerald Ford accused two Senate Democrats—Fulbright and Edmund Muskie of Maine—"of undermining American support for Israel."[118] In a reversal of conventional wisdom at the time, conservatives were putting liberals on the defensive about U.S. support for Israel.

Nixon recognized that conservatives, not liberals, had emerged as Israel's more reliable friends. In a memorandum for Kissinger in March 1970, Nixon described "the danger for Israel of relying on the prominent liberal and dove senators of both parties to come through in the event a crisis arose." The liberal response to the Vietnam War weighed heavily on Nixon's mind. "When the chips are down they [liberal and dove senators] will cut and run," said Nixon, "not only as they are presently cutting and running in Vietnam, but also when any conflict in the Mideast stares them straight in the face." According to Nixon, Israel's "real friends (to their great surprise) are people like Goldwater, Buckley, RN et al., who are considered to be hawks on Vietnam but who, in the broader aspects, are basically not cut-and-run people whether it is in Vietnam, the Mideast, Korea, or any place else in the world."[119]

Despite his support for Israel, Nixon continued to fear that weapons sales, pushed by Congress, would undermine peace negotiations. During a National Security Council (NSC) meeting on July 16, Nixon recommended that Joe Sisco fly to Israel to discuss negotiations and Israel's need for additional aircraft. The timing was especially important for Nixon because Congress would be out of session "for the best part of August." Nixon said that "we are not going to have a policy governed by domestic political opinion, but we do have 'more running room' when Congress is out of session, particularly on the aircraft question." Nixon asked that Sisco keep "a very low-profile" and "suggested that Mr. Sisco go out the following week and then stay there until Congress gets out of town." Nixon added, "Don't promise them a damn thing. This is not going to be a free ride this time. From now on it is quid pro quo."[120]

For her part, Israeli Prime Minister Meir also recognized that U.S. conservatives had become the better friends of Israel. The New Left was becoming increasingly hostile toward "imperialistic" Israel, and anti-Semitism was rising in the United States following the 1967 war.[121] Some American Jews took issue with Meir for her praise of Nixon, but she responded, "Have you any liberals who can supply us with Phantoms? My business as Prime Minister is to ensure that we have Phantoms and that we have the answers to missiles and that if we are going to lose lives in the next war we have a chance to win."[122]

Conservative congressional support for military sales to Israel continued to grow. Robert S. Allen, correspondent for *The Christian Science Monitor,* wrote that a "Republican Revolt" had started over the administration's unwillingness to sell more Phantoms to Israel. Allen noted that Senator Scott and Representative Ford had both publicly urged the administration to sell sixty Phantoms to Israel. "Particularly incomprehensible and infuriating to Republican Congressional leaders," wrote Allen, was Nixon's support for Rogers. Republicans hoped that Nixon would be responsive to Senate advice and overrule Rogers as he had "done on virtually all other major policies."[123]

In order to spur the administration into action, Jackson felt it was necessary to offer another amendment that specifically earmarked $250 million, taken from the $500 million authorized by the Jackson amendment, for the sale of Phantom fighters to Israel. But he added that if "funds are authorized and appropriated in a timely fashion, and if they are expanded for the purpose of providing these vital planes, I would adjust my amendment accordingly and as the situation dictates."[124]

Rogers continued to resist the call for more Phantom sales because the administration believed that the military balance of power was still in Israel's favor.[125] However, behind the scenes, rumors circulated that Nixon was considering taking Rogers off the Middle East and replacing him with Kissinger, which meant a stronger pro-Israel tilt from the State Department.[126]

The Senate responded in October by passing a bipartisan resolution, supported by seventy-eight senators, that urged the administration to provide Israel with more Phantoms, "without further delay."[127] Senate Majority Leader Mike Mansfield (D-MT) and Fulbright opposed the resolution, as well as liberal Republicans George Aiken and John Sherman Cooper.[128] Although it simply expressed the sense of the Congress (as in 1968), the resolution also publicly affirmed broad, bipartisan Senate support for Phantom sales to Israel.

Jackson followed up the resolution by making good on his earlier threat. On November 23, the Senate voted 82–14 in favor of a Jackson amendment to a $70.2 billion defense appropriations bill, which again set aside $500 million in military credit sales to Israel but earmarked half to be used for Phantom sales. The favorable Senate vote came after Rogers met with eight senators and again refused to sell any more Phantoms to Israel.[129] The State Department predictably expressed a negative view of the Jackson amendment, arguing the administration had already requested $300 million in military credit sales through pending legislation. Ultimately, the Jackson amendment was removed from the Defense Appropriations Act (the House never voted on the amendment) after a Senate-House conference committee report determined that "the same sum was available to Israel in the continuing resolution for foreign aid pending before both Houses." Basically, since the Jackson amendment from the previous year had already been approved by Congress with $500 million for military credit sales set aside, the second Jackson amendment was deemed unnecessary.[130]

Nixon finally agreed to sell more Phantoms to Israel in December 1971. The decision to sell Phantoms in September 1970 came on the day that the Jackson amendment was passed; the decision in December 1971 came on the heels of a nonbinding resolution passed in October 1971 and the revised Jackson amendment that passed in November. While congressional opposition to the administration was not the only factor that influenced Nixon to finally agree to more Phantom sales in December 1971, it was almost certainly an important one.[131]

Along with congressional insistence on increased military sales, Nixon's shift was influenced by at least two other factors as well. First, military sales and the peace process were inextricably linked, and the Phantoms had always been a bargaining tool for the Nixon administration—to maintain leverage with Israel while also appeasing Arab states and the Soviet Union by not ramping up the arms race in the Middle East. In November 1971, Israel informed the U.S. government that it could not engage Egypt in peace discussions regarding the Suez Canal without a deal on the Phantoms. Additionally, Israel "sought assurances that the United States would restrict itself to a passive role in the negotiations and specifically would not put forward any compromise proposals."[132] Thus, the decision by Nixon removed an obstacle to peace negotiations. By January 21, after securing new shipments of Phantoms and U.S. neutrality in negotiations, the Meir government agreed to participate in talks with Egypt through Jarring.[133] The Israeli flexibility was rewarded with an agreement that more than doubled the expected jet sales. Rather than offering to sell eighteen Phantoms and thirty-six Skyhawks, as expected, the administration agreed to sell forty-two Phantoms and ninety Skyhawks over the following two to three years.[134]

Second, Nixon's shift demonstrated how domestic politics can influence foreign-policy decisions. Since 1972 was an election year, Nixon believed that a Middle East peace plan had to wait until after the election. During the Moscow summit in May 1972, when the United States and the Soviet Union signed the Strategic Arms Limitation Treaty (SALT) agreement, Nixon told Soviet leadership that the Middle East had to be put on ice because "we can't settle before the [presidential] election, but after that we can make progress in a fair way."[135] Therefore, releasing the jets to Israel in the first part of 1972 did not compromise peace prospects, in Nixon's mind anyway, because the issue could not be resolved for the next year. Moreover, such a move by Nixon would generate a certain amount of goodwill from American Jewish Zionists that could translate into more votes for Nixon and the Republican Party come November 1972, which it probably did.[136] Though on October 2, a month before the election, Alan Cranston (D-CA) took Nixon to task while speaking on the Senate floor. Cranston reminded his colleagues that while Nixon stressed his pro-Israel position for the upcoming election, his first three years in office were marked by "the infamous Rogers plan," "incessant State Department pressure on Israel," and "dribbles of vital military aid which the administration begrudgingly granted only under the steady hammering of the Congress."[137]

By selling more Phantoms to Israel, Nixon managed to simultaneously start and stop the peace process. Israel agreed to participate in negotiations with Egypt through Jarring, and Sadat, despite his public denunciations of U.S. support for Israel, was eager to restart negotiations. Kissinger received Egyptian National Security Advisor Hafiz Ismail for a private meeting in late February 1973, part of a backchannel effort to establish closer U.S.-Egypt relations and make progress toward peace. Ismail conveyed Sadat's urgent desire to end the conflict and the Egyptian president's expectations for a state of peace by the end of September. Ismail went so far as to indicate that Egypt would sign a separate peace agreement with Israel, including free passage through the Suez Canal and acceptance of "legitimate concerns" of Israel's security. But Kissinger doubted the sincerity of the Egyptian proposal, particularly its plan of "normalization" of relations with Israel, which fell short of recognizing the State of Israel. Kissinger, who never seriously considered the Egyptian proposals, balked at the opportunity to oversee far-reaching peace agreements between Israel and Egypt.[138]

With more Phantoms on the way, Israel did not feel the need to negotiate. When Nixon pushed Meir to "get off dead center" in negotiations on March 1, 1973, Meir declined and referred to Israel's military superiority, thanks to the Phantoms. "We never had it so good," she said. "The planes are coming in and we are okay through '73."[139] Time would tell, however, that Israel was not okay through 1973.

Conclusion

Strong congressional insistence on substantial military sales to Israel weakened the Nixon administration's ability to facilitate a peace agreement. The shift in Nixon's policy bedeviled Rogers's successor—Henry Kissinger—who also found it difficult to get the Israelis to go along with the U.S. peace process without having leverage over Israel with military sales. Once Israel had a generous package deal involving Phantoms and Skyhawks and U.S. aid to Israel sharply increased, the slow-moving peace process stalled, and war broke out in October 1973.

Jackson's amendment represented a turning point with regard to increased congressional assertiveness in the making of U.S.–Middle East policy, and U.S. foreign policy more generally. Congress flexed its muscles over U.S. policy toward Israel at particularly important times in the peace process. In turn, Nixon's willingness to ask Congress for larger military packages for Israel was certainly influenced by Jackson's insistence on the full $500 million being authorized annually. Even as Nixon attempted to prevent arms sales to Israel from ballooning, Jackson continued to insist on larger aid packages for Israel. His original amendment was extended for an additional year in 1972, and then again in 1973 for an additional two years.[140] In order to fully understand why U.S. military aid to Israel took off during Nixon's first term and remained high in the years afterward, the influence of the legislative branch demands consideration.

3

Stepping Forward?

Congress, the Nixon Administration, and Step-by-Step Diplomacy

The congressional role in U.S.-Israel relations advanced in late 1973. Congress passed an emergency aid bill for Israel that totaled $2.2 billion in order to offset Israel's losses in the 1973 Arab-Israeli War and also to provide for more purchases of U.S. weaponry. Several legislators, especially William Fulbright, objected to the pro-Israel tilt of the aid request, along with the administration's questionable defense of such a large number. But the voices of opposition could not match the chorus of support for Israel from both sides of the political aisle, and the aid bill cleared both chambers of Congress by landslide votes.

Nixon requested the $2.2 billion from Congress, which points to the importance he afforded Israel as a regional ally. But Nixon's request needs to be contextualized. In the throes of the Watergate debacle, the massive aid request also worked to distract attention from his domestic troubles and likely aimed to generate congressional support for his beleaguered presidency by asking for legislators to participate in foreign-policy decision-making, a point of contention between the two branches. Aware of the strong pro-Israel sentiment of Congress, Nixon had to know legislators would assist Israel in its hour of need; the move would also attract overwhelming support from Jewish Americans. Additionally, Nixon wanted to have leverage for peace discussions by being able to dangle grants in front of Israel if it went along with U.S. diplomacy. Moreover, according to the *New York Times,* Nixon made the "clear suggestion . . . that all of the $2.2-billion would not necessarily be needed but was being requested to demonstrate both to the Soviet

Union and the Arab countries the determination of the United States not to let Soviet military shipments to Egypt and Syria upset the military balance."[1] In line with that perception, the administration did not even try to justify more than half of the amount in conversations with the House subcommittee that considered the request.

But Congress approved the full amount anyway. During the course of debates about the emergency aid bill, legislators perpetuated the argument that Israel needed the enormous amount of aid—and quickly—in order to feel strong enough to engage Arab states in peace discussions. Congress hurried to approve Israel's aid bill on the day before the convening of a Geneva peace conference, which aimed to restart the peace process. Yet during the months that followed, Nixon and Kissinger, who became secretary of state in September 1973, moved instead to threaten to withhold military aid from Israel due to its uncompromising position in peace discussions. Nixon feared that if Israel had too much military aid it would be less willing to return territory occupied in 1967. As in the years immediately before (and after) the 1973 war, presidents feared the development of a fortress mentality in the minds of Israeli officials and sought to limit U.S. military aid to remind Israel of the need to more actively pursue peace.

While the first half of this chapter explores the congressional role in allocating unprecedented military aid for Israel, the second half details the Nixon administration's efforts to facilitate peace agreements.[2] The 1973 Arab-Israeli War—and more importantly for the United States, an oil embargo—forced the administration to become more involved in the peace process. Kissinger employed step-by-step diplomacy, a piecemeal approach to peace, in order to improve U.S.-Arab relations, provide a foundation for an overall peace based on U.N. Resolution 242, and ameliorate the toxic psychological environment of mistrust. Ultimately, the administration tried to balance a U.S.-Israel special relationship and strategic alliance with an effort to establish stronger U.S.-Arab relations, which proved to be a difficult task.

In his memoirs, Kissinger refers to criticisms for not pursuing an immediate comprehensive settlement in the aftermath of the 1973 war.[3] He offers valid reasons for not choosing that path. Israel rejected a return to the 1967 borders and "adamantly" refused to give back the Old City of Jerusalem, and Arab states would not accept this refusal. Israel was preparing for elections in December 1973, which meant no cabinet would have the authority to negotiate a comprehensive settlement. On the Arab side, a comprehensive agreement required consensus by all parties involved, which meant radical forces could veto any such agreement. The Soviet Union would support the Arab position and seek maximum gains, thereby further extending its influence. In such a situation, Europe and Japan would support the Arab position for fear of a crippling oil embargo, which would leave the United States isolated.[4] Almost certainly, any attempt for an immediate settlement would have quickly fallen apart and furthered the risk of war and, possibly, of superpower confrontation.

Step-by-step diplomacy produced two important disengagement agreements (Israel-Egypt in January 1974 and Israel-Syria in May 1974) and the reestablishment of diplomatic relations between the United States and several Arab countries. But after the Israel-Syria agreement, step-by-step diplomacy lost momentum. Nixon's position became as untenable as Saigon's, and presidential misdeeds undermined the capacity of the executive branch to conduct such delicate and complicated diplomacy. Pro-Israel lobbying forces started to play an even larger role in influencing U.S. decision-making in order to relieve pressure on Israel, an important factor that has been understated in scholarship.[5] It would be left to Gerald Ford's administration, a caretaker presidency, to see through the most intricate and sincere U.S. diplomatic effort to resolve the Arab-Israeli conflict, a process that began in October 1973.

The Aid Package

Egypt and Syria attacked Israel on October 6, 1973, the Jewish holiday of Yom Kippur, which started the 1973 Arab-Israeli War. During the first few days of the war Egyptian forces successfully crossed the Suez Canal and advanced into the Sinai Peninsula, while Syrian forces recaptured territory in the Golan Heights. The Arab armies received substantial support from the Soviet Union, which airlifted military aid to both countries. To reverse the tide of the war, the United States enacted its own airlift to Israel. The American airlift changed the course of the war as Israeli forces, initially driven back, regrouped and pushed Egyptian and Syrian armies back to the prewar lines. In response to the airlift, as well as a proposed multibillion-dollar American aid package for Israel, the Arab member states of the Organization of Petroleum Exporting Countries (OPEC) placed an embargo on oil to the United States and restricted the oil flowing to Western Europe and Japan.

The combatants agreed to a cease-fire on October 22, but the integrity of the cease-fire quickly deteriorated as Israeli forces encircled the Egyptian Third Army, cut off from escape and resupply. After a Soviet message to Nixon suggested the possibility of unilateral Soviet military intervention to relieve the besieged Egyptian Army, followed by Kissinger's elevating the DEFCON level from 4 to 3, a second cease-fire took hold on October 25.

The Nixon administration intentionally delayed a resupply of Israel. The administration hoped to advance détente with the Soviet Union, and rearming Israel threatened to damage that effort. Many U.S. officials believed that Israel would easily win the confrontation anyway, given its swift success in 1967 and U.S. military support, and therefore did not feel any urgent need to supply Israel. Nixon believed "that only a battlefield stalemate would provide the foundation in which fruitful negotiations might begin."[6] Therefore, he hoped to avoid making Israel feel too strong in war so it would be more inclined to seek peace in its aftermath. According to William Quandt, the administration felt the status quo prior to the war gave incentive for an Arab attack. Quandt further reasoned that the administration wanted to avoid upsetting U.S.-Arab relations, which had started to improve, and particularly to avoid a confrontation with oil-producing Arab states, and that an Arab attack on occupied territory was different from an attack on Israel's "recognized borders."[7] Craig Daigle has convincingly argued that Anwar Sadat felt the need to use war—not to defeat Israel, but to create a "crisis of détente"—in order to restart the peace process.[8]

At the outset of the war, several legislators stood in support of Israel. Sen. George McGovern (D-SD) called on American policy to affirm diplomatic support for Israel in the United Nations and "to provide Israel with military supplies in the full amounts required to deter further aggression." Sen. Richard Schweiker (R-PA) referenced his strong support for "the partnership of military aid between our Government and Israel" and stated his intention to work for a "sense of the Senate" resolution in support of "our full diplomatic support" for Israel. Senators Schweiker and Abraham Ribicoff (D-CT) noted the importance of expanded borders, which enabled Israel to absorb the Arab attack. Sen. John Tunney (D-CA) argued for "our support of Israel's military security and territorial sovereignty," which provided "a bulwark of stability in that area."[9] Representatives Lawrence Coughlin (R-PA) and Frank Brasco (D-NY) compared the Arab attack to Pearl Harbor. For Coughlin, Israel was a bastion of democracy, which demanded U.S. moral support. Brasco denounced those in favor of an evenhanded policy, especially "some political figures" and a "new type of radical intellectual . . . . which views the Western World as inherently corrupt."[10]

While Nixon refrained from sending military supplies, many members of Congress urged the president to change course and provide Israel with more weapons, especially Phantoms. Sen. Frank Church (D-ID) noted the Soviet military resupply of Egypt and Syria and called on the United States to "see to it that Israel is promptly supplied with such replacement of equipment as she may need to defend herself." Referencing the spirit of the Nixon Doctrine and pervasive fears of another Vietnam-type situation, Church pointed out that Israel did not ask for "a single American soldier" but "only for the tools with which to fend off this attack." Rep. Jonathan Bingham (D-NY) also called for a resupply of Israel to offset Soviet armaments and sent Nixon a letter to make that point. Rep. Clarence Long (D-MD) felt that "Congress and the entire American community has no alternative but to give all the help to Israel that it possibly can."[11] Sen. Walter Mondale (D-MN) said, "I hope and pray that the administration has taken whatever steps are necessary to insure that Israel is promptly resupplied with any equipment she needs to defend herself against this mammoth replenishment of Arab forces by the Soviets." Tunney further argued that "Israel cannot fight the Soviet Union along with the Arab States." Rep. Jack Kemp (R-NY) blamed the Soviets (not Scoop Jackson) for ruining détente.[12] Rep. Bertram Podell (D-NY) also wanted to end détente and to resupply Israel to the point of military superiority.[13]

Legislators also introduced nonbinding legislation to push the president to arm Israel. On October 9, Rep. William Lehman (D-FL) urged his "fellow Congressmen to join me in insisting that the U.S. Government immediately release to Israel all aircraft, tanks, and other military equipment" contracted but not yet delivered to Israel. Lehman saw "much in common" between America and Israel—"a home for the persecuted" and "a free democracy"—and introduced a "sense of the Congress" resolution that called for immediate delivery of all weapons already sold to Israel.[14] The resolution drew many cosponsors, especially from representatives of states with large numbers of Jewish Americans: New York Democrats Bertram Podell, Bella Abzug, Herman Badillo, and Lester Wolff; New York Republicans Angelo Roncallo and Hamilton Fish; as well as Jerome Waldi (D-CA) and Joe Moakley (D-MA). Clarence Long, who introduced a similar concurrent resolution on October

10, also sent a telegram to Kissinger that encouraged "prompt review of Israel's military and economic aid, with view to asking Congress for all additional help required." An article from the October 1973 issue of *Congressional Quarterly* claims that "a 36-hour lobby phone blitz by AIPAC" inspired many legislators to implore the Nixon administration to rearm Israel.[15]

On October 14, the Nixon administration initiated a resupply of Israel.[16] The Jackson amendment from 1970 explicitly provided a congressional mandate to empower the president to furnish "to Israel the means of providing for its own security." Therefore, Nixon did not need any further authorization to transfer enormous amounts of weapons to a country engaged in a war. Israel's struggles against Egypt and Syria surprised U.S. officials and required some type of military support in order to ensure Israel's survival. The administration had refrained from airlifting aid in an effort to preserve détente and to remind Israel of the need to pursue peace agreements in the war's aftermath. But the administration could not let Israel be overrun, and also wanted to keep the Soviet Union at a disadvantage in the region and felt compelled to counter the Soviet resupply of Arab military stores.

The American airlift to Israel required refueling somewhere in Europe, but U.S. officials struggled to find allies willing to cooperate. Although 1973 was supposed to be "The Year of Europe"—an attempt to revitalize U.S.-European alliances strained by diverging national interests and the war in Vietnam—by October 1973, the allies across the Atlantic had drifted further apart. The economies of Western Europe relied much more heavily on Middle Eastern oil than the United States did, and European leadership did not want to undertake measures that could lead to diminished oil supplies from the Arab Middle East. The United States, based on an agreement with Portugal, shared a military base on the Azores Islands. But Portugal declined to authorize the Americans to use the base for refueling. Nixon, infuriated by the Europeans and determined to help Israel hold the line in war, reportedly yelled in a meeting, "Fuck the Portuguese!" The American airlift subsequently refueled in the Azores.[17]

Congress voiced its approval of Nixon's decision to help Israel. Two days after the start of the airlift, Elizabeth Holtzman (D-NY) cosponsored a resolution with House Majority Leader Thomas "Tip" O'Neill (D-MA) that expressed "House support for strengthening Israel's defense in its efforts to repel the recent Arab attacks."[18] Mario Biaggi (D-NY) also joined as cosponsor to the resolution.[19] The Senate likewise expressed strong bipartisan backing for

Israel. In support of the resupply, Hubert Humphrey (D-MN) joined with sixty-six other senators in submitting a resolution on October 18 "to urge the continued transfer to Israel of Phantom aircraft and other equipment."[20] Sen. Charles Mathias (R-MD) supported the resolution and arms for Israel to offset Soviet weapons to Arab states but added, "I must say that I regret with all my heart the necessity for doing so." Mathias then offered his own "parallel resolution" that stressed the importance of negotiations.[21]

A few legislators advocated for a more balanced policy but lacked support in Congress. Rep. Steve Symms (R-ID) voiced his concern that legislators were "fanning the flames of war in the Middle East." He argued that the United States had no "business interfering in Middle Eastern policy," much like Vietnam "12 years ago." He further noted the irony "that many former Vietnam war doves have now jumped to their feet to demand U.S. aid to Israel."[22] On October 17, Rep. Paul Findley (R-IL), one of the loudest voices in the House in favor of evenhandedness, mourned the fact that the "carefully balanced policy which the President charted and has pursued in the Middle East for the past 5 years is fast being destroyed."[23] The next day Findley met with Nixon, who said the United States intended to "carry out the provisions of U.N. Resolution 242 in the Middle East." Nixon even "authorized" Findley to quote him "directly," much to Findley's delight, given that, according to Findley, "U.S. references to the return of occupied lands have become infrequent and muted."[24] Rep. Jim Johnson (R-CO) denounced "the inflamed rhetoric of war . . . being heard in the Chambers of the Congress" and argued, "To provide arms support for one side during a war is an act of war." He regarded U.S. military support of Israel as "not just acts of friendship toward Israel—they are also acts of war toward Egypt and Syria and the other Arab countries now involved in the war."[25] Sen. James McClure (R-ID) pointed to the need to address Palestinian grievances and Arab territory occupied by Israel. He did not blame the recent hostilities on Arab states or Israel but instead criticized American foreign policy: "One of our grave mistakes has been in giving the Israelis the impression that with a total commitment from the United States she is invincible—that there has been no reason to negotiate."[26] In another statement, McClure echoed Symms by saying, "It is ironic that last week's dove is suddenly this week's hawk."[27]

Nixon had to request congressional assistance to finance the resupply. The administration proposed separate legislation for emergency aid, rather than an amendment to the existing Foreign Aid Authorization Bill, because that bill was being held up in a Senate-House conference committee stalemate. On October 19, Nixon requested $2.2 billion in emergency aid for Israel, along with $200 million for Cambodia. By that point, the resupply of Israel had already cost nearly $1 billion. Thus, the $2.2 billion aid bill provided for the existing amount, along with an additional $1.2 billion. The White House described the $2.2 billion request as a "ceiling," and the *New York Times* stated, "Early reaction on Capitol Hill indicated that the aid to Israel will be readily approved, although perhaps not for the full amount requested by the Administration. Privately some pro-Israeli Senators expressed surprise at the size of the request and suggested it exceeded Israel's needs."[28]

In response, the Arab member states of OPEC announced an embargo on all oil to the United States and drastically cut back oil to Western Europe and Japan. The move aimed to persuade Western countries to side with Arab states regarding occupied territories and the Palestinians. Japan issued a statement endorsing the Arab interpretation of Resolution 242, and the countries of the European Community issued a statement on November 6 that supported "a pro-Arab stance demanding an Israeli withdrawal from the occupied territories."[29] Less than two weeks later, OPEC announced that Europe would be excluded from December production cuts.[30] Similar to what some commenters have called "Suez in reverse," European powers were distancing themselves from the United States and its widely unpopular policies in the Middle East, a profound reversal of earlier situations when the United States sought to distance itself from unpopular European policies, like Suez in 1956.[31]

The oil embargo worsened an already-existing energy crisis in the United States. By 1973, U.S. domestic oil production had decreased while consumption reached all-time highs. According to Daniel Yergin, during the early 1970s "the phrase 'energy crisis' began to emerge as part of the American political vocabulary."[32] In April 1973, amidst ongoing energy concerns and a likely shortage of gasoline for the summer driving season, President Nixon abolished the quota system established by Eisenhower.[33] Like Europe and Japan, the United States looked to the Middle East and its large oil deposits as a way to satisfy energy needs. During the summer of 1973, U.S. imports had risen to 6.2 million barrels per day, up from 4.5 million per day in 1972 and 3.2 million in 1970.[34]

The oil embargo "shocked" the international market and worsened a growing economic crisis in the United States. In August 1971, the United States pulled out of the Bretton Woods Agreement that had served as the foundation for the post-WWII economic order. Massive debt due to the Vietnam War and Great Society programs led to increased inflation and the overvaluation of the dollar. During the years of the Bretton Woods Agreement, the dollar was pegged to the price of gold, and the world's major currencies were pegged to the U.S. dollar. But the overvaluation of the dollar, along with dwindling gold supplies in the United States and lack of confidence in the dollar abroad, forced the Nixon administration to float the dollar, meaning it would fluctuate based on market demand. Americans confronted rising inflation and rising energy prices while the economy stagnated, creating what some have called stagflation. The oil embargo exacerbated these existing conditions, which further weakened the administration's position and thereby complicated the American effort to mediate the Arab-Israeli conflict. The importance of oil forced the administration to become more active in mediating a solution.

The congressional body continued to exhibit solid bipartisan support for Israel, regardless of the oil weapon. Sen. Birch Bayh (D-IN) commended Nixon for responding favorably to the legislators "who had recommended military aid for Israel" and argued in favor of separating the $2.2 billion to Israel from the administration's request for $200 million for Cambodia.[35] (Congress would indeed separate the two proposals.) Rep. Robert Drinan (D-MA) noted that as of October 23, 224 representatives had cosponsored a House "resolution supporting the administration's decision to supply Israel with aircraft and arms."[36] Representative Lehman and Sen. Adlai Stevenson III (D-IL) reminded their respective chambers of the differences between Israel and Vietnam and acknowledged the legitimacy of the Vietnam doves who supported military aid to Israel.[37] Humphrey and Mondale called for both military and nonmilitary aid to Israel. Humphrey also applauded the administration's bill, which "carries out the clear intent" of the Senate resolution "now cosponsored by 70 Members of this body."[38] Ribicoff felt "it is important to acknowledge the identity of interests between the United States and Israel and to make certain that Israel receives the support it needs to gain a lasting peace."[39] Rep. Ed Koch (D-NY) submitted to the *Congressional Record* his October 30 letter to Nixon that lauded the president for his support of Israel.[40] Three Republican representatives from New York—James Grover, John Wydler, and Angelo Roncallo—all submitted to the *Record* Rep. Gerald Ford's (R-MI) pro-Israel address to the United Jewish Appeals, which took place on November 26.[41] Although he was a long-time supporter of Israel, Ford's speech may have been self-serving as it coincided with congressional consideration of his appointment to the vice presidency.

Legislators refused to be cowed into abandoning Israel because of the oil weapon. Representative Brasco countered newspaper columnists who portrayed Israel as a liability and instead derided both "Arab oil blackmail" and oil companies who cared only for "profit at all costs" within an atmosphere of an "orgy of greed."[42] Representative Podell warned against sacrificing Israel for oil. For Podell, "The future of our country and that of Israel, our close friend and ally for over 25 years, are inextricably intertwined."[43] Rep. Philip Ruppe (R-MI) voiced his concerns about the oil embargo but added, "I am certainly not suggesting that we negotiate the security of Israel for the sake of our energy needs."[44] Mondale argued that even though the United States needs fuel, "American foreign policy cannot yield to blackmail over oil."[45]

Support for Israel also came from legislators on behalf of organized labor. According to record clippings submitted to the *Congressional Record,* delegates to an AFL-CIO convention called on union members to help "speed generous help to the cause of peace and freedom which Israel is now defending so courageously against terrible odds." Israeli Prime Minister Golda Meir phoned AFL-CIO President George Meany "to express appreciation for the support given Israel by the American labor movement."[46] Representative Badillo communicated to the House the strong backing of American labor, rooted in the close historical relationship between the AFL-CIO and Histadrut.[47] Rep. James Corman (D-CA) similarly noted that the American Legion supported arms for Israel.[48]

A few legislators qualified their support for the aid bill. On October 23, Abzug spoke in favor of the bill but also noted Nixon's ulterior motive: "It is evident, however, that the President was attempting to use our justified concern over the outcome of this war to mute criticism of his shocking defiance of the court and his firing of the special prosecutor."[49] Only three days earlier, on the day that Kissinger flew to Moscow to work out a cease-fire to the 1973 war and OPEC announced a full embargo on the United States, Attorney General Elliot Richardson and Deputy Attorney General William Ruckelshaus resigned from their positions rather than fire the Watergate Special Prosecutor Archibald Cox (who was appointed by Richardson), on what came to be known as the Saturday Night Massacre. Only weeks before, Spiro Agnew had resigned as vice president amidst accusations of bribery and tax evasion. The vice presidency remained vacant for nearly two months as Ford's confirmation by the House did not happen until December 6. (The Senate confirmed Ford's appointment on November 27.)

While Nixon defied Congress and Watergate investigators, legislators moved to restrict the president's ability to wage war without a congressional declaration. In 1972, Sen. Jacob Javits (R-NY) first introduced a bill that, in a slightly different form in 1973, came to be called the War Powers Act. The resolution, which aimed to avoid another Vietnam scenario, granted the president only a ninety-day grace period to deploy U.S. combat troops abroad without congressional authorization. Congress passed the resolution and, as expected, Nixon vetoed it. But the veto came just days after the Saturday Night Massacre, which ensured a passionate congressional rebuttal to Nixon's action. Both the Senate and the House voted to override Nixon's veto, and the War Powers Act became law on November 7.[50]

Nixon and Kissinger met with Senator Javits on November 12 to cultivate support for the aid request. Javits was one of the leading pro-Israel voices in the Senate and at times acted as a go-between for the administration and American Jewish Zionists, as well as Israel. Nixon recognized the importance of U.S. weapons sales to Israel and pointed out that the United States was "the only country in the world supporting Israel. This doesn't mean Israel is wrong but that we must do our best to work out a settlement so one isn't forced on them. Without arms, Israel is finished." Nixon then added that U.S. aid saved Israel, and Javits responded by saying, "Your standing in the Jewish Community is great," and he stroked Nixon's ego by adding, "You personally saved Israel." Both Nixon and Kissinger asked Javits to support the administration's request of $2.2 billion in emergency aid for Israel. Javits said he would and added, "I tell Israel the relations of conservative Republicans, and you, to Israel. I will fully cooperate."[51]

The war in East Asia continued to cast a long shadow over the White House as South Vietnam had been in a free fall since U.S. troops were withdrawn in March 1973. Rep. Joseph Maraziti (R-NJ) and Sen. Mark Hatfield (R-OR) voiced their concerns about the possibility of U.S. troops being used in the Middle East, especially in light of the Vietnam War and following Nixon's veto of the War Powers Act.[52]

The struggling economy also created unease for such a large aid bill. Maraziti did not object to the sale of arms to Israel, but he did object to Congress's giving the president the possibility to use the aid bill as grants to Israel. In that case, "the American taxpayer may be asked to foot the bill of a war effort in which they again do not want to become involved."[53] Up to that point, all U.S. military aid to Israel had been in the form of loans. Rep. Harold Runnels (D-NM), reflecting a broader congressional concern with better regulating defense spending, stated, "I am for finding a suitable arrangement to help Israel, but I do not like, nor will I vote for a proposition in which there is such hurried and free wheeling talk of a billion here and a billion there."[54]

Some legislators outwardly opposed the aid bill. The most eloquent opposition came from William Fulbright. The Democrat from Arkansas spoke of a political and moral commitment to the survival of Israel, but not its territorial conquests in 1967 and 1973. Fulbright called on Israel to "give up the chimera of absolute military security through the occupation of territory . . . and at long last take steps to redress the great wrong done to the Palestinian people." As in his fight over the Phantoms a few years earlier, Fulbright again voiced his support of the Nixon administration, saying it had "proceeded on the proper course." The problem, according to Fulbright, was congressional interference that removed "the incentive for a compromise that this administration has been seeking to bring about."[55]

James Abourezk, the first-term Democratic senator from South Dakota (and also the first Arab American U.S. senator), shared in Fulbright's view of U.S.–Middle East relations.[56] According to Abourezk, "We need not sacrifice our friendship with Israel to maintain good relations with the Arab world, but we should not be so foolish so as to turn our backs on people who want our friendship." He warned against "blindly" pouring more arms into the Middle East, which he likened to "pouring gasoline on a fire that is already burning much too fiercely." For Abourezk, weapons did not equate to security: "If Israel is to have security, that means she must get along with her Arab neighbors."[57]

McClure also pushed for a balanced policy, and on the Senate floor on December 6 he criticized the pro-Israel bias of news reporting. The following day he noted that Israel's Labor Party reportedly adopted a platform of "territorial compromise" in upcoming negotiations. He wondered, "If the Israelis themselves can consider new positions, such as withdrawing from occupied Arab lands, why can't we?"[58] Israeli Deputy Prime Minister Yigal Allon and Foreign Minister Abba Eban, two left-leaning moderates in the Meir cabinet, both publicly supported flexibility in negotiations in order to advance the peace process.[59] Eban delivered a speech to the Conference of Presidents and stressed, according to American documentation, that "Israel must undertake far-reaching conceptual reassessment" and avoid being misled by "fringes of [the] political spectrum" where "some illusions were sprouting."[60] By early January, "a public opinion poll showed that 82.8 percent of Israelis interviewed favored some territorial concessions for peace—an increase of 36 percent since November. The President underlined this and wrote 'okay' in the margin."[61]

Opposition in the House came primarily from Findley, along with John Rarick (D-LA) and Harold Royce (H. R.) Gross (R-IA). On October 25, Rarick criticized the "peace-hawks" who denounced U.S. involvement in Vietnam for being "an immoral war," but regarding U.S. support for Israel, "suddenly sprouted a completely new set of feathers and now bear a striking resemblance to hawks." He questioned the moral logic of the peace-hawks and argued that "national policy should not be one of pro-Israel, or pro-Arab for that matter. It should simply be pro-American."[62] He also emphasized the need to address Palestinian grievances.[63] On November 30, Gross criticized the U.S. government for going "overboard when it singlehandedly and unilaterally intervened in behalf of one country" in the Middle East. That same day, Findley told the House, "The United States must have a balanced policy in the Middle East, not to protect oil supplies, but because such a policy is right."[64]

The emergency aid bill for Israel moved out of the House Foreign Affairs committee on December 4 by a vote of 33–1 and moved to a House vote on December 11. Findley offered one last challenge. Even though the bill said nothing about policy, for Findley, "it is nevertheless thunderous as a policy statement." He then proposed an amendment to include explicit reference to U.N. Resolution 242, which he hoped "would place the prestige of the House of Representatives behind fairness and evenhandedness as the basis of our Middle East policy."[65]

The ambiguity of 242 continued to confuse U.S. officials. On November 27, Nixon and Kissinger had met with bipartisan congressional leadership, during which Rep. Samuel Stratton (D-NY) asked for Kissinger to explain the significance of 242. Kissinger replied, "In the family—242 doesn't mean a thing." Nixon quipped, "It means 1967 for the Arabs and for Israel it means what they have plus ten percent." Obviously annoyed, Fulbright added, "It is not right to say 242 doesn't mean anything." But Nixon pointed out, "It means different things to different people. To us it means what is negotiated." U.S. officials narrowly believed they could work only as a mediator between the parties, rather than force acceptance of a U.S. proposal in a manner similar to what Eisenhower had done. Kissinger reminded the meeting that "a settlement has to cost Israel some territory. That is why we are for 242. It avoids our having to come down on one side or the other." The participants in the meeting all seemed to agree that Israel needed to make substantial territorial concessions in line with implementation of Resolution 242.[66]

But Congress refused to accept Findley's amendment that tied U.S. aid to Israel with support for the implementation of 242. Wolff noted that Findley had raised his amendment at the committee level, and it was overwhelmingly rejected. Thomas Morgan (D-PA), chairman of the Foreign Affairs Committee, urged defeat of the Findley amendment.[67] Despite vocal support from David Dennis (R-IN), Clement Zablocki (D-WI), Richard Ichord (D-MO), and Henry Smith (R-NY), the amendment failed by a large margin, 82–334.[68]

Opposition to the actual emergency aid bill came from several additional representatives. Robert Kastenmeier (D-WI) regarded the legislation as "more fuel to fan the flames of war."[69] Ronald Dellums (D-CA) rejected the "illusion that our only duty to Israel is just to send off a shipment of arms so that the Israelis and the Arabs can kill each other more efficiently."[70] Chalmers Wylie (R-OH) opposed the bill on the grounds that peace cannot come through "continual rearming of nations at war."[71] Representatives Gross and Runnels also spoke against the aid bill.[72]

Lee Hamilton (D-IN), who chaired the House subcommittee that considered the aid bill, offered a poignant critique. He rose in support but protested the figure of $2.2 billion and took the administration to task for not offering a valid justification for such a large amount of money. He acknowledged the use of approximately $1 billion already given to Israel during the course of war but blasted the administration's rationale for requesting the additional $1.2 billion. In fact, no rationale was supplied. Instead, the administration justified the $1.2 billion based on one vague word: "imponderables." The administration made no effort to itemize or detail the need for the extra $1.2 billion, more than half of a gargantuan level of aid, beyond anything the United States had ever allocated in one lump sum, which adds credence to the notion that Nixon did not expect Congress to authorize the full amount. Moreover, Hamilton felt that the aid bill exuded pessimism about prospects for peace. For Hamilton, the "request is so large, so poorly justified, so militantly defended by some that it frankly makes it very difficult to vote for the request even if Members, like myself, want to support Israel and assure its deterrent strength."[73] Burt Talcott (R-CA) echoed Hamilton's concerns. He voted for the bill but questioned "the adequacy of the justification for this huge sum of money."[74]

Despite a small amount of opposition and some finely argued reservations, the House passed the aid bill by a landslide vote, 364–52. Strong support came from representatives on both sides of the aisle, and particularly from Northeast Democrats: House Majority Leader Tip O'Neill (MA), Mario Biaggi (NY), and William Cotter (CT).[75] Matthew Rinaldo (R-NJ) voiced his support the day before the vote and noted with pride "that the Union Lodge of B'nai B'rith has named me man of the year for 1973."[76] Some representatives, like Benjamin Gilman (R-NY), argued, "Anything less than a totally secure military force will severely restrict and hamper Israel's negotiating power in the forthcoming Geneva peace talks." Others, such as Peter Frelinghuysen (R-NJ), argued that the aid bill aimed "to maintain a reasonable military balance in order to prevent a conflagration" and "should not be interpreted as a slap at the Arab States."[77] The next day, Shirley Chisholm (D-NY), similar to other Vietnam doves, cited her "conscience and heart" as her rationale for voting against aid for the "insane war in Southeast Asia" but for aid to Israel, "which would best insure a lasting peace that will benefit all parties."[78]

On the same day the House passed the emergency aid bill it also passed the Jackson-Vanik amendment, which tied U.S.-Soviet economic relations to the free emigration of Soviet Jews to Israel. In 1972, Scoop Jackson tried to use Soviet restrictions on emigration on all its citizens as a way to scuttle the SALT (Strategic Arms Limitation Talks) agreement between the United States and the Soviet Union. While arms control was a crucial component of Nixon's détente, the relaxation in tensions also threatened defense contracts for Jackson's home state of Washington.

Although he lost the battle on SALT, Jackson eventually focused on only Jewish emigration as a way to continue to hammer away at détente.[79] The administration hoped to grant the USSR most favored nation (MFN) trade status in order to advance détente and increase American exports to a very large market during hard economic times.[80] But the USSR had imposed a "diploma tax" on anyone who wished to emigrate since they had received the benefits of public education, part of a broader Soviet effort to appease its Arab clients and enact oppressive measures against Soviet Jews in the aftermath of the 1967 war. The tax was ostensibly to make up for costs of education, though in all likelihood it was meant to slow the "brain drain" from the Soviet Union. Even though Moscow repudiated the measure, Jackson cosponsored an amendment with Rep. Charles Vanik (D-OH) that denied MFN status to any nonmarket (that is, communist) economy that placed restrictions on emigration. As with Jackson's amendment in 1970, Amos Eiran, the Israeli liaison to Congress, played a vital role in proposing and advancing the legislation.[81] Jackson, a Cold War liberal, sought to weaken détente while further endearing himself to many in the American Jewish community and Israel to prepare for another run at the White House in 1976.

Jackson's efforts certainly got Nixon's attention. The president told Senator McClure and Deputy Assistant for National Security Affairs Brent Scowcroft, "I want the Cabinet out to kick Jackson in the tail. Jackson is trying to take all the heat off the Jews and put it on the Soviet Union." He reminded the two American officials that "the goal is . . . a procedure that Israel will begin to withdraw from the occupied territories."[82] Much to Nixon's chagrin, the Jackson-Vanik amendment, advanced by anti-détente and pro-Israel legislators and attached to a U.S.-Soviet trade bill, cleared the House by another lopsided vote, 319–80.[83] On December 12, Representative Drinan called the passage of the two bills on the same day "a happy coincidence."[84]

Both actions of Congress—the emergency aid bill and the Jackson-Vanik amendment—significantly contributed to the tightening of relations between the United States and Israel, and also revealed the ability of Congress to use Israel to impact U.S. foreign policy on a broader scale. The aid bill pointed to the importance of the special relationship and a strategic alliance, but also something more. The roughly $1 billion used in the resupply did in fact ensure Israel's right to exist, while additional monies could be explained by a strategic relationship. But an additional $1.2 billion without adequate justification—indeed, without even a valid attempt by the administration to justify the amount—pointed to the gradual development of a new U.S.-Israel relationship, something that exceeded special and strategic reasoning. The amendment to the trade bill had nothing to do with Israel's survival, little strategic value for U.S.-Israel relations, and possibly hurt the U.S. economy. Instead, it primarily served Jackson's political ambitions. It also demonstrated that the U.S. Congress could use Israel to challenge U.S. foreign policy. The Jackson-Vanik amendment was a direct attack on Nixon's policy of détente.

Leading up to the day of the Senate vote on the aid bill, Abourezk, Fulbright, and McClure led the fight against its passage. Abourezk emphasized the need to address Palestinian grievances and submitted a statement by the National Conference of Catholic Bishops that called for a "comprehensive political solution" that included recognition of the rights of both Israel and Palestinian Arabs based on U.N. Resolution 242.[85] Fulbright cited Representative Hamilton's concerns about the administration's lousy justification for the aid level. Fulbright called the bill "ill-timed and ill-advised" and asked that a vote be postponed until the next legislative session, which would follow the Geneva conference. He again voiced his support of Nixon and Kissinger in their efforts to seek a settlement based on Resolution 242 and contended that passage of the bill would announce the abandonment of an evenhanded policy. McClure rose in support of Fulbright's statement and in opposition to the aid bill.[86] Senators Hatfield and Quentin Burdick (D-ND), on separate occasions, echoed Hamilton's objection to the administration's inadequate justification for $2.2 billion, and both would vote against the bill.[87]

The Senate considered the emergency aid bill on December 20, 1973, the day before the start of the Geneva peace conference. Humphrey opened the discussion by stumping in support to make Israel feel strong enough to take risks in the upcoming peace negotiations.[88] This drew objections from Abourezk and Fulbright. Abourezk argued that U.S. arms facilitated, rather than prevented, the outbreak of war. He cited Hamilton's objection to the aid total and also noted, "History has shown that the weapons certainly do not come in handy as guarantors of peace, but as tools of ever larger and more costly wars."[89]

Fulbright made an even more pointed rejection of Humphrey's psychological argument. He first reasoned that Israel can get as many weapons as it wants at any point in the future, a valid point agreed to by the senator from Minnesota. Fulbright then argued that the purpose should not be to make Israel feel strong enough to make peace, but to make Israel know it needs to return land. On that point the two senators disagreed. Fulbright put it bluntly: "Are we or are we not prepared to live up to what we profess to have: an evenhanded policy designed to bring about peace in that area under the guidelines set down in resolution 242?"[90]

He proceeded to offer three amendments. The first, and most significant, tied U.S. funds to fulfillment of U.N. Resolution 242. But the Senate, like Fulbright's Foreign Relations Committee that first considered the bill, voted to table the three amendments. Humphrey noted that Israel had supported Resolution 242 and was committed to implementing it, and the Senate wanted to quickly approve the bill in order to assist Israel (and Kissinger) at Geneva.[91] Javits also pointed out that the Foreign Relations Committee had approved the bill without amendments, 15–2.[92] Fulbright made one last appeal. He felt "that the Senate has taken leave of its senses. The threatening recession and the serious disruption of our economy are the price we are beginning to pay for 15 years of making extreme and unwise policies both foreign and domestic."[93]

But like sentiment in the House, broad bipartisan support for Israel in the Senate led to passage of the emergency aid bill by an overwhelming margin, 66–9.[94] Additionally, the House agreed with the Senate and approved an increase in the possible grant total to Israel from $1 billion to $1.5 billion.[95]

President Nixon would use the additional grants as incentives for Israel to go along with American diplomacy in the months ahead. Yet even with the aid bill, Nixon worried about Israeli stubbornness in peace negotiations. According to a December 20 message from Scowcroft to Kissinger, Nixon recommended that "we should move cautiously in sending more supplies and equipment at the present time . . . we may want to expedite shipments later on but right now he [Nixon] did not wish to build Israel up to enhance their intransigence."[96] Here again, it seems that Nixon did not expect Congress to approve of the entire amount. The president also appeared to be shaken by all of the challenges facing the White House. Scowcroft informed Kissinger that "the President has seemed irritable over the past few days and this afternoon looked very tired. He almost fell asleep during [Secretary of Defense James] Schlesinger's briefing."[97]

The Difficult Road to Geneva

While the U.S. Congress, and the Senate in particular, aimed to pass the emergency aid bill to support U.S. and Israeli efforts at Geneva, actually convening a conference proved to be a difficult task. To give the appearance of progress to Arab states in order to lift the oil embargo, Kissinger planned to have a ceremonial peace conference, a forum for the combatants to meet, air grievances, and move forward with talks that would hopefully lead to peace. Although a multilateral conference, the "purpose was to use it as a framework for an essentially bilateral diplomacy."[98] Following the conference, Kissinger intended to employ step-by-step diplomacy to strengthen the existing cease-fire, improve U.S.-Arab relations, end the oil embargo, reduce Soviet influence in the region, and provide Israel with an opportunity to withdraw from the occupied territories. However, getting all the combatants to attend the conference was another matter.

Kissinger traveled to the Middle East in early November to improve the status of U.S.-Arab relations and to create regional support for the U.S. effort. After brief stops in Morocco and Tunisia, he met with Egyptian President Anwar Sadat in Cairo to discuss the peace process. Kissinger then mediated a six-point agreement between Israel and Egypt that was signed on November 11 that reaffirmed the cease-fire and allowed for the movement of nonmilitary supplies.[99] Implicitly, Israel and Egypt agreed to future disengagement even before negotiating the details to such agreements. Those negotiations would soon follow.

The agreement revealed the strengthening of U.S.-Egypt relations, a central goal of both Nixon's and Sadat's foreign policies. Sadat had removed Soviet advisers from Egypt in 1972 in order to develop stronger ties with Washington. He sent Nixon a note during the 1973 war that demanded U.S. involvement in the peace process, a dramatic overture considering Egypt had severed diplomatic ties with the United States during the 1967 war and never reestablished them. But Nixon reminded Sadat "that the only thing the United States could guarantee was that it was fully committed to advancing a process that would lead to a diplomatic agreement."[100] Nevertheless, Kissinger regarded Sadat's move as a "breakthrough" because he "staked his policy on the American connection," thereby moving further away from Moscow.[101] Sadat told Kissinger, "Never forget, Dr. Kissinger. I am making this agreement with the United States, not with Israel."[102] Egypt and the United States agreed to resume diplomatic relations.[103]

After scoring success on the Israel-Egypt front, Kissinger traveled to Riyadh to meet with King Faisal, one of the most dependable friends of the United States, about the oil embargo and step-by-step diplomacy. The most influential member of OPEC, Saudi Arabia had a commitment to the Palestinian cause that had long complicated relations with Washington.[104] The king admitted that Saudi Arabia felt "embarrassed" because it valued U.S. friendship and certainly desired oil revenues; however, the king "needed some proof of tangible progress before a proposal to sheath the oil weapon could be put forward to the other Arab states."[105] The answer to both the American and Saudi problems was step-by-step diplomacy. Faisal reportedly blessed Kissinger's diplomatic approach, thereby clearing a big hurdle in the Arab world.[106]

Syria wanted to strengthen relations with the United States more than attend a peace conference, especially one that did not promise peace. Like Egypt, Syria had severed diplomatic relations with the United States during the 1967 war. And like Sadat, Syrian President Hafez al-Assad had expressed interest in developing better relations.[107]

That suited Kissinger well. Syria did not need to attend the conference, but it did need to participate in step-by-step diplomacy. Kissinger hoped Assad, like Sadat, would leave the Soviet camp for the American one. The best way to "loosen" Syrian ties with the Soviet Union, according to Kissinger, was "by giving Damascus a stake in closer ties with the United States."[108] Assad would not attend a conference until first completing a disengagement agreement with Israel, but more significantly, he agreed to the concept of step-by-step diplomacy.[109]

That left the tricky question of Palestinian representation. A meeting of Arab heads of state in Algiers at the end of November declared the Palestine Liberation Organization (PLO) to be the "sole" representative of the Palestinians. But according to Kissinger, "The idea of a Palestinian state run by the PLO was not a subject for serious discourse."[110] He told Abba Eban, "Our policy was based on Jordan, not the Palestinians."[111] Kissinger regarded PLO interests as "incompatible with the interests of any of the parties to the Middle East conflict." Most problematic, the PLO refused to accept U.N. Resolution 242 or recognize the right of Israel to exist, which made negotiations practically impossible. Thus, Kissinger's diplomacy would discuss Palestinian refugees only in the context of a Jordanian-Palestinian arrangement and, presumably, only through official channels with Amman. But Jordan did not fight in the 1973 war and would seem out of place at a conference designed to bring together the combatants from the recent war, as well as diplomacy based on disengagement agreements.

By not recognizing the legitimate aspirations of Palestinians for a separate nation-state, and by not recognizing the political authority of the PLO, Kissinger's perspective revealed fundamental flaws of the U.S. position. As historian Paul Chamberlin has shown in his study of the PLO, high-ranking officials like Yasser Arafat had moderated their behavior and seemed ready to become engaged in peace discussions. Chamberlin further suggests that in the aftermath of the 1973 war, the U.S. missed an opportunity to resolve the Arab-Israeli conflict by not considering a political solution apart from Jordan.[112] Others have argued that the administration considered a "Palestinian option" before, during, and after Black September 1970 but favored the Jordanian option, first, because King Hussein indicated that Jordan would recognize the State of Israel, which Palestinian leadership consistently refused to do, and second, because Israel would not accept a separate Palestinian state while Palestinians would accept nothing less.[113] Refusing to engage Palestinian political representation outside of a Jordanian connection may have ensured the collapse of the peace process. But at the same time, engaging the PLO in no way ensured a peaceful comprehensive settlement to the conflict, either.

Upon returning from his trip, Nixon and Kissinger met with bipartisan congressional leadership on November 27 to lay out the administration's plan for the peace process. Kissinger explained that the plan aimed to woo moderate Arabs to work through the United States in order to get concessions from Israel, thereby decreasing the influence of the USSR and increasing the prestige of the United States. Regarding Israel, Kissinger argued that the Israeli position had been based on military supremacy but, after the 1973 war, the Israelis "now know they can't do that."[114]

From the perspective of U.S. officials, American Jewish Zionists complicated the Israeli position. Senate Minority Leader Hugh Scott (R-PA) asked Kissinger, "Are the Israelis more or less intransigent than American Jews?" Kissinger said, "Less . . . Israel's position has evolved and they are willing to talk about things. But the American Jews are so tough and tend to hypo the Israelis and give them illusions." Senator Fulbright asked, "Isn't that an illusion?" Kissinger responded, "It is in this Administration." Fulbright shot back, "Not in Congress."[115]

Kissinger managed to convene a conference at Geneva on December 21, under the auspices of the U.N. Secretary General, with the United States and Soviet Union as cochairs. But the conference also revealed serious problems as only Israel, Jordan, and Egypt attended. For a time, it looked as if Israel would not attend at all.[116] Its political situation was in flux as Prime Minister Golda Meir's government faced an election at the end of December. Both Nixon and Kissinger pressured and pleaded with the Israelis to get them to join the conference, which they ultimately did.[117] Jordan's role in future negotiations would be limited at best, and excluding the PLO from the negotiating process undermined the legitimacy of Palestinian interests. Syria refused to attend, although it agreed to engage Israel in discussions. Only Sadat appeared satisfied with the status of the peace process and the prospects for moving forward.

Stepping Forward

Step-by-step diplomacy aimed to improve U.S.-Arab relations and pressure Israel to give up territory taken in 1967. Nixon and Kissinger would work hard to achieve these goals. And in time, pro-Israel lobbyists and Israeli officials would work hard to undermine both objectives.

As U.S. diplomacy cautiously stepped forward, certain pro-Israel forces worried the administration. Shortly before the Geneva conference, Kissinger sent word to the White House that he believed the "Jewish community" planned to "split him from the President," based on reports coming from the Israeli embassy.[118] Senator Javits sent a message to Kissinger, warning him not to accept any invitations to see Jewish groups without first speaking with Javits, who claimed to have important information.[119] Kissinger agreed to "not plan a program or meetings with Jewish leaders without first seeking the Senator's advice."[120] In response, Javits sent word that he was "concerned that other elements of the Jewish community might get their noses out of joint because this group would be only a partial representation of the elements which you need to contact." Furthermore, Javits recommended that Kissinger "survey carefully all the elements of influence in the Jewish community in this area and then make your contacts with them on a carefully planned basis."[121] Javits and Kissinger both recognized that the American Jewish Zionists wielded a significant degree of power, and Scowcroft agreed "to make no dinner engagements for Jewish groups without further word from you."[122]

Kissinger met with Jewish American leadership soon after Geneva and argued that Israel needed to take advantage of the situation and move toward full peace agreements. The meeting included some of the most influential American Jewish Zionists—Max Fisher (major Republican Party fundraiser), Jacob Stein (president of the President's Conference [NY]), Arthur Hertzberg (president of the American Jewish Congress), Rabbi Israel Miller (Zionist Federation of America), Herman Weisman (president of the Zionist Organization of America), Daniel Bloomberg (president of B'nai B'rith), along with several other leading figures. Kissinger told the group that "the Yom Kippur war was a disaster for Israel" and that Israel no longer enjoyed a decisive military advantage. The international community—not just the Soviet Union, but Europe and Japan as well—were lining up against the Israeli position. "Our strategy now will gain time," said Kissinger, "if it works." But Kissinger warned, "I won't kid you—Israel must make sacrifices. It is the condition of its survival. I guarantee you, if Israel continues to stay on the October 6 borders, in ten years it will be bled to death or destroyed."[123]

Kissinger revealed one of the central purposes of step-by-step diplomacy in the meeting—to shield Israel from external pressures in order to give Israel time to prepare itself to move forward with a substantial land-for-peace exchange. Step-by-step diplomacy did not aim to keep Israel in the occupied territories; it aimed to give Israel a chance, if it wanted one, to get out. Kissinger regarded a significant Israeli withdrawal as vital to Israeli security.

As Kissinger tried to implement his diplomacy in a way that excluded the Palestinians, Senator Abourezk undertook efforts to strengthen U.S. ties with the Arab world, and particularly with the PLO. In early 1974, at the behest of the Interior Committee on which he served, Abourezk undertook a three-week tour of the Middle East to meet with oil-producing states and became the first elected U.S. official to visit Iraq after it broke diplomatic relations with the United States during the 1967 war.[124] He argued that in order to stabilize its oil policy, the United States must discontinue its "one-sided" backing of Israel and seek a just settlement to the Palestinian refugee situation. During the trip, Abourezk also "became the first American to hold discussions with the Palestine Liberation Organization in the course of an official visit to the Middle East."[125] Upon his return he wrote to Kissinger and testified to an Arab "reservoir of good will toward America." He urged Secretary Kissinger to engage the Arab world in sincere peace discussions.[126] Kissinger did indeed plan to strengthen U.S. ties with the Arab world, but not with the PLO.

Kissinger used "shuttle diplomacy" to negotiate an agreement between Israel and Egypt, called Sinai I, on January 18, 1974.[127] Meir's Labor Alignment coalition managed to hold onto power after a strong challenge from the newly formed Likud Party during the December 31 Knesset elections, which made the Israeli position more stable.[128] After shuttling between Cairo and Jerusalem for about a week, Kissinger facilitated an agreement that included a reduction in force levels and a more substantial disengagement of military forces; a U.N. buffer zone would fill in between Israeli and Egyptian forces on the east side of the Suez Canal.

American officials expected the oil embargo to be lifted after the agreement. Nixon, of course, longed for good news to deliver to the American public and planned to make the announcement during his upcoming State of the Union address. But the embargo continued. King Faisal had effectively given a "veto to states with unsatisfied claims," and on January 21, Assad demanded that the oil weapon be used on Syria's behalf.[129] In other words, Assad wanted movement toward a peace agreement before he would consent to lifting the oil embargo.

Kissinger continued to push the Israelis to use the opportunity presented by step-by-step diplomacy to move bilaterally in a way that dealt comprehensively with all the details. Near the end of his January trip, he met with moderate Israeli officials, including Yigal Allon, Abba Eban, and Simcha Dinitz, and encouraged Israel to move forward with a peace plan. Kissinger offered his assessment: "I thought at the end of October you were in bad shape politically. I think now you have an extraordinary chance. You can deal with each of these countries separately and give each of them something they want, and they will never get together again."[130]

To get the oil flowing, Nixon wrote to Faisal on February 7 that he planned to push hard for a substantial Israeli withdrawal and claimed that lifting the embargo would help to achieve that goal.[131] The next day Nixon sent word to Faisal through Ambassador James Akins that reiterated that message: "I will not be swayed by domestic political considerations. I recognize that the government did not do enough in the Middle East during my first term but I am determined now that the Middle East be settled." But Nixon claimed that he needed the embargo lifted to lessen domestic pressures. In particular, "Congress and the press will make it extremely difficult for me to make progress. . . . I am out on a limb—I have been there before—but I want us to be able to work together for a settlement."[132]

Like Nixon, Golda Meir faced domestic political problems. She refused "to consider a national unity government including Likud, reportedly describing that prospect as a 'disaster' for Israel as it would block negotiating prospects and threaten Israel's positive relations with the U.S."[133] A month earlier, Likud leader Menachem Begin had criticized the Sinai agreement and warned the fragile Israeli government against entering into long-term agreements based on Israeli withdrawals.[134] The role of the National Religious Party, traditionally aligned with the Labor Party, added to the rightward drift in Israeli politics. According to Meir, "the entire right wing had now combined into a bloc of its own. A coalition would have to be formed again, and it would clearly be a back-breaking job to form it, since the religious bloc, which was a traditional coalition partner of ours, was itself deeply divided on the question of who should lead it and what its policy should be at this tremendously difficult time."[135] The hardline shift convinced longtime politicians Shimon Peres and Moshe Dayan to not take part in the cabinet, even after personal pleas by Meir. Therefore, Meir was forced to form a minority government that, according to an American intelligence report, "would be able to make the necessary decisions concerning a disengagement with Syria. After that, however, the decisions on a broader settlement are expected to be more difficult."[136] Feeling the political tide turning against her, Meir tendered her resignation on April 11 and agreed to lead a caretaker government until a successor was chosen.[137] Israel, like the United States, lacked a strong leader.

Negotiating an agreement between Israel and Syria—"two mortal enemies," according to Kissinger—promised to be difficult.[138] Historically, Palestine had been a part of Greater Syria. But the European mandate system following World War I led to the separation of Palestine from Syria, and Trans-Jordan from both Palestine and Syria. Thus, many Syrians viewed Israel as an illegitimate state that usurped a Palestinian state, itself an illegitimate creation of the European nation-state model. From the Israeli side, Syria constituted the most belligerent Arab neighbor, bent on demolishing Israel. While Kissinger shuttled between Damascus and Jerusalem in February, Syria and Israel exchanged daily artillery fire across the cease-fire lines.[139]

Aside from tough negotiations between enemy states, Nixon and Kissinger continued to face challenges from Scoop Jackson and American Jewish Zionists. In the Senate, Jackson pressed forward with his effort to link MFN status for the Soviet Union to freedom of emigration. Jackson's effort troubled the administration because U.S. diplomacy had already severely diminished Soviet involvement in the peace process. As Kissinger said in a meeting with GOP congressional leadership, "We can't frustrate them in every area." As for the "Jewish community," according to Nixon, "They are worse than Jackson." The president wondered, "Isn't it better for the U.S. to have influence with its [Israel's] enemies than the Soviet Union? Israel says all it needs is weapons."[140] Nixon's comments reflected a similar Saudi concern—that Israel wanted to undermine the "American-Arab rapprochement." In particular, the Saudis were incensed by Meir's declaration in early February that Israel will "never give up Golan."[141]

Despite these challenges, progress on the Israel-Syria front produced the desired result. The Arab members of OPEC lifted the oil embargo on March

18. While that was a major achievement, U.S. officials still needed to make sure that another embargo would not follow, which meant finding a way to continue the peace process and prevent another war and included a step toward peace between Israel and Syria.

The administration stressed the importance of improved U.S.-Arab relations to congressional leadership, and the challenge of American Jewish Zionists. Nixon commented at a meeting on April 24, "We are at a watershed period in foreign policy, in a period when often we are tied exclusively to Israel. We are now developing a relationship of friendship with the whole area. It's not to get the Soviet Union out—that is self-defeating—but to have us in." Kissinger pointed out that the administration requested $250 million in aid for Egypt and $100 million in a contingency fund for Jordanian and Syrian projects. Egypt needed U.S. support because Sadat no longer relied on the Soviets, and Kissinger planned to make that point "with the American Jewish leaders" too. But Nixon bemoaned the influence of American Jewish Zionists. "The most unreasonable people supporting Israel," said Nixon, "are not their government, but the American Jewish community." To mute domestic criticisms and offer incentives for Israel, Nixon planned to allocate the additional $500 million in credits "after a continuation of the negotiation"—meaning a successful Israel-Syria disengagement agreement.[142]

Although legislators argued in late 1973 that massive military aid would strengthen Israel's bargaining position and facilitate peace agreements, the Nixon administration took the opposite path in 1974. During a shuttle trip in early May, Kissinger floated to Nixon the idea of freezing aid to Israel as a way to soften its position. He sent a message to Scowcroft: "I must be assured of the President's support if the Israelis should reject our position. We may even have to threaten the Israelis with a cutoff of our aid. You should confirm with [White House Chief of Staff Alexander] Haig that I can count on the President's support for such measures and advise me."[143]

Nixon was only too ready to support Kissinger's idea. He sent a letter to Meir on May 4, warning that Israel should not jeopardize U.S. peace efforts in the region, and that the United States may have to reexamine its relationship with Israel.[144] (In doing so, Nixon foreshadowed Ford's decision the following March to freeze aid shipments to Israel and reassess U.S.–Middle East policy.) On May 10, Nixon sent word to Kissinger through Scowcroft that "he fully supported your tough stance with the Israelis and that you should know that his support for continued aid to Israel, also in the event of any new hostilities, is fully conditioned on their taking a reasonable posture in your present negotiations." Nixon offered to write Meir another letter, if Kissinger felt that would help.[145]

But the threats by Nixon and Kissinger did not have the desired effect. Kissinger blamed Israeli intransigence on four factors—"domestic divisions in Israel"; "a deliberate attempt to wreck our Arab policy"; "Israeli assessment of presidential paralysis—the last message from the President brushed off with disdain by the PM"; and "Israeli apparent belief that they have established a direct pipeline to the Pentagon." While Kissinger felt that the first three factors had to be dealt with after his current shuttle, the final factor could be handled immediately. He, therefore, instructed Haig to get in touch with Defense Secretary Schlesinger and have him "hold up all new commitments. Also delay administratively all pipeline items. We can then review the entire situation after my return."[146]

Nixon's reply, consistent with many of Nixon's venting sessions about Israel, again supported Kissinger's position. Scowcroft messaged Kissinger that Nixon "called again to say that he wanted by the end of the day a listing of all forms of aid to Israel which were under his authority to terminate. He said to tell you that you should make it unmistakably clear, if you reach that point, that the Israelis will be immediately shut off completely, without a nickel."[147] The message echoed two similar messages from the day before. Another Nixon message related that he intended to "cut off every bit of aid to Israel under his authority" if negotiations failed. Nixon added that the disengagement between Syria and Israel "was not the end of the line but merely a step toward a permanent settlement in which we would support them for a full solution to the problem."[148] Later that day, Scowcroft informed Kissinger of another Nixon phone call, during which he again said he planned to cut off all aid to Israel if negotiations broke down.[149]

While Nixon and Kissinger tried to pressure Israel, one powerful pro-Israel organization took aim at Kissinger in an effort to discredit him and undermine the U.S.-led peace effort. Herman Edelsberg, executive director of the International Council of B'nai B'rith, sent a confidential memorandum to the "Board of Governors" on May 7, which discussed "Tasks Confronting B'nai B'rith."[150] Such documents are difficult to come across, and this one seems to brag about the power of pro-Israel organizations and their ability to influence U.S. policy. Whether or not the document accurately reflects the power of an organization like B'nai B'rith is hard to say. But Fulbright, who in 1977 received the memorandum from Norman Dacey, chairman of The American Palestine Committee, called it "quite a remarkable document."[151]

Edelsberg recognized the importance of the legislative branch and discussed different ways of impacting certain congressional elections. As opposed to the president, legislators can serve unlimited terms. In order to determine which candidates to support, Edelsberg referenced "a meticulous and continuous survey of congressional voting records, together with both public and private statements made by individual Senators and Congressmen." Using that information, a "detailed study of electoral prospects" was nearing completion, which could "show where Jewish campaign contributions can be most judiciously placed." The memo recommended to "use all available forms of pressure, both on and off the record, to secure the desired results." One particular senator had drawn the ire of pro-Israel forces—William Fulbright—the senator who received the memo. "As an example of the political potentialities," wrote Edelsberg, "it can already be said that all the indications suggest that our actions in support of Governor Bumpers will result in the ousting of Mr. Fulbright from his key position in the Senate." Indeed, Fulbright lost his nomination bid a few weeks later. Edelsberg noted that Fulbright's defeat "will represent a meaningful victory for the Jewish cause in the struggle against skeptical elements in the State Department and elsewhere."[152]

Influencing U.S. policy at its highest levels of operation required a working relationship with individuals committed to advancing a position in line with certain pro-Israel lobbying forces. Edelsberg pointed to Scoop Jackson and Defense Secretary Schlesinger. Jackson's support for Israel had "endeared him to all Jews," and as the 1976 presidential election loomed in the future, Edelsberg argued that "it is necessary to redouble efforts in his support." Schlesinger equaled a link to the Pentagon. But aside from Schlesinger and Jackson, Edelsberg feared that sentiment was turning against Israel. Therefore, he noted that "we must seek other means of access to the Joint Chiefs of Staff."[153] He stressed the importance of continued military aid from the United States.

The document also highlighted the effectiveness of pro-Israel lobbying efforts and the perceived need to discredit Kissinger. According to Edelsberg, "recent events have shown that selective and measured pressure in decision-making areas of the U.S. Government can induce the desired results. As B'nai B'rith activists, it is our duty to maintain that pressure to secure the greatest possible U.S. support for Israel's needs."[154] The memorandum clearly indicated the willingness and ability of a pro-Israel organization to attack Nixon and Kissinger in an effort to relieve pressure being placed on Israel through step-by-step diplomacy. According to Edelsberg,

> Examples of the political success that the type of pressure mentioned above can achieve may be drawn from the Watergate scandal. B'nai B'rith can claim to have contributed to a situation in which the early ouster of President Nixon from the White House looks assured. The strong likelihood that Vice President Ford will succeed to the Presidency offers us new opportunities of more actively influencing U.S. policy in the Middle East, as well as on the whole range of issues that concern American Jewry. Indeed, the prospective President's "open mind" on foreign affairs may provide something of a blank sheet on which to impress our views. Nevertheless, we are still confronted by obstacles, and we must plan carefully in advance so as to place ourselves in a position to remove them or to soften their resistance.[155]

Edelsberg viewed step-by-step diplomacy, in particular, as a major threat. "In the view of the International Council, the chief of these obstacles is the present course of U.S. foreign policy, the brain child of Dr. Kissinger." In order to counteract Kissinger's diplomacy, the International Council recommended following one of two courses—either pressure Kissinger directly to get him "to change course," or try "to undermine the prestige he currently enjoys." Edelsberg recommended pursuing both aims simultaneously and then potentially switching to just one course if it seemed more useful. "But the Kissinger policies will not just go away," he warned. Therefore, "efforts must be made to tie him more closely to the Watergate scandal. B'nai B'rith research units should not find this task beyond their scope." He recommended, "The support which we have always enjoyed with the mass media must be developed."[156]

Previous attempts had been made to link Kissinger to Watergate, such as when he negotiated Sinai I in January 1974.[157] But soon after the May 7 document, a similar effort to connect Kissinger to the illegalities of the White House occurred while he shuttled between Syria and Israel. On May 12, the *Boston Globe* reported that Kissinger may have committed perjury when asked by the Senate Foreign Relations Committee about his role in wiretaps. A May 17 *New York Times* piece accused Kissinger of "prolonging his shuttle diplomacy in order to avoid the even more complicated and poisonous controversies of Washington."[158] According to Kissinger, "by May 22 this had become a general theme taken up by both the CBS and NBC television correspondents of my shuttle."[159] In his memoirs, Kissinger referenced an article from "the left-wing magazine *New Times*" that claimed, "The honeymoon is over for Henry Kissinger. There are signs that the media is [*sic*] going after him for the first time."[160] To counteract the stories, the White House press office acknowledged that Nixon had specifically asked Kissinger to stay in the Middle East until he reached an agreement. But in trying to protect Kissinger, the plan actually backfired as it undermined one of Kissinger's negotiating tactics—threatening to pack up and leave. Kissinger expressed his dissatisfaction in an urgent cable to Scowcroft.[161]

Kissinger managed to navigate domestic and regional problems as Syria and Israel consented to an agreement on May 31. Israel committed itself to withdraw from all the territory taken in the 1973 war, along with Quneitra, capital of the Golan, in return for prisoners of war. As in Sinai I, the Golan Heights had been divided into Israeli and Syrian zones with a substantially reduced military presence, separated by a U.N. presence in between; the main difference was that each side had two separate zones, rather than one, on each side of the buffer zone.[162] Yitzhak Rabin, former chief of staff and ambassador to Washington, officially became prime minister on June 3, only three days after Israel announced it had reached a disengagement agreement with Syria.

Soon after, Kissinger buckled under the pressure of ongoing questions about his role in wiretapping, and his credibility more generally. During a June 6 press conference, one journalist asked Kissinger if he had retained counsel for a possible perjury indictment. Kissinger responded that he had not, and that he would "answer no further questions on the topic." By evading questions, Kissinger encouraged more attacks, which followed. "The June 6 press conference opened the floodgates," said Kissinger. "There was next to no coverage of the foreign policy questions and answers."[163] Over the next several days, leading newspapers, especially the *New York Times* and *Washington Post,* along with leading news magazines, like *Time* and *Newsweek,* published stories that tried to connect Kissinger to Watergate.[164] By June 11, "the leading news media of the United States . . . had taken the position that serious new evidence had raised suspicion of perjury requiring a new investigation." Clearly overcome with frustration, Kissinger fired back during his press conference in Salzburg: "I do not believe that it is possible to conduct the foreign policy of the United States under these circumstances when the character and credibility of the Secretary of State is at issue. And if it is not cleared up, I will resign."[165] Kissinger's threat managed to rally support for his efforts and stem the tide of criticisms, and an August 6 report from the Senate Foreign Relations Committee absolved Kissinger of any wrongdoing connected to wiretaps or perjury. After attacking the use of unnamed sources, Kissinger says his "relations with the media never fully recovered." But Kissinger maintained (and perhaps with Watergate's "Deep Throat" in mind), "I continue to believe that anonymous accusers give journalists a power no branch of government possesses and expose public officials to much scurrilous abuse by individuals whose motives—and veracity—escape examination."[166]

To build on the momentum of the Israel-Syria agreement, and while Kissinger sought to offset persistent questions about his credibility, the embattled Nixon traveled to the Middle East in early June 1974. The president certainly hoped to distract people's minds from the Watergate fiasco, but the trip also came on the heels of an impressive moment in U.S. diplomatic history. Kissinger managed to bring Israel and Syria, two bitter enemies, to an agreement that for decades restored the armistice between the countries. The disengagement was the second in an effort to build momentum toward implementation of Resolution 242 as part of a comprehensive peace based on bilateral agreements. And while Nixon looked for anything to save his beleaguered presidency, he also genuinely wanted to advance the peace process. By visiting the Middle East, he sought to capitalize on the momentum created by the recent success while diverting attention away from his domestic troubles. And as a briefing paper for Kissinger noted, "perhaps the main purpose of the trip was to strengthen our bilateral relations with the nations of the Middle East."[167]

Prior to his trip, Kissinger sent Nixon a memorandum about the status of Middle East negotiations and certain points to make with Israeli officials. The memo stressed the importance of maintaining momentum, arguing that the United States and Israel needed to "develop a common strategy for keeping the present diplomatic process going."[168] Kissinger noted that some time needed to pass in order for the Syrian disengagement to take hold, "but we cannot lose momentum altogether." Kissinger recognized that Israeli officials would likely press Nixon about commitments regarding the Golan Heights, Jerusalem, final borders, or Palestinian refugees, and he advised the president to resist making such commitments. Instead, he recommended that Nixon mention that the final peace needed to be "worked out in direct negotiations. The U.S. has produced the framework for those negotiations."[169]

Nixon continued to have concerns about more weapons for Israel. In his memoirs, Nixon recalled a June 5 meeting with American Jewish Zionist leadership that left him "disturbed by what I considered to be their short-sighted outlook." According to Nixon, "I pointed out that hardware alone to Israel was a policy that made sense maybe five years ago but did not make sense today," and "I made it very clear there is going to be no blank check in our conversations with the Israelis." Furthermore, Nixon argued that "the only long-term hope lies in reaching some kind of settlement now while they can operate from a position of strength."[170]

Nixon received a warm welcome wherever he traveled in the Middle East, especially in Cairo and Damascus. In Cairo, more than a million people flooded the streets to see the U.S. president. On June 16, Nixon and Assad agreed to resume normal diplomatic relations between the United States and Syria. For Nixon, the "strengthening of our bilateral relations" included "educational and cultural exchanges," and Nixon invited Assad to visit the United States, which he accepted.[171] The dramatic transition to normal diplomatic relations was perhaps best expressed by Assad's son, Bashar al-Assad, who succeeded his father as president in 2000 and remains president despite an ongoing civil war. In conversation with his father in June 1974, the younger Assad said, "This Nixon who is coming, isn't he the one who you have said is the foreign devil and the tool of the Jews? How come you are inviting him here?"[172] Like Sadat, the older Assad wanted to work more closely with the United States than with Israel. "The Syrian Arab Republic," said Assad, "declares its readiness to pursue its sincere and constructive cooperation with the Government of the United States of American for laying down the firm basis for a just and lasting peace in the Middle East region."[173]

But the most important question remained unanswered—what was the next step in step-by-step diplomacy? Nixon proved unable the lay the groundwork for an Israel-Jordan agreement. According to Richard Thornton, the U.S. effort to pursue an agreement with Jordan "fell upon deaf ears in Israel." The main problem, according to Thornton, was the weak leadership of the new Rabin cabinet.[174] When Rabin assumed the prime minister position in early June, his cabinet reflected the deep divide between the left and right as the moderate Yigal Allon served as foreign minister while the hawkish Shimon Peres served as defense minister; Rabin oftentimes filled a middle position between the two. Sometimes referred to as the Triumvirate, Rabin, Peres, and Allon shared power in the cabinet. Rabin did not have the authority to follow a course of his choosing that may have included an effort to engage Jordan. Peres explained to Senator Javits during the latter's trip to Israel in July that he was "puzzled" by the U.S. effort to bring Israel and Jordan together for an agreement, noting that he and other Israeli leaders were planning for the next agreement to be a second step with Egypt.[175]

Jordan did not seem particularly interested in moving forward with peace negotiations, either. According to a journalist who cited "reliable Israeli sources," Moshe Dayan met with King Hussein near the end of May and proposed an agreement based on Jordanian civilian control of the West Bank and an Israeli military presence.[176] But Hussein refused the offer, perhaps uncomfortable with a substantial increase of Palestinians determined to obtain a nation-state inside Jordan's borders, especially after Black September, and also the domestic challenges of allowing an Israeli military presence.

Nevertheless, the administration continued to press the Jordanian option. A cable from Kissinger to the U.S. ambassadors in the Middle East stressed the importance of a Jordanian agreement and the willingness of the administration to pursue a peaceful resolution to the conflict. "As for U.S. policy on further Israeli withdrawals from occupied territories," said Kissinger, "we continue to support and work for comprehensive Middle East settlement . . . and have made clear we view disengagement agreements so far achieved as only first steps toward final just and durable peace." Kissinger also added that the administration sought an Israel-Jordan agreement based on "our recognition that any peace settlement must take into account legitimate interests of Palestinian people."[177] Nixon recognized that Jordan came last in step-by-step diplomacy because the three most difficult issues—West Bank, Jerusalem, and Palestinian refugees—all involved Jordan.[178] The Israeli political situation promised to be a complication, and Israeli officials expressed a desire "to wait two or three years." But Nixon said bluntly in late July, "We can't wait. It won't be in the next 2–3 weeks, but we must move."[179] Nixon planned to use economic incentives to spur bilateral agreements between Israel and Egypt and Israel and Syria, which "is why we are setting up cooperative commissions for both of them. That is why we have asked for aid for them—we want to give them a stake in continuing to work with us."[180]

But Nixon never had a chance to follow through on his peace-making efforts as Watergate finally forced the president's resignation on August 9.

The elevation of the unelected Ford included keeping Kissinger as a holdover for both of his duties—Secretary of State and National Security Advisor. It would be up to the Ford administration to see through Kissinger's diplomacy in the Middle East.

Conclusion

The U.S. government moved from lavishing Israel with weapons in late 1973, to threatening to withhold them in May 1974. Overwhelming bipartisan support for Israel in Congress resulted in passage of a $2.2 billion emergency military-aid bill. But as Fulbright argued, Congress could have waited to vote on the aid until after the Geneva conference, or limited the amount to $1 billion and offered more to Israel on a case-by-case basis. Fulbright hoped that by denying Israel such an enormous aid package the U.S. government could signal to Israel the need to compromise in peace discussions. But several important legislators, especially Humphrey, countered by arguing that Israel needed the enormous amount of military aid immediately, despite poor justification from the executive branch, in order to take risks in peace negotiations. Nixon and Kissinger soon discovered that, with so much military firepower, Israel seemed less interested in making territorial compromises. Therefore, Nixon and Kissinger went so far as to threaten to withhold further military aid to soften Israel's position during negotiations with Syria, which substantiated Fulbright's argument.

Nixon aimed to implement an evenhanded policy that still regarded Israel as a strategic ally in the Cold War. During his first term, Nixon tried to avoid selling more Phantoms to Israel. During his truncated second term, Nixon steadily applied pressure on Israel to leave the territories. Combined with the administration's lack of justification for more than half of the $2.2 billion and the threat to withhold weapons during Israel-Syria negotiations, Nixon's October aid request seems especially self-serving.

The U.S. plan put forward by Nixon and Kissinger succeeded in advancing the major goals of step-by-step diplomacy: it strengthened the cease-fire from the 1973 war, improved U.S.-Arab relations, ended the oil embargo, reduced Soviet influence in the region, and provided Israel with an opportunity to withdraw from the occupied territories. But on numerous occasions, U.S. officials expressed more concern with the "illusions" and intransigence of American Jewish Zionists than with Israeli officials. Documentation shows that a powerful international organization like B'nai B'rith actively sought to work against U.S. policy. Moving forward, both Congress and pro-Israel lobbyists would continue to influence policymaking in the Middle East.

Nixon's position steadily deteriorated throughout the period of step-by-step diplomacy, to the point that Meir, according to Kissinger, brushed off Nixon's threat to withhold aid in early May. When he resigned in August, the White House remained only a shell of what it had been in 1968 or 1972. The unelected Ford inherited one of the most ambitious diplomatic schemes during the Cold War. One can only wonder what would have happened with the peace process if Nixon had not been dragged down by Watergate.

4

The Spirit of the 76

The Israeli Embassy, Congress, and President Ford's Reassessment

Gerald Ford had always wanted to become Speaker of the House. But historical events pushed him in a different direction, first to vice president and then to president. Known to be a supporter of Israel while serving in the House, Ford soon discovered that foreign policy concerns looked much different from inside the White House than from inside the Capitol building.

The experienced legislator's presidency witnessed continuing conflicts with Congress, especially in the realm of foreign policy.[1] The midterm elections that took place shortly after Richard Nixon's resignation brought the "class of 1974" to Washington, D.C., which included many first-time legislators who, according to Loch K. Johnson, "came to Congress with what they considered a mandate to clean up the government."[2] In his memoirs, Kissinger recalled this "new and extremely liberal Congress," headed by George McGovern, was nearly constantly at odds with the Ford White House.[3] In particular, Congress challenged the White House over foreign-policy issues, which had been the sacred realm of the executive branch. Ford remembered in a 2003 interview, "There was, I thought, an unfortunate encroachment by the Congress on foreign power action by the United States. . . . Congress was trying to claw its way into the foreign policy arena, and that inevitably was a potential encroachment on presidential power."[4] Just as with the two previous administrations, conflict between the two branches continued in the area of U.S.–Middle East relations.

President Ford declared a "reassessment" of U.S.–Middle East policy in March 1975, which included the suspension of new arms deals with Israel, slowed the delivery of arms already in the pipeline, and ushered in one of the most contentious periods in U.S.-Israel relations. After negotiations for a Sinai II agreement failed that March, Ford and Kissinger privately blamed Israel for sabotaging the peace talks with Egypt and publicly insinuated that Israel bore responsibility for the breakdown of talks. They believed that Israel aimed to remain in the occupied territories and stymied disengagement talks with Egypt to resist movement toward a broader peace that would have meant relinquishing most of the territory taken in 1967. The administration desperately needed another agreement to advance the momentum created by Kissinger's step-by-step diplomacy, and both Ford and Kissinger wanted a notable achievement to bolster Ford's chances of election in 1976. The diplomatic process tried to shield Israel from external pressures—especially the Soviet Union and Europe—to give back territory until Israel was prepared to do so. But U.S. officials expected Israel to eventually return the vast majority of the lands. Thus, reassessment was a way of punishing Israel for not going along with American diplomacy, which had been designed by Kissinger to benefit both Israel and the United States.

Reassessment brought about a fierce public relations campaign from Israel. In certain situations, Israel has used *hasbara,* or general political public relations, to influence public opinion and policy decisions in the United States. Peter Hahn discusses several *hasbara* efforts by Israel during the presidencies of Harry Truman and Dwight Eisenhower in his book *Caught in the Middle East,* as well as in a separate article based on research conducted at the Israel State Archives in Jerusalem.[5] Rather than disseminating ideological messages or propaganda, a *hasbara* campaign advances the Israeli position through meetings with U.S. government officials, coordination with American Jews, messages through the press, and lectures given by Israeli officials. As happened during the Truman and Eisenhower administrations, the Israeli *hasbara* in the spring of 1975 meant a head-on collision with the Ford administration.

Relying on research gathered at the Israel State Archives, this chapter charts the efforts of the Israeli embassy in Washington, D.C. to influence U.S. policy between late March and late May 1975, the main period of reassessment.[6] The embassy worked tirelessly to explain the Israeli position to U.S. congressional leadership and also used meetings with congressional assistants and lower-level officials from the executive branch to access important information. The embassy coordinated its efforts with American Jewish

Zionist leadership, and at times Israeli Ambassador Simcha Dinitz even prepared individuals for their meetings with Ford and Kissinger. Ultimately, the efforts of the embassy led to a May 21 letter signed by seventy-six senators that undercut Ford's desire to withhold weapons to soften the Israeli position. Referred to by some Israeli officials at the time as "the spirit of the 76," the letter was a tremendous achievement for Israel, thanks in large part to Dinitz, who first proposed the idea of such a letter to Foreign Minister Yigal Allon in late April.

Scholars are divided about Ford's reassessment, especially the impact of the Senate letter. Steven Spiegel claims the letter mattered little because Ford and Kissinger had already determined to restart step-by-step diplomacy.[7] On the other hand, William Quandt believes the letter forced the administration to recognize that further pressure on Israel would be "politically counterproductive," and consequently the administration had no choice but to resume step-by-step diplomacy in the absence of an obtainable peace agreement.[8] Salim Yaqub sees Ford's reassessment as "political theater," believing that Kissinger meant only to shield Israel from external pressures in order to secure indefinite Israeli occupation of the disputed territories.[9] In that case, domestic politics mattered little because U.S. officials would not force a peace agreement on Israel. Galen Jackson argues that domestic politics, and in particular the activities of the Israel lobby, shaped the administration's approach to peacemaking, but the administration decided to not have a showdown with Israel largely because Kissinger feared rising anti-Semitism in the United States.[10]

The letter mattered a great deal, not for its impact on whether or not the administration decided to shelve step-by-step diplomacy and move to a comprehensive peace conference at Geneva, but because it forced the Ford White House to make unprecedented commitments to Israel as part of the Sinai II agreement. U.S. officials, above all else, feared the outbreak of another war and all that would go with it. Another war likely meant another oil embargo, which would severely threaten the economic health of the United States and the Western World, and maybe even lead to superpower confrontation. The region had seen five wars in less than thirty years, and three wars in less than ten years—1948–1949, 1956, 1967, 1969–1970, and 1973—and Moscow had threatened unilateral military intervention in 1967 and 1973. Kissinger's diplomacy had only disengaged the combatants, and without at least another step forward, U.S. officials believed war to be a legitimate possibility. Also important, Kissinger wanted to continue to draw Egypt closer to the United

States and needed to show Sadat that U.S. diplomacy could deliver. The letter mattered because it denied the Ford administration the ability to pressure Israel into making an agreement with Egypt. Therefore, the Ford White House had to buy the Sinai II agreement with substantial American promises of material aid and political protection, which, moving forward, formalized a significant change in the U.S.-Israel relationship. Dinitz and the Israeli embassy, both aside from and in coordination with the Israel lobby, played a vital role in this development.

A ferocious, behind-the-scenes battle developed between Israel and the United States for the heart of the peace process, which threatened to damage U.S.-Israel relations, U.S.–Middle East relations, and Israel-Egypt relations. Israel successfully used its *hasbara* campaign to challenge an exceptionally weak presidential administration during a difficult time. Ford had to navigate the fall of Saigon and a sluggish economy, both blamed on inept executive leadership. At the same time, pro-Israel forces aimed to reframe the nature of reassessment to prevent the deterioration of U.S.-Israel relations and that proved able to use Congress to secure future aid agreements and deliveries. Given the sour relations between the legislative and executive branches, as well as the strong pro-Israel tilt of the legislature, congressional officials were very willing to challenge presidential foreign policymaking. The State of Israel clearly influenced Congress and public opinion, which in turn impacted U.S. foreign policy in nontrivial ways. In particular, the "spirit of the 76" letter demonstrated not only the significant power of the Israel lobby in shaping U.S.-Israel relations, but also the increasing power of Congress in affecting U.S. foreign policy.

A Second Israel-Egypt Agreement?

Foreign policy was not Ford's area of expertise. While in the House of Representatives, he had supported Nixon's policies in East Asia and was known to be a good friend of Israel.[11] Otherwise, his position on foreign policy matters was unknown. Lacking experience, Ford trusted Kissinger to take charge of U.S. foreign policy, especially in the Middle East.

Step-by-step diplomacy became increasingly ineffective after the agreement between Israel and Syria. Having disengaged belligerents in the Sinai Peninsula and Golan Heights, the peace process demanded some type of agreement involving the West Bank. That, however, meant introducing the

Palestinian question to the peace process, which would make negotiations even more fragile.

An interim agreement between Israel and Jordan never came to fruition. On October 28, 1974, the Arab League summit assembled in Rabat, Morocco, and unanimously endorsed the PLO as the sole representative of the Palestinians.[12] The move was a deliberate attack on step-by-step diplomacy; Arab leaders wanted an immediate, comprehensive agreement rather than the more methodical, piecemeal approach. In other words, the patience afforded Kissinger by Arab leaders immediately after the 1973 war had grown thin. If the PLO represented the Palestinians, then Jordan would have no authority to negotiate any settlement involving the West Bank.

Refusing to deal with the PLO was fine with Kissinger. He regarded the organization as being too radical and potentially harmful to his diplomatic process. Step-by-step diplomacy fed slowly off victories but starved quickly with defeats. It was not in America's best interest to begin negotiations with a loose-cannon organization. After all, the PLO concerned itself more with disrupting diplomacy than in negotiating an agreement with Israel, which the PLO would not recognize as a legitimate state anyway. A simple misunderstanding, if not handled properly, could undermine the entire process. Additionally, the PLO was widely known to use terrorism for political means. For that reason and others, the United States did not recognize the political legitimacy of the PLO, which made negotiations practically impossible.[13]

Even before the meeting in Rabat, Kissinger received word of a possible second disengagement agreement developing between Israel and Egypt. The Egyptians wanted the strategically important Mitla and Gidi passes in the Sinai, along with control over the Abu Rudeis and Ras Sudr oil fields; the fields provided Israel with 50 percent of its total oil needs.[14] Kissinger made two separate trips to the Middle East—one in February and one in March—to bring the two sides closer together, all to no avail.

Kissinger had two main reasons for pursuing another round of Israel-Egypt negotiations. Following the staggering Democratic successes in the 1974 midterm elections, Kissinger likely hoped to secure a Middle East agreement to help Ford and fellow Republicans in the 1976 elections. Even more important, the Ford administration had to find some way to prevent a backslide into war. Stagnation of the peace process would not be tolerated by Egypt, a point made clear by Anwar Sadat in October 1973 when he chose a surprise attack on Israel to restart the stalled peace process. With West Bank negotiations on hold, Kissinger needed another partner to keep "stepping" toward peace.

But Kissinger did not expect such strong Israeli resistance to an agreement. Negotiations failed due to a seemingly small misunderstanding. Although Israel hoped for an Egyptian pledge of nonbelligerency, Israeli Prime Minister Yitzhak Rabin had stated during an interview in February that Israel would give up the specific territory in return for an Egyptian commitment to not go to war, or threaten with force, as part of an effort to reach peace.[15] But the Israeli negotiating team caught Kissinger by surprise in March when it insisted that Egypt agree to nonbelligerency. For Sadat, that meant acceptance of the status quo, which he recognized would alienate the Arab world. So Sadat rejected the Israeli proposal and instead offered "nonuse of force," which in turn met with an Israeli rejection. As negotiations headed for collapse, not even a stern letter from President Ford on March 21 moderated the Israeli position.[16] Disengagement talks quickly deteriorated and fell apart.

Looking deeper, however, reveals that the failure of negotiations had much more to do with the peace process as a whole than with a single disengagement agreement between Israel and Egypt. Ford and Kissinger badly needed an agreement to keep stepping forward, and they felt betrayed by the Israelis. When House Majority Leader Tip O'Neill met with Rabin in early April, he mentioned that, according to Ford, Israel was told twenty-four times before Kissinger's March shuttle that it would not receive nonbelligerency from Egypt as part of an agreement, and each time Israel said to continue with negotiations.[17] When Israel demanded nonbelligerency during Kissinger's shuttle, the administration interpreted the demand as an attempt to sabotage negotiations. The breakdown in talks killed momentum toward a general peace agreement. For their part, Israeli officials stressed the problem of giving something tangible to Egypt, like land in the Sinai Peninsula, in return for political pledges from an Egyptian leader that had recently attacked Israel on Yom Kippur. Israel needed to be persuaded through economic and political incentives, rather than be pressured by them, in order for an agreement to come to fruition.

Reassessment

President Ford, who in his autobiography remembers being "mad as hell" because of Israeli "stalling," responded with a reassessment of U.S.–Middle

East policy.[18] Reassessment included an immediate freeze on U.S. aid to the region and halted step-by-step diplomacy while the administration contemplated the possibility of ending Kissinger's diplomacy and moving to a general settlement at a Geneva conference. Neither Israel nor the United States wanted to transition immediately to a general agreement. A Geneva conference meant a potentially larger role for Moscow, and Ford and Kissinger were likely reluctant to convene a peace conference given the weakened image of the United States during the fall of Saigon, as well as Ford's less-than-powerful status as a caretaker president. Israel would resist a comprehensive settlement, which meant domestic political problems for Ford and Kissinger. Reassessment was clearly designed to put pressure on Israel to pursue negotiations in such a way that invited broader peace discussions down the road.

At 8:00 a.m. on March 24, Ford and Kissinger met with bipartisan congressional leadership to discuss reassessment. Kissinger said, "After the October [1973] war it was the unanimous conclusion of the world community that Israel should return to the '67 borders. In the face of that we cooperated in a strategy with Israel to reduce Soviet Union influence in a step-by-step process. I must emphasize that every step was coordinated and usually at the instigation of Israel."[19] Ford followed by stating that the United States did not blame Israel for the failure of negotiations (Ford publicly called Israel "inflexible"), adding, "We have to take a new look, assess the situation and any relations with all the parties. Such an assessment will start today. We undertook a massive effort, with the best intentions, support of the people and Congress. For us not to reassess the situation would not be responsible."[20] Senate Democratic Majority Leader Mike Mansfield (D-MT) agreed, "You have no choice but to reassess."[21] Mansfield communicated being "deeply depressed," with "grave concern at the rigidity of Israel." He wondered about the Israelis: "Are they expressing a death wish?"[22]

Ford and Kissinger, despite their bland public rhetoric, privately fumed about Israeli intransigence. Ford favored a full peace settlement. He told Kissinger bluntly, "We must move comprehensively." Kissinger warned his president that Israel "will attack you," but Ford stood resolute. "I know they will hit us," he said, "but I kind of enjoy a fight when I know I am right."[23] Kissinger too was fed up with the Israelis. The next day he lamented "the unraveling of our Middle East policy," saying, "Israel has treated us as no other country could." He blamed Israel for attempting "to blow up our Middle East strategy."[24]

The administration recognized the power of pro-Israeli forces and their ability to influence U.S. policy. On the morning of March 26, Kissinger informed Ford that Senator Jacob "Javits came in very threatening. If we went after Israel, he and [Senator Abraham] Ribicoff would come after me. He said our interests are identical with Israel." Kissinger blamed "three million Israelis" for "running American foreign policy. We are giving aid to Israel at a rate which would be unbelievable for any other country."[25] The next morning Kissinger told Ford, "It is not a friendly misunderstanding. If the Jewish Community comes after us, we will have to go public with the whole record." Ford addressed the issue of Israeli influence on both branches of government during a National Security Council meeting. He told Secretary of Defense James Schlesinger, "As I recall my own experiences as a Congressman, the Israeli representatives float very freely on Capitol Hill. Now we can't do anything about that with Congress. But I have the impression the Israeli representatives are almost as free in many Departments as they are with Congress. You must try to control that." Schlesinger responded, "It is very difficult to handle." But Ford maintained, "The proper relationship should be businesslike but arms-length and aloof."[26]

The Ford administration threatened Israel with the possibility of a comprehensive settlement, but Kissinger knew the pitfalls along that path. Almost inevitably, the conference in Geneva would devolve into a wild shouting match. Israel would refuse to seat the PLO, which in Arab eyes represented the Palestinian people and, therefore, needed to participate in the discussions. The Soviets, acting as a lawyer and adviser for Arab nations, would clamor for an immediate Israeli withdrawal. Pressure would also come from Europe and Japan over energy concerns. No longer in control of the process, the influence of the United States would be neutralized, to a significant degree, by world opinion. The result would likely be another war and oil embargo.

But another option existed: the United States could simply pressure Israel to withdraw from the occupied territories by refusing any further military aid. In the words of Kissinger, the United States was "literally their [Israel's] only friend in the world."[27] This intimate relationship was reflected in the staggering figures of U.S. aid to Israel. Following the 1973 war, the United States appropriated $3.3 billion in assistance to Israel. Of that total, nearly $2.8 billion was for military assistance, while the remaining $500 million was for economic aid. Specifically, the United States sent 700 tanks,

55,147 anti-tank missiles, 2,583 trucks, 76 cargo carriers, an assortment of aircraft (F-4, A-4, and C-130) totaling 162 units, along with other various items.[28]

Ford intended to withhold further military aid as a way to persuade Israel to reconsider its inflexible position. Based on U.S. intelligence, Kissinger estimated that military assistance had put Israel "in a position to fight an intensive war for almost four weeks without resupply."[29] Kissinger observed that "Israel is, for the first time, vulnerable economically, and continuing U.S. assistance is essential because Israel is running an annual budget deficit of over $2 billion which it expects the U.S. Government to cover."[30] And Ford was prepared to refuse further aid until Israel proved more forthcoming in peace negotiations. Freezing U.S. aid to Israel was the bite that complemented the bark of reassessment.

On April 14, Ford and Kissinger met with four Middle East ambassadors (Kenneth Keating, Israel; Hermann Eilts, Egypt; Thomas Pickering, Jordan; and Richard Murphy, Syria) to discuss the feasibility of a comprehensive settlement. Kissinger mentioned either trying for an agreement similar to the one sought in March or going for a more substantial interim step. But of all the options, he concluded, "The best is to come up with a comprehensive plan. It would give us something to stand on with the Arabs. We would be taking on the Israelis, but for something more significant than the line through the passes. It would make the interim stages easier under an overall umbrella."[31] Keating, who also favored a comprehensive plan, cited the economic impact of reassessment: "Economically, they [Israel] are in serious trouble. Forty percent of their budget goes to defense. Inflation is running 30–40%."[32] Ford vowed, "Until we get progress there will be no request for Israeli aid. If Congress tries to force it, I will veto it."[33]

Kissinger divulged Israel's intention of keeping large tracts of land taken during the 1967 war. He estimated that Israel intended to keep "half the Golan, a third of the Sinai, and a third to a half of the West Bank"[34]—not to mention full control of Jerusalem. Such a position was in direct violation of the spirit of U.N. Resolution 242 and a rebuke of the land-for-peace process established by U.S. diplomacy. He later said that Israel wanted peace with the Arabs and aid from the United States, but "they don't want to pay a price."[35] The vast majority of the United Nations wished Israel to withdraw to essentially its 1967 borders, and the United States sought the same objective but allowed Israel to move slowly toward that goal. Yet Israel seemed convinced it could have both territory and peace, which the Arab states would never allow. U.S. officials expected a modest adjustment to borders, but also that Israel would withdraw to roughly the status quo prior to the 1967 war.

From the Israeli perspective, the occupied territories served a variety of useful purposes. For one, Israel believed the territories offered a heightened degree of security. The surprise attack on Yom Kippur demonstrated the need for expanded borders; if Israel had withdrawn from the territories, the attack could have reached Jerusalem or Tel Aviv. Religious considerations fueled the occupation of the West Bank, and especially all of Jerusalem; Jerusalem was the holiest Jewish city, which at long last had been brought back into the fold. In addition, Israel hoped the seizure of territory would produce economic benefits, especially with the oil fields in the Sinai.

When King Hussein of Jordan visited Washington on April 29, his comments focused on the impossibility of peace without an Israeli withdrawal. "From the Arab point of view," said Hussein, "it is a question of territory or peace. The combination for the Israelis of territory and peace is an impossibility."[36] He went on to say, "The Israelis are masters at long-range planning. . . . They have been able to obtain and build up great military strength superior to what they have ever had before. But with all that military strength, they cannot guaranty a peace in the area."[37] The king feared that the moment for constructing a lasting peace may be lost: "The Arab leaders and people are losing hope, and I find the situation very, very alarming. We may now be facing our last chance to make progress for the area and the world."[38]

Kissinger knew the king's assessment of Israeli intentions was probably right. He slammed the Israeli position in a memo for Ford just a week prior to the meeting with Hussein. Citing a statement made by Israeli Defense Minister Shimon Peres, Kissinger claimed the Israelis wanted "an Egyptian-Israeli second-stage agreement as a means of avoiding having to move in any serious way in any other negotiations for as long as possible."[39] The Israelis were probably "trying to stall through the presidential elections of 1976," aware that Ford would be reluctant to tackle such a divisive issue.[40] Kissinger argued that "Israel would like to 'take Egypt out of the war' alone; however, Sadat could not long survive making a separate peace."[41] And he reminded Ford, "The basic point to keep in mind is that Israel wants to keep half of the Golan Heights and a third of the Sinai for security purposes, plus a third to a half of the West Bank and all of Jerusalem for security, religious, and economic reasons."[42] He countered this position by saying, "Changes in Israel's 1967 boundaries will be an inconsequential addition to Israel's security, particularly in an era of modern weapons, if Israel's increasingly powerful Arab neighbors are bent on Israel's destruction over an historical period."[43] In fact, Kissinger held Israel responsible for the 1973 war, saying "that the Israeli strategy of standing pat and playing for time—of making ostensibly conciliatory statements about wanting a settlement but actually standing fast in the hope of forcing Arab territorial concessions—had produced the stalemate which led eventually to the October 1973 war."[44] In conclusion, Kissinger recommended, "On balance, the greatest advantage seems to lie with trying for an overall settlement."[45]

But to impose a full settlement on Israel, Kissinger advised Ford, "We would also have to develop firm Congressional and public support in the U.S. for this course, which Israel may attempt to slow." To do so, Kissinger informed the president, "the basic choice the U.S. faces is whether to opt for a course that masks the real Israeli strategy or one that deals openly with the issues that must be resolved if there is to be a peace settlement. If we are to choose the latter course, we will have to take into account the additional factor that the Jewish leadership in the United States will add a vocal and highly organized voice in support of what will be firm Israeli opposition to this course."[46] Armed with blunt facts, the administration could potentially rally the political support necessary to impose a settlement on Israel and bring the conflict nearer to a close.

The day after King Hussein's visit to the White House, Saigon capitulated to North Vietnamese forces, and the undeclared Vietnam War finally ended. The bad blood between the executive and legislative branches engendered by the Vietnam War carried over into other areas of U.S. foreign policy, including the Middle East. Just when the Ford administration needed the support of Congress and a unified American front to execute its foreign policy, Congress was poised to continue its trend of challenging the executive branch and asserting more influence on foreign-policy matters.

The Israeli *Hasbara*

In response to reassessment, Israel launched *hasbara* to make its case directly to Congress, the president, and the American people. Israel's *hasbara* had three main goals. First, to turn the foreign-aid spigot back on; second, to eliminate the appearance of divisions between the United States and Israel, which Israeli officials speciously argued could have invited an attack from Arab states; and third, to prevent the Ford administration from forming a new Middle East policy without influence from, or at least coordination with, Israel. Kissinger recalled President Ford's being especially irritated when Israeli ambassador Simcha Dinitz returned to the United States before Kissinger after the failure of negotiations in order to coordinate an Israeli strategy with American Jewish Zionist leadership.[47]

Dinitz found himself in an unusually powerful position for an ambassador. As the former director general and political adviser for Golda Meir, Dinitz was well informed about Israeli policy with respect to the peace process and U.S.-Israel relations. The unstable Israeli political situation made Dinitz's position even more powerful. At the end of May 1974, right after the Israel-Syria agreement, Yitzhak Rabin succeeded Meir as prime minister. But Rabin only narrowly defeated Shimon Peres for the position, and he felt obligated to include Peres in the cabinet, which he did as minister of Defense; additionally, Yigal Allon, another important Israeli politician, became minister of Foreign Affairs. The absence of a clear-cut leader in the Israeli government opened the door for an experienced politician like Dinitz to exert more influence as an ambassador in Washington.

Dinitz worked with other Israeli officials, especially David Turgemon and Zvi Rafiah, who were political consultants for the Israeli embassy in Washington. Rafiah went to Washington in the summer of 1973 to "institutionalize the Congressional Liaison Office of the Embassy." He served as a liaison between the Israeli embassy and both Houses of Congress and worked to develop positive relations with both political parties.[48] Israeli officials met with an assortment of U.S. political leaders—from the White House, State Department, Defense Department, Pentagon, and Congress, as well as influential American Jewish Zionists—and reported back to the Israeli government the contents of their conversations. In doing so, the embassy helped to supply the Israeli government with crucial information about developments within the U.S. government, as well as the mood of public opinion, while also putting out the Israeli position.

On March 24, the day after the announcement of reassessment, Turgemon met with Arthur Horton, deputy of Robert Oakley. (Oakley worked in the NSC for Brent Scowcroft.) Horton, who asked that their conversation "be kept very private," related that Kissinger believed an agreement could have been reached, but divisions within the Israeli cabinet prevented one from happening. Peres, in particular, seemed opposed to the agreement. Kissinger believed Israel was trying to play for time—to take Egypt out of the war while Israel increased its military forces.[49] Horton also spoke about a potential change in U.S.-Israel relations and said that "Israel will have to work hard to present its point of view in front of the Congress," and not "in the direction of Senator [Charles] Percy (R-IL) but rather Senator [Daniel] Inouye (D-HI)."

Not all senators, including Percy, supported the Israeli line. As the minority leader of the Senate Subcommittee on Near Eastern Affairs, Percy supported a comprehensive peace plan that included a homeland for Palestinians, which he clearly stated in a congressional report released on April 21.[50] Percy recognized that no lasting peace could ignore the Palestinians, who lay at the heart of the conflict. "What is critically important now," Percy argued, "is to resolve this central political, historical and emotional Palestinian 'problem,' for until it is successfully resolved—until, I believe, the Palestinians are given a homeland of their own—there will be no peace in the Middle East, no security for Israel, no end to the killing."[51] Percy predicted neither peace nor security for Israel "until she withdraws from most of the lands she has occupied since the 1967 war."[52] He went so far as to suggest a foundation for an eventual Palestinian state: Gaza and the West Bank, as 390,000 and 640,000 Palestinians lived in those respective areas.[53] By acquiring Gaza and the West Bank, the Palestinian nation would have the actual land necessary to seriously petition the United Nations for statehood. Percy's position was at odds with the Israeli position that sought to prevent the creation of a Palestinian state.

Sen. George McGovern (D-SD), chair of the same Senate subcommittee, submitted his own report on May 23.[54] McGovern and Percy put forward similar plans for the Palestinians and border disputes, although McGovern called for Palestinian self-determination rather than possession of land, which did not preclude a Jordanian option. McGovern asked that Israel publicly "acknowledges the right of the Palestinian people to live on the West Bank and in Gaza."[55] The senators' positions echoed, in essence, the Johnson administration's principles of territorial integrity and political independence for all people in the Middle East, principles that had gone unfulfilled. In return for a peace treaty and recognition of statehood, Israel would be able "to enter into a territorial settlement approximating the 1967 borders with practical modifications."[56] Rather than criticize Israel, McGovern criticized Kissinger and his step-by-step method. McGovern offered a useful analogy: "I believe that a 'step-by-step' approach to peace is not now possible in the Middle East until the general outline of a final settlement is worked out . . . it is not practical to mount a ladder until there is a definite structure against which to lean the ladder."[57] McGovern argued to first outline a final peace settlement and then step toward a common goal, which resembled Secretary of State Rogers's failed plan during Nixon's first term. But Israel had balked at that idea because with the final arrangements predetermined, negotiations seemed trivial.

While Percy and McGovern appeared to break with Israel's position, Senator Inouye and many other legislators proved willing to help advance the Israeli position vis-à-vis the administration's harder line. Dinitz reported to Jerusalem the details of his successful meetings with numerous senators and representatives. His meeting with Inouye went well, and Inouye even offered to arrange meetings between Dinitz and "senators who are not known to be big supporters of us." Dinitz met with William Broomfield (R-MI), the ranking member of the House Committee on International Relations and a friend of President Ford. According to Dinitz, Broomfield and other members "accepted my suggestion" that Sadat manipulated the recent negotiations—to present the Egyptian side as desiring peace—to win public support in the United States, but not an agreement.[58] Senator Humphrey, known for being a strong supporter of Israel, "said we're completely okay, and this he also expressed to the *New York Times*—that the Congress will not move even an inch from its support of Israel." Humphrey also claimed that Israel had strong support in the Senate Foreign Relations Committee, on which Humphrey served, especially after Fulbright's reelection defeat. Sen. Richard Stone, a freshman Democrat from Florida, offered his help. He reiterated Inouye's support and reported to Dinitz that "Inouye told him that he will help us in the aid request of 1976." Sen. Hugh Scott feared that liberals who supported Israel were being adversely affected by a neo-isolationism due to the Vietnam War; nevertheless, he told Dinitz that he "is supporting us and we should not fear. He will continue being our friend."[59]

The Ford administration recognized the success of Israel's *hasbara.* Joseph Sisco, Undersecretary of State for Political Affairs and respected adviser of Kissinger, called Dinitz on March 26, obviously annoyed by conversations he had that day with senators and representatives. Sisco said they all asked him the same questions: "Why were the talks suspended and why don't they continue?"[60] These points went to the core of the Israeli *hasbara*—establishing that there was no reason to suspend the talks, that Kissinger had acted hastily, and that there was no reason for them not to continue. Sisco informed Dinitz that Kissinger would not renew his mission until Israel put forth practical ideas for moving forward. Dinitz asked whether he meant procedure or substance. Sisco replied substance and asked his words to be forwarded to Israel.[61]

Dinitz continued to meet with senators, like John Tower (R-TX), member of the Armed Services Committee.[62] Dinitz "briefed him on our position" and "made it clear that at a certain point the Egyptians stopped negotiating and turned to dictations, part of the assumption that they can manipulate the difficulties of America in different arenas to pressure Israel." Tower responded favorably and mentioned, "I always said it and I'll say it today, Israel cannot agree to any arrangement which does not include tenable and defensible borders."[63]

The embassy also used the legislative branch to gauge the perspective of the White House. Rafiah cabled information he obtained from a conversation with Richard Perle, assistant to Senator "Scoop" Jackson.[64] (Perle would go on to be an influential voice in the administrations of Ronald Reagan and George W. Bush.) Perle and nine other senators' assistants had been briefed at the White House by Harold Saunders, Middle East analyst in the State Department. Although Saunders did not blame Israel for the breakdown in the talks, "he did leave the clear impression that Israel should have accepted the Egyptian proposal. Saunders said that the Egyptians were not unreasonable." Moreover, Saunders pointed out that Israel's reasons for rejecting the Egyptian proposal seemed minor compared to the potential consequences of the failure of peace talks. Perle reported that Saunders's message was well received and that "people taking part in the meeting felt that Israel was to blame."[65]

Dinitz offered his overall assessment of the situation to Foreign Minister Allon in a March 28 cable, based on information from White House briefings to Congress, meetings with senators and representatives, and meetings with members of the press.[66] Ford was angry at Israel, not because Israel pursued its own national interest, but because Israel failed to appreciate the difficult position of the White House on both the domestic and foreign fronts. "All the American international affairs," wrote Dinitz, "along with huge difficulties in domestic affairs, are destabilizing his position in the U.S. at a time when he needed more than ever success in the Middle East." Ford bristled at Israeli ingratitude, given all the American political and material support. Dinitz noted the strong support of Congress but also a sense of disappointment about the failure of peace talks. Many members of Congress voiced concerns about a long stalemate that could lead to war and, importantly, an oil embargo. Most of the congressional criticisms, however, blamed the administration for ending peace discussions too quickly. Dinitz believed that the administration had started to moderate its statements both publicly and privately, not ascribing blame to anyone, because of the influence of Congress, which pressed the administration to reaffirm its friendship with Israel.[67]

Dinitz noted the success of Israel's *hasbara*. He intended to continue "our *hasbara* line" that advanced four main ideas: an explanation of the Israeli position in the recent negotiations, support for the continuation of the U.S. process, appreciation for Kissinger and his efforts, and a belief that talks failed "because of Egypt's rigid position and our hint that Egypt was trying to manipulate the tough situation of the U.S. to dictate conditions to Israel and the U.S. instead of negotiating. [This argument was received well by the Congress and the press.]" Thus, not only did Israel take advantage of the political turmoil of the United States, it also blamed Egypt for doing the very same thing. Dinitz even suggested that if Israel tried to take on President Ford and Kissinger, "We can maybe even bring about the fall of State Secretary." But then he questioned, "Would it serve our interests?" Dinitz recommended not going in that direction because the next Secretary of State might be worse for Israel.[68]

In addition to its *hasbara,* Dinitz suggested Israel do something more. "I think we need to sincerely consider political maneuvers that will benefit us in the short and long term," he wrote.[69] Dinitz wondered "if Egypt does not give much in return, will we be able to get anything in return from America in the field of bilateral relations as a compensation?"[70] Israeli officials continued to stress the problem of giving up something tangible, like land in the Sinai, for Arab promises to avoid attacking Israel, especially given the lack of trust.

Dinitz regularly prepped individuals for their meetings with administration officials, like Detroit oil magnate Max Fisher. Fisher was a longtime friend of Ford, significant contributor to the Republican Party, and influential American Jewish Zionist. Fisher met several times with Ford over the course of reassessment, as well as with Rabin, Allon, Peres, and Meir.[71] Dinitz reported to Allon, "I prepared Fisher for his meeting with the President. Fisher met the President and I received the final report. Kissinger and Scowcroft were also in the meeting. It was serious but also very friendly. The President was very serious but somber. He said a major opportunity had been missed."[72] Fisher reported that Ford was angry because he feared the U.S. position in the Middle East was collapsing, and Kissinger was obviously upset and rarely talked. After the meeting, Fisher said the Secretary "looked as if the whole world had turned around against him."[73]

American documentation tells a similar story. Fisher argued, "The reassessment raises too many fears. This weakens the hand of what you are doing in diplomacy." But Ford defended his position: "Henry and I have spent more time on this than on any other foreign policy issue. We put my credibility on the line and it was a hell of a disappointment." He went on to say that "nothing has hit me so hard since I've been in this office," and although Israel wanted to avoid a comprehensive settlement, "We see no alternative now to Geneva."[74]

Dinitz and Fisher demonstrated that, at least during the reassessment period, the State of Israel worked in close coordination with American Jewish Zionist leadership. On April 7, Dinitz talked with Fisher for an hour on a public phone. During their conversation, Dinitz "advised Fisher not to speak only with Kissinger, but also have a conversation with the President. . . . Then I reiterated the main points he should raise in front of the President, and to uproot the thought that he was misled by us. Fisher promised he would."[75]

The embassy worked to gather information about the ongoing reassessment. On March 30, Dinitz sent word that, based on information from "a very reliable source," the Pentagon was in the process of creating a report about the balance of power in the Middle East, specifically designed to "justify an immediate halt to all aid to Israel."[76] Dinitz noted, however, the report was only at the working level and in no way represented a decision.[77] Two days later, Turgemon followed up with a more detailed report of the reassessment, based on his meeting with Phillip Stoddard, deputy head of the Middle East and South Asia in the State Department. From their conversation, Turgemon reported that those responsible for writing papers about the reassessment, from the working level of the State Department and other branches of the administration, were to hand in their papers by April 5. That would be followed by a period of analyzing and summarizing the material, and then conclusions and recommendations. The administration deliberately made a short deadline because they did not want too much time to pass without action.[78]

Turgemon spent considerable time discussing the broader picture with Stoddard. The reassessment, Stoddard claimed, had two strategic goals. First, "to show Israel that it should have hopped on the train while it was still in the station, and not try to catch it after it left." When given another chance, Israel should "climb on the train at the station." Second, to reevaluate U.S. policy in the Middle East in general, and with each country specifically—topics such as weapons sales to Iran and Saudi Arabia, the positions and policies of each country, as well as potential pressures that could influence Syrian President Hafez al-Assad and Sadat, the policy of the USSR, and what America would do if another war erupted in the Middle East. Stoddard intimated a crucial point to Turgemon—the chief goal of U.S. policy was to prevent war because "the U.S. government does not see much chance to solve the conflict."[79] Indeed, U.S. officials recognized the important difference between the presence of peace and the absence of war.

While U.S. officials contemplated a new policy, Dinitz received a message that questioned Israel's effort to play for time. According to Ephraim Evron, deputy director general of the Foreign Ministry, "We want to make clear that we are not negotiating to just buy time, and that *this time* [italics added] our goal is to make progress."[80] The message echoed Sisco's earlier request to have Israel create substantive peace plans.

Kissinger rightly believed that Israel sought to use Congress to influence policy and attack the administration. According to an unnamed source, Kissinger informed Republican and Democratic legislators on March 31 that "the intention of Israel is to cause damage to the Administration, and it is doing it through an effort to influence the Congress directly while bypassing the White House and State Department, and while taking advantage of the election year." Kissinger felt that Israel was trying to make the United States look like a "paper tiger," and that the United States "needs to develop a new foreign policy, and to take a middle ground position with all the parameters of 242." According to the report, no one in the meeting challenged his statements or disagreed with the need to develop a new strategy.[81] Although it is unknown who took part in the meeting, such a message reflects a growing uneasiness on the part of some congressmembers to take on the administration over U.S. foreign policy in the Middle East. When Tip O'Neill met with

Prime Minister Rabin in early April, he reminded Rabin that Israel "could not have a finer friend in Congress than me." However, he cautioned Rabin: "Do not underestimate Kissinger with the Congress. He mesmerizes the Congress when he performs in front of them." O'Neill recognized the challenging circumstances for Israel: "I appreciate the power of the Jewish lobby, but the Jewish lobby never stood in front of a crisis like this one."[82]

Kissinger met with influential American Jewish Zionists, and the records of their discussions speak to the inner turmoil Kissinger felt as an American Jew and as U.S. Secretary of State. The records also show that several American Jews resented Kissinger's efforts to continually highlight his Jewishness.

Kissinger vented his frustrations to four prominent Jewish intellectuals on March 30—Elie Wiesel, Hans Morgenthau, Max Kampelman, and John Stoessinger.[83] "Kissinger opened with horrid depictions of Israeli intransigence," according to a report written by Israeli diplomat Mordechai Gazit, and twice complained that in twenty-four meetings Israel never once demanded nonbelligerency. He saw Israel making a "historic disaster" because U.S. support for Israel could not continue as it had in the past, and anti-Semitism was rising in the United States. Kissinger claimed the existence of Israel to be in jeopardy. Wiesel, who survived Auschwitz, was especially disturbed by Kissinger's portrayal of the situation. He asked the Secretary if he, as a Jew and historian, had trouble sleeping at night. Kissinger answered that he did not sleep well. But Kissinger reminded the group, "After all, I am Jewish. As long as I am Secretary of State there never will be another Czechoslovakia," referring to appeasement.[84]

The question remained about how to move forward in light of the breakdown of talks. He asked if American Jews would accept U.N. Resolution 242 as the basis of negotiations. "Wiesel said that if the government of Israel will agree to it, so will American Jews. The most important thing is Jerusalem—it must stay in the hands of Israel. Kissinger said, okay."[85]

Kissinger continued to complain behind the scenes to influential American Jewish Zionists about Israel's *hasbara.* He met with Fisher and Rabbi Israel Miller, chairman of the Presidents Conference, and again bemoaned Israel's efforts to mislead the administration, which damaged U.S. prestige. Miller grew irritated when Kissinger claimed that, to a certain extent, he felt happy because as a Jewish State Secretary, the heavy responsibility to protect Israel was off his shoulders. Miller sharply reminded Kissinger that responsibility sits on the shoulders of every Secretary of State, and "he as a Jew should see this as an honor and not just as a burden." Miller then explained that, as a Jewish American leader, he felt he was "sitting on a volcano," trying to prevent eruptions from prominent Jews directed at President Ford and Secretary Kissinger. Kissinger asked what he could do to help, and Miller said to "cool it." Additionally, Kissinger agreed to have Sisco brief the Conference of Presidents about the administration's policy.[86] Later in April, Kissinger was reportedly bitter and angry when talking with Nahum Goldmann, founder and president of the World Jewish Congress. Kissinger accused Israel of being shortsighted, saying that "Israel lost a rare opportunity to have negotiations that would have led to taking Egypt out of the war."[87] Thus, in retrospect, Kissinger's devotion to a comprehensive peace effort seems circumspect at best, or perhaps Kissinger changed his opinion based on his audience.

Obviously perturbed by the administration and especially by Kissinger, leaders of the major Jewish organizations in the United States held an informal meeting at Fisher's flat in New York in early April. The participants viewed the administration as increasingly hard to defend (especially to "friends and activists" involved with Jewish organizations) because of public statements suggesting Israel was to blame for the failure of negotiations. The participants agreed that Kissinger needed to be talked to in a "straightforward" manner and to be "brought back down to Earth." Fisher appeared very firm about the need to keep a united Jewish front and not publicly criticize Israel, but rather to voice criticisms privately to Israeli leadership. Fisher also believed that "a responsible Israeli leadership should consider the influential position and perspective of the American Jewish leadership."[88]

Right around the same time, Kissinger held a stormy meeting with an angry Arthur Goldberg, former Supreme Court Justice and ambassador to the United Nations who helped draft U.N. Resolution 242.[89] Goldberg fumed about a *New York Times* report about Kissinger's meeting with the "Eastern Political Establishment," which included Cyrus Vance, George Ball, McGeorge Bundy, and others not known for being strong supporters of Israeli policy. According to Dinitz, based on his phone conversation with Goldberg, Kissinger began the meeting with Goldberg by claiming "the entire purpose of his policy and as a Jew are to help Israel and to make sure nothing bad will happen to her. Goldberg stopped him and told him, don't tell me that shit. Are you forgetting who you are talking to? Do you think you are talking to the press or Jewish leadership? You are talking to someone who was in a Cabinet. Representative in the U.N. and member of the Supreme Court, in a higher rank than you are. I am a proud Jew and I am not interested to know what you are doing as a Jew and not doing as a Jew. I am talking to you from American interests."[90] Kissinger, reportedly embarrassed, apologized and said he would rather resign than have an anti-Israel policy. Goldberg scolded him again and said, "If you want to resign, then resign. America will continue without you. I resigned from the Supreme Court and America continued to exist. America is big enough and strong enough and does not depend on one person."[91]

Dinitz continued to coordinate with Jerusalem about using American Jewish Zionist leadership to meet with U.S. officials. On April 7, Jerusalem asked Dinitz, "Did you activate, maybe you have already done it, Dave Ginsberg to meet Cyrus Vance and McGeorge Bundy; Ted Sonnenfeld to see Averell Harriman and Dean Rusk. These were the people in the group with whom the State Secretary met. And also Dave Fortis to see McNamara?"[92] Dinitz replied, "I'm in contact with Dave Ginsberg and I'm activating him. He's also one of the main people giving us information about the group Kissinger is meeting."[93]

Dinitz reported a long conversation between Kissinger and Leonard Garment, who briefly served as White House counsel for Nixon during his last few months as president. Garment, like Fisher, reported Kissinger to be "a broken person," and that in all his years he could not recall Kissinger in such "a difficult personal and mental state." Kissinger referred to Rabin, Allon, Dinitz, and members of the Israeli negotiating team as "his brothers." (He noticeably failed to mention Peres.) Kissinger feared that because Israel did not go along with step-by-step diplomacy, both the United States and Israel would lose all control over negotiations. Therefore, he believed the best thing to do was to restart the American initiative and avoid Geneva (that is, a multinational Middle East peace conference). Kissinger told Garment, "As a Jew he has only one goal and that is the safety and integrity of Israel. As an American State Secretary he has believed and will believe that the safety and integrity are basic principles of American policy." Garment reminded Dinitz that "with all of our rightful criticism of Kissinger, one needs to remember he is paranoid and does not control himself. But he is also, above all, the best friend Israel has ever had in the administration."[94]

When Kissinger met with Dinitz on April 7, he asked to speak privately for twenty minutes before the meeting began. Obviously angry, Kissinger referenced the Israeli *hasbara* and threatened to turn the tables and "release a white paper about the Israeli policy and its behavior." But Dinitz shot back that the reason for the entire blowup was Kissinger—he could have acted differently when negotiations were suspended but, instead, chose to confront Israel. Kissinger admitted that he overreacted, but it reflected the deep pain he felt. And since that time, he had been portrayed by the Jewish and Israeli media as an enemy of Israel. He reminded Dinitz, "I treated you with more trust than most of my colleagues at work. I showed you messages, telegrams, and wires from the Soviet Union and Egypt." He told Dinitz that he had offered his resignation to Ford, but that Ford refused to accept it. "I will not agree being Secretary of State," said Kissinger, "when I see how things are going and what Israel is bringing on herself." According to Dinitz, Kissinger "said in a crying voice, I was a Jew before I was an American and now you are making me the scapegoat!" Kissinger informed Dinitz that "of all the countries in the world, Israel is to him most important and added, I am part of the Jewish nation and have no closer people than the leaders of Israel and their ambassador here."[95] In doing so, Kissinger revealed that he was clearly too close to the situation to effectively serve as a U.S. Secretary of State.

Dinitz continued to prepare American Jewish Zionists for meetings with the administration, such as Garment and Fisher for their meeting with Kissinger, and Fisher for another meeting with Ford. Dinitz also reported that the two had met with White House Chief of Staff Donald Rumsfeld and told him to have the president make a public statement indicating that the reassessment was not directed against Israel. The two also reported talking with Senator Javits, and Javits also agreed to talk with Ford about releasing a public statement to that effect.[96] According to an assistant of Javits who asked not to be quoted, although the senator supported Kissinger, he was "very annoyed by the Secretary blaming Israel, that he is creating such a big kerfuffle, and that he is behaving like a small child who is unhappy because people are not responding to his wishes."[97] Dinitz again contacted Fisher on April 23 to ask him to press Ford about the frozen shipments of aid. Although Fisher related that he could not call on the president specifically about that matter, he would find a way to reach him. Dinitz and Fisher agreed to coordinate and plan for the meeting when Fisher returned to Washington the following week.[98]

The Israeli *hasbara* clearly managed to get the Israeli message out for U.S. public consumption. Dinitz reported being in a "maximum *hasbara* effort and there are already practical results." Perhaps chief among them was rattling Kissinger, who complained about Israel's sending lecturers all over the

United States, mostly former generals and all hardliners. Kissinger reportedly called Dinitz "a determined hardliner and he is doing *hasbara* campaign in Congress, the press, and amongst the American Jews."[99] Dinitz met for an hour and a half with James Reston of the *New York Times,* who told Dinitz that Israel's arguments were being well received in public opinion, namely, that the responsibility for sour relations with Israel lay at the doorstep of the administration, and it was up to the administration to make it right. Reston "said the friendship for Israel in the U.S. is very deep and extensive."[100] The embassy also reported that NBC had sent out a questionnaire about the U.S.-Israel relationship, and the results were to be published on radio and television before President Ford's speech that night. It seemed to the embassy that NBC was "considering the opportunity of making a television program about the *hasbara* attack in the U.S.—How many lectures were sent, etc. We will inform when we know more."[101]

Israeli officials continued to meet with senators and representatives in order to generate more support for Israel. Senator Bumpers, who defeated Fulbright in the Democratic primary in Arkansas, emphasized his support for Israel in a meeting with Abba Eban, longtime Israeli politician and diplomat.[102] So did Sen. Robert Griffin (R-MI), friend of President Ford and Max Fisher, and member of the Foreign Relations Committee. Griffin reminded Eban "that the tendency of the Congress is to work independently in the issue of foreign affairs," which complicated the situation for Kissinger.[103] When Eban met with Sen. Stuart Symington (D-MO), Symington said that even though he was fond of Kissinger, the Secretary should not have reacted the way he did.[104]

The meeting with Symington revealed the two-way street of interest between Israel and legislators. Eban raised the question about a delay on deliveries of the F-15 Eagle fighter jets, made by McDonnell Douglas in Symington's home state of Missouri. Although Ford called for a freeze on arms sales and shipments, the order had been placed before reassessment, with delivery to happen at some point in the future. According to the report, "Symington called immediately one of the bosses at McDonnell who told the senator the following—Israel is supposed to get 25 planes [and possibly 50] at the rate of 2 to 3 a month beginning in mid-1976." However, the official at McDonnell confirmed that there were delays. "Symington responded with anger" and said that if they did not deal with the delay immediately Israel would not get the planes for many years. After that, Symington wanted to speak with Sisco about the same issue but could not reach him, and then promised to report to Eban about his talk with Sisco. At that point, "the senator started to talk about the great virtues of the planes."[105]

Dinitz recognized that Israel had to walk a fine line, careful to not be seen as attacking the president. Tip O'Neill told Dinitz that he had "the impression that Israel and the Jewish lobby want to have a direct fight with the President and Secretary within the Congress and using the Congress." According to Dinitz, "O'Neill advised us not to do this terrible mistake."[106] O'Neill recognized that Congress and the president were divided by Vietnam and that when the 1976 election came around, O'Neill, a Democrat, would fight against any Republican. But until then, O'Neill warned against taking on the president. Dinitz disingenuously assured him that Israel had no intention of taking on Ford or Kissinger inside or outside of Congress.[107]

Kissinger continued to voice his frustrations about the Israeli *hasbara*. In a secret meeting with Foreign Minister Allon and other Israeli and U.S. officials, Kissinger told the meeting that when any country disagrees with U.S. policy, it should handle the issue through diplomatic channels and not launch a public relations campaign. If Israel continued to try to undermine the Ford administration, Kissinger again threatened to release a fact sheet about Sinai II discussions and U.S.-Israel relations.[108] However, just over a week later, Lawrence Eagleburger, executive secretary to the Secretary of State and future Secretary of State for George H. W. Bush, told an Israeli official to ignore Kissinger's threats about a white paper.[109]

Dinitz reported back to Jerusalem a humorous story about how easily Israel could influence a senator's stated position. Senator Stone called Dinitz on April 22 and told the ambassador that he and six other new senators planned to meet with Kissinger at the State Department. Stone asked if he should bring up any certain topics with Kissinger, and Dinitz responded that he should ask about delays pertaining to shipments of the F-15 fighter jets, along with other topics. After the meeting, Stone told Dinitz he had made a slight error. Dinitz wanted Stone to ask Kissinger about the visit of an Air Force delegation to talk about the F-15s; Stone mistakenly asked Kissinger about training Israeli pilots to fly F-15s. Kissinger, naturally, had no idea what Stone was talking about. However, he did indicate, like Symington, that there were production delays of the F-15s and that Israel would not start receiving them until the following year. Nevertheless, Stone managed to invent a topic for discussion with the Secretary of State, based on his misunderstanding of instructions from the Israeli ambassador. Ironically, given the misstep, Dinitz reported that "Stone told me that he does not believe a word of the Secretary."[110]

The Israeli embassy continued to quietly collect information about the Ford administration. Dinitz relayed reports that Ford did not intend to run for president in 1976, and he, therefore, felt free from domestic pressures in order to pursue the national interest in foreign policy. According to Dinitz, rumors had swirled for some time that Ford would not run in 1976, primarily because of the poor U.S. economy and health concerns about his wife, Betty. Dinitz rightly pointed out that a decision had not been made and noted that Ford was starting to think independently (that is, independently of Kissinger) on matters relating to foreign relations.[111]

Dinitz sent another periodic assessment to Foreign Minister Allon on April 28. He noted that both Houses of Congress maintained their traditional support. Additionally, "liberals and isolationists" had started to articulate the differences between East Asia and the Middle East, even as Saigon fell. But he feared Congress would not support a large aid request for Israel. According to Dinitz, "This development is not due to the suspension of talks, but rather a result of the financial crisis and by the fact that the Congress is more meticulous and critical of expenses, and foreign aid in particular." Dinitz also reported that even pro-Israel congressional members voiced their concerns about stalemate and the suspension of talks because the region could erupt into war and further erode the U.S. position. Dinitz reminded Allon that even with strong support from Congress, the president determines and implements foreign policy. However, he added that "Congress has helped in the past and could help in the future."[112]

Even more than misunderstandings and sour relations, Dinitz feared the formulation of a new U.S. policy less favorable to Israel. He no doubt expected foreign aid to resume, especially with strong support for Israel in Congress. But if the administration created a new policy, one not based on step-by-step diplomacy or a deliberate avoidance of the core issues at the heart of the peace process, then Israel would inevitably be in a disadvantageous position. He noted that even with influence in the American "public sphere" specifically related to its *hasbara,* Israel needed to assert itself into the "political sphere." In particular, Israel needed to decide if it wished to renew the U.S. initiative and enter into a separate agreement with Egypt or go to Geneva and try to negotiate a general agreement that included all participants in the conflict.

Dinitz mentioned that he favored an interim agreement, but that with each passing day that step seemed less likely, and a general agreement more likely. Therefore, Israel needed to develop a dialogue about an agreement with Egypt and push the administration to offer tangible benefits in return for an Israeli withdrawal and political declarations from Egypt.[113]

Increasingly, however, Dinitz worried that a Middle East settlement seemed to be moving toward the 1967 borders with an independent Palestinian state. Dinitz reminded Allon that Kissinger had told Israel a few times that such a scenario would be the beginning of the end for Israel. And without greater Israeli assertiveness in the political sphere, "such a maneuver will receive not only an international consensus but will also receive wide support in the U.S. [I dare to say there will be a few Jews, and even important ones, that will agree to such a formula.]"[114]

Therefore, Dinitz recommended that Israel abandon its policy of intentionally buying time and communicate "concrete" suggestions to the administration. According to Dinitz, "I do feel that the end of buying time is getting near and what we wanted to do by delays is no longer preventable, and what we succeeded in delaying by shutting up may evolve into a policy." Basically, Dinitz feared that a new strategy—and ultimately, policy—would be created with or without Israeli participation. He finished his lengthy assessment with a reminder: "One thing that we cannot do anymore is that we cannot avoid discussing the core issues. We cannot believe by not talking to the Americans we can avoid the development of a process. The policy and the process will be created with us or without us. I believe it will be better with us."[115]

The Spirit of the 76

Dinitz sent word to Jerusalem about his new plan to use Congress to influence U.S. policy. "After a long conversation I had with Congress members and consultation I had with Morris Amitay [executive director of AIPAC], and Rafiah, I have raised the thought about trying to organize a letter from the senators to the President. Evaluation of experts and from first approaches to senators' assistants, it is believed that it is possible reach approximately 70 signatures on the letter." Dinitz even included a first draft. He mentioned the obvious advantages of such a letter. But in all likelihood it would be seen as a direct attack on the administration, "even with the careful phrasing of the letter and the gentle tone." Therefore, Dinitz recommended that "the Embassy of Israel and the government of Israel will not be related to this letter in anyway whatsoever," meaning that Israeli manipulation of U.S. politics needed to be kept from public knowledge.[116] The letter gradually evolved into one of the strongest congressional challenges to U.S. foreign policy in the Middle East up to that time, as well as efforts to negotiate peace in the region.

A few days before, while attending a bar mitzvah at Dinitz's house on April 26, Kissinger had warned against personalizing the conflict and attacking himself or the president. Kissinger mentioned that he and his assistants did not agree with the Israeli position that Egypt had been rigid in negotiations, and he suggested that Israeli officials like Dinitz should consider why good friends of Israel, like Ford, Vice President Nelson Rockefeller, Kissinger, Nancy Kissinger, General Scowcroft, and Eagleburger, changed their positions to negative after the March discussions. The Secretary pointed out that Rabin was mistaken if he thought he could repeat "the 1971 tricks"—when Rabin was ambassador to the United States—and Israel managed to abort the plans of Jarring, Rogers, and Sisco. Kissinger admitted that in 1971 he helped Israel thwart those plans and initiatives. "But today the situation is different," reported Evron. "Kissinger is now the Secretary of State and consultant to the President, and things have changed in the international arena." Kissinger also warned that Dinitz mistook Israeli influence in Congress. "There are quite a few powerful congressmen and senators who like to say positive things to the Ambassador," Kissinger said, but in discussions with the State Secretary they said other things.[117]

Robert Oakley revealed to Turgemon that the administration felt handcuffed by the fallout from the Vietnam War, anti-administration domestic politics, and congressional involvement in foreign affairs influenced by pro-Israel lobbying. Nevertheless, the administration needed movement toward peace. He told Turgemon that "for the past 18 months Israel had consistently asked for military and economic aid and no pressure from the U.S. so that Israel could enter into peace negotiations. Then Oakley said, look where it has gotten us." Oakley claimed that the administration found it difficult to consider new initiatives in the Middle East "due to the domestic embarrassment of the Watergate affair and the tragedy of Vietnam." Moreover, relations with Congress worsened every day, and Oakley lamented the absence of leadership within Congress. The midterm elections in 1974, shortly after

Nixon resigned from the presidency, brought many new senators and representatives to Washington, which also resulted in the old leadership's losing its strength and position. Due to that turnover, the administration found it hard to "communicate with the Congress and to influence it."[118]

Israel continued to monitor the public mood and note the importance of domestic factors for U.S. foreign policy. A report written by Joseph Ben-Aharon to Prime Minister Rabin on May 18 explained that the situation in the Middle East had been "swallowed" by the fall of Saigon and the end of the Vietnam War.[119] In trying to better his image, Ford requested aid to assist refugees, but Congress denied the budget request. Given economic troubles and increasing unemployment, Congress felt that the average citizen would not support aid to refugees of an unpopular war during an economic crisis.[120]

The report, which analyzed U.S. public opinion toward Israel, mentioned that the fall of Saigon actually allowed the administration to focus its efforts on other foreign-policy issues. However, according to Ben-Aharon, "Israel needs to convince the American public that it will fight its own wars and all it needs is military support. The normal citizen in America will accept American aid to Israel as long as he feels Israel is the underdog against Arab oil and the Russians, but nevertheless tries to reach peace."[121] Moreover, there appeared to be "no change in the infrastructure of support for Israel in the non-Jewish American public." The report claimed that two famous (and, unfortunately, unnamed) professors at Harvard "who are calling for more 'balanced' policy in the Middle East have regrettably admitted to me that public support is almost naught."[122] The report also warned about a "rise in Arab and pro-Arab activity, especially on campuses," and that Arab propaganda had become more "sophisticated." The economic recession had forced some private universities to search for financial support, which attracted oil money from Arab states that asked in return to teach more "about the Arab and Muslim world." Therefore, the report spoke to the "need to strengthen the Jewish and pro-Israel elements on campuses, and the need for general renovation of the Hillel system in the campuses."[123]

Rumors started to circulate about wavering congressional support for Israel. In the opinion of Samuel H. Goldberg, deputy assistant secretary for Congressional Relations in the State Department, the Vietnam War and Watergate affair had created a "certain tiredness in Congress," which contributed to growing support for a more balanced policy in the Middle East in which the United States would not tilt toward either Israel or the Arabs. In his estimation, support for a balanced policy had risen after the 1973 war from 2 percent to 10 percent; obviously, though, support for Israel remained high. In addition to Vietnam and Watergate, Goldberg also noted that the intense pressure on senators and representatives to advance a pro-Israel agenda had started to create some disillusionment. According to Goldberg, "One of the problems is many Congress members have this complication of feeling like captives caged by the Jewish lobby." Specifically, Goldberg said that "Senator Percy is generally a friend of Israel and Goldberg considers his recent statements as part of his attempt to get out of the captivity of the Jewish lobby."[124]

But Dinitz continued to report strong congressional support for Israel. According to Sen. Sam Nunn (D-GA) and Rep. Elliot Levitas (D-GA), the backing of Israel after the fall of Vietnam appeared to be more "concrete and assured." The congressmen saw no similarity between Israel and Vietnam, and Levitas claimed that if "Israel was not included in the recent foreign aid bill, only 60 of 435 would have voted for it." Indeed, many legislators would not approve a foreign-aid bill that did not provide adequate aid to Israel. While the situation in East Asia had convinced some senators and representatives to reduce foreign aid, many had determined "to enlarge the defense budget to signal to the international community that the U.S. is not disarming itself."[125] Sen. Richard Schweiker (R-PA) claimed that there was "no decline in U.S. support in Congress for Israel" and that Senator Percy was "a lone case." Schweiker admitted that the poor economic situation in the United States influenced "congressional members' attitudes to foreign aid, but that aid to Israel will continue."[126]

The letter proposed by Dinitz in late April finally came into play. On May 8, Kissinger informed Ford that two senators, Javits and Scoop Jackson, "are circulating a letter on the Hill supporting secure defensible borders" for Israel and insisting "the U.S. must give military support regardless of what Israel does because it is a bastion of democracy."[127] The letter evolved into an attack on the Ford administration's foreign policy and gained broad senatorial support. On May 19, Rafiah sent word that fifty-six senators had agreed to sign the letter, and the following day he reported that the number had jumped to seventy-two.[128] On May 21, Rafiah communicated that seventy-five senators had agreed to sign the letter and that a press conference would be scheduled the next day at 11:00 a.m.[129]

Ford recalls in his memoirs, "On May 21, I received a letter signed by seventy-six Senators urging me to 'be responsive' to Israel's request for $2.59 billion in military and economic aid. Although I said publicly that I welcomed the letter as an expression of Senate sentiment, in truth it really bugged me. The Senators claimed the letter was 'spontaneous,' but there was no doubt in my mind that it was inspired by Israel."[130] Ford's suspicion is confirmed by Israeli Prime Minister Yitzhak Rabin, who cites the letter as being the result "of our public campaign in the United States."[131] Israeli documents show that Dinitz led the effort.

The letter did not directly attack the administration, but indirectly the letter threatened the president's foreign-aid request and signaled the end of Ford's reassessment. The letter referenced the Vietnam War and how the United States needed reliable allies like Israel, as well as congressional participation in foreign policy. According to the letter, peace in the Middle East required Ford to request enough foreign aid "that Israel obtain a level of military and economic support adequate to deter a renewal of war by Israel's neighbors. Withholding military equipment from Israel would be dangerous, discouraging accommodation by Israel's neighbors and encouraging a resort to force." The letter included a thinly veiled threat for President Ford: "Within the next several weeks, the Congress expects to receive your foreign aid requests for fiscal year 1976. We trust that your recommendations will be responsive to Israel's urgent military and economic needs." In other words, unless Ford's foreign-aid request included Israel at a level acceptable to Congress, it would not clear the Senate. Regarding reassessment, "We urge you to make it clear, as we do, that the United States acting in its own national interests stands firmly with Israel in the search for peace in future negotiations, and that this premise is the basis of the current reassessment of U.S. policy in the Middle East."[132] With more than three-quarters of the upper chamber of Congress calling for the renewal of aid shipments to Israel, while also advancing the Israeli *hasbara* position regarding the suspension of negotiations, Ford's reassessment, for all practical purposes, was over. The administration would have to find a way to forge an agreement without the threat of withholding weapons from Israel.

Israeli officials regarded the letter as a tremendous achievement. According to Dinitz, the letter reaffirmed the importance of military and economic aid for Israel at a crucial time. Ten freshmen senators signed the letter, which demonstrated that the new class of senators would support Israel. The letter made headline news in major newspapers during the midst of reassessment. Dinitz recognized that the letter signaled to the world that U.S. support for Israel had not lessened.[133] Allon wrote back, "Dinitz, I would like to convey my appreciation to you and the friends from the Embassy, and especially Morris Amitay and his assistants for the impressive and encouraging accomplishment. . . . This statement of support for Israel, which itself is important, has a special meaning considering the recent political developments."[134]

Understandably, the Ford administration seethed at the challenge to presidential foreign policymaking. According to Sidney Sober, deputy assistant Secretary of State for Near East and South Asian Affairs, U.S. officials viewed the letter as an attack on the administration, and Israel needed to be aware of that. "He [Ford] personally does not see it as completely negative," reported Turgemon, "but many people in the Administration are quite upset." Sober also warned to not mess with Kissinger or criticize him in public because he was the most powerful person. Turgemon said Israel would not do that, and it appreciated "all the good efforts he has done in the past." Turgemon told Sober that the letter was not an attack on the administration, but importantly, the letter disproved the writings of "certain reporters that said there was a change in the U.S.-Israel relationship."[135]

Not all senators supported the Israeli maneuver, even those who signed the letter. After signing, some senators "told journalists privately that they had been pressured to vote against their own best judgment, and expressed admiration for the few senators who resisted."[136] In his memoirs, Sen. James Abourezk recalls how pro-Israel lobbyists manipulated the political climate by stressing the upcoming presidential election for two Democratic hopefuls—George McGovern and Ted Kennedy. According to Abourezk, "Lobby operatives took the letter to Senator George McGovern's staff, telling them that Senator Ted Kennedy had already signed it, and that McGovern shouldn't be the only prospective presidential candidate left off the list. Then producing McGovern's signature, they confronted Kennedy's staff with the same ultimatum."[137] Abourezk also mentions that one unnamed senator signed the letter against his better judgment but did so because he received several phone calls from American Jews who had actively worked in his campaign and who wanted him to sign the letter.[138] Abourezk was one of the most vocal critics of U.S. foreign policy in the Middle East, which likely skewed his outlook; however, Galen Jackson, in his article about domestic politics and Sinai II, similarly explains that many senators wavered back and forth about signing the letter.[139] Despite reservations, though, more than three-quarters of the Senate added their signatures.

After signing, McGovern inadvertently articulated the confusing nature of the letter. He said, "It would be folly for Israel to assume that American support means approval of the existing boundaries in the Middle East. The present boundaries are not defensible; they are a virtual assurance of continued conflict. . . . In return for . . . recognition, Israel must agree to return the occupied territories and must accept Palestinian self-determination, including the right to a political entity of their own."[140] Yet the letter did precisely what McGovern had hoped to avoid. By its attacking the White House's reassessment and essentially guaranteeing Israeli military aid shipments, Ford and Kissinger lost the only leverage they had in negotiations—weapons.

Shortly after the letter, a *New York Times* article by Terence Smith sent the Israeli embassy into a frenzy. The article claimed that the senatorial letter, which Israeli officials happily referred to as "the spirit of the 76," convinced the Rabin administration that it could continue to ignore the repeated requests by the Ford administration to come up with new ideas and move forward with the peace process.[141] The day that the article appeared, Rafiah sent word that "Israel needs to immediately deny the Terry Smith article." According to Rafiah, the letter had been "sold" to the senators by claiming that it would allow Israel to enter into negotiations. The assistants of Jackson, Javits, Clifford Case (R-NJ), and Birch Bayh (D-IN) all informed Rafiah that Israel needed to deny the article. Richard Perle, Jackson's assistant, "said that although he agrees Israel should not come with new suggestions, publicizing the theme in the manner it was done in the *New York Times* will be very damaging."[142]

Dinitz also recognized the need for restraint. He informed the Foreign Ministry that the embassy in Washington would not publish "an explosive paper" that was "a clear attack on Sadat prior to his meeting with Ford" in Salzburg, Austria, set to happen in early June. The paper suggested even more military support from the United States, but since "the Embassy had been trying to downplay that point," Dinitz said he would not publish the letter.[143] In all likelihood, Dinitz realized that enough had been accomplished through Israel's *hasbara* campaign and the Senate letter, and attempting to undermine Sadat's position would have perhaps alienated even more senators and representatives in the aftermath of the Terence Smith article. Israel still needed to work with Sadat—as well as the U.S. government—in order to advance Israeli interests.

Conclusion

Israel proved remarkably able to influence domestic political opinion in the United States. Through meetings with U.S. government officials and members of the press and coordination with American Jewish Zionists, Israeli officials managed to keep abreast of developments in the public and political spheres in order to undertake measures to better the Israeli position. The Israeli *hasbara* resulted in a forceful senatorial letter that ended Ford's pressure on Israel.

The first meeting between Ford and Sadat took place that June in Salzburg, a springboard to the next round of negotiations for a Sinai II agreement. Israel and Egypt would agree to Sinai II in early September, which is discussed in the next chapter. The key to the entire agreement—the crucial element that was absent in March 1975—was a set of executive agreements concluded by the Ford administration with Israel. The administration promised to Israel billions of dollars in military and economic aid, ended the freeze on new arms shipments, vowed to not recognize the PLO until it accepted U.N. Resolution 242, and agreed to carefully coordinate strategy for any potential Geneva conference—all for a disengagement agreement unconnected to any future peace plan.[144] The U.S.-Israel agreements established a much higher baseline of U.S. material support for Israel for decades to come. Quite certainly, the Israeli embassy, Israel lobby, and U.S. Congress played crucial roles in this development.

Salim Yaqub, Steven Spiegel, and Galen Jackson all downplay the importance of the Senate letter. The letter may not have changed the minds of Kissinger and Ford about whether or not to pursue a comprehensive peace in the spring of 1975. But without the threat of a potential Geneva conference or the withholding of military aid, Israel extracted very significant concessions from the United States for another disengagement agreement. The Senate letter forced the administration to stop pressuring Israel and instead resort to enticing Israel with enormous aid packages and political pledges. Egypt could not give Israel what it really wanted—weapons and powerful political support in the international arena. That, along with removing Egypt from the larger Arab war with Israel, was what Sinai II was all about for Israel. It is difficult to imagine that the U.S. government would have sacrificed so much political and economic leverage over Israel if not for Israel's *hasbara* campaign and the activities of the Israeli embassy. If the Senate letter did not matter, or if Congress did not influence presidential policymaking in significant ways, one has to wonder why the State of Israel worked so hard and went to such lengths to influence policy through Congress, especially with the "Spirit of the 76."

Kissinger's memoirs, unfortunately, are silent about his meetings with American Jewish Zionist leadership and Israeli officials during reassessment.[145] That casts serious doubt on the accuracy of Kissinger's recollections in his memoirs and also points to the importance of non-U.S. documentation.

When thinking about the influence of domestic politics on the Sinai II agreement, consider a counterfactual possibility: What would have happened if seventy-six senators had signed a letter demanding *no* military aid for Israel until it agreed to sincere, substantive peace discussions?

Sen. J. William Fulbright with King Faisal of Saudi Arabia, taken in Riyadh, November or December 1972. (J. William Fulbright Papers, Third Accession, 144-C, Series 19, Box 115, Folder 8. Special Collections, University of Arkansas Libraries, Fayetteville.)

Sen. Henry M. Jackson, with staff members Dorothy Fosdick and Richard Perle, meeting with a military official, possibly Rear Admiral James B. Linder, during a tour of the aircraft carrier U.S.S. *Forrestal,* possibly in Norfolk, VA, November 13, 1972. Fosdick was a foreign policy expert and longtime adviser to Jackson; Perle would become an important neoconservative and work with both the Ronald Reagan and George W. Bush administrations. (University of Washington Libraries, Special Collections, UW40111.)

Photograph of Sen. J. William Fulbright taken during interview about Middle East speech, Summer 1970. (J. William Fulbright Papers, Second Accession, 144-B, Series 86, Box 1a, Folder 1. Special Collections, University of Arkansas Libraries, Fayetteville.)

Sen. Henry M. Jackson shaking hands with Israeli Prime Minister Golda Meir during a visit to the U.S. Embassy in Tel Aviv, Israel, February 22, 1972. (University of Washington Libraries, Special Collections, UW27852z.)

Sen. Henry M. Jackson talking with Israeli Minister of Defense Moshe Dayan and former Chief of Staff of the Israel Defense Forces (IDF) Haim Bar-Lev during a trip to Tel Aviv, Israel, 1972. (University of Washington Libraries, Special Collections, UW40110.)

Photograph of Sen. James Abourezk, undated. (James G. Abourezk Papers, Archives and Special Collections, University Libraries, University of South Dakota.)

Photograph of Amos Eiran taken during interview with author. Eiran served as Israel's liaison to the U.S. Congress, 1966–1972, and Director General for Prime Minister Yitzhak Rabin, 1974–1976. Eiran is holding the original Senate roll call for the Jackson-Vanik amendment, which he received as a gift from Scoop Jackson. The bottom reads: "76 yeas 9 nays / To Amos Eiran – with great admiration and respect from his friend Henry M. Jackson." (Author's collection.)

Israeli Ambassador Simcha Dinitz meeting with President Gerald Ford and Secretary of State and National Security Advisor Henry Kissinger on Ford's first day as president, August 9, 1974. (Courtesy Gerald R. Ford Presidential Library.)

Kissinger briefing Ford on unsuccessful Middle East peace talks, March 23, 1975. (Courtesy Gerald R. Ford Presidential Library.)

Kissinger and Ford meeting with bipartisan congressional leadership to discuss the suspension of peace talks and Ford's declared "reassessment" of U.S. foreign policy in the Middle East, March 24, 1975. (Courtesy Gerald R. Ford Presidential Library.)

Ford shaking hands with Max Fisher, March 27, 1975. The two met to discuss U.S.-Israel relations in light of Ford's reassessment. (Courtesy Gerald R. Ford Presidential Library.)

Ford and Kissinger review a map of the Sinai Peninsula with bipartisan congressional leadership during a meeting about the Sinai II Disengagement Agreement, September 4, 1975. (Courtesy Gerald R. Ford Presidential Library.)

5

The Sinai II Agreements of 1975

A New Relationship

The 1975 Sinai II disengagement agreement, which redrew the military map in the Sinai Peninsula and transferred the Abu Rudeis and Ras Sudr oil fields from Israel to Egypt, was more than just a bilateral agreement between Israel and Egypt.[1] In addition to being a crucial stepping-stone to Camp David a few years later, the Sinai II agreement consisted of a U.S. pledge to man an early warning station in the Sinai Peninsula and a series of secret executive agreements that the Ford administration negotiated with both Israel and Egypt. The secret agreements with Israel included multiyear, multibillion-dollar military sales and a vow to not advance any future peace proposals without Israeli approval. Previously, U.S. presidents had tried to pressure Israel by either denying weapons sales or threatening to withhold them. But after the May 1975 Senate letter, the administration had to use weapons sales as inducements for peace, rather than restrict weapons to moderate Israel's bargaining position. The agreements clearly favored Israel, spelled doom for the peace process, and signaled the solidification of a new relationship between the United States and Israel.

Most historians are probably unaware of the congressional response to Sinai II because the topic has not been given much attention. Former White House Middle East expert Harold Saunders addressed congressional influences on U.S. foreign policy in the Middle East from 1973 to 1984, including a brief section on Sinai II.[2] A few authors have dedicated at least a chapter within a larger work to Sinai II, but little emphasis is placed on the executive agreements.[3] Surveys of U.S.–Middle East relations, such as Michael Oren's *Power, Faith, and Fantasy,* overlook the importance of Sinai II.[4]

The lack of historical attention may derive from a scarcity of scholarship about the expanded use of executive agreements in foreign policy.[5] The new commitments to Israel came during a period of intense congressional efforts to reassert Congress's authority in both war-making and treaty-making, a push-back against the so-called Imperial Presidency. Scholarship about the Imperial Presidency first emerged in response to the Vietnam War and roughly thirty years later in response to a controversial war in Iraq, with the lion's share of attention devoted to the topic of war-making.[6]

Yet making an international commitment constitutes one of the most important elements of foreign policy in which Congress (and in the case of treaties, the Senate), according to the Constitution, should participate. While the conflicts in Vietnam and Iraq involved questionable war-making procedures by presidents, they also involved substantial American commitments to South Vietnam and post–Saddam Hussein Iraq, too.

For the first few decades of the Cold War, Congress had taken issue with the prolific use of executive agreements made by the White House that bypassed senatorial consultation and consent.[7] In fact, the U.S.-Israel agreements came just after Congress had considered legislation to create a possible legislative veto of any executive agreement within the first sixty days—the Executive Agreements Review Act of 1975. The Ford administration concluded the agreements in secret, out of view of Congress and the American public. In the aftermath of Vietnam, the move reminded Congress of the potential dangers of unchecked executive power.

But when issues involve Israel, Congress cares less about the extent of presidential power and more about the direction of U.S. policy. Congress has demonstrated a general inclination to go along with presidential policies that favor Israel, and ultimately, legislators acceded to the administration's secret agreements. Before doing so, though, numerous legislators argued that Ford needed to seek the advice and consent of the Senate for such wide-ranging commitments to Israel, which resembled a treaty, and many voiced serious reservations about such massive commitments without any congressional debate about, or approval of, the agreements. Some questioned the implications of the agreements, which pointed to a new type of relationship between the two countries. An amendment to a resolution that authorized the use of U.S. technicians in the Sinai formally stipulated that Congress did not approve of the executive agreements. But technically, the administration did not need congressional approval, and Congress essentially gave its tacit approval when it appropriated funds in 1976.

While the Senate letter of May 1975 forced the administration to buy the Sinai II agreement, Kissinger's negotiation of Sinai II put legislators in an uncomfortable position. If Congress did not approve of a resolution to sanction the use of U.S. technicians in an early-warning station in the Sinai Peninsula, then the Sinai II agreement between Israel and Egypt would not be implemented. But by passing the resolution, Congress, in effect, authorized the secret executive agreements made by Kissinger, which included a substantive change in the U.S.-Israel relationship. Beyond a moral commitment to Israel's survival or a strategic alliance, with Sinai II, the United States committed itself to meeting Israel's future economic and military needs, and also to Israel's continued occupation of lands taken in 1967. The executive agreements marked an enormous shift in U.S. policy, and the U.S. government arrived there, not by intent, but out of desperation, in an effort to preserve its position in the Middle East and prevent another war in the region, after several years of conflict between the executive and legislative branches regarding U.S.-Israel relations.

Executive Agreements and the Congressional Response

While not flashy or exciting, executive agreements are instrumental tools of presidential foreign policymaking. Sinai II included executive agreements that formally transformed the U.S.-Israel relationship and, therefore, requires a brief discussion about congressional efforts to restrict the use of such agreements prior to September 1975.

An executive agreement is "considered interchangeable with treaties in the legal sense, both domestically and internationally," but does not require the consent of the Senate.[8] Executive agreements have been used for about two centuries, but only sparingly until the Cold War. They allowed for a flexible yet credible response to communist activity overseas, and in a timely and legitimate manner. In 1935, the U.S. government entered into 25 treaties and 10 executive agreements, but in 1946 the ratio was 19 treaties to 139 executive agreements. During the five years from 1969 through 1973, the U.S. government agreed to a total of 80 treaties and 1,087 executive agreements.[9] Most executive agreements have been minor, unimportant items, and considering the sheer number each year, congressional oversight of each agreement was simply impossible. But at times, from the perspective of legislators, executive agreements resembled treaties and should have been submitted to the Senate as such.

Bypassing congressional participation naturally produced backlash on Capitol Hill. The first major congressional action was the failed Bricker Amendment of the 1950s, which aimed to limit the president's ability to enter into international commitments without congressional approval of executive agreements.[10] In the years leading up to the Executive Agreements Review Act of 1975, Congress passed a series of resolutions that either directly or indirectly affected executive agreements. The most significant, the Case-Zablocki Act of 1972, required the president to report all such agreements within sixty days of their commencement. The Nixon White House offered little resistance because the legislation did nothing to constrain the president's ability to enter into executive agreements; instead, the act simply required a sharing of information between the executive and legislative branches.

Sen. Sam Ervin Jr. (D-NC) went further than Case. He sponsored a bill in April 1972 that included a possible legislative veto of an executive agreement within sixty days by concurrent resolution of both Houses of Congress. As Arthur Schlesinger Jr. points out, Congress believed "it could best restrain the Presidency by enacting specific legislation in the conspicuous fields of presidential abuse."[11] Ervin had served as chair of the Senate Watergate Committee and took on Nixon over the issue of executive privilege on several occasions; the bill about executive agreements was part of Ervin's ongoing attempt to create a better balance of power between the two branches.[12] But since the Ervin bill sought to regulate all executive agreements, it failed to attract support, and no action was taken in the 92nd Congress. Ervin reintroduced his bill in July 1974, just months before he retired from the Senate. A slightly amended measure passed the Senate on November 21, 1974, but ultimately died in the House Rules Committee.[13]

The Ervin bill inspired several other pieces of legislation that would ultimately comprise the Executive Agreements Review Act of 1975. During March 1975, Congress considered six separate bills about executive agreements, two in the Senate and four in the House.[14] Thomas Morgan (D-PA), chair of the International Relations Committee, introduced a bill much like the Ervin bill that proposed a legislative veto of an executive agreement during the first sixty days. Different from the Ervin bill, however, was that "the measure is limited to those agreements which involve significant national commitments abroad."[15] Clement Zablocki (D-WI), cosponsor of the Case Act, joined with Morgan in proposing the legislation, as did twenty-six other representatives. "Much in the spirit of the War Powers Act," remarked Zablocki on the House floor, "the enactment of this bill would allow Congress to reassert its Constitutionally-mandated powers by requiring the Executive Branch to submit to Congress for review each executive agreement concerning a national commitment."[16]

The Senate Subcommittee on Separation of Powers, part of the Judiciary Committee, considered the two senatorial bills about executive agreements during the course of four scheduled hearings (May 13, 14, and 15, and July 25, 1975). The subcommittee was chaired by Sen. James Abourezk (D-SD). In his opening statement, Abourezk defended both the constitutionality of the proposed legislation as well as the broader congressional desire to play a more direct role in American foreign policy, especially in light of executive abuses of power.[17] Particularly irritating to Abourezk was a recent revelation of undisclosed executive agreements made by President Nixon with South Vietnam President Nguyen Van Thieu. The *New York Times* published a 1973 correspondence between the two leaders on May 1, 1975, just two weeks before the hearings. Nixon had pledged that if North Vietnam violated the Paris cease-fire accords, the United States would "take swift and severe retaliatory action" and would "respond with full force."[18] The secret agreement made by Nixon was technically an executive agreement, which brought into sharp focus (at least for Abourezk and the subcommittee) the need for stronger congressional control of executive agreements.

But the hearings revealed little legal support for the pending legislation. Supreme Court Justice Antonin Scalia, who at the time served as assistant Attorney General, voiced his opposition. Although he did notice substantive differences between the pending legislation and the 1972 Ervin bill, which had not been endorsed by the Senate, Scalia still deemed the legislation to be constitutionally defective.[19] He did, however, open the door to a different congressional approach. He recommended that Congress not try to regulate *all* executive agreements but instead offer challenges on a case-by-case basis. A specific situation may present itself in which Congress disagrees with the president, and the nature of the agreement invites congressional participation. In that case, congressional oversight may be both constitutional and prudent. Scalia also pointed out that a joint resolution would be a more appropriate tool to challenge an executive agreement, rather than a concurrent resolution or single-chamber resolution, because the president can veto the legislation. Therefore, if Congress could override the president's veto, then the process would still be constitutional.[20] Nevertheless, the hearings failed to produce support for the proposed legislation.

Sinai II—A Purchased Agreement

Congress's increasing antipathy toward executive agreements suggested an imminent showdown between the two branches over the Ford administration's negotiation of Sinai II. Shortly after the final Senate hearing, the Ford White House successfully mediated another step between Israel and Egypt, signed on September 4, 1975. Like the previous two disengagement agreements, Sinai II did little to change the status quo in the Middle East. Egypt regained control of the strategic Mitla and Gidi passes in the Sinai Peninsula, along with the oil fields, in return for an Egyptian commitment to resolve any conflict by peaceful means. The Israeli military line in the Sinai moved approximately ten miles back, leaving the position to be filled by the Egyptians. The limited zone was demilitarized to no more than eight thousand troops in eight battalions, with seventy-five tanks and seventy-two short-range artillery pieces. The United States agreed to man and supervise an early-warning system in the buffer zones as spelled out in detail in the agreement.[21]

In order to make the deal acceptable to both parties, the administration entered into secret executive agreements with both Israel and Egypt. The agreements with Israel proved to be far reaching and open ended and put Israel in a far stronger position than any of its Arab neighbors, or all of its Arab neighbors combined. The United States committed itself to meeting Israel's future economic and military needs, completing the process begun on May 21, and military aid to Israel would thus eclipse the $1 billion mark. The United States also pledged to not advance any steps in the peace process without first consulting with Israel, and to not recognize the PLO prior to its recognition of Israel and acceptance of U.N. Resolution 242. In other words, the Ford administration agreed to billion-dollar weapons sales to Israel without any expectation of additional steps in the peace process. Further, the administration agreed to compensate Israel for oil lost by giving up the oil fields and agreed to consider selling both F-16 fighter jets and Pershing ground-to-ground missiles, the missiles being originally designed to carry nuclear warheads. With Egypt, the United

States promised to promote future negotiations between Syria and Israel, to provide assistance for the early-warning system, and to consult with Egypt on any Israeli violations of the agreement, and reaffirmed its policy of assisting Egypt in its economic development.[22] In total, the U.S. pledged to provide approximately $600 million in aid to Egypt, and nearly $2.5 billion in aid to Israel.

Reading between the lines of Sinai II, the United States obviously purchased the interim step. The Ford administration paid a high price to salvage the remnants of its Middle East policy. Using secret agreements, aid packages, and questionable promises, the presidential approach to the Middle East looked eerily similar to a path followed in East Asia, and all without a clear, attainable vision of the future. Yet the interim agreement gave the appearance of another step being taken toward a final settlement to appease the Arab members of OPEC, which also wanted to avoid another embargo. It also brought Israel and Egypt closer together, which made another war far less likely, and strengthened the U.S.-Egypt relationship, a central goal of Kissinger.

The U.S.-Israel agreements were a vital component of Sinai II, and Israel managed to get the tangible benefits sought by Dinitz the previous spring. According to Amos Eiran, who served as the director general for Prime Minister Yitzhak Rabin from 1974 to 1976, "Without the Israeli-American understanding, I don't think that the Egyptian-Israeli agreement would have ever been achieved." Eiran admitted that part of the reason for the breakdown in negotiations in March was because Israel wanted something tangible in another agreement with Egypt. When negotiations restarted that summer, Israel asked the United States for concrete commitments. Eiran said, "We wanted a solid commitment from the U.S. Nobody assured us, this is the end of wars. Who knows? Another revolution in Egypt and the Muslim Brothers will be in power. It would be a very difficult situation."[23]

The agreements formalized the end of reassessment and promised to be costly for the United States. The *New York Times* noted the end of the weapons ban in a short article published on September 7. According to Israeli sources, negotiations had already begun on providing new weapons to Israel, including "F-16 warplanes, Lance ground-to-ground missiles, and laser guided bombs," some of the most sophisticated weaponry in the American arsenal.[24] William Drummond argued in a *Los Angeles Times* article (reprinted in the *Washington Post*) that according to official American sources the secret agreements empowered Israel to dictate the course of the peace process moving forward.[25] A *Chicago Tribune* piece questioned the mounting costs of the agreement. "It started out at about $3 billion; but as the dust settled, this turned out to be for just the first year, bringing the cost of the three-year agreement to something like $9 billion." Of the aid, more than two-thirds was destined for Israel, less than one-third to Egypt.[26] According to a report from the Congressional Budget Office, for the first five years the cost to the United States "could reach over $15 billion." The assessment pointed out the monumental significance of the agreements, which called "upon the United States to be 'fully responsive' to Israel's defense, energy, and economic needs 'on an on-going and long-term basis.'"[27] Through the end of the decade, annual U.S. military aid to Israel would be one-half military grants and one-half military loans, apart from aid connected to the Camp David agreement.

American popular approval was lacking. A Gannett News Service (GNS) national poll, conducted on September 3–4 and based on phone calls to one thousand voting-age Americans, reflected little support for the agreement, especially the substantial aid packages. Regarding just the U.S. technicians, only 28 percent supported the plan, while 41 percent opposed it, and 18 percent said their opinions hinged "upon the conditions under which the Americans are deployed." Regarding the proposal for "$2.5 billion in military and economic aid to Israel during the next year," just 24 percent approved and 64 percent disapproved; 12 percent expressed no opinion. While Republicans favored sending the technicians and Democrats/Independents were slightly opposed, opposition to the aid packages to Israel cut "across party lines, with Republicans almost as heavily opposed as Democrats."[28]

A Brewing Conflict

From the perspective of many members of Congress, the agreements constituted national commitments and represented another example of unchecked presidential power in foreign affairs. Although Congress failed to muster support for legislation that regulated all executive agreements, Sinai II offered Congress an opportunity to regulate executive agreements on a case-by-case basis.

Legislators bristled at the secret nature of the agreements. After the Pentagon Papers and Watergate, Congress wanted to make foreign policy more transparent and accessible to the public. Sen. Clifford Case (R-NJ) released a statement that stated, "It is my belief that there is no such thing as a valid secret United States commitment." Such commitments, according to Case, "require the approval of the Congress and the American people."[29] A White House document recognized "bipartisan concern about the secret elements of the agreement." Many congressional members did not "wish to be party to a secret agreement because of post-Vietnam fears" and thus wanted "to make public as much as possible of the entire agreement."[30] Complicating the situation, newspapers published details of the secret agreements on September 16, which added to the atmosphere of mistrust swirling about Washington. In an effort to advance an image of transparency, on October 3 the Senate Foreign Relations Committee "voted 12 to 2 to release the attached documents provided by the Department of State in connection with the Sinai disengagement proposal," thereby making public the secret agreements.[31]

Legislators also resented another set of substantial executive agreements not being submitted to Congress as treaties, especially given congressional efforts to check executive power. The White House submitted to Congress only the portion of the agreement about U.S. participation in the early-warning station. The White House informed the relevant committees in the House and Senate about U.S. pledges to Israel and Egypt but did not see the need to submit these agreements for ratification by Congress. In the case of the Sinai technicians, however, the White House wanted congressional approval.

The debate about sending U.S. personnel to the Sinai Peninsula, along with secret presidential commitments, understandably drew comparisons to Vietnam. Ford and Kissinger tried to allay congressional fears in a meeting with bipartisan leadership on September 4. Ford called U.S. participation "absolutely crucial to the settlement."[32] House Speaker Carl Albert (D-OK) reminded the meeting about "when Secretary of State [John Foster] Dulles urged the Congress to approve sending 800 technicians to South Vietnam."[33] But Albert also noted the difference in the two situation because "both sides have requested our participation, and we are not putting Americans into an active conflict. These Americans will be civilians, not military." Senate Majority Leader Mike Mansfield (D-MT) offered a more pointed critique than Albert: "I am very much concerned that the United States for the first time is making a commitment of personnel to the Middle East. Whether they are military or civilian is beside the point." Between the promise of U.S. personnel and substantial aid packages, Mansfield argued, "All of this seems to me to be a pretty stiff price to pay for a very small withdrawal."[34]

Relevant committees in both Houses of Congress conducted hearings about Sinai II. The House Committee on International Relations went first on September 8, 11, 18, and 25, and the Senate Foreign Relations Committee followed shortly thereafter on October 6 and 7. Ostensibly to discuss sending two hundred U.S. civilians to man an early-warning station in the Sinai, the discussions usually focused on secret executive agreements and prospects for peace in the Middle East.

The first witness to appear before the House committee was Henry Kissinger. He addressed the charge that the United States purchased Sinai II and did not deny it. "I have read in the press," said Kissinger, "many statements to the effect that the United States bought this agreement in the Sinai by the promise of military and economic aid to both of the parties."[35] Kissinger reminded the committee that "economic and military aid to Israel has been an unchallenged premise of every known aid bill before every Congress. More frequently than not, the Congress has increased the administration request."[36] He referenced the senators' May letter to Ford, which called for the type of aid involved in Sinai II. Regarding Egypt, Congress had appropriated $250 million in foreign aid the previous year, and the Ford administration had been "planning for a substantial increase in this amount without the agreement."[37] According to Kissinger, the additional funds required would be "relatively small."[38]

While Kissinger made legitimate points, he also seriously understated the significance of the executive agreements. The United States effectively agreed to align its foreign policy goals in the Middle East with Israel's, which meant not pursuing a multilateral peace at Geneva, nor recognizing the PLO. While a strategic alliance involved coordination with Israeli officials about foreign-policy goals, it in no way required U.S. submission to Israeli insistence on the indefinite occupation of the West Bank and Jerusalem, which offered virtually no security benefits. Additionally, the White House agreed to provide Israel with oil in the event of an embargo and compensation for giving up the oil fields, along with a pledge to consider selling F-16 planes, as well as Pershing missiles that could potentially carry a nuclear warhead. Such a move would send more sophisticated weaponry to the Middle East and in a way that further weighed the military scale in Israel's favor and extremely reduced the prospect of a broader peace. The substantial aid packages were extraordinarily expensive and did not guarantee a peaceful resolution of the conflict but, rather, its continuation. When Kissinger communicated to the

House that Sinai II did not represent much change from envisioned aid packages, he made a fair point. But he also fudged the truth.

The wounds from the Vietnam War ran deep in the congressional body. Undersecretary of State Joe Sisco pleaded with the House committee, saying the administration was "going to extraordinary length in trying to share this information with the committee and the Congress because we were very, very conscious of the atmosphere that exists in our country. We have all gone through a pain and an anguish in terms of Vietnam and there isn't any family in this room that hasn't been touched by the Vietnam situation." Sisco was cognizant of the strain between the two branches of government when he said, "I know there isn't a great deal of trust in this town but I hope that we can begin to develop the kind of confidence between the executive branch and the legislature which I think is necessary for us to move together as a country."[39]

The House committee voiced its frustration with executive secrecy. In his first meeting, Sisco had asked for, and received, an executive session by a vote of 18–1, during which he informed the committee about the details of the executive agreements. But two days before his second meeting, the details appeared in the press.[40] This upset the committee, which is why Sisco's motion for executive session on September 18 was voted down.[41] The committee questioned the administration's desire for secrecy in light of the press leaks and grilled Sisco on certain portions of the agreement, like the Pershing missiles and oil commitments to Israel. Sisco remained tight-lipped in open session but claimed to be willing to offer more discussion in executive session. Thus, several representatives indicated their hope that the committee could meet in executive session before voting on a joint resolution.

Following the House hearings, *Washington Post* reporters Roland Evans and Robert Novak noted that "the Sinai agreement comes before Congress at a time when the congressional grab for power over foreign policy is reaching white-hot intensity."[42] They also hypothesized that Israel might want to scuttle Sinai II since "President Ford has ended the Israeli arms embargo and new weapons are flowing to Israel." The authors cited a "congressional insider" who related, "Israel's strategy seems to be changing. They seem to be doing exactly nothing to lobby Congress on the technicians. Considering Israel's real power up here, it's funny nothing is happening." Moreover, the two chambers appeared to be pursuing different tracks. The House committee sought to separate the issue of U.S. technicians from the rest of the executive agreements; therefore, the vote would be on only the technicians and nothing else. But the Senate committee wanted to package the technicians with the rest of the agreements and, therefore, vote on all elements of the agreement.[43] Time would tell that the House recommendation would move forward.

The House committee must have been satisfied with the answers it received from Sisco in executive session. On October 2, the committee discussed a resolution cosponsored by Morgan and ranking minority member William Broomfield (R-MI) permitting U.S. participation in the Sinai early-warning station. After adopting four amendments, Morgan introduced the draft as a joint resolution, and the measure passed the committee the following day by a unanimous vote, 31–0.[44]

The Senate Foreign Relations Committee followed with its own hearings, which promised to be more detailed than those in the House. Foreign Relations had voted to make public the U.S. secret agreements just days before the hearings and, therefore, could ask more searching questions in open session.

The first witness to testify before the Senate committee was James Abourezk, who chaired the subcommittee review of executive agreements. Abourezk generally sought to cultivate better relations with the Arab world and did not shy away from conflict with the executive branch. He had voiced strong objections to the emergency aid bill to Israel in 1973, and following William Fulbright's exit from the Senate in 1974, Abourezk emerged as the most vocal senator in support of an evenhanded policy in the Middle East.[45] In the upcoming Senate debate about the resolution to approve technicians, Abourezk would again challenge the pro-Israel drift of U.S. policy.

Abourezk wanted to restrict weapons sales to all countries engaged in the conflict, including Israel. In January 1975, he had released a statement that criticized the Ford administration's decision "to provide antitank missiles to Lebanon in order to defend against American tanks already supplied to Israel." Foreshadowing future conflict in Lebanon, American weapons had been used by Israel in southern Lebanon, which begat the Lebanese request for American anti-tank missiles. Abourezk first "pointed out that U.S. law prohibits arms shipments to any nation using our arms to commit aggression against another country." He then questioned, "How in the name of sanity can our government continue to violate the law by furnishing arms to Israel, then compound the foolishness by shipping arms to the nations being attacked by Israel?"[46]

Abourezk often wrote newspaper articles and made Senate speeches that questioned the U.S. commitment to Israel. The *New York Times* published an Abourezk article in January 1975, submitted to the *Congressional Record,* that pushed the executive branch to engage the PLO in direct discussions. Abourezk's article came in response to a December 9 Senate letter to Ford, signed by seventy-one senators, that denounced the PLO and its leader, Yasser Arafat. The December letter also reiterated the United States's "long-standing commitment to Israel's security by a policy of continued military supplies and diplomatic and economic support." Abourezk cautioned against "cavalier" actions of the Senate. He pointed to the self-interested motivations of some legislators: "Open-ended Congressional support for anything Israel wishes to do, or not do, may satisfy a constituency, or it may even see Israel through a military victory or two. But such political and military largess can only insure Israel's survival for a short time."[47] Abourezk referenced the ongoing moderation of the PLO (also noted years later in a scholarly work by Paul Chamberlin) and the need to address Palestinian grievances and border disputes.[48] Otherwise, war could re-erupt. Abourezk reminded his readers, "An oil embargo would result from even a minimum military confrontation." Thus, without dealing with the core problems in the Middle East, the United States threatened its own economic interests.[49]

Abourezk wrote a stinging criticism of Sinai II, published in the *Washington Post* and also submitted to the *Congressional Record.* He accused the administration of using Sinai II to advance Ford's reelection in 1976 and argued that the agreement "formalized the Middle East status quo" by "splitting off Egypt from the Arab bloc; isolating the Palestinians, resulting in an increased militancy on their part, and by pouring American weapons and money into Israel." Abourezk recognized that "Israel can now avoid any further pressure which the U.S. could have exerted to force her to face all of the issues which constitute the Middle East conflict." Abourezk also referenced a *Time Magazine* quotation from an Israeli "high-level government official," who stated: "The interim agreement has delayed Geneva, while at the same time assuring us arms, money, a coordinated policy with Washington and quiet in Sinai. Relatively speaking, we gave up a little for a lot." Moreover, during the first year of the agreement, "Kissinger has agreed to provide Israel with about $2.3 billion American taxpayer's dollars." Referencing Israeli influence on Congress, Abourezk predicted that "Israel will receive from the United States treasury in excess of $11 billion in the next five years." All in all, "We are indeed giving far too much for far too little."[50]

In his testimony to the Senate Foreign Relations Committee in October 1975, Abourezk pointed out that "the Sinai agreement is a major benchmark, a plateau of involvement by the United States at a level not reached before."[51] Asked if he supported the portion of the agreement that provided for U.S. personnel in the Sinai, Abourezk rejected the proposal for two main reasons. First, he felt that putting "Americans in the middle of the two combatants in the Middle East" was unwise and unnecessary because "there are other technicians in the world aside from American employees who can listen and who can run electronic gear just as well as our people can."[52] Second, he regarded the Sinai II agreement as a step in the wrong direction because it did not force Israel to give up more territory, and he therefore opposed the agreement generally.[53]

Though not in the majority, Abourezk was not alone, either. Several senators and other witnesses voiced objections about an interim agreement that could paralyze, rather than advance, the Arab-Israeli peace process (in particular, George McGovern and George Ball). Outside of the hearing, Fulbright voiced his concerns in a *Christian Science Monitor* article, saying the United States paid too high of a price and should have sought a "full Mideast accord."[54]

Sen. Thomas Eagleton (D-MO) made a procedural critique regarding "the status of international agreements consummated in the absence of congressional approval," which was at the heart of the 1975 debate about executive agreements.[55] The absence of a legislative veto, according to Eagleton, had led to "the Executive's usurpation of the Senate's treaty power."[56] Eagleton hoped the executive agreements with Israel and Egypt would create "a renewed effort to provide Congress with the mechanism necessary to reassert our legitimate powers in this area."[57] In the end, Eagleton told the committee that the executive agreements should have been submitted as treaties, but he nevertheless offered his support only for the resolution that provided for the early-warning system, apart from the more significant aid packages and pledges.[58]

Kissinger appeared immediately after Eagleton and met with the committee for a lengthy session. He pointed out that some of the executive agreements were binding, while others were assurances of "good faith." However, the White House refused to make public legal adviser Monroe Leigh's memorandum, which discussed the legality and extent of commitments of the U.S. government for each of the separate executive agreements.[59] In response to Leigh's memorandum, the assistant Counsel for the Office of Legislative Counsel, Michael J. Glennon, responded that of the four secret agreements, only one was a valid executive agreement, two were problematic, "and one was beyond the power of the President to enter into without the advice and consent of the Senate."[60] Despite reservations, the Senate Foreign Relations Committee recommended passage of the resolution regarding the technicians on October 7.

The joint resolution included several safeguards approved at the committee level, which signaled congressional concerns with Sinai II. One amendment required the president to provide Congress with written updates every six months in order to keep Congress apprised of any developments and the possibility of withdrawing U.S. personnel as soon as possible. George McGovern proposed a similar amendment during Senate debate on October 8, which was printed and ordered to lie on the table, that emphasized the need to work for a comprehensive peace.[61] He feared war would resume without a full agreement that addressed the Israeli occupation and Palestinian refugees. In that case, "it is hardly likely that the superpowers . . . will be able to remain uninvolved," and "it can be rated a virtual certainly [*sic*] that another war will immediately trigger a new oil embargo with far more devastating economic consequences than the 1973 embargo for the entire world."[62] Second, a concurrent resolution could force the president to recall the technicians, which extended the thinking of the War Powers Act. A third amendment included a final section that explicitly stated that approval of the early-warning station did not mean approval of any other agreements. In H. J. Resolution 683 (1975), Section 5 states, "The authority contained in this joint resolution to implement the 'United States Proposal for the Early Warning System in Sinai' does not signify approval of the Congress of any other agreement, understanding, or commitment made by the executive branch."[63]

The Congressional Debate

Congress debated the Sinai II agreement at length between October 6 and 9. Several senators, especially Abourezk, Joe Biden (D-DE), and Fritz Hollings (D-SC), voiced serious concerns about the executive agreements. But the prospect of a potential war proved to be too dangerous for many legislators to vote against the resolution, despite their misgivings about the executive agreements.

Abourezk and Biden both criticized the Senate for hurrying to pass the resolution. Abourezk sparred with Mansfield about the "big rush." Mansfield, who admitted he did not vote for the resolution in the Foreign Relations Committee, did not see the need to extend debate "when I think everybody's mind is made up."[64] Biden took issue with Humphrey's insistence that the Senate needed to pass the resolution immediately in order to ensure the success of Sinai II and prevent a war. Biden cited with disdain the Ford administration's insistence "that we must move promptly. Otherwise, we run the risk of war breaking out and being responsible for that occurring."[65] Like Biden, many legislators commented on how they felt trapped by the agreement—if they did not pass it soon, then the failure of the agreement, and perhaps war, would be blamed on Congress. Biden also responded to the argument that Anwar Sadat needed Congress to pass the resolution quickly. He included a September 15 quote from Sadat, during which the Egyptian president said he was "not concerned at all" about Congress moving slowly on the resolution. Biden wondered why "everyone in this room is telling us, the committee was telling us," that Sadat "was in such jeopardy if we did not move immediately," when "he does not say he is in such jeopardy."[66]

Biden's main problem with the resolution was the executive agreements. He noted, "I have been a fairly strident opponent of the resolution," and "The placement of the 200 technicians in the Sinai is not the issue at all." He argued that "we are also voting to approve, through a backdoor measure, all of those agreements which have been initialed by this administration," along with Israel and Egypt. "So we are not just voting on the 200 technicians; we are voting on much more than that."[67] Biden's comment hit the mark. Once the U.S. Congress approved of the technicians—even if it did not explicitly approve the executive agreements—those agreements would still be signed by the relevant parties as part of Sinai II and become operative policy of the United States moving forward.

Biden did not necessarily disagree with the substance of the agreements but, rather, the manner in which the administration subverted the Senate's constitutional authority on treaty-making. He admitted, "I support many of the provisions." However, given that "an executive agreement has the full force and effect of a treaty in international law and is domestically a binding national commitment," Biden felt that "it is totally inappropriate for us to vote into effect those provisions without having adequate extensive debate on the impact . . . because the President plans on binding the United States of

America with those provisions."[68] Thus, Biden's concern with the insistence on prompt passage of the resolution was rooted in his broader procedural concern with lasting, binding commitments made by the United States, resembling treaties, that did not receive adequate senatorial advice and consent.

Biden, as did many legislators, derided the administration for its secrecy. He felt the U.S. government had not "learned one of the lessons" of the Vietnam experience. Biden said, "I am about to state what the true lesson of Vietnam should have been, and that is that the American people are not prepared to, are not willing to, and will not submit to extensive commitments to foreign countries without first being fully aware of what the commitments are, and the degree to which the U.S. Government is bound by those commitments." By voting in favor of the resolution, Biden reasoned that the American people would again be asked to adhere to commitments to foreign nations—primarily Israel, but also Egypt—without being aware of the nature of the commitments.[69] Although Biden's Foreign Relations Committee voted to make public the secret agreements, the Ford administration still regarded them as classified. Therefore, the administration refused to release Monroe's legal analysis about which agreements were binding and which were not. The American people lacked the ability to properly gauge the extent of U.S. commitments that had the potential to impact future presidencies and generations.

Fritz Hollings took up where Biden left off with a colorful, comical, and lengthy rebuke of Sinai II. He first submitted an amendment that reaffirmed U.N. Resolution 242 as the basic policy of the United States, and then predicted that "the opposition is going to say, 'Let's not have any amendments, we must hurry; we are trying to save Sadat,' and so on." But for Hollings, "it is the old Gulf of Tonkin syndrome, if I ever heard it."[70] Hollings demanded that Israel give back the territory taken in 1967. Clearly fed up with Israel's unwillingness to relinquish land, he asked the Senate, "Remember that shibboleth they had over there about defensible boundaries? Even the Suez Canal is not defensible. Sharm al-Sheikh is an outpost. I could take it with a company from Parris Island this afternoon, and the Senator from New Jersey could take it back from me with two companies tomorrow afternoon." For Hollings, the only secure and recognized boundaries, as stated in 242, "are the pre-1967 boundaries. But no one wants to talk about that now. No one wants to ask Israel about that." He wondered, "What is the American policy position, if it is not the withdrawal of Israeli Armed Forces from the territories occupied in the recent conflict? But for all they can run around the mulberry bush, no one has asked that question, or even asked Israel, 'Would you agree to that?'" Hollings justified, "That is the reason we raise the amendment."[71]

Hollings spoke out against stationing technicians and "the general atmosphere created by the whole spate of agreements recently negotiated by Secretary of State Kissinger." He sympathized with the American people, who "have a right to be confused as to just where we are in terms of our Middle East policy. Testimony given by the administration to the Foreign Relations Committee has an eerie, Alice-in-Wonderland quality about it." He went on to clarify, "I have never heard of such a situation as grown men sitting in the Foreign Relations Committee, saying, 'Everybody off Sadat's back. Time is of the essence. We have to rush this thing on through and put people in the middle of the combat zone and then say they are noncombatants, and do not worry.'" Hollings argued, "If that is the case, then they are not worth a tinker's hurrah, and they ought not to put them in there in the first place." He denounced the "Mickey Mouse rinkydink" diplomacy of Henry Kissinger and the "pea-in-the-shell trick movements before the Foreign Relations Committee, to bring it out on the floor and adopt the posture of no amendments because the House is going to adjourn tomorrow."[72]

Hollings also noted the erosion of popular support for the Sinai accords. He claimed, "People the nation over suspect that these latest agreements are not in the interest of an overall settlement. Anyone who has traveled back home, or looked at his mail, knows whereof I speak." He perceptively added that the U.S. commitment to Israel had not "disappeared" or "diminished" at all. "Rather it is the suspicion that we are going about fulfilling that commitment in the wrong way. And if that suspicion is given soil to grow in, then one day the commitment itself may begin to erode. That would be a sad day for Israel. It would be sad for America, too." He called his amendment "vitally necessary" because "if we continue to be deflected in the quest for an enduring peace, the Middle East will explode with a bang sufficient to involve us all in the costliest kind of war." He implored the Senate to adopt his amendment, though he clearly realized it would not, "and we are just going to ram this thing through."[73] Though it may go without saying, when the time came, Hollings voted against the resolution.

Senator McClure commended the senator from South Carolina and spoke in favor of the Hollings amendment. McClure feared that U.S. policy had changed with the Sinai II agreement and that "it must be inferred that we are abandoning the goal of U. N. Resolution 242." McClure, like Hollings, struck at the heart of the matter. He pointed out a "troublesome matter" about the U.S.-Israel relationship, "that the whole basis of the United States-Israel commitment has been a moral commitment. It has not been a legally binding document. It has been a moral commitment on our part to the continued existence of the nation of Israel."[74] The resolution before the Senate, in McClure's view, signaled a massive transformation of the U.S.-Israel relationship.

Javits argued against the Hollings amendment. As he did during debates about the emergency aid bill in 1973, Javits noted that Israel had already agreed to 242. Further, he did not want to include an amendment that could lead to defeat of the bill because that could mean another war. He added that the House would recess for two weeks, and if the Senate included an amendment, then the House would not be able to weigh in on the resolution until it returned. Like Humphrey, Javits emphasized the need to pass the resolution quickly, which meant no amendments. Unfortunately for Hollings and his supporters, the amendment was tabled, 54–28.[75]

Discussion in the House resembled that in the Senate. Morgan called on the House to pass the resolution immediately. He reminded his colleagues of the possibility of another war in the region. He implored the House to approve the resolution "quickly," otherwise "there is a possibility that the entire agreement could be in trouble."[76]

But numerous representatives lodged their concerns about the agreement. Clarence Zablocki cosponsored an amendment with Paul Findley, which was defeated during committee debate, to limit the agreement to twenty-four months. Zablocki noted his serious reservations about U.S. policy. He referenced that morning's *Washington Post,* which claimed Kissinger had told the Senate that congressional approval of the technicians "would bring into effect other agreements . . . that make commitments and assurances legally binding on the United States." He further added that Kissinger claimed "existing American policy" was based on the May letter from seventy-six senators that called for "substantial military and economic aid" for Israel. Kissinger used that letter to justify the massive aid agreement with Israel connected to Sinai II. Zablocki asked, "Are we agreeing to that" as existing American policy? He said, "These are the reasons why this open-ended authorization resolution has given me great concern." That rationale explained Zablocki's effort for trying to limit the agreement to twenty-four months. He ended by reiterating his worry that by "blindly" agreeing to the technicians, "without any reservations, and giving an open-ended authorization, we may rue the day. We may buy a short-term peace at tomorrow's peril."[77] Findley added that the pressure to pass the resolution quickly, based on questionable assurances from the executive branch, reminded him of the Tonkin Gulf Resolution—"the mood was support the President, get behind him at this moment of great delicacy." Numerous congresspeople, in light of Vietnam, voiced worries about section 10 of the secret U.S. assurances to Israel, which suggested the United States may use military action, if necessary, to protect Israel.[78]

Concerns came from many additional representatives. David Obey (D-WI) resented that Congress needed to pass the resolution to ensure the success of the Sinai II agreement. He felt faced with a "'damned if you do and damned if you don't' situation" and worried that "Israel has the impression that they can get virtually anything they want out of this Congress in the way of an aid bill."[79] John Dent (D-PA) cautioned, "Once we start providing billions, it will not stop." He wondered, "What will have to be paid for the loss of the buffer land area? Will it be billions or trillions of dollars of planes, guns for Israel?"[80] Jim Johnson (R-CO) opposed the resolution because arguments in favor "are at best flimsy" and because of "the language of escalating commitment on the part of the United States to Israel." Like Senator McClure, Johnson observed that the U.S. commitment to Israel had moved from ensuring its survival to providing "defense, energy, and economic needs," "military supply needs," "oil requirements," and more.[81] Richard Ichord (D-MO) could not vote for the resolution without the Findley-Zablocki amendment so that the United States could avoid becoming the "sole guarantor of peace for this region."[82] Elmer "Bud" Shuster (R-PA) opposed the resolution due to its cost, "given our problems here in America," and worried about U.S. involvement in a military conflict in the region.[83] Joe Skubitz (R-KS) noted that approving the technicians meant the enactment of the executive agreements and wondered, "What's next?" He cited an October 1 article from the *Washington Post,* which said, "Israel needs the agreement as its ticket to the billions in aid and the political partnership it seeks from Washington."[84] Charles Grassley (R-IA) also spoke out against the resolution and argued that congressional approval meant the executive branch "will have a blank check to continue their policies in the future."[85] The previous day, Robert Kastenmeier (D-WI) chastised Ford for supporting a multibillion-dollar aid plan for Israel when he "cannot bring himself to support expenditures for feeding hungry children and for assisting malnourished pregnant women," referring to Ford's rejection of the National School Lunch and Child Nutrition Act Amendments of 1975.[86]

Some representatives supported the resolution but voiced serious reservations. Edward Derwinski (R-IL) supported passage but cited deep concern about placing American technicians in the Sinai and called on Congress to "make it very evident that in endorsing the stationing of U.S. technicians . . . it is not giving its approval to any other agreement which American negotiators might have initiated or concluded."[87] Lee Hamilton's (D-IN) support included "major concerns," such as the extent of commitments, the administration's secretive approach, "the very high price Americans are being asked to pay for what appears to be small progress toward peace," and he stated that some of the U.S.-Israel agreements may be "premature" given the many outstanding issues in the region. He hoped the U.S. government would avoid making "too many commitments" and "maintain flexibility" in order to promote "a lasting Middle East peace." He also stipulated that Congress needed to carefully consider billion-dollar aid to Israel at the right time.[88] Elizabeth Holtzman (D-NY) supported the resolution, albeit with "a number of reservations," as did Marilyn Lloyd (D-TN), who referenced being "deeply concerned by the content and language" of the secret agreements. Margaret Heckler (R-MA), planned "to vote for this resolution, but with very serious reservations."[89] Allan Howe (D-UT) rose in support but admitted to being "personally very disturbed" about the secret agreements, in particular, the pledge to meet "Israel's military, economic, and energy needs." He regarded the agreements as treaties that "should be presented to the Senate for ratification in the same manner as any other treaty."[90] Timothy Wirth (D-CO) supported the resolution but added, "I would emphasize, as others have, that by consenting to this provision of the Sinai agreement, we do not imply our consent to any other promises."[91]

Despite opposition, reservations, and another attempted amendment from Findley, broad support for the resolution carried it to passage. Numerous representatives cited the avoidance of war as the primary justification for their support. Wayne Hays (D-OH), for example, said, "One can call it buying peace, or whatever; but whatever it is, the price is going to be very, very cheap compared to a war." Hays also cited the May letter from the seventy-six senators "demanding that we give to Israel $2.75 billion worth of arms" and said that Kissinger's commitment to Israel was less than that, "more in the area of $2.3 billion."[92] For Edward Biester (R-PA), "the alternative of continued, escalating conflict is clearly unacceptable."

Findley submitted the same amendment to the House that had been defeated at the committee level—to end the resolution after two years. Zablocki rose in support and voiced his concern with "the sweeping, open-ended commitment of military, economic, and oil aid to Israel . . . which puts the United States in the position of long term obligation to Israel even if Israel refuses to negotiate with the Arabs."[93] Several representatives objected to the amendment. Hays claimed the amendment would "destroy the resolution" and "destroys the chance for peace." Jonathan Bingham (D-NY) said it amounted to a "rejection of the resolution." Benjamin Gilman (R-NY), Samuel Stratton (D-NY), and Dante Fascell (D-FL) all rose in opposition to the Findley amendment, which was defeated, 122–287.[94] Shortly after, the joint resolution easily cleared the House, 341–69.[95]

The following day, many senators voiced similar concerns to those of their House counterparts. Mansfield compared passage of the resolution to the Tonkin Gulf Resolution and also argued that voting for the technicians would be committing the United States "to this entire package of agreements and the significant change in American policy they represent."[96] Humphrey tried to downplay the connection to Tonkin Gulf by noting that both Israel and Egypt had asked the United States to be involved, as opposed to the situation between North and South Vietnam. But Dick Clark (D-IA) agreed with Mansfield and tried to offer a clarification to Humphrey. Echoing Findley from the day before, Clark said, "It is not the content, but, rather, the haste with which these are being considered and with which—that is the comparison—with which the Gulf of Tonkin was being considered."[97] Soon thereafter, the Senate passed an amendment that required a vote on the resolution before 4:00 p.m. the following day.[98]

Several senators tried to amend the resolution, but to no avail. Abourezk tried to recommit the resolution as a treaty, but the measure failed, 9–85.[99] Biden, Clark, Floyd Haskell (D-CO), and Adlai Stevenson III (D-IL) co-sponsored an amendment to declassify Monroe Leigh's legal memorandum about the secret agreements, but Humphrey moved to table the amendment, and the Senate agreed, 59–32. The same group of senators submitted an amendment to include three specific points that stated any assurance made by a U.S. official to Israel or Egypt: "1) is simply a statement of the present intentions of the executive branch; 2) is not binding under domestic or international law; and 3) may not be construed as limiting the freedom of the United States in pursuing its national interest in the Middle East."[100] Biden sought to formally stipulate that the resolution would "not set in motion any commitments which (1) the Congress has not had an opportunity to pass on and, (2) equally important which the American people have not been informed about."[101] But Humphrey moved to table that amendment, too, and the Senate again agreed, 51–32.[102] Jesse Helms (R-NC) submitted an amendment for a one-year limit on the technicians. Abourezk, obviously perturbed by the consistent tabling of amendments, said he felt such a move was "personally offensive" and noted that the amendments would be defeated anyway. Nevertheless, Humphrey again successfully tabled the amendment; Helms did not feel the need to request the yeas and nays.[103] Charles Mathias (R-MD) offered, and then withdrew, an amendment to end the resolution on February 1, 1977, unless extended by a joint resolution.[104] Robert Dole (R-KS) submitted and withdrew a sense of the Senate resolution that called on the president to request that Western Europe, Japan, and the United Nations share in providing assistance to Israel and Egypt.[105]

Beyond amendments, a few senators spoke of serious misgivings about the resolution. Biden again denounced the "backdoor" approval of other commitments connected to approval of the technicians and told his colleagues that by approving of the resolution, "we are saying that the Executive, the President of the United States, has the right to do every one of the things that are set out in the agreement."[106] Harry Byrd Jr. (D-VA) refused to vote for the open-ended commitments "when the dangers ahead seem without limit."[107] Stevenson opposed the resolution because its approval would "trigger secret, dangerous and expensive commitments."[108]

As representatives had in the House, many senators supported the resolution with reservations. Clark voted for the resolution "with the greatest reluctance" and with "grave misgivings about the nature and extent of the commitments to which we may be binding this Nation in the agreements with Israel and Egypt."[109] James Pearson (R-KS) supported the approval of the technicians but not the additional secret commitments.[110] Robert Morgan (D-NC), who replaced Sam Ervin in the Senate, decided to vote for the resolution only "after a great deal of soul searching." He said, "There is no doubt this is one of the hardest decisions we have had to make," and argued that the United States needed "to take advantage of the slightest possibility that there can be peace in the Middle East. If we do not seize the advantage, and war results, there will not be the slightest practical advantage to us."[111] Thomas McIntyre (D-NH) supported the resolution with a "sense of dissatisfaction." He felt that several of the Senate amendments had merit, and if enacted they would have alleviated legitimate concerns. But the Senate did not have enough time to approve amendments because that would require a conference, and given the House recess, that path seemed impractical.[112] Charles Percy (R-IL) thought the resolution would prevent a "catastrophic" war, and Edward "Ted" Kennedy supported the resolution because he felt it advanced the cause of peace.[113] Joseph Montoya (D-NM) also voted in favor of the resolution with "reservations."[114] Howard Baker (R-TN), although he supported the resolution, called Sinai II the "Sinai Dis-Agreement" because of the questions raised, "questions that go to the very foundations of our national foreign policy and to the foundations of the relationship between the Congress and the executive."[115] As in the House, the resolution easily cleared the Senate, 70–12. Ford signed it into public law on October 13, 1975.

Conclusion

The executive and legislative branches walked out of step in the area of U.S.–Middle East foreign policy. After the Senate refused to allow the Ford administration to withhold weapons from Israel, the administration felt obligated to buy the Sinai II agreement. In order to preserve the agreement between Israel and Egypt, Kissinger forced Congress to acquiesce to the open-ended executive agreements with Israel. As a result, the United States and Israel formalized the establishment of an uneasy alliance in the fall of 1975, which would come to define U.S.-Israel relations in the decades to follow.

Congress reserved the right to revise the executive agreements by way of its appropriations power but essentially approved of the aid packages to Israel and Egypt by allocating significant amounts to both countries in the next fiscal year. Representative Morgan and six other members of the House Committee on International Affairs traveled to the Middle East in January 1976, and the group found a sincere desire for peace in Egypt and Israel.[116] Strong support for Israel in the House led to passage of the 1976 International Security Assistance Act, which included aid for Israel, despite congressional efforts to limit foreign military aid. According to Marvin Feuerwerger, "all members who asserted that they voted for the bill because of the Sinai agreement claimed to have done so because they believed it fostered regional peace." Also important, "the feeling of the congressional leadership concerning the importance of aid to Israel for the security of the foreign aid program was reflected in the words of one leader who—despite his own private misgivings about the level of assistance pledged to Israel—promised to fight for that assistance: 'We've got to pass a foreign aid bill, and money for Israel is instrumental in helping get that bill passed.'"[117] Tip O'Neill recognized the importance of House support for Israel. He offered a floor amendment to the 1976 Second Concurrent Budget Resolution that included "funding for Tennessee Valley Authority, as well as job and education programs," along with the "funding required to implement the Sinai agreement and carry out Middle East aid programs." The amendment narrowly passed, thanks to strong liberal support, and the budget resolution passed, too. O'Neill cleverly took advantage of legislative support for Israel as a means to get funding for domestic programs that otherwise, in all likelihood, would not have cleared the House.[118]

While the president has the right to enter into executive agreements, Congress still possesses the ability to potentially veto that action on a case-by-case basis. (This would become evident in the Iran Nuclear Agreement Act of 2015.) Even if the president promises a certain amount of aid to a country, Congress must still "authorize" the agreement through direct legislation or appropriations the following year. Otherwise, Congress can effectively veto the agreement by denying aid. Congress possessed the right to challenge or even undo the executive agreements connected to Sinai II through its appropriations power. But it never did.

Despite its successful efforts to restrict the president's ability to wage war, Congress proved willing to allow for an empowered executive branch to unilaterally make significant national commitments since presidential policy favored Israel. Rather than challenge the White House on massive foreign-aid requests, which it had done with South Vietnam, Angola, and Turkey, or by way of the War Powers Act, Congress instead rewarded Israel and Egypt with combined aid packages totaling billions of dollars, all while the American economy sank further into a severe recession. Sinai II represented a new era in U.S. foreign policy in that Congress cut back on virtually all foreign aid except that to the Middle East, which portended the volatility and importance of the region for the foreseeable future.

From the perspective of the executive branch, Sinai II must have been bittersweet. On the one hand, Ford and Kissinger managed to negotiate another step between Israel and Egypt, the prospects of which had seemed quite dim the previous March. In doing so, the administration managed to avert another war in the Middle East and preserve the American position vis-à-vis the Soviet Union. President Ford, never known for his foreign-policy adroitness, once remarked that Sinai II was "a great achievement—one of the most historic in this decade and perhaps in this century."[119]

But on the other hand, Congress took over five weeks to permit U.S. technicians in the Sinai and refused to explicitly endorse the far-reaching secret agreements. On top of that, the congressional approval of technicians included a possible legislative veto through a concurrent resolution similar to the War Powers Act. When talking to Ford about Congress and Sinai II, Kissinger complained, "What they are doing to the Sinai agreement is unbelievable. It is the greatest achievement since the opening to China and all that is happening is they are pissing all over it."[120] While Ford, and to a lesser extent Kissinger, overstated the significance of Sinai II, one can understand why Kissinger felt Congress had watered down the achievement.

Congress did not abridge the core elements of Sinai II, though. As in the years before and the years to come, support for Israel proved to be the key element to congressional participation in Middle East affairs. Sinai II did in fact lead to another peace agreement, though not the one hoped for by either the executive or legislative branch. Instead of a comprehensive peace, the Arab-Israel peace process evolved into a bilateral peace agreement between Israel and Egypt at Camp David a few years later, while the main issues of the conflict (Palestinians and borders) persisted.

Conclusion

A Separate Peace

Following the secret agreements of Sinai II, the executive branch did not possess the necessary leverage to pressure Israel into a broader peace plan. Billion-dollar weapons sales had become a matter of fact, regardless of Israel's willingness to compromise in peace discussions and return the occupied territories, especially the West Bank.

But President Jimmy Carter did manage to negotiate a landmark peace agreement between Israel and Egypt, an impressive achievement that brought peace to two warring states. Despite its importance, however, scholarship has been critical of the Camp David Accords, pointing out that Carter lacked the ability to compel Israel into making larger concessions concerning the West Bank and the Palestinians and instead had to settle for a separate peace between Israel and Egypt. Scholars emphasize the significance of Congress, domestic politics, as well as Carter's decision to skirt the issue of Palestinian self-determination.[1]

Carter, similar to the presidents before him, tried to chart an evenhanded course. He told Egyptian Foreign Minister Ismail Fahmy in September 1977, "I have no embarrassment in saying that we are even-handed. I have made this clear. Some of my positions have been unpopular in Israel, but I am very eager for an agreement."[2]

Congress continued to push for enormous arms sales to Israel. A November 1976 transition paper informed the president-elect of the strong support for Israel in the Senate Foreign Relations Committee and House International Relations Committee. Carter expected the Senate committee to ask for a presidential commitment to "fund fully Israel's arms purchases" and "to avoid the imposition of a settlement on the Israelis," and the House committee to "press for maximum funding of Israel's arms purchases."[3] Carter got what he expected. Based on solid bipartisan support for Israel, the two committees, and in fact both Houses of Congress, broadly supported arms sales to Israel without an imposed settlement.

President Carter, who pledged to restrict U.S. weapons sales abroad, followed the trend established by previous presidents and used arms agreements as inducements for peace. In September 1978, he arranged for Israeli and Egyptian officials to meet at Camp David for peace talks. Israeli Prime Minister Menachem Begin and Egyptian President Anwar Sadat agreed to a plan for peace between their two countries. With the Camp David Accords, U.S. military aid to Israel reached $4 billion in 1979, with $1 billion initially budgeted and another $3 billion connected to the peace agreement. A memo from William Quandt, who headed the Middle East Desk at the National Security Council, to National Security Advisor Zbigniew Brzezinski stated that "the total of resources (goods and services) which we will transfer to Egypt and Israel over the next three years will be almost $13 billion, of which over $3.5 billion will be financed directly by the U.S. taxpayer."[4] In addition to peace with Israel, Egypt entered into an expanded security relationship with the United States that included weapons sales and services.

But the Palestinians, due to maneuvering by Begin, were denied a state or political autonomy. A second agreement negotiated at Camp David, not linked to the Israel-Egypt peace treaty, was a "Framework for Peace in the Middle East." The American team ultimately agreed to eliminate explicit language regarding Israeli withdrawal from the West Bank and Gaza and, according to Quandt, "artfully obstructed" future negotiations involving the Palestinians.[5] The framework stipulated that a five-year transition administration would be formed by Israel, Egypt, and Jordan, and that Palestinians in the West Bank and Gaza might participate in the Egyptian and Jordanian delegations. The framework itself depended on voluntary Palestinian involvement in an election process that sidestepped any meaningful kind of Palestinian autonomy, and only in the third year would discussions move onto the final status of the West Bank and Gaza. In short, the framework proved to be an insult to the Palestinians, generally ignored Syria, the Golan Heights, and Jerusalem, and was negotiated apart from the Israel-Egypt peace agreement.

Carter felt he needed to get some kind of agreement—both to avoid war and in order to bolster his own political standing. He could not extract any meaningful compromise from Begin, so he compelled Sadat to abandon the larger Arab cause for Egypt's future.

Carter enjoyed widespread domestic acclaim for Camp David. Members of Congress and the media lauded the president's accomplishment. Following the summit, a Gallup poll showed that Carter's approval rating had jumped from 45 percent to 56 percent. Carter remembered a meeting with American Jewish Zionist leadership as being "delightful, full of fun and good cheer, and we welcomed it because it was so rare."[6] But according to Quandt, who participated in the Camp David talks, domestic advisers—not his foreign policy advisers—counseled Carter to leave Camp David with a success, suggesting that the president's domestic position outweighed his foreign-policy goals.[7]

Rather than pave the way for a broader peace in the region, Camp David ensured the continuation of conflict for future decades. Carter, and most U.S. officials, were prepared to live with a separate peace and let the other problems persist. The Arab-Israeli conflict mattered only as much as it affected U.S. energy concerns, the Cold War, and American hegemony in the region. Peace between Israel and Egypt ensured enough stability to continue to have access to Middle Eastern oil and to keep the Soviets at bay. The United States could remain the dominant power in the region and do so with much stronger bilateral relations with Israel and with Egypt.

Carter tried unsuccessfully to salvage a comprehensive peace in the aftermath of the September 1978 talks at Camp David. But the White House had burned bridges with congressional leadership and American Jewish Zionist leadership over a package arms deal involving Israel, Egypt, and Saudi Arabia several months before Camp David.[8] According to Steven Spiegel, that incident "severely damaged the president's Jewish support," and Carter "never fully recovered politically from this episode."[9] Carter had no influential domestic friends to support his cause, and his repeated calls for Israeli compromises on territory and Palestinians fell on deaf ears. On November 8, Carter confided to his diary, "It's obvious the Israelis want a separate treaty with Egypt, to keep the West Bank and Gaza, [and] to get as much money as possible from us."[10] Brzezinski figured, "Begin feels he can get away with almost anything."[11]

At a meeting in Baghdad that November, the Arab League denounced the Camp David Accords. The members of the League (minus Egypt, which did not attend) voted to punish Egypt if it actually signed the peace agreement with Israel: they pledged to move the Arab League headquarters away from Cairo, suspend Egypt from the League, and boycott Egyptian companies that did business with Israel.[12] Neither Saudi Arabia nor Jordan—the two closest Arab friends of the United States—supported the accords. Palestinians, of course, rejected them.[13]

Three months after Camp David, Israel started to build more settlements in the West Bank, which made future negotiations involving Palestinians much more difficult. The Carter team believed that Begin had agreed at Camp David to a long-term freeze on settlement building. But the Israeli team argued that the agreed-to freeze would last only three months. Spiegel states, "Carter subsequently blamed Begin's 'broken promise' for the Jordanian and Saudi refusal to back Camp David."[14]

Sadat felt even more isolated and demanded a stronger linkage to the Palestinians before signing a peace agreement with Israel. But the Israelis balked, and the Americans could do nothing. Then in December, Sadat threatened to not exchange ambassadors with Israel until there was some movement toward Palestinian autonomy in Gaza. But Israel balked at this proposal, too. Returning from a meeting in Jerusalem, an American senior official blamed Israel for obstructionism. The situation seemed much as it had in March 1975, but this time the administration did not "reassess" U.S.–Middle East policy. Nevertheless, according to Spiegel, "Leading American Jews and their allies attacked the administration's operating style in statements, articles, and meetings."[15] The administration acquiesced to Israel's insistence that peace with Egypt would not be linked in any meaningful way to the Palestinians.

As Israel and Egypt worked to hammer out the final details of a peace treaty acceptable to both sides, the Middle East appeared combustible. The Iranian Revolution reached a tipping point, and the shah was forced to flee Iran in January 1979. The overthrow of the shah marked the end of the U.S.-Iran relationship, which had served as a bedrock of American Middle East foreign policy for nearly three decades. OPEC raised prices by 14.5 percent, which reminded U.S. officials of the importance of the Saudi relationship and the need to avoid another embargo.[16] A civil war continued to rage in Lebanon, exacerbated by the ongoing plight of the stateless Palestinians. In February 1979, war broke out between North and South Yemen. That same month, Saudi Crown Prince Fahd refused to visit Washington for fear of being identified with the United States.[17] Peace between Israel and Egypt became even more important as U.S. foreign policy in the Middle East unraveled.

Carter also had to worry about his reelection campaign. In the 1978 midterms, Democrats lost fifteen seats in the House and three seats in the Senate, despite the Democratic president's accomplishment at Camp David. While they were still in control of both the House and Senate, 1980 promised to be a challenging year for Democrats. Ed Sanders noted in early February 1979, "Support for us in the Jewish community at the moment is minimal," and he urged Carter to appeal to the Democratic allegiance of many American Jews in preparation for the 1980 elections.[18] To push Israel over Palestinian self-determination would have threatened Carter's chances of reelection. According to Quandt, during a meeting on February 19, "Carter stated clearly that he did not want a public confrontation with Israel."[19]

In late March, Begin and Sadat signed an Israel-Egypt peace treaty on the White House lawn, witnessed by Carter. The Arab League, true to its word, suspended Egypt and moved its headquarters from Cairo to Tunis. Saudi Arabia resented the American willingness to sacrifice the Palestinians for a separate peace and feared a weakening of American resolve after the inability of the United States to save the shah (and South Vietnam). American relations with Jordan "deteriorated to their lowest point" due to Hussein's refusal to join peace talks.[20] The peace process proved to be a battle between Israel and the United States as much as between Israel and Arab states. Israel had won easily, which left U.S.-Arab relations in miserably poor shape.

The United States could pressure no one other than Anwar Sadat. Sadat needed the United States; both his domestic and international plans depended on a close relationship. The Carter administration could not force Begin to soften his stance, especially with the amounts of U.S. weapons being sold to Israel. Nor could the administration convince Arafat to recognize Israel or accept U.N. Resolution 242, and no other Palestinian representative than the PLO could be found. Jordan preferred to remain aloof of peace negotiations. Syria, for its part, refused to take another partial step toward accord with Israel. The toppling of the shah's regime in Iran further complicated energy concerns and U.S. policy in the Middle East, which pointed to the need for a closer relationship with Saudi Arabia and another regional power like Egypt. For the United States, at least in the short term, a separate peace was far better than the possibility of another war and all that would go with it.

The other elements of the conflict, including the Palestinians, simply did not matter that much to many U.S. officials.

Sadat tried to pursue peace with Israel and concomitantly assure the Arab states that Egypt would continue to fight for Palestinian rights and the 1967 borders. Economic concerns proved to be most important. According to Sadat, the Egyptian government "had, with crass stupidity, copied the Soviet pattern of socialism, although we lacked the necessary resources, technical capabilities, and capital."[21] The constant drain on an ill-conceived economic structure was obviously defense spending. As long as Israel remained in the Sinai, the Egyptian military had to be heavily funded for the possibility of war. The wars in 1967 and 1973 showed that surprise was to the aggressor's advantage, so the potential defender needed to be prepared. But if Sadat could somehow bring peace to Egypt, he would no longer need to allocate excessive funding for defense purposes. Sadat could then work to fix an economy that, five days before the October War, "had fallen below zero."[22] Similar to Carter, Sadat believed he could not leave Camp David in September 1978 without an agreement, even though he threatened to do exactly that. Sadat felt trapped into signing an agreement that left an abyss between Egypt's national achievements and its view of itself as leader of the Arab world.

Sadat paid a high price for making a separate peace with Israel, while the Palestinian question—intentionally avoided by Kissinger—remained unanswered at Camp David. Seen as willing to sacrifice the larger Arab cause, Egypt was expelled from the Arab League from 1979 to 1989, and Sadat was assassinated by the terrorist group Egyptian Islamic Jihad in October 1981. While Israel and Egypt have managed to avoid any conflicts after agreeing to peace, the slow pace of the peace process after the Camp David Accords led directly to the First Intifada (1987–1993), and the failure to build on peaceful measures in the 1990s, which culminated again at Camp David, led to the Second Intifada (2000–2005).

Camp David, for all its merits, reflects a mixed bag of successes and failures, and rather evenly so. On the one hand, while a disastrous agreement for the Palestinians and Syria, Camp David secured peace between two warring countries that stabilized part of a volatile region. Major conflicts in 1956, 1967, 1969–1970, and 1973 all involved Israel and Egypt. Since Camp David, the two have maintained a cold peace, and the United States has continued to rely on both countries as regional allies. The Camp David Accords strengthened economic and security ties between the United States and Israel and further enabled the United States to sell massive amounts of weapons to Egypt, which completed the Soviet removal from that country and solidified the U.S.-Egypt relationship.

But on the other hand, while a significant agreement for Israel, Egypt, and the United States, Camp David guaranteed that the core issues of the conflict would remain unaddressed, which furthered an existing resentment within the Arab world for U.S. foreign policy. With Egypt no longer at war with Israel, and with Israel receiving a steady stream of the world's most technologically sophisticated weapons, the peace process ground to a halt after Camp David. Israel took war to the PLO in Lebanon in the hopes of extinguishing the Palestinian nationalist movement, which did not work. Only in the 1990s, after the end of the Cold War, a Palestinian uprising (intifada), and the successful U.S.-led war against Iraq, would the peace process start again, only to falter in 2000, ironically at Camp David. Israel has managed to hold onto the West Bank and deny a Palestinian state from forming, while Hamas and Hezbollah call for the destruction of Israel. As Nasser and other Arab leaders learned in 1967 (and hopefully these organizations will soon realize), such violent rhetoric will always be met by American pledges of allegiance to Israel. That is the essence of the special relationship. An attack that threatens Israel's existence would be like an attack on the United States, and the response would be similar.

By the time of the signing of the Israel-Egypt peace agreement in 1979, the United States could boast impressive achievements in the region: it had successfully contained communism, offset the power of the oil weapon through its relationship with Saudi Arabia and energy diversification, strengthened ties with Egypt, and established an enduring relationship with Israel. But this was all accomplished at the expense of Arab demands, like the return of all lands taken by Israel in 1967 and Palestinian grievances, and at the consequence of widespread dissatisfaction in the Arab world, which contributed to a pervasive anti-Americanism that fueled radicalism in the region and beyond. The United States became enmeshed in the Middle East during the 1970s, with both partial achievements and partial failures, and in ways that plague us up to the present day.

Conclusion

This work aims to correct, at least in part, the imbalance in scholarship that devotes near-exclusive attention to presidential policies and downplays the influence of the legislative branch on U.S.–Middle East relations. When issues involve Israel, and with the activities of the Israel lobby, Congress becomes a major player in U.S. foreign policy. Most Americans do not realize how important Congress is in the relationship between the United States and Israel.

Domestic politics and the legislative body always affect the foreign policy of a democracy. But in the case of U.S.-Israel relations, focusing on the interplay of domestic and foreign politics and extrapolating the impact of Congress on U.S. foreign policy have particular relevance. The changes in U.S.-Israel relations between 1967 and 1975 had a long-lasting impact on U.S.–Middle East relations and U.S. foreign relations more broadly. Certainly, international developments, as in Vietnam and elsewhere, impacted U.S. relations with the Middle East. Geopolitical concerns and pursuit of the national interest obviously drove foreign-policy considerations, and a strong Israel—the main noncommunist, pro–United States stalwart in the Middle East—certainly benefited the U.S. position in the Cold War. But the perception of U.S. national security interests in the Middle East, by high-ranking political leaders in both the executive and legislative branches, played out in a domestic setting that witnessed an unusually active Congress. While the president leads in foreign affairs, Congress holds the power to demand participation when it sees fit. And by focusing on domestic politics and the activities of U.S. officials, people—more than abstract conceptions of power—drive the historical narrative. The situation clearly illustrates that domestic politics and Congress always matter to some degree for U.S. foreign relations, and did particularly during the 1970s.

Rather than presidents' willfully seeking a closer relationship with Israel, instead, Congress pressured increasingly weak presidencies to move closer to Israel. Presidents Johnson, Nixon, Ford, and Carter all tried to maintain an evenhanded policy in the Middle East. Johnson, who felt strong basic sympathies with Israel, also agonized over selling offensive weapons and sought to prevent a strategic relationship from forming. Nixon tried to mend relations with Arab states and often vented his frustrations about Israel for its tough stance in peace negotiations. In May 1974, Nixon went so far as to threaten Prime Minister Meir with no further weapons sales if Israel did not demonstrate more of a willingness to compromise. Ford actually did freeze military aid to the Middle East in the spring of 1975, only to be thwarted by the actions of the Senate. The Senate letter of May 1975 not-too-subtly indicated that the Senate would reject any presidential foreign-aid request that did not arm Israel to Congress's satisfaction. Like all presidents, Ford had to consider how decisions regarding Israel would affect his ability to conduct U.S. foreign policy in other areas. Carter seemed determined to battle the Israel lobby over weapons sales to the region and in the process alienated American Jewish Zionists and legislators—the very base of support he needed in order to pressure Israel into a comprehensive peace agreement. But Carter's inability to facilitate a lasting regional peace was hurt as much by Sinai II as by his own clumsiness in foreign affairs.

The U.S. Congress, not the presidency, pushed for a decidedly pro-Israel foreign policy. The aforementioned presidents tried to keep Israel at arm's length. But an activist Congress, empowered by the Vietnam War and increasingly influenced by the Israel lobby, redirected presidential initiatives from evenhandedness and toward an uneasy alliance with Israel that included billion-dollar weapons sales regardless of movement in the peace process. Presidents, Congress, and Israeli officials all recognized that the only way the United States could force Israel to go along with presidential efforts to forge a comprehensive peace was by withholding weapons. Consecutive administrations tried to pressure Israel to leave the occupied territories, primarily by threatening to restrict weapons sales. But Congress would not have it. Congress ensured that Israel would receive unprecedented levels of American-made weaponry and thereby empowered Israel to dominate regional diplomacy. At the end of the day, U.S. presidents basically threw up their hands and realized that U.S. policy would become more pro-Israel, like it or not, and that going with that development was the path of least resistance.

Between 1967 and 1980, the power of the presidency, relative to Congress, certainly ebbed. The embattled Johnson chose to not run for the office in 1968. Richard Nixon, at the peak of step-by-step diplomacy, had to resign in 1974. If one considers a counterfactual—if Watergate had never happened and Nixon had carried out a powerful second term—one has to imagine that Richard Nixon would have made Israel play ball according to the rules of the U.S. president. Gerald Ford was never elected on a presidential ticket and served as a caretaker president. Jimmy Carter won his election on being a Washington outsider and proved unable to advance a coherent foreign policy. Only with Ronald Reagan's election in 1980 did the power of the presidency rebound. But even then, Reagan still had to do battle with Congress over U.S. foreign policy, most notably with the Boland Amendments and Iran-Contra.

Presidential weakness furthered the influence of Congress on U.S.-Israel relations and the peace process. Legislators used a combination of policy initiatives and displays of public support to challenge the White House when it tried to pressure Israel by threatening to withhold weapons. The congressional uproar over military sales began during Johnson's presidency and escalated over the next decade. Congress advanced a pro-Israel position that was probably more in line with U.S. popular opinion at this time than the White House's insistence on an evenhanded regional policy, which points to the importance of domestic politics. Legislators perpetuated a narrative that military aid to Israel should be given generously so that Israel would feel strong enough to negotiate peace. This proved to be an unwise policy as Israel used American arms to seek peace with only Egypt, and as a way to remain in the West Bank. Strategically, arming Israel helped to contain communism in the Middle East, a region that took on greater importance in light of the situation in East Asia. But arming Israel also provided convenient ammunition to Islamic fundamentalists, which would complicate U.S. foreign policy in the Middle East for decades to follow. A paradox emerged: Congress became involved in foreign relations to restrain presidential excesses and then pushed hard for the president to arm Israel excessively.

The crucial period of executive-legislative tension came during the Ford presidency, which, in relation to Congress, was the weakest of the Cold War. Domestically and internationally, the White House lacked trust and prestige. For the United States, step-by-step diplomacy aimed for improved relations with the Arab world and a peace program to allow Israel to eventually remove itself from the occupied territories. Kissinger, while an ardent supporter of Israel, still wanted it to leave the vast majority of territories taken in 1967; he also recognized the importance of improved Arab relations with the United States and with Israel. But the escalation of U.S. political and military support for Israel undermined these objectives. The Ford administration believed it needed another interim agreement between Israel and Egypt in 1975 to keep the struggling peace process alive and to bring Cairo closer to Washington. Most important, the tenuous cease-fire from the 1973 war seemed likely to come undone without another agreement, which would mean another war. And with another war came the possibility of superpower confrontation and almost certainly another crippling oil embargo that could have severely weakened the integrity of Western economies. Ford could not withhold weapons sales to Israel at a pivotal moment, even if that meant the end of a comprehensive peace process. The administration had no choice but to do whatever was necessary to get an agreement between Egypt and Israel in order to avoid a war that carried with it the possibility of catastrophic consequences.

Why did the president not ignore Congress and just withhold weapons from Israel anyway? For one thing, the Middle East is not the only foreign-policy concern of the United States. The president must work with Congress on a host of issues beyond the Middle East and has to consider the possible political consequences of challenging Israel. This became especially true in the context of the Vietnam War and its aftermath—the president is not an imperial ruler but an elected representative in a democracy. In May 1975, the Senate reminded Ford that his general foreign-aid request required congressional approval, and that approval hinged on the continuation of arms for Israel. Political consequences can be felt at the ballot boxes too. The president must keep in mind both reelection and midterm elections, which can sway the political makeup of Congress. Party politics matter, and Israel has managed to cultivate broad bipartisan support in the United States. Even though presidents preferred to follow an evenhanded policy in the Middle East, Congress made that politically unwise and practically impossible. Presidents proved willing to accept low-level conflict so long as it did not compromise other U.S. interests in the region. And if that meant billion-dollar weapons sales and the militarization of the region, then so be it.

Israel was in no hurry to reach another agreement with Egypt, and unable to withhold weapons sales, the Ford administration instead had to buy Sinai II and steer the peace process down a narrow path that culminated at Camp David. In order to get Israel to agree to another step with Egypt in September 1975 the White House had to enter into several far-reaching executive agreements with Israel, and Congress felt obligated to pass a resolution that indirectly authorized the agreements. In effect, U.S. military aid to Israel became detached from any movement in the peace process, which altered Johnson's policy of arming Israel in order to generate movement toward a broad peace.

The executive agreements connected to Sinai II, which have been underappreciated and understudied, represent a benchmark in U.S.-Israel relations that require a rethinking of the U.S.-Israel narrative. Based on material aid alone—regardless of the important politically oriented executive agreements, which certainly impacted the peace process—the U.S.-Israel relationship entered into a new period as Sinai II established a much higher baseline for future aid packages. (The emergency aid related to the 1973 war was case-specific and did not constitute an annual change in U.S. assistance to Israel.

In the next fiscal year, U.S. military support dipped back down to $300 million.) Since the Sinai II agreement, annual U.S. military aid to Israel has never fallen below $1 billion. Economic aid, which also rose significantly, remained high until the 2000s. In addition, U.S. assistance after Sinai II became one-half loans and one-half grants, rather than almost exclusively loans. Over time, more and more U.S. assistance would take the form of grants. Unable to pressure Israel, U.S. policymakers instead went all in on the side of Israel.

U.S. and Israeli officials understood that the executive agreements were extraordinarily important. Numerous legislators voiced serious reservations with Sinai II because of the U.S. pledges that constituted a marked change in the relationship between the United States and Israel. According to Amos Eiran, Israel would not have entered into another agreement with Egypt if not for the American commitments to Israel. Israeli officials no longer had to fight for U.S. support—they could count on it. American officials started to treat Israelis as close friends rather than bazaar hagglers, just as Ephraim Evron requested of the Johnson administration in 1967.

The executive agreements did not come out of nowhere; they came after several years of organized and intensive Israeli efforts to gain greater access to U.S. weapons and to lessen political pressure to leave the occupied territories. Thus, the agreements represent the culmination of a process. After Sinai II, Israel managed to take Egypt out of the larger Arab war against Israel, which significantly diminished the possibility of another Arab attack. This enabled Israel to follow a path that involved indefinite occupation of the West Bank and the denial of a Palestinian state from forming.

When Gerald Ford left Washington in early 1977, he bequeathed to Jimmy Carter a powerful informal alliance between the United States and Israel that would bedevil Carter and his administration, just as it did those of Nixon and Ford, when pushing for peace agreements. According to Morris Amitay, executive director of AIPAC from 1974 to 1980, Congress continued to play a crucial role during the Carter years and the search for peace in the Middle East. Following the death of Carter's Secretary of State Cyrus Vance in 2002, Amitay commented that Israeli activists had not often interacted with Vance. According to Amitay, "the watchword then was to use Congress to influence policy."[23]

Given President Donald Trump's decision in May 2018 to undo Barack Obama's executive agreement with Iran regarding the Iranian nuclear program, one might be tempted to think that an executive agreement is easy to revoke. It is not. An executive agreement is considered to be interchangeable with a treaty, which is the most binding American international commitment. Revoking an executive agreement runs the risk of weakening American credibility abroad and generating domestic backlash. In the case of Sinai II, the Ford administration's executive agreements with Israel came only months after the fall of Saigon. Neither Ford nor his successor, Jimmy Carter, could reverse an American agreement with Israel and save face in the international community during the Cold War. How could any ally trust the United States after it first abandoned South Vietnam and then reneged on an agreement with Israel? American credibility was already soiled because of Vietnam; it would have been ruined by rescinding the executive agreements with Israel. Moreover, given Israel's ability to catalyze broad support in Congress and among the American public, it would have been political suicide for Carter to ignore or repeal the executive agreements.

Presidents may not like previous executive agreements, but almost always they try to honor them. Jimmy Carter did not like the Sinai II executive agreements, but he still upheld them. However, he did try to create wiggle room for his own diplomatic initiatives. He tried to issue a joint communiqué with the Soviet Union about the peace process in 1977. But that was denounced by legislators, Israeli officials, and American Jewish Zionists, for one, because it reintroduced the USSR into the peace process, and two, because it violated Ford's agreement to not take any steps without coordinating with Israel. Carter agreed to not recognize the PLO, but he still developed backchannel dialogue with PLO officials. Carter agreed to the weapons arrangement connected to Sinai II, but he also used sales to Israel as a way to confront the power of the Israel lobby and bully through Congress a package agreement that included controversial weapons for Saudi Arabia. Carter did not agree with the Ford administration's decision about U.S.-Israel relations, and his administration worked to redirect U.S. foreign policy with respect to the peace process, but Carter still honored and worked within the broad parameters of the previous administration's executive agreements. And with Camp David, Carter also discovered the challenges in trying to get Israel on board with American foreign policy without significant political and material commitments.

This work highlights the important agency of non-U.S. actors in the making of foreign policy, which fits into a developing trend in historiography concerned with non-U.S. agency.[24] Israeli officials connected to the Israeli embassy in Washington (especially Simcha Dinitz) built upon existing institutional relations in the U.S. capital, which allowed Israeli officials to meet with and influence members of both branches of government, especially the legislative branch. Dinitz played a heretofore unnoticed role in the reassessment period. While the divided Israeli cabinet of Yitzhak Rabin, Shimon Peres, and Yigal Allon all jockeyed for power, the former foreign minister and longtime politician Dinitz used the opportunity to take the lead in shaping Israel's relations with the United States from a position far removed from Jerusalem, and at a particularly important time.

This work also sheds more light on how a foreign government can exercise influence on the U.S. political system. Pro-Israel lobbying managed to generate considerable pressure on legislators to mobilize a congressional defense against the president's desire to follow a balanced policy in the Middle East. In order to better address the impact of pro-Israel lobbying, it requires a more evenhanded assessment of how and why such lobbying begets the results it does. In the case of Israel, the embassy in Washington, D.C. spearheaded an effort to reverse Ford's reassessment, restart foreign aid, and lessen U.S. political pressure on Israel, and Israeli officials worked closely with American Jewish Zionist leadership to advance that effort. Discussions about the influence of the Israel lobby in the United States should consider the involvement of the State of Israel and its embassy in Washington, D.C. in shaping lobbying efforts by American Jewish Zionists.

But it was not simply an Israeli tail wagging the American dog. U.S. legislators used Israel to their advantage, too. Scoop Jackson always wanted to be president, and he made calculated political decisions in his support for Israel, especially regarding weapons sales and the emigration of Soviet Jews. He tried to shape a presidential campaign around a pro-labor and traditional Democratic position on domestic issues, with a strong Cold War and pro-Israel foreign policy. Jackson realized the potential political advantages of endearing himself to the American Jewish community, and as late as October 1975, he was still thought to be the frontrunner for the Democratic nomination for the 1976 presidential election. And not just Jackson—Hubert Humphrey, Stuart Symington, Jacob Javits, Abe Ribicoff—the list goes on. Legislators are happy to advance a pro-Israel position, regardless of the impact on the Middle East or other U.S. interests, because they are generally concerned with representing their constituencies and getting reelected. Moreover, Congress used Israel as a means to play a larger role in directing U.S. foreign policy during a period of increased legislative assertiveness. The Jackson-Vanik amendment, in particular, used the plight of Soviet Jews as an opportunity to make a direct attack on the Nixon administration's policy of détente. In 1976, Tip O'Neill used congressional support for Israel to secure funding for liberal domestic projects.

Yet one has to wonder, why such extreme support? Assistance for Israel is one thing, but billion-dollar military aid and international protection for the occupation of Arab lands are entirely different. Military aid and weapons sales came about rather naturally due to the special relationship and did not spring up independently from it. But *that much* military aid? Is any amount of military aid an expression of the special relationship? Is any amount of military aid an expression of a strategic alliance? At what point does U.S. support damage other U.S. interests, as well as the pursuit of peace? That is the crux of the matter. U.S. military aid for Israel moved well beyond a moral commitment to Israel's survival or any strategic rationale and instead provided the ammunition for an indefinite occupation of certain Arab lands. Israel managed to have its cake and eat it, too—billion-dollar military assistance from the United States without pressure to leave the territories. The U.S. government, regardless of congressional insistence, was going to sell weapons to Israel. But the extent of weapons sales that ballooned during this period, and often the timing of such sales, undercut peace discussions. And Congress, more than the executive branch, was responsible.

One important reason for such overwhelming support is that Congress does *not* conduct the foreign relations of the United States. Congressional officials can use the State of Israel to further their own domestic agendas and do so without the responsibility of having to try to facilitate peaceful relations between Arabs and Israelis. The president must try to be balanced in foreign affairs to promote international stability and advance the national interest; legislators need not be balanced. They can stump for lopsided weapons sales to Israel without having to actually conduct peace negotiations.

Regarding Congress and foreign policy, other fundamental problems persist. Legislators do not have access to privileged information regarding foreign-policy issues and, in general, seem to not understand regional nuances. Legislators often lack the personal or institutional preparation to become intricately involved in foreign policy. The congressional assertiveness of the late 1960s and the 1970s grew out of necessity, due to Vietnam and the excesses of the Imperial Presidency. In the process, legislators forayed into an area in which many lacked experience—foreign policy. Many congressional officials probably misread the diplomatic environment and undertook actions that happened to sever U.S. military aid to Israel from any movement in the peace process. (Take, for example, George McGovern's decision to sign the May 1975 letter. He subsequently stated that Israel must return the occupied territories and accept Palestinian self-determination.) Congress denied the president the necessary leverage—the ability to withhold weapons—to pressure Israel into being more forthcoming in peace negotiations. If he tried, Congress would threaten to kill the foreign-aid request in order to change the president's behavior.

The United States has continually armed both Arabs and Israelis while proving unable to lead the peace process to a satisfactory conclusion, and at times weapons sales and peace discussions take place simultaneously. That, naturally, has necessitated more diplomacy and more weapons sales, with results that continue the ongoing cycle.

A seventh-grade social studies class from Wahiawa, Hawai'i, made a similar observation in a March 1975 letter to Hawai'i's Republican senator Hiram Fong. The students perceptively asked their senator why the United States tried to pursue diplomacy and at the same time trained Israeli and Arab soldiers how to use American-made weapons. The class wondered, "Why are we doing this? On the one hand we are sending Kissinger to the Middle East to help bring peace and on the other we are teaching both sides how to fire missiles."[25] From the pencils of babes.

The United States played Cold War politics while trying to mediate a regional dispute, all while taking a pro-Israel position. The situation was bound to be problematic for all parties involved.

Rather than use weapons as inducements for peace, U.S. officials could have decided to withhold weapons sales from Israel and force it to accept a settlement that included the demarcation of final borders and that addressed Palestinian grievances, and in a way that intentionally avoided PLO participation. Quite certainly, the PLO enjoyed substantial support in the occupied territories, from Arab governments, and even in the international arena. But U.S. officials could have denied weapons sales to Israel until it proved willing to relinquish the West Bank and East Jerusalem to King Hussein. If Jordan proved able to secure an agreement that returned such important territories for some type of Palestinian state or legitimate autonomy, the intransigence of the PLO would have been out of step with broad popular opinion, thereby undercutting its political viability. U.S. military aid empowered Israel to the point that it felt able to refuse to return these territories, which strengthened the PLO's uncompromising position and added to its popular appeal. The proliferation of weapons sales to Israel undermined the peace process as much as the absence of PLO participation. As in East Asia, U.S. officials sought to use a preponderance of American military power in the Middle East to bring about a favorable situation. In neither case did the effort work well.

Now, in the post–Cold War international environment, titanic levels of U.S. military aid to Israel are not really justifiable on national-security grounds (or any grounds) and are counterproductive. The U.S. policy of arming Israel to the teeth, which started in the 1970s, set up a dynamic that propelled future U.S. arms sales to Israel into the post–Cold War era, long after the Cold War justification melted away. At this point, though, Israel can secure weapons from a collection of suppliers, including Russia and China, along with its own weapons manufacturing base that has received substantial funding from the United States. But it does not need to. Beginning in 2019, the United States government has agreed to grant Israel nearly $4 billion of military aid per year over the next ten years.

In conclusion, between 1967 and 1975, the United States and Israel together laid the foundation for an uneasy alliance. Beginning with the policy established by President Johnson in 1967, American officials decided to support Israel's occupation, which to a great extent exists still today, in order to pressure Arab states to finally make peace with Israel. Until that time, American arms would need to flow to Israel, regardless of the impact on peace discussions or U.S.-Arab relations. The special and strategic elements remained a part of U.S.-Israel relations, but U.S.-Arab relations suffered from an unspoken American commitment to an indefinite occupation of Arab lands and a willingness to disallow a Palestinian state from coming into existence. Presidents have encouraged Israel to return territories and move to a two-state solution, but they lack the ability to pressure Israel to do something it perceives to be against its interests. Israelis need only to point to ongoing calls by Palestinian leadership for Israel's destruction to defend its continued occupation. Even still, Israel understands it needs U.S. support and wants to refrain from undertaking any measures that might lead to an erosion of that support. This all has created an uneasiness between the United States and Israel, tension between the United States and European states, and conflict between Congress and the Executive over U.S. support for Israel.

Although some criticisms of Israel's occupation certainly have merit, the situation also begs a crucial question that, to this day, lacks an adequate answer—with whom can Israel negotiate? Corruption has plagued Palestinian leadership, and the broader Palestinian negotiating position has been undermined by terrorist attacks and a refusal to openly and consistently accept the legitimacy of the State of Israel. Rockets from Hamas, border attacks from Hezbollah, and a potential nuclear threat from Iran only add to Israel's insecurity. The Middle East is a tough neighborhood, and optimism must be tempered by realism. However, a discussion about a possible negotiating partner for Israel also presumes that Israel has an honest intention to negotiate away occupied territories in order to secure peace. That scenario seems unlikely.

While Egypt and Israel agreed to peace in 1979, and Jordan and Israel in 1994, the core issues of the conflict persist and threaten both regional and international stability. Certainly, blame can be spread all around. It can be placed on Lyndon Johnson for his shortsightedness, the U.S. Congress for its overenthusiastic support of Israel, Israelis and Arabs for pushing maximalist demands, and the United States and the Soviet Union for dumping weapons into a volatile region for their own selfish purposes. Regardless of blame, the facts on the ground clearly reflect the failure of U.S. diplomacy to secure peace and justice in the Middle East.

Acknowledgments

I have worked on this project, off and on, for the past fifteen years. I am indebted to so many people who have helped me along the way—too numerous to remember, and I apologize for my forgetfulness.

At the University of Kansas, I had the pleasure of working with Theodore Wilson, who advised my master's work and guided me into the fascinating and turbulent arena of U.S.–Middle East relations. Thank you also to Donald Worster and Paul Kelton, along with Nicole Anslover, Brady DeSanti, Ryan Schumacher, David Trowbridge, and Sally Utech. A special thank you to Ethan Schmidt for his encouragement and support throughout my graduate career.

At West Virginia University, I owe a debt of gratitude to James Siekmeier, whose expertise, guidance, and friendship played a crucial role in the completion of my manuscript and in my development as a professional historian. Thanks to Elizabeth Fones-Wolf, who provided many suggestions and continues to be a wonderful mentor. Thank you also to Katherine Aaslestad, Ken Fones-Wolf, Joseph Hodge, Scott Crichlow, and Macabe Keliher for all of their encouragement and feedback, along with Zack Levenson for his research assistance. Thanks as well to all of my friends from Morgantown.

I have benefited from the help of some outstanding scholars at various institutions. At Vanderbilt University, Thomas Schwartz has been a constant source of support, advice, and encouragement, for which I am very grateful. At the University of Haifa, Zach Levey offered valuable thoughts for how to improve my manuscript, and he and his family made my wife and me feel so welcome in Haifa during the course of my fellowship. During my time in Israel I benefited from the advice of Abraham Ben-Zvi, Ehud Eiran, Gadi Heimann, and Rob Geist Pinfold. A special thanks to Amos Eiran for graciously agreeing to an interview. Thank you also to Jonathan Matthews for all of his assistance while researching at the Israel State Archives. Thank you to the University Press of Kentucky, two blind readers of my manuscript, and particularly, Sarah Olson, Natalie O'Neal, and Anthony Chiffolo, for their advice and editorial assistance. Thanks also to Craig Daigle, Salim Yaqub, Robert David Johnson, Douglas Little, Peter Hahn, Daniel Hummel, and Olivia Sohns.

I have received much institutional support to complete my project. The WVU History Department generously provided funding that enabled me to research at presidential libraries, archives holding papers of individual senators, and especially my trip to the Israel State Archives in Jerusalem. At WVU, I benefited from the support of the Arlen G. & Louise Stone Swiger Doctoral Fellowship, as well as the WVU Foundation Distinguished Doctoral Fellowship. The WVU Eberly College of Arts and Sciences also contributed funding for several research and conference trips. Thank you to the Schusterman Center at Brandeis University for granting me a faculty fellowship to participate in the Summer Institute for Israel Studies. I was fortunate to be a Fulbright Israel Postdoctoral Fellow 2018–2019, which provided me with financial and intellectual support in order to complete my research and writing, and I am very grateful for that as well. Many thanks to the United States-Israel Educational Foundation, and especially Noa Turgeman and everyone with Fulbright Israel. Thanks also to the University of Haifa for hosting and funding me as a Fulbright scholar. And thank you to the Gerald R. Ford Presidential Foundation, which funded two research trips to the Gerald R. Ford Presidential Library in Ann Arbor, Michigan.

Like all historical researchers, I am indebted to archivists. A special thanks to Geir Gundersen and Elizabeth Druga at the Gerald R. Ford Presidential Library. The archivists at the Ford Library are outstanding. A big thank you to Thomas Eisinger at the Center for Legislative Archives at the National Archives in Washington, D.C. Thank you also to the excellent archivists at the presidential libraries of Lyndon Johnson, Richard Nixon, and Jimmy Carter; at the Israel State Archives; and at the University of Washington, University of South Dakota, University of Arkansas, and Princeton University.

I would not be here without my parents, Myron and Janice Kolander. Their love and support have been central to my life and vital to my success. I am so proud of my son, Luke, and very thankful for the many ways that he brings joy to my life. I am overjoyed to have a beautiful baby girl, Elaine, who recently joined our family. Thank you to my siblings who always look out for their little brother—my brother, Kyle, and his family, Danielle, Will, and Olivia Kolander, and my sister, Kari, and her family, Eric and Finn McCrady. Thank you to the Runges, the Martens, the Newlands, the Poes, and Larry Eckert as well. My grandmothers, Elvera Eckert and Elaine Kolander, continue to shower me with kindness and wisdom, and for that I am fortunate. Thank you to my friends for your encouragement.

I am very blessed to have a beautiful wife who loves me so well—thank you, Eliza. In addition to unwavering support, Eliza also offered important assistance to my work, such as brainstorming ideas, reading and suggesting revisions to parts of the manuscript, making charts, and listening to me drone on and on about U.S.-Israel relations. And thanks to all the wonderful people I have forgotten to mention!

Last and most important, thanks and praise to GOD. I am so grateful for the multitude of wonderful blessings in my life, more grateful than I can adequately express.

Notes

Introduction

1. Redfa's story was the basis for the 1988 movie, *Steal the Sky.* Author Interview with Amos Eiran, Dan Accadia Herzliya Hotel, Herzliya, Israel, May 6, 2019. Eiran served as Israel's liaison to Congress from 1966 to 1972, and director general for Prime Minister Yitzhak Rabin from 1974 to 1976.

2. Dennis Ross, *Doomed to Succeed: The U.S.-Israel Relationship from Truman to Obama* (New York: Farrar, Straus and Giroux, 2015); Steven L. Spiegel, *The Other Arab-Israeli Conflict: Making America's Middle East Policy, from Truman to Reagan* (Chicago: University of Chicago Press, 1985); William B. Quandt, *Peace Process: American Diplomacy and the Arab-Israeli Conflict Since 1967,* 3rd ed. (Washington, D.C.: Brookings Institution, 2005); and George Lenczowski, *American Presidents and the Middle East* (Durham, NC: Duke University Press, 1990).

3. Walter LaFeber, Richard Polenberg, and Nancy Woloch, *The American Century: A History of the United States since the 1890s,* 7th ed. (Armonk, NY: M. E. Sharpe, 2013); and Thomas G. Paterson, et al., *American Foreign Relations, Volume Two,* 7th ed. (Boston: Wadsworth, 2010).

4. Peter L. Hahn, *Caught in the Middle East: U. S. Policy toward the Arab-Israeli Conflict, 1945–1961* (Chapel Hill: The University of North Carolina Press, 2004). "Evenhanded" is often used as shorthand to mean a policy that favored neither Israel nor Arab states.

5. Douglas Little, *American Orientalism: The United States and the Middle East since 1945,* 3rd ed. (Chapel Hill: The University of North Carolina Press, 2008); Abraham Ben-Zvi, *Decade of Transition: Eisenhower, Kennedy, and the Origins of the American-Israeli Alliance* (New York: Columbia University Press, 1998).

6. Warren Bass, *Support Any Friend: Kennedy's Middle East and the Making of the U.S.-Israel Alliance* (Oxford, UK: Oxford University Press, 2003); and Yaacov Bar-Siman-Tov, "The United States and Israel since 1948: A 'Special Relationship'?" *Diplomatic History* vol. 22, issue 2 (Spring 1998): 231–62.

7. David Schoenbaum, *The United States and the State of Israel* (Oxford, UK: Oxford University Press, 1993); Craig Daigle, *The Limits of Détente: The United*

States, the Soviet Union, and the Arab-Israeli Conflict, 1969–1973 (New Haven, CT: Yale University Press, 2012); and Salim Yaqub, "The Weight of Conquest: Henry Kissinger and the Arab-Israeli Conflict," in *Nixon in the World: American Foreign Relations, 1969–1977,* edited by Fredrik Logevall and Andrew Preston, 227–48 (Oxford, UK: Oxford University Press, 2008).

8. Salim Yaqub, *Imperfect Strangers: Americans, Arabs, and U.S.-Middle East Relations in the 1970s* (Ithaca, NY: Cornell University Press, 2016), 239–75; and William Quandt, *Camp David: Peacekeeping and Politics* (Washington, D.C.: The Brookings Institution, 1986).

9. John Lehman, *The Executive, Congress, and Foreign Policy: Studies of the Nixon Administration* (New York: Praeger Publishers, 1974); Thomas M. Franck and Edward Weisband, *Foreign Policy by Congress* (Oxford, UK: Oxford University Press, 1979); Edmund S. Muskie, Kenneth Rush, and Kenneth W. Thompson, eds., *The President, the Congress, and Foreign Policy: A Joint Policy Project of the Association of Former Members of Congress and the Atlantic Council of the United States* (Lanham, MD: University Press of America, Inc., 1986); Thomas E. Mann, ed., *A Question of Balance: The President, the Congress, and Foreign Policy* (Washington, D.C.: The Brookings Institution, 1990); and John Spanier and Joseph Nogee, eds., *Congress, the Presidency and American Foreign Policy* (New York: Pergamon Press Inc., 1981).

10. Robert David Johnson, *Congress and the Cold War* (Cambridge, UK: Cambridge University Press, 2006). According to Johnson, "Policy toward certain regions, especially the Middle East, largely fell outside of the Cold War framework because of the Arab-Israeli conflict, the role of oil diplomacy, the activities of the Israeli lobby, and the emergence of terrorism in the mid-1970s" (xxv).

11. Marvin C. Feuerwerger, *Congress and Israel: Foreign Aid Decision-Making in the House of Representatives, 1969–1976* (Westport, CT: Greenwood Press, 1979); and Mohamed Rabie, *The Politics of Foreign Aid: U. S. Foreign Assistance and Aid to Israel* (New York: Praeger Publishers, 1988).

12. Harold H. Saunders, "The Middle East, 1973–1984: Hidden Agendas," in *The President, the Congress, and Foreign Policy: A Joint Policy Project of the Association of Former Members of Congress and the Atlantic Council of the United States,* edited by Edmund S. Muskie, Kenneth Rush, and Kenneth W. Thompson, 175–205 (Lanham, MD: University Press of America, Inc., 1986).

13. Arthur M. Schlesinger Jr., *The Imperial Presidency* (Boston: Houghton Mifflin Company, 1973.

14. Bruce J. Schulman, *The Seventies: The Great Shift in American Culture, Society, and Politics* (New York: Free Press, 2001); Daniel J. Sargent, *A Superpower Transformed: The Remaking of American Foreign Relations in the 1970s* (New York: Oxford University Press, 2015); and Yaqub, *Imperfect Strangers.*

15. Jeremy M. Sharp, "U. S. Foreign Aid to Israel," Congressional Research Service, June 10, 2015, accessed online June 17, 2017, https://www.fas.org/sgp/crs/mideast/RL33222.pdf.

16. Peter Baker and Julie Hirschfeld Davis, "U. S. Finalizes Deal to Give Israel $38 Billion in Military Aid," *New York Times,* September 13, 2016, accessed online June 8, 2017, https://www.nytimes.com/2016/09/14/world/middleeast/israel-benjamin-netanyahu-military-aid.html?_r=0.

17. John J. Mearsheimer and Stephen M. Walt, *The Israeli Lobby and U. S. Foreign Policy* (New York: Farrar, Straus and Giroux, 2007), 5.

18. For other works critical of the Israel lobby, see George W. Ball and Douglas B. Ball, *The Passionate Attachment: America's Involvement with Israel, 1947 to the Present* (New York: Norton, 1992); Edward Tivnan, *The Lobby: Jewish Political Power and American Foreign Policy* (New York: Simon and Schuster, 1987); and Paul Findley, *They Dare Speak Out: People and Institutions Confront Israel's Lobby* (Westport, CT: Lawrence Hill, 1985, 1989, 2003).

19. Robert H. Trice, "Interest Groups and the Foreign Policy Process: U. S. Policy in the Middle East," *Sage Professional Papers: International Studies Series, Volume 4* (Beverly Hills: Sage Publications, Inc., 1976), 37.

20. Mearsheimer and Walt, 5.

21. Walter Hixson, *Israel's Armor: The Israel Lobby and the First Generation of the Palestine Conflict* (New York: Cambridge University Press, 2019).

22. Spiegel, 159.

23. "The Israeli Lobby: Instant Votes When Needed," *Congressional Quarterly,* October 27, 1973, page 2858, University of South Dakota, University Libraries, Archives and Special Collections, James G. Abourezk Papers (hereafter JGAP), Box 837, Mideast Peace Settlement 1975. Kenen created the American Zionist Committee that became AIPAC and continued to lead the organization until 1974.

24. Ibid.

25. Stephen Walt, "America Is Wide Open for Foreign Influence," *Foreign Policy,* April 9, 2019, accessed online June 28, 2019, https://foreignpolicy.com/2019/04/08/america-is-wide-open-for-foreign-influence/.

26. Mitchell Bard, *The Water's Edge and Beyond: Defining the Limits to Domestic Influence on United States Middle East Policy* (New Brunswick, NJ: Transaction Publishers, 1991), 33.

27. Michelle Mart, *Eye on Israel: How America Came to View Israel as an Ally* (Albany: State University of New York Press, 2006).

28. Ibid., 67.

29. A recent work by Amy Kaplan also analyzes the deep cultural connections between Americans and Israelis. Amy Kaplan, *Our American Israel: The Story of an Entangled Alliance* (Cambridge, MA: Harvard University Press, 2018).

30. Johnson, xxi.

31. Daniel G. Hummel, *Covenant Brothers: Evangelicals, Jews, and U.S.-Israeli Relations* (Philadelphia: University of Pennsylvania Press, 2019); Timothy P. Weber, *On the Road to Armageddon: How Evangelicals Became Israel's Best Friend* (Grand Rapids, MI: Baker Academic, 2004); Stephen Spector, *Evangelicals and Israel: The Story of American Christian Zionism* (Oxford, UK: Oxford University Press, 2008);

Victoria Clark, *Allies for Armageddon: The Rise of Christian Zionism* (New Haven, CT: Yale University Press, 2007); Angela M. Lahr, *Millennial Dreams and Apocalyptic Nightmares: The Cold War Origins of Political Evangelicalism* (Oxford, UK: Oxford University Press, 2007); and Donald Wagner, "Evangelicals and Israel: Theological Roots of a Political Alliance," *Christian Century,* November 4, 1998, vol. 115, issue 30.

32. Hummel, 5. In his book, Hummel uses biblical quotes from the New International Version (NIV), "which most evangelicals adopted as their preferred translation in the 1970s" (248).

33. Edward Said, *Orientalism* (New York: Pantheon Books, 1978).

34. Douglas Little, *American Orientalism: The United States and the Middle East since 1945,* 3rd ed. (Chapel Hill: The University of North Carolina Press, 2008).

35. Melani McAlister, *Epic Encounters: Culture, Media, and U. S. Interests in the Middle East, 1945–2000* (Berkeley: University of California Press, 2001).

36. *Imperfect Strangers,* 55–86, 255–61, 276–301.

37. Ibid., 7.

38. Ibid.

39. Ibid., 11.

40. Ibid., 12.

41. Ibid., 13–14, 145–82.

42. Salim Yaqub, *Containing Arab Nationalism: The Eisenhower Doctrine and the Middle East* (Chapel Hill: The University of North Carolina Press, 2004), along with *Imperfect Strangers;* Roham Alvandi, *Nixon, Kissinger, and the Shah: The United States and Iran in the Cold War* (Oxford, UK: Oxford University Press, 2014); and Paul Chamberlin, *The Global Offensive: The United States, the Palestine Liberation Organization, and the Making of the Post-Cold War Order* (Oxford, UK: Oxford University Press, 2012).

1. Johnson, Congress, and the Special Relationship

Parts of this chapter first appeared in Kenny Kolander, "The June 1967 Arab-Israeli War: Soviet Policy by Other Means?" *Middle Eastern Studies* vol. 52, issue 3 (May 2016): 402–18.

1. Michael B. Oren, *Six Days of War: June 1967 and the Making of the Modern Middle East* (Oxford, UK: Oxford University Press, 2002); Richard Parker, *The Politics of Miscalculation in the Middle East* (Bloomington: Indiana University Press, 1993); William Roger Louis and Avi Shlaim, eds., *The 1967 Arab-Israeli War: Origins and Consequences* (New York: Cambridge University Press, 2012); Yaacov Ro'i and Boris Morozov, eds., *The Soviet Union and the June 1967 Six Day War* (Stanford, CA: Stanford University Press, 2008); and Galia Golan, "The Soviet Union and the Outbreak of the June 1967 Six-Day War," *Journal of Cold War Studies* vol. 8, no. 1 (Winter 2006): 3–19.

2. Zach Levey, "The United States' Skyhawk Sale to Israel, 1966: Strategic Exigencies of an Arms Deal," *Diplomatic History* vol. 28, issue 2 (April 2004): 255–76.

3. Walter Hixson, *Israel's Armor: The Israel Lobby and the First Generation of the Palestine Conflict* (New York: Cambridge University Press, 2019).

4. Steven L. Spiegel, *The Other Arab-Israeli Conflict: Making America's Middle East Policy, from Truman to Reagan* (Chicago: University of Chicago Press, 1985); William B. Quandt, *Peace Process: American Diplomacy and the Arab-Israeli Conflict since 1967,* 3rd ed. (Washington, D.C.: Brookings Institution Press, 2005); and Mitchell Bard, *The Water's Edge and Beyond: Defining the Limits to Domestic Influence on United States Middle East Policy* (New Brunswick, NJ: Transaction Publishers, 1991), 189–211.

5. Jeffrey K. Sosland, *Cooperating Rivals: The Riparian Politics of the Jordan River Basin* (Albany: State University of New York Press, 2007).

6. Douglas Little, *American Orientalism: The United States and the Middle East since 1945,* 3rd ed. (Chapel Hill: University of North Carolina Press, 2008), 279. Fatah is also called the Palestine National Liberation Movement.

7. Ibid., 280.

8. Hixson, 147–53. See also Olivia Sohns, "The Future Foretold: Lyndon Baines Johnson's Congressional Support for Israel," *Diplomacy & Statecraft* 28: 1, 57–84. In addition to cultural affinity, Sohn's work also points to the importance of Congress in shaping U. S. foreign policy. In this case, through the experiences of LBJ as Senate majority leader.

9. Spiegel, 123.

10. Ibid.

11. Ibid.

12. Levey, 259–60.

13. Gadi Heimann, "From Friendship to Patronage: France-Israel Relations, 1958–1967," *Diplomacy & Statecraft* vol. 21, issue 2 (June 2010): 240–58; Gadi Heimann, "From 'Irresponsible' to 'Immoral': The Shifts in de Gaulle's Perception of Israel and the Jews," *Journal of Contemporary History* vol. 46, no. 4 (October 2011): 897–919.

14. Levey, 261; Spiegel, 131–32.

15. Hixson, 153–59.

16. Levey, 262–63. News of the secret Israel–West Germany tank deal leaked in early 1965, and West German officials feared that the tank deal would lead Arab states to recognize East Germany.

17. Spiegel, 134.

18. Levey, 265–67.

19. Ibid., 267.

20. Ibid.

21. Arthur Schlesinger Jr., *The Imperial Presidency* (Boston: Houghton Mifflin, 1973).

22. Johnson, 142.

23. Levey, 270. "Bundy Meeting Selected Congressmen," August 12, 1965 (emphasis in original), Lyndon B. Johnson Presidential Library (hereafter LBJL), White House Central Files, Confidential File. Bard also references the Bundy meeting (195).

24. 112 *CR,* 89th Congress, 2nd Session, 1733 (February 1, 1966).

25. Levey, 270. Memorandum from the President's Deputy Special Assistant for National Security Affairs (Komer) to President Johnson, February 8, 1966, *The Foreign Relations of the United States* (hereafter *FRUS*), 1964–1968, Vol. XVIII, Arab-Israeli Dispute, 1964–1967; Document 267 (emphasis in original).

26. Levey, 270.

27. Ibid., 273.

28. Ibid.

29. 112 *CR,* 89th Congress, 2nd Session, 24531–24532 (September 29, 1966).

30. 112 *CR,* 89th Congress, 2nd Session, 28946 (October 22, 1966).

31. Clea Lutz Bunch, "Strike at Samu: Jordan, Israel, the United States, and the Origins of the Six-Day War," *Diplomatic History* vol. 32, issue 1 (January 2008): 55–76; Hixson, 163–65.

32. Avi Shlaim, *The Iron Wall: Israel and the Arab World* (New York: W. W. Norton & Company, 2000), 236–41; Hixson, 162–73.

33. "Memorandum from Secretary of Defense McNamara to President Johnson," April 17, 1967, *FRUS,* 1964–1968, Volume XVIII, Arab-Israeli Dispute, 1964–1967, Document 405. McNamara was referring to a memo in February 1967 from the Joint Chiefs of Staff: "Memorandum from the Joint Chiefs of Staff to Secretary of Defense McNamara," February 2, 1967, *FRUS,* 1964–1968, Volume XVIII, Arab-Israeli Dispute, 1964–1967, Document 387.

34. "Memorandum from the Under Secretary of State (Katzenbach) to President Johnson," May 1, 1967, *FRUS,* 1964–1968, Volume XVIII, Arab-Israeli Dispute, 1964–1967, Document 415.

35. Hixson, 171.

36. Malcolm Kerr, *The Arab Cold War, 1958–1967: A Study of Ideology in Politics,* 2nd ed. (New York: Oxford University Press, 1967).

37. 113 *CR,* 90th Congress, 1st Session, 13318 (May 19, 1967).

38. 113 *CR,* 90th Congress, 1st Session, 13808 (May 24, 1967).

39. 113 *CR,* 90th Congress, 1st Session, 13573 (May 23, 1967).

40. 113 *CR,* 90th Congress, 1st Session, 13775 (May 24, 1967).

41. 113 *CR,* 90th Congress, 1st Session, 13398, 14540 (May 22, June 1, 1967).

42. 113 *CR,* 90th Congress, 1st Session, 13546, 13557 (May 23, 1967).

43. 113 *CR,* 90th Congress, 1st Session, 13482 (May 23, 1967).

44. 113 *CR,* 90th Congress, 1st Session, 13320 (May 19, 1967).

45. 113 *CR,* 90th Congress, 1st Session, 13324 (May 22, 1967).

46. 113 *CR,* 90th Congress, 1st Session, 13480 (May 23, 1967).

47. 113 *CR,* 90th Congress, 1st Session, 13324 (May 22, 1967).

48. 113 *CR,* 90th Congress, 1st Session, 13573 (May 23, 1967).

49. 113 *CR,* 90th Congress, 1st Session, 13318, 13398 (May 19, 22, 1967).

50. Quandt, 41.

51. 113 *CR,* 90th Congress, 1st Session, 14580 (June 5, 1967).

52. Ibid.

53. 113 *CR,* 90th Congress, 1st Session, 14603 (June 5, 1967).

54. 113 *CR,* 90th Congress, 1st Session, 14617 (June 5, 1967).

55. 113 *CR,* 90th Congress, 1st Session, 14581 (June 5, 1967).

56. 113 *CR,* 90th Congress, 1st Session, 14663 (June 5, 1967).

57. Hixson, 173–84.

58. John J. Mearsheimer and Stephen M. Walt, *The Israeli Lobby and U. S. Foreign Policy* (New York: Farrar, Straus and Giroux, 2007), 121.

59. Ibid., 121–22.

60. Ibid., 45.

61. Hixson, 191–97. I intentionally use the term *American Jewish Zionists* rather than *American Jewish community* or *American Zionists. American Jewish community* suggests that all American Jews are Zionists, which they are not, or that all American Jews support the political efforts of Jewish lobbyists, which they do not. *American Zionists* can also mean non-Jewish Zionists, particularly evangelical and fundamentalist Christians. Although at times I use the phrase *American Jewish community,* I try to use *American Jewish Zionists* when the context specifically involves issues pertaining to the State of Israel, rather than more general Jewish issues. However, if a direct quote uses the phrase *American Jewish community* or *American Zionists,* I have included it as such.

62. Editorial Note, June 7, 1967, *FRUS,* 1964–1968, Volume XIX, Arab-Israeli Crisis and War, 1967, Document 164.

63. Message from Larry Levinson and Ben Wattenberg of the White House Staff to President Johnson, June 7, 1967, *FRUS,* 1964–1968, Volume XIX, Arab-Israeli Crisis and War, 1967, Document 198.

64. Ginsburg to Bundy, Memorandum for the Vice President, June 17, 1967, LBJL, National Security Files (hereafter NSF), National Security Council History (hereafter NSCH), Box 19, Middle East Crisis, Volume VII, Appendix I(4)-J.

65. 113 *CR,* 90th Congress, 1st Session, 14745 (June 6, 1967).

66. 113 *CR,* 90th Congress, 1st Session, 14774 (June 6, 1967).

67. 113 *CR,* 90th Congress, 1st Session, 14800 (June 6, 1967).

68. 113 *CR,* 90th Congress, 1st Session, 14864 (June 6, 1967).

69. 113 *CR,* 90th Congress, 1st Session, 15084 (June 7, 1967).

70. 113 *CR,* 90th Congress, 1st Session, 14865 (June 6, 1967).

71. 113 *CR,* 90th Congress, 1st Session, 14905 (June 6, 1967).

72. 113 *CR,* 90th Congress, 1st Session, 15122 (June 7, 1967).

73. 113 *CR,* 90th Congress, 1st Session, 17313 (June 26, 1967).

74. Read to Bundy, "An Approach to Political Settlement in the Near East," June 8, 1967, LBJL, NSF, NSCH, Box 19, Middle East Crisis, Volume VII, Appendix I(4)-J.

75. Zbigniew Brzezinski, "The Middle Eastern Crisis: The U. S. Should Take an Explicit Stand," June 14, 1967, LBJL, NSF, NSCH, Box 19, Middle East Crisis, Volume VII, Appendix I(4)-J.

76. Memorandum from the Board of National Estimates to Director of Central Intelligence Helms, June 1, 1967, *FRUS,* 1964–1968, Volume XIX, Arab-Israeli Crisis and War, 1967, Document 126.

77. Intelligence Memorandum Prepared in the Central Intelligence Agency, June 3, 1967, *FRUS,* 1964–1968, Volume XIX, Arab-Israeli Crisis and War, 1967, Document 143.

78. Hixson, 203.

79. 113 *CR,* 90th Congress, 1st Session, 15131, 15255, 15261 (June 8, 1967).

80. 113 *CR,* 90th Congress, 1st Session, 15261 (June 8, 1967).

81. 113 *CR,* 90th Congress, 1st Session, 21326 (August 3, 1967).

82. Hixson, 203.

83. 113 *CR,* 90th Congress, 1st Session, 23606 (August 22, 1967).

84. 113 *CR,* 90th Congress, 1st Session, 15067 (June 7, 1967).

85. 113 *CR,* 90th Congress, 1st Session, 15068 (June 7, 1967).

86. 113 *CR,* 90th Congress, 1st Session, 15180 (June 8, 1967).

87. 113 *CR,* 90th Congress, 1st Session, 15210 (June 8, 1967).

88. 113 *CR,* 90th Congress, 1st Session, 15069, 15074 (June 7, 1967).

89. Hixson, 210.

90. 113 *CR,* 90th Congress, 1st Session, 15132 (June 8, 1967).

91. 113 *CR,* 90th Congress, 1st Session, 15133 (June 8, 1967).

92. 113 *CR,* 90th Congress, 1st Session, 15213 (June 8, 1967).

93. 113 *CR,* 90th Congress, 1st Session, 15271 (June 8, 1967).

94. 113 *CR,* 90th Congress, 1st Session, 15948 (June 15, 1967).

95. 113 *CR,* 90th Congress, 1st Session, 15956–15957 (June 15, 1967).

96. Avi Raz, "The Generous Peace Offer that Was Never Offered: The Israeli Cabinet Resolution of June 19, 1967," *Diplomatic History* vol. 37, issue 1 (January 2013): 456–83; Hixson, 218.

97. Shaiel Ben-Ephraim, "Distraction and Deception: Israeli Settlements, Vietnam, and the Johnson Administration," *Diplomatic History* vol. 42, issue 3 (June 2018): 456–83; Hixson, 222–30.

98. 113 *CR,* 90th Congress, 1st Session, 14864 (June 6, 1967).

99. 113 *CR,* 90th Congress, 1st Session, 15529 (June 12, 1967).

100. 113 *CR,* 90th Congress, 1st Session, 15272, 15484, 15848, and 16346 (June 8, 12, 14, and 19, 1967).

101. 113 *CR,* 90th Congress, 1st Session, 15298 (June 8, 1967).

102. 113 *CR,* 90th Congress, 1st Session, 15367 (June 12, 1967).

103. 113 *CR,* 90th Congress, 1st Session, 17678 (June 28, 1967).

104. 113 *CR,* 90th Congress, 1st Session, 17305–17312 (June 26, 1967).

105. 113 *CR,* 90th Congress, 1st Session, 17313 (June 26, 1967).

106. 113 *CR,* 90th Congress, 1st Session, 17427–17430 (June 27, 1967).

107. Spiegel, 158.

108. 113 *CR,* 90th Congress, 1st Session, 20752 (August 1, 1967).

109. 113 *CR,* 90th Congress, 1st Session, 22092 (August 9, 1967). The United Arab Republic existed between 1958 and 1961 and included the states of Egypt and Syria. Tower likely meant Egypt, though he may have been referring to Syria, too.

110. 113 *CR,* 90th Congress, 1st Session, 22096–22097 (August 9, 1967).

111. 113 *CR,* 90th Congress, 1st Session, 22097 (August 9, 1967).

112. 113 *CR,* 90th Congress, 1st Session, 23963–23964 (August 24, 1967).

113. 113 *CR,* 90th Congress, 1st Session, 22096 (August 9, 1967).

114. 113 *CR,* 90th Congress, 1st Session, 23968 (August 24, 1967).

115. 113 *CR,* 90th Congress, 1st Session, 23970 (August 24, 1967).

116. 113 *CR,* 90th Congress, 1st Session, 23970–23972 (August 24, 1967).

117. Spiegel, 155; Quandt, 46.

118. Spiegel, 155.

119. Shlaim, 258–59.

120. Hixson, 222.

121. "Letter from President Johnson to King Faisal," September 25, 1967, *FRUS,* 1964–1968, Volume XIX, Arab-Israeli Crisis and War, 1967, Document 447.

122. "Telegram from the Department of State to the Embassy in Jordan," September 29, 1967, *FRUS,* 1964–1968, Volume XIX, Arab-Israeli Crisis and War, 1967, Document 452.

123. "Memorandum of Conversation," September 25, 1967, *FRUS,* 1964–1968, Volume XIX, Arab-Israeli Crisis and War, 1967, Document 448.

124. "Telegram from the Department of State to the Embassy in Israel," September 29, 1967, *FRUS,* 1964–1968, Volume XIX, Arab-Israeli Crisis and War, 1967, Document 451.

125. "Notes of a National Security Council Meeting," September 13, 1967, *FRUS,* 1964–1968, Volume XIX, Arab-Israeli Crisis and War, 1967, Document 438.

126. "Memorandum from the Under Secretary of State for Political Affairs (Rostow) to Secretary of State Rusk," September 18, 1967, *FRUS,* 1964–1968, Volume XIX, Arab-Israeli Crisis and War, 1967, Document 441.

127. "Telegram from the Department of State to the Embassy in Israel," September 29, 1967, *FRUS,* 1964–1968, Volume XIX, Arab-Israeli Crisis and War, 1967, Document 451.

128. "Memorandum of Conversation," October 3, 1967, *FRUS,* 1964–1968, Volume XIX, Arab-Israeli Crisis and War, 1967, Document 453.

129. "Memorandum from the President's Special Assistant (Rostow) to President Johnson," October 3, 1967, *FRUS,* 1964–1968, Volume XIX, Arab-Israeli Crisis and War, 1967, Document 455.

130. "Memorandum from the President's Special Assistant (Rostow) to President Johnson," October 9, 1967, *FRUS,* 1964–1968, Volume XIX, Arab-Israeli Crisis and War, 1967, Document 462.

131. "Memorandum of Conversation," October 4, 1967, *FRUS,* 1964–1968, Volume XIX, Arab-Israeli Crisis and War, 1967, Document 456.

132. "Telegram from the Mission to the United Nations to the Department of State," October 3, 1967, *FRUS,* 1964–1968, Volume XIX, Arab-Israeli Crisis and War, 1967, Document 454.

133. "Memorandum from the President's Special Assistant (Rostow) to President Johnson," September 12, 1967, *FRUS,* 1964–1968, Volume XIX, Arab-Israeli Crisis and War, 1967, Document 437.

134. 113 *CR,* 90th Congress, 1st Session, 26439 (September 21, 1967).

135. 113 *CR,* 90th Congress, 1st Session, 27777–27778 (October 4, 1967).

136. 113 *CR,* 90th Congress, 1st Session, 28724–28726 (October 11, 1967).

137. 113 *CR,* 90th Congress, 1st Session, 28994 (October 16, 1967).

138. "Memorandum from the President's Special Assistant (Rostow) to President Johnson," October 9, 1967, *FRUS,* 1964–1968, Volume XIX, Arab-Israeli Crisis and War, 1967, Document 463. In an earlier memorandum, Rostow also noted that McNamara wanted the freeze to continue in order to not upset legislators regarding military sales. "Memorandum from the President's Special Assistant (Rostow) to President Johnson," September 22, 1967, *FRUS,* 1964–1968, Volume XIX, Arab-Israeli Crisis and War, 1967, Document 445.

139. "Memorandum from the President's Special Assistant (Rostow) to President Johnson," October 12, 1967, *FRUS,* 1964–1968, Volume XIX, Arab-Israeli Crisis and War, 1967, Document 468.

140. "Memorandum of Conversation," October 13, 1967, *FRUS,* 1964–1968, Volume XIX, Arab-Israeli Crisis and War, 1967, Document 473.

141. "Memorandum of Conversation," October 18, 1967, *FRUS,* 1964–1968, Volume XIX, Arab-Israeli Crisis and War, 1967, Document 477.

142. 113 *CR,* 90th Congress, 1st Session, 29614 (October 23, 1967).

143. 113 *CR,* 90th Congress, 1st Session, 29878 (October 24, 1967).

144. 113 *CR,* 90th Congress, 1st Session, 29916 (October 25, 1967).

145. 113 *CR,* 90th Congress, 1st Session, 29975 (October 25, 1967).

146. 113 *CR,* 90th Congress, 1st Session, 30015 (October 25, 1967).

147. 113 *CR,* 90th Congress, 1st Session, 30012–30013 (October 25, 1967).

148. Bard, 198.

149. Ibid., 198–99.

150. Ibid., 199.

151. "Memorandum of Conversation," January 7, 1968, *FRUS,* 1964–1968, Vol. XX, Arab-Israeli Dispute, 1967–1968, Document 39.

152. Ibid. Spiegel also says, "The White House had hinted that the president wanted congressional support before proceeding with the sale" (161).

153. "Memorandum of Conversation," January 8, 1968, *FRUS,* 1964–1968, Vol. XX, Arab-Israeli Dispute, 1967–1968, Documents 40 and 41.

154. Bard, 203.

155. Spiegel, 160.

156. Robert David Johnson, "Lyndon Johnson and Israel: The Secret Presidential Recordings," Research Paper No. 3, July 2008, 94; accessed online April 22, 2019, https://www.tau.ac.il/humanities/abraham/publications/johnson_israel.pdf. Hixson also includes this quote but says that Johnson made up his mind to sell the Phantoms as early as January (231–34).

157. Quandt, 47–48; Hixson, 230–34.

158. 114 *CR,* 90th Congress, 2nd Session, 2422–2424 (February 7, 1968).

159. 114 *CR,* 90th Congress, 2nd Session, 3287 (February 19, 1968).

160. 114 *CR,* 90th Congress, 2nd Session, 10423 (April 24, 1968).

161. Spiegel, 161.

162. Ibid.

163. Bard, 196–97.

164. Spiegel, 161; Bard, 202.

165. Spiegel, 162.

166. Bard, 201.

167. 114 *CR,* 90th Congress, 2nd Session, 22102 (July 18, 1968).

168. Bard, 202.

169. Mearsheimer and Walt, 118.

170. Spiegel, 162.

171. 114 *CR,* 90th Congress, 2nd Session, 24516–24520 (July 31, 1968).

172. Spiegel, 161.

173. Spiegel, 162; Bard, 202–3.

174. Spiegel, 162–63.

175. 114 *CR,* 90th Congress, 2nd Session, 27509 (September 18, 1968). As Spiegel notes, AIPAC also claimed credit for the favorable party platforms (162).

176. 114 *CR,* 90th Congress, 2nd Session, 27670, 28484, 28635 (September 19, 26, 1968).

177. 114 *CR,* 90th Congress, 2nd Session, 27635–27636 (September 19, 1968).

178. 114 *CR,* 90th Congress, 2nd Session, 28249–8250, 28502, 28635, 29510–29511 (September 25, 26, 27, and October 3, 1968).

179. Spiegel, 160–61.

180. Ibid., 163.

181. Bard, 202–4.

182. Ibid., 204.

183. 114 *CR,* 90th Congress, 2nd Session, 30432, 30557, 30567 (October 10, 1968).

184. Spiegel, 163.

185. Bard, 189–211; David Rodman, "Phantom Fracas: The 1968 American Sale of F-4 Aircraft to Israel," *Middle Eastern Studies* vol. 40, no. 6 (November 2004): 130–44.

186. Bard, 204.

187. Ibid.

188. Johnson, 143.

189. Spiegel, 159.

190. Ibid.

2. Phantom Peace

Parts of this chapter first appeared in Kenneth Kolander, "Phantom Peace: Henry 'Scoop' Jackson, J. William Fulbright, and Military Sales to Israel," *Diplomatic History* vol. 41, issue 3 (June 2017): 567–93.

1. Douglas Little, *American Orientalism: The United States and the Middle East since 1945,* 3rd ed. (Chapel Hill: University of North Carolina Press, 2008).

2. Nixon made several derogatory remarks about Jews during his presidency, which were recorded on White House Tapes released by the National Archives.

3. Ronald Drucker, "McDonnell F-4 Phantom: Essential Aircraft in the Air Warfare in the Middle East," *HistoryNet,* June 12, 2006, accessed on August 18, 2015, http://www.historynet.com/mcdonnell-f-4-phantom-essential-aircraft-in-the-air-warfare-in-the-middle-east.htm.

4. The standard biographies for the two influential senators are Robert Gordon Kaufman, *Henry M. Jackson: A Life in Politics* (Seattle: University of Washington Press, 2000), and Randall Bennett Woods, *Fulbright: A Biography* (Cambridge, UK: Cambridge University Press, 1995).

5. John J. Mearshimer and Stephen M. Walt, *The Israel Lobby and U. S. Foreign Policy* (New York: Farrar, Straus and Giroux, 2007).

6. Craig Daigle, *The Limits of Détente: The United States, the Soviet Union, and the Arab-Israeli Conflict, 1969–1973* (New Haven, CT: Yale University Press, 2012); David Korn, *Stalemate: The War of Attrition and Great Power Diplomacy in the Middle East, 1967–1970* (Boulder, CO: Westview Press, 1992); and Boaz Vanetik and Zaki Shalom, *The Nixon Administration and the Middle East Peace Process, 1969–1973* (Chicago: Sussex Academic Press, 2013).

7. Noam Kochavi, *Nixon and Israel: Forging a Conservative Partnership* (Albany: SUNY Press, 2009).

8. Daigle, 39.

9. Ibid., 55–56, 83–89.

10. Daigle, 83–98; Schoenbaum, 173.

11. Quandt, 67.

12. Ibid., 68–69.

13. Daigle, 98–105.

14. Daigle, 87; Dima P. Adamsky, "Disregarding the Bear: How U. S. Intelligence Failed to Estimate the Soviet Intervention in the Egyptian-Israeli War of Attrition," *Journal of Strategic Studies* vol. 28, issue 5 (2005): 803–31; and Dima P. Adamsky, "'Zero-Hour for the Bears': Inquiring into the Soviet Decision to Intervene in the Egyptian-Israeli War of Attrition, 1969–70," *Cold War History* vol. 6, no. 1 (February 2006): 113–36.

15. "Nixon's Answer to Israel: What It Is and Why," *New York Times,* March 22, 1970, accessed online with ProQuest, January 25, 2015.

16. David E. Rosenbaum, "U. S. Appears to Speed Up Plane Shipments to Israel," *New York Times,* July 13, 1970, accessed online with ProQuest, January 25, 2015.

17. Ibid., 17.

18. Daigle, 16.

19. Kaufman, 176.

20. Ibid.

21. Ibid.

22. Woods, 669.

23. William Fulbright, "A New Internationalism," speech delivered to Yale University, April 4, 1971, University of Arkansas Libraries, Special Collections, J. William Fulbright Papers [hereafter JWFP], Box 33, Series 72:10. J. William Fulbright, *The Crippled Giant: American Foreign Policy and Its Domestic Consequences* (New York: Vintage Books, 1972).

24. Kaufman, 140–45.

25. Robert David Johnson, *Congress and the Cold War* (Cambridge, UK: Cambridge University Press, 2006), 184.

26. Johnson, 120, 161–64.

27. Kaufman, 13.

28. "Statement of Senator Henry M. Jackson for the Near East Report," May 24, 1972, University of Washington Libraries, Special Collections, Henry M. Jackson Papers [hereafter HMJP], Accession No. 35606, Box 9, Folder 9/92.

29. Kaufman, 39.

30. Ibid., 48, 103.

31. Woods, 221.

32. Ibid., 259.

33. Ibid., 311.

34. Ibid., 311.

35. Kaufman, 177.

36. Woods, 454–55.

37. Fulbright to Dr. H. E. Hyder, June 14, 1967, JWFP, Box 40, Series 48:15.

38. Fulbright to John Fistere, December 15, 1969, JWFP, Box 40, Series 48:15.

39. Fulbright quote taken from R. I. Brougham, Letter to the Editor, *The Middle East Newsletter* vol. IV, nos. 1 & 2 (March 1970), JWFP, Box 40, Series 48:15.

40. Fulbright to John Fistere, December 15, 1969, JWFP, Box 40, Series 48:15.

41. Fulbright to David A. Shapiro, June 13, 1967, JWFP, Box 40, Series 48:15.

42. Daigle, 103.

43. "Jackson Criticizes Fulbright," *Washington Post,* August 30, 1970, HMJP, Accession No. 35604, Box 252, Folder 252/9.

44. Quandt, 72–76.

45. American Orientalism, 102.

46. Memorandum of Conversation, "President's Meeting with his Foreign Intelligence Advisory Board," June 5, 1970, *Foreign Relations of the United States* [hereafter *FRUS*], 1969–1976 Vol. XXIV, Middle East Region and Arabian Peninsula, 1969–1972; Jordan, September 1970, Document 23.

47. Ribicoff to Fulbright, May 26, 1970, JWFP, Box 40, Series 48:15.

48. 116 *CR,* 91st Congress, 2nd Session, 18536–18537 (June 4, 1970).

49. "Section 501 of the Defense Procurement Act, 1971 (The Jackson Amendment)," HMJP, Accession No. 35606, Box 6, Folder 6/96.

50. "Senator Jackson's Mid-East Amendment Adopted by Committee," HMJP, Accession No. 35606, Box 7, Folder 7/80.

51. Author Interview with Amos Eiran, Dan Accadia Herzliya Hotel, Herzliya, Israel, May 6, 2019.

52. Ibid.

53. Ibid.

54. Ibid.

55. Ibid.

56. "Panel Oks U. S. Aid: Assist Israel," *The Light,* San Antonio, TX, June 18, 1970, HMJP, Accession No. 35604, Box 252, Folder 252/9.

57. J. W. Fulbright to John Stennis, June 26, 1970, HMJP, Accession No. 35606, Box 48, Folder 48/9.

58. Ibid.

59. Robert S. Allen and John A. Goldsmith, "Plane Sales to Israel," *Herald,* Everett, WA, July 6, 1970, HMJP, Accession No. 35604, Box 252, Folder 252/9.

60. Johnson, 172.

61. Daigle, 129.

62. Ibid.

63. "A Letter to the President Supporting a Firm U. S. Policy in the Middle East . . . From 72 Members of the Senate," July 30, 1970, HMJP, Accession No. 35606, Box 6, Folder 6/96.

64. 116 *CR,* 91st Congress, 2nd Session, 26743 (July 31, 1970).

65. 116 *CR,* 91st Congress, 2nd Session, 27823–27824, 27832–27833 (August 7, 1970).

66. 116 *CR,* 91st Congress, 2nd Session, 26662–26663 (July 30, 1970).

67. 116 *CR,* 91st Congress, 2nd Session, 28125–28126 (August 10, 1970).

68. 116 *CR,* 91st Congress, 2nd Session, 26913, 26943–26944 (July 30, 1970).

69. Daigle, 135–38.

70. 116 *CR,* 91st Congress, 2nd Session, 29537–29538 (August 20, 1970).

71. 116 *CR,* 91st Congress, 2nd Session, 29538 (August 20, 1970).

72. 116 *CR,* 91st Congress, 2nd Session, 29558–29561 (August 20, 1970).

73. 116 *CR,* 91st Congress, 2nd Session, 29754–29755 (August 21, 1970).

74. "Old Myths and New Realities—II: The Middle East," August 24, 1970, JWFP, Box 36, Series 71:30; 116 *CR,* 91st Congress, 2nd Session, 29796–29813 (August 24, 1970).

75. Woods, 584–86.

76. 116 *CR,* 91st Congress, 2nd Session, 30708 (September 1, 1970).

77. 116 *CR,* 91st Congress, 2nd Session, 30710 (September 1, 1970).

78. 116 *CR,* 91st Congress, 2nd Session, 30712 (September 1, 1970).

79. "Jackson Criticizes Fulbright," *Washington Post,* August 30, 1970, HMJP, Accession No. 35604, Box 252, Folder 252/9.

80. "Military Bill Is OK'd After Senate Beats War Funds Cutoff," *The Providence Journal,* September 29, 1970, HMJP, Accession No. 35604, Box 252, Folder 252/10.

81. Hedrick Smith, "U. S. to Give Israel 18 More A-4 Jets," *New York Times,* November 13, 1970, accessed online with ProQuest, February 5, 2015.

82. Daigle, 140.

83. Ibid., 141.

84. "U. S. Plan for Military Aid for Israel Boosted," *Scranton Tribune,* September 29, 1970, HMJP, Accession No. 35604, Box 252, Folder 252/10.

85. "Sen. Jackson Will Tour Israeli Sites," *Washington Post,* November 4, 1970, HMJP, Accession No. 35604, Box 252, Folder 252/11.

86. "Unofficial Transcript of Senator Henry M. Jackson's News Conference, November 12, 1970, at the American Embassy, Tel Aviv," HMJP, Accession No. 35604, Box 252, Folder 252/11.

87. "Jackson Popular in Israel for Strong Pro-Israel Stand," *Intermountain Jewish News,* Denver, CO, November 27, 1970, HMJP, Accession No. 35604, Box 252, Folder 252/11.

88. Ibid.

89. "Reassuring but Hardly Surprising," *Evening Journal,* Wilmington, DE, November 16, 1970, HMJP, Accession No. 35604, Box 252, Folder 252/11.

90. William Beecher, "U. S. Officials Say Israelis Will Get 180 Modern Tanks," *New York Times,* October 24, 1970, accessed online with ProQuest, February 5, 2015; and Hedrick Smith, "U. S. to Give Israel 18 More A-4 Jets," *New York Times,* November 13, 1970, accessed online with ProQuest, February 5, 2015.

91. Zach Levey, "Anatomy of an Airlift: United States Military Assistance to Israel during the 1973 War," *Cold War History* vol. 8, no. 4 (November 2008): 481–501.

92. "The Middle East and American Security Policy: Report of Senator Henry M. Jackson to the Committee on Armed Forces, United States Senate, December 1970," p. 8, HMJP, Accession No. 35605, Box 319, Folder 319/6.

93. Ibid., 21.

94. Ibid.

95. Ibid., 22.

96. "Senator Tells Israel to Seek Roll-Back," *The Jewish Chronicle,* Kansas City, MO, November 13, 1970, HMJP, Accession No. 35604, Box 252, Folder 252/11.

97. "Jackson Holds Israel Credits Are Inadequate," *Jewish Week and American Examiner,* New York, NY, February 4, 1971, HMJP, Accession No. 35604, Box 252, Folder 252/12.

98. "Senator Jackson Critical of Middle East Budget Request," January 31, 1971, HMJP, Accession No. 35606, Box 8, Folder 8/25.

99. "American Policy and Middle East Security," by Senator Henry M. Jackson, Address to B'nai B'rith Inaugural Israel Bond Dinner, February 7, 1971, HMJP, Accession No. 35606, Box 8, Folder 8/26.

100. Rowland Evans and Robert Novak, "Nixon's Noose on Israel," *Washington Post,* February 19, 1971, HMJP, Accession No. 35604, Box 252, Folder 252/12.

101. Fulbright to David G. Nes, December 1, 1970, JWFP, Box 40, Series 48:15.

102. Fulbright to The Honorable M. Kamel, December 28, 1970, JWFP, Box 40, Series 48:15.

103. Quandt, 87–92.

104. Daigle, 163.

105. Ibid., 166.

106. Ibid., 166–68.

107. Philip Warden, "Rogers' Proposal Stupid—Jackson," *Chicago Tribune,* March 18, 1971, HMJP, Accession No. 35604, Box 254, Folder 254/3.

108. "Javits, Jackson Take Issue with Rogers' Mideast Stand," *News Miner,* Fairbanks, AK, March 23, 1971, HMJP, Accession No. 35604, Box 254, Folder 254/3; 117 *CR,* 92nd Congress, 1st Session, 4535–4537 (March 2, 1971); 117 *CR,* 92nd Congress, 1st Session, 7081 (March 18, 1971); and 117 *CR,* 92nd Congress, 1st Session, 7766 (March 24, 1971).

109. Philip Warden, "Fulbright Backs Nixon on Mideast," *Chicago Tribune,* March 24, 1971, HMJP, Accession No. 35604, Box 254, Folder 254/3.

110. Thomas B. Ross, "Rogers Will Brief Entire Senate on Middle East," *Houston Chronicle,* March 25, 1971, HMJP, Accession No. 35604, Box 252, Folder 252/12.

111. Ibid.

112. Tad Szulc, "U. S. Aides Clarify Views on Mideast," *New York Times,* March 25, 1971, HMJP, Accession No. 35604, Box 254, Folder 254/3.

113. R. H. Shackford, "Rogers Retreats on Mideast Plan," *The Pittsburgh Press,* March 26, 1971, HMJP, Accession No. 35604, Box 254, Folder 254/2.

114. Lewis Gulic, "Rogers Details U. S. Aim in Mideast Peace," *The Salt Lake City Tribune,* March 26, 1971, HMJP, Accession No. 35604, Box 254, Folder 254/2.

115. 117 *CR,* 92nd Congress, 1st Session, 17355–17356 (June 1, 1971).

116. Staff Correspondent, "American Political Left Splits on Israel Position," *The Christian Science Monitor,* Boston, MA, March 29, 1971, HMJP, Accession No. 35604, Box 254, Folder 254/3.

117. "Remarks of Senator Henry M. Jackson (D., WASH.)," April 28, 1971, HMJP, Accession No. 35606, Box 8, Folder 8/54; "Senator Urges U. S. Scrap Rogers Formula for Middle East Peace," *Hebrew Watchman,* Memphis, TN, April 29, 1971, HMJP, Accession No. 35604, Box 254, Folder 254/3; and "U. S. Senators Agree Israel to Stand Pat," *Jewish Chronicle,* Dayton, OH, May 6, 1971, HMJP, Accession No. 35604, Box 254, Folder 254/3.

118. George Sherman, "Israel Gets Bipartisan Boost," *The Evening Star,* Washington, D.C., May 1, 1971, HMJP, Accession No. 35604, Box 254, Folder 254/3.

119. Richard Nixon, *The Memoirs of Richard Nixon* (New York: Grosset & Dunlap, 1978), 481. See also Memorandum from President Nixon to the President's Assistant for National Security Affairs (Kissinger), Washington, March 17, 1970, *FRUS,* 1969–1976, Vol. XXIII, Arab-Israeli Dispute, 1969–1972, Document 102.

120. Memorandum for the Record, San Clemente, July 16, 1971, *FRUS,* 1969–1976, Vol. XXIII, Arab-Israeli Dispute, 1969–1972, Document 243.

121. Melvin I. Urofsky, *We Are One! American Jewry and Israel* (Garden City, NY: Anchor Press, 1978), 370.

122. Ibid., 388.

123. Robert S. Allen, "Republican Revolt Brewing Over Failure to Sell F-4s to Israel," *Appeal-Democrat,* Marysville, CA, September 13, 1971, HMJP, Accession No. 35604, Box 254, Folder 254/4.

124. "To Maintain a Balance in the Middle East," p. 5, Remarks by Senator Henry M. Jackson, Senate Floor, September 23, 1971, HMJP, Accession No. 35606, Box 8, Folder 8/94.

125. Marquis Childs, "Rogers to Israelis: No More Planes," *The Detroit News,* September 30, 1971, HMJP, Accession No. 35604, Box 254, Folder 254/4.

126. Robert S. Allen, "Pressure on Rogers," *Tulsa World,* October 15, 1971, HMJP, Accession No. 35604, Box 254, Folder 254/4.

127. "78 Senators Urge Jets for Israel," *Washington Post,* October 16, 1971, HMJP, Accession No. 35604, Box 254, Folder 254/4.

128. John W. Finney, "78 Senators Ask Phantom Jets for Israel," *New York Times,* October 16, 1971, HMJP, Accession No. 35604, Box 254, Folder 254/4.

129. "Senate Votes $500m Credit for Israel Jets, Arms," *Boston Globe,* November 24, 1971, HMJP, Accession No. 35604, Box 254, Folder 254/4.

130. "$500 Million Still Available," *Jewish World,* Albany, NY, December 23, 1971, HMJP, Accession No. 35604, Box 254, Folder 254/4.

131. Kochavi, 4–5, 21–24.

132. Terrence Smith, "Decision to Resume Sales of F-4's to Israel Reported," *New York Times,* December 31, 1971, accessed online with ProQuest, January 30, 2015.

133. Bernard Gwertzman, "Israel Is Termed Ready for Talks," *New York Times,* January 22, 1972, accessed online with ProQuest, January 30, 2015.

134. William Beecher, "U. S. to Supply Israel 42 Phantom Jets," *New York Times,* February 6, 1972, accessed online with ProQuest, January 31, 2015.

135. Daigle, 224.

136. Ibid.

137. 118 *CR,* 92st Congress, 2nd Session, 33037–33045 (October 2, 1972).

138. Daigle, 250–58.

139. Ibid., 258.

140. "Selected Senate Actions Concerning Israel," JWFP, Box 41, Series 48:15.

3. Stepping Forward?

1. John W. Finney, "Nixon Asks $2.2 Billion in Emergency Aid for Israel," *New York Times,* October 20, 1973, accessed online February 14, 2019, https://www.nytimes.com/1973/10/20/archives/nixon-asks-22billion-in-emergency-aid-for-israel.html.

2. Steven Spiegel, *The Other Arab-Israeli Conflict: Making America's Middle East Policy, from Truman to Reagan* (Chicago: The University of Chicago Press, 1985); William B. Quandt, *Peace Process: American Diplomacy and the Arab-Israeli Conflict since 1967,* 3rd ed. (Washington, D.C.: Brookings Institution Press, 2005); Richard C. Thornton, *The Nixon-Kissinger Years: Reshaping America's Foreign Policy,* 2nd ed. (St. Paul, MN: Paragon House, 2001).

3. Henry Kissinger, *Years of Upheaval* (New York: Simon & Schuster, 1982), 615.

4. Ibid.

5. Henry Kissinger does not address the impact of the pro-Israel lobby in *Years of Upheaval,* and Steven Spiegel minimizes the role of the lobby in his work *The Other Arab-Israeli Conflict.* John Mearsheimer and Stephen Walt pay little attention to step-by-step diplomacy in *The Israeli Lobby and U. S. Foreign Policy* (New York: Farrar, Straus and Giroux, 2007). Mitchell Bard does not address the influence of the lobby on step-by-step diplomacy in *The Water's Edge and Beyond: Defining the Limits to Domestic Influence on United States Middle East Policy* (New Brunswick, NJ: Transaction Publishers, 1991). See also Edward Tivnan, *The Lobby: Jewish Political Power and American Foreign Policy* (New York: Simon & Schuster, 1987).

6. Spiegel, 248–49.

7. Quandt, 106.

8. Craig Daigle, *The Limits of Détente: The United States, the Soviet Union, and the Arab-Israeli Conflict, 1969–1973* (New Haven, CT: Yale University Press, 2012), 8.

9. 119 *CR,* 93rd Congress, 1st Session, 33152–33153, 33160 (October 8, 1973).

10. 119 *CR,* 93rd Congress, 1st Session, 33460, 33472–33473 (October 9, 1973).

11. 119 *CR,* 93rd Congress, 1st Session, 33291, 33350–3351 (October 9, 1973).

12. 119 *CR,* 93rd Congress, 1st Session, 33773, 33817–33818 (October 11, 1973).

13. 119 *CR,* 93rd Congress, 1st Session, 34161, 34388 (October 15–16, 1973).

14. 119 *CR,* 93rd Congress, 1st Session, 33417–33418 (October 9, 1973).

15. "The Israeli Lobby: Instant Votes When Needed," *Congressional Quarterly,* October 27, 1973, page 2,858, University of South Dakota, University Libraries, Archives and Special Collections, James G. Abourezk Papers [hereafter JGAP], Box 837, Mideast Peace Settlement 1975.

16. Zach Levey, "Anatomy of an Airlift: United States Military Assistance to Israel during the 1973 War," *Cold War History* vol. 8, no. 4 (November 2008): 481–501.

17. Author Interview with Amos Eiran, Dan Accadia Herzliya Hotel, Herzliya, Israel, May 6, 2019.

18. 119 *CR,* 93rd Congress, 1st Session, 34389–4390 (October 16, 1973).

19. 119 *CR,* 93rd Congress, 1st Session, 34764 (October 18, 1973).

20. 119 *CR,* 93rd Congress, 1st Session, 34614 (October 18, 1973).

21. 119 *CR,* 93rd Congress, 1st Session, 34617–34618 (October 18, 1973).

22. 119 *CR,* 93rd Congress, 1st Session, 33916 (October 12, 1973).

23. 119 *CR,* 93rd Congress, 1st Session, 34491 (October 17, 1973). Since his exit from the House of Representatives in 1983, Findley has authored two books about U.S.-Israel relations that criticize the influence of the pro-Israel lobby and the pro-Israel bias of U. S. foreign policy. See *They Dare Speak Out: People and Institutions Confront Israel's Lobby* (Westport, CT: Lawrence Hill, 1985, 1989, 2003), and *Deliberate Deceptions: Facing the Facts about the U.S.-Israeli Relationship* (New York: Lawrence Hill, 1993, 1995).

24. 119 *CR,* 93rd Congress, 1st Session, 34708 (October 18, 1973).

25. 119 *CR,* 93rd Congress, 1st Session, 34486–34487 (October 17, 1973).

26. 119 *CR,* 93rd Congress, 1st Session, 34616–34617 (October 18, 1973).

27. 119 *CR,* 93rd Congress, 1st Session, 34679 (October 18, 1973).

28. John W. Finney, "Nixon Asks $2.2 Billion in Emergency Aid for Israel," *New York Times,* October 20, 1973, accessed online December 6, 2019, https://www.nytimes.com/1973/10/20/archives/nixon-asks-22billion-in-emergency-aid-for-israel.html.

29. Daniel Yergin, *The Prize: The Epic Quest for Oil, Money & Power* (New York: Free Press, 1991), 629; Rudiger Graf, "Making Use of the 'Oil Weapon': Western Industrialized Countries and Arab Petropolitics in 1973–1974," *Diplomatic History* vol. 36, issue 1 (January 2012): 203.

30. Ibid.

31. "The Year of Europe?" *Foreign Affairs,* January 1974, accessed online March 25, 2015, http://www.foreignaffairs.com/articles/24476/z/the-year-of-europe.

32. Yergin, 590.

33. Ibid.

34. Ibid., 591.

35. 119 *CR,* 93rd Congress, 1st Session, 34813–34814 (October 23, 1973).

36. 119 *CR,* 93rd Congress, 1st Session, 34852 (October 23, 1973).

37. 119 *CR,* 93rd Congress, 1st Session, 34951, 35098 (October 24, 26, 1973).

38. 119 *CR,* 93rd Congress, 1st Session, 35334 (November 5, 1973).

39. 119 *CR,* 93rd Congress, 1st Session, 35417 (October 30, 1973).

40. 119 *CR,* 93rd Congress, 1st Session, 35465 (October 30, 1973).

41. 119 *CR,* 93rd Congress, 1st Session, 38533–38534, 38776–38777, and 39104–39105 (November 28, 29, and 30, 1973).

42. 119 *CR,* 93rd Congress, 1st Session, 36418–36419 (November 7, 1973).

43. 119 *CR,* 93rd Congress, 1st Session, 36886 (November 13, 1973).

44. 119 *CR,* 93rd Congress, 1st Session, 34932 (October 24, 1973).

45. 119 *CR,* 93rd Congress, 1st Session, 39137 (December 3, 1973).

46. 119 *CR,* 93rd Congress, 1st Session, 35504 (October 30, 1973).

47. 119 *CR,* 93rd Congress, 1st Session, 36734–36735 (November 12, 1973).

48. 119 *CR,* 93rd Congress, 1st Session, 38274–38275 (November 27, 1973).

49. 119 *CR,* 93rd Congress, 1st Session, 34856 (October 23, 1973).

50. Robert David Johnson, *Congress and the Cold War* (Cambridge, UK: Cambridge University Press, 2006), 190–93.

51. Memorandum of Conversation, Nixon, Kissinger, Javits, and Scowcroft, November 12, 1973, Richard Nixon Presidential Library [hereafter RNPL], National Security Council Files [hereafter NSCF], Presidential/HAK MEMCONS, Box 1027, Folder—MEMCONS April–Nov 1973, HAK and Presidential [1 of 5].

52. 119 *CR,* 93rd Congress, 1st Session, 35015–35016, 35267 (October 25, 30, 1973).

53. 119 *CR,* 93rd Congress, 1st Session, 35015 (October 25, 1973).

54. 119 *CR,* 93rd Congress, 1st Session, 39753 (December 5, 1973).

55. 119 CR, 93rd Congress, 1st Session, 36482–36483 (November 9, 1973).

56. Abourezk's parents were Lebanese.

57. 119 *CR,* 93rd Congress, 1st Session, 36482 (November 9, 1973).

58. 119 *CR,* 93rd Congress, 1st Session, 40020–40021, 40167–40168 (December 6, 7, 1973).

59. Memorandum from Harold Saunders and William Quandt to Secretary Kissinger, November 30, 1973, RNPL, NSCF, Harold H. Saunders Files/Middle East Negotiation Files, Box 1179, Folder—ME—1973 Peace Negotiations, Nov. 28–30, 1973 [1 of 7].

60. Diplomatic Cable from American Embassy in Tel Aviv to Secretary of State, November 28, 1973, RNPL, NSCF, Harold H. Saunders Files/Middle East Negotiation Files, Box 1179, Folder—ME—1973 Peace Negotiations, Nov. 28–30, 1973 [1 of 7].

61. Brent Scowcroft to Henry Kissinger, January 11, 1974, RNPL, NSCF, Henry A. Kissinger Office Files, HAK Trip Files, Box 43, Folder—HAK Trip Europe & Mid East Jan 10–20, 1974, TOHAK 1–70 [2 of 3].

62. 119 *CR,* 93rd Congress, 1st Session, 35189 (October 25, 1973).

63. 119 *CR,* 93rd Congress, 1st Session, 35864 (November 1, 1973).

64. 119 *CR,* 93rd Congress, 1st Session, 38832, 38870 (November 30, 1973).

65. 119 *CR,* 93rd Congress, 1st Session, 40837 (December 11, 1973).

66. "Bipartisan Leadership Meeting," November 27, 1973, RNPL, NSCF, Presidential/HAK MEMCONS, Box 1027, Folder—MEMCONS April–Nov 1973, HAK and Presidential [1 of 5].

67. 119 *CR,* 93rd Congress, 1st Session, 40841–40842 (December 11, 1973).

68. 119 *CR,* 93rd Congress, 1st Session, 40837–40838, 40840 (December 11, 1973).

69. 119 *CR,* 93rd Congress, 1st Session, 40826 (December 11, 1973).

70. 119 *CR,* 93rd Congress, 1st Session, 40827 (December 11, 1973).

71. 119 *CR,* 93rd Congress, 1st Session, 40835 (December 11, 1973).

72. 119 *CR,* 93rd Congress, 1st Session, 40835–40837 (December 11, 1973).

73. 119 *CR,* 93rd Congress, 1st Session, 40821–40822 (December 11, 1973).

74. 119 *CR,* 93rd Congress, 1st Session, 40829 (December 11, 1973).

75. 119 *CR,* 93rd Congress, 1st Session, 40829, 40832 (December 11, 1973).

76. 119 *CR,* 93rd Congress, 1st Session, 40603–40604 (December 10, 1973).

77. 119 *CR,* 93rd Congress, 1st Session, 40819 (December 11, 1973).

78. 119 *CR,* 93rd Congress, 1st Session, 41216 (December 12, 1973).

79. Johnson, 199–200.

80. Mitchell Bard, *The Water's Edge and Beyond: Defining the Limits to Domestic Influence on United States Middle East Policy* (New Brunswick, NJ: Transaction Publishers, 1991), 65–90; Spiegel, 223.

81. Author Interview with Amos Eiran, Dan Accadia Herzliya Hotel, Herzliya, Israel, May 6, 2019.

82. Memorandum of Conversation, Nixon, McClure, and Scowcroft, December 18, 1973, RNPL, NSCF, Presidential/HAK MEMCONS, Box 1027, Folder—MEMCONS December 1973, HAK and Presidential [1 of 2].

83. 119 *CR,* 93rd Congress, 1st Session, 40805 (December 11, 1973).

84. 119 *CR,* 93rd Congress, 1st Session, 41188 (December 12, 1973).

85. 119 *CR,* 93rd Congress, 1st Session, 41607–41609 (December 14, 1973).

86. 119 *CR,* 93rd Congress, 1st Session, 41964–41969 (December 17, 1973).

87. 119 *CR,* 93rd Congress, 1st Session, 41998–41999, 42788–42789 (December 17, 20, 1973).

88. 119 *CR,* 93rd Congress, 1st Session, 42761–42762 (December 20, 1973).

89. 119 *CR,* 93rd Congress, 1st Session, 42763 (December 20, 1973).

90. 119 *CR,* 93rd Congress, 1st Session, 42764–42765 (December 20, 1973).

91. 119 *CR,* 93rd Congress, 1st Session, 42771 (December 20, 1973).

92. 119 *CR,* 93rd Congress, 1st Session, 42775 (December 20, 1973).

93. 119 *CR,* 93rd Congress, 1st Session, 42788 (December 20, 1973).

94. 119 *CR,* 93rd Congress, 1st Session, 42788 (December 20, 1973).

95. 119 *CR,* 93rd Congress, 1st Session, 42823 (December 20, 1973).

96. Brent Scowcroft to Henry Kissinger, December 20, 1973, RNPL, NSCF, Henry A. Kissinger Office Files, HAK Trip Files, Box 42, Folder—HAK Trip Europe & Mideast Dec. 3–22, 1973, TOHAK 34–185 [1 of 2].

97. Ibid.

98. Kissinger, 755.

99. Along with defusing tensions, the Kilometer 101 agreement committed Israel and Egypt to return to the October 22 cease-fire lines "in the framework of agreement on the disengagement and separation of forces under the auspices of the UN." Ibid., 641.

100. Yehuda Blanga, "'The Russians Are Coming, the Russians Are Coming': American Management of the Crisis Associated with Ending the October 1973 War," *Middle Eastern Studies* vol. 49, issue 4 (2013): 569.

101. Kissinger, 644.

102. Ibid., 643.

103. Grasping for any kind of good news, Nixon hoped to deliver the message to the American people. Sadat and Kissinger agreed "that the announcement would be made jointly at the White House and in Cairo." But during a press conference, Kissinger was specifically asked if the United States and Egypt planned to resume diplomatic relations. "Mindful of Nixon's wrath but reluctant to lie," said Kissinger, "I squirmed and said nothing. Sadat had no such inhibitions. 'We will have news for you later in the day, be patient,' Sadat boomed, all but giving the game away." Ibid., 644.

104. Maurice Labelle Jr., "The Only Thorn: Early Saudi-American Relations and the Question of Palestine, 1945–1949," *Diplomatic History* vol. 35, issue 2 (April 2011): 257–81.

105. Kissinger, 664.

106. Ibid., 665.

107. Untitled document ("Sanitized Copy"), November 7, 1973, RNPL, NSCF, Henry A. Kissinger Office Files, HAK Trip Files, Box 40, Folder—HAK Trip, Cairo-TS.

108. Kissinger, 782.

109. Ibid., 784.

110. Kissinger, 625.

111. Ibid.

112. Paul Chamberlin, *The Global Offensive: The United States, the Palestine Liberation Organization, and the Making of the Post-Cold War Order* (Oxford, UK: Oxford University Press, 2012), 218–56.

113. Simen Zernichow and Hilde Henriksen Waage, "The Palestine Option: Nixon, the National Security Council, and the Search for a New Policy, 1970," *Diplomatic History* vol. 38, issue 1 (2014): 182–209.

114. "Bipartisan Leadership Meeting," November 27, 1973, RNPL, NSCF, Presidential/HAK MEMCONS, Box 1027, Folder—MEMCONS April–Nov 1973, HAK and Presidential [1 of 5].

115. Ibid.

116. Israeli officials indicated that they would not attend until Syria gave a list of Israeli POWs and allowed the Red Cross to tend to those prisoners.

117. Quandt, 138–41.

118. Diplomatic Cable, Eagleburger to Scowcroft HAKTO 49, December 16, 1973, RNPL, NSCF, Henry A. Kissinger Office Files, HAK Trip Files, Box 42, Folder—HAK Trip Europe & Mideast Dec. 8–22, 1973, TOHAK 1–88 [2 of 2].

119. Diplomatic Cable, Eagleburger to Scowcroft, December 11, 1973, RNPL, NSCF, Henry A. Kissinger Office Files, HAK Trip Files, Box 42, Folder—HAK Trip Europe & Mideast Dec. 8–22, 1973, TOHAK 1–88 [1 of 2].

120. Diplomatic Cable, London HAKTO 18 to Eagleburger, December 13, 1973, RNPL, NSCF, Henry A. Kissinger Office Files, HAK Trip Files, Box 42, Folder—HAK Trip Europe & Mideast Dec. 8–22, 1973, TOHAK 1–88 [1 of 2].

121. Diplomatic Cable, Scowcroft to Kissinger, December 13, 1973, RNPL, NSCF, Henry A. Kissinger Office Files, HAK Trip Files, Box 42, Folder—HAK Trip Europe & Mideast Dec. 8–22, 1973, TOHAK 1–75 [1 of 2].

122. Ibid.

123. Memorandum of Conversation, Henry Kissinger, Max Fisher, et al., December 27, 1973, Kissinger Transcripts in Proquest-Chadwyck's Digital National Security Archive, accessed on June 30, 2014.

124. News Release, December 11, 1973, JGAP, Box 1042, Mideast Crisis.

125. "Interview with Abourezk," JGAP, Box 866, P.L.O.: Key to Peace 1/75.

126. Abourezk to Kissinger, February 8, 1974, JGAP, Box 689, Middle East—General Material 1973–74 Trip. Lee Egerstrom, "No Yielding in Abourezk Visit, Say Iraqi Officials," January 9, 1974, *Aberdeen American News,* JGAP, Box 689, Middle East—General Material 1973–74 Trip.

127. Kissinger would shuttle between Middle East capitals to negotiate with heads of state and negotiating teams, serving as an intermediary between two parties. He used shuttle diplomacy to negotiate a cease-fire to end the Yom Kippur War and then for all three disengagement agreements. This feature of his personal style of diplomacy is often mentioned in connection with step-by-step diplomacy, but the two are separate ideas. The former involves his movement between cities on behalf of other parties, while the latter refers to his diplomatic method for resolving the Arab-Israeli conflict.

128. Likud is the conservative, right-wing party in Israel that won the 1977 elections, which was the first time that the political left was defeated in Israel.

129. Kissinger, 893.

130. Memorandum of Conversation, Kissinger, Allon, Eban, Dinitz, et al., January 20, 1974, RNPL, NSCF, Henry A. Kissinger Office Files, Country Files—Middle East, Middle East HAK Trip December 1973 Miscellaneous Papers to JORDAN June 1974 The President, Box 140, Folder—NSCF: Country Files: Middle East, Sec. Kissinger's Middle East Trip Jan 11–20, 1974 (2 of 2)[2 of 2].

131. Nixon to Faisal, February 7, 1974, RNPL, NSCF, Henry A. Kissinger Office Files, Country Files—Middle East, Palestinians to Secretary Kissinger's Trip

to the Middle East, November 5–10, 1973, Box 139, Folder—NSCF: Country Files: Middle East, Saudi Arabia (2 of 3), [Dec 73—Feb 74] (2 of 3).

132. Scowcroft to Akins, February 8, 1974, RNPL, NSCF, Henry A. Kissinger Office Files, Country Files—Middle East, Palestinians to Secretary Kissinger's Trip to the Middle East, November 5–10, 1973, Box 139, Folder—NSCF: Country Files: Middle East, Saudi Arabia (2 of 3), [Dec 73—Feb 74] (2 of 3).

133. Memorandum for Secretary Kissinger from The Situation Room, February 26, 1974, RNPL, NSCF, Henry A. Kissinger Office Files, HAK Trip Files, Box 44, Folder—HAK Trip Mid East & Europe TOHAK 1–50, Feb 25–Mar 4, 1974 (2 of 2).

134. Reportage, Comment on Signing of Disengagement Agreement, "Likud Against Speedy Agreement," January 17, 1974, RNPL, NSCF, Henry A. Kissinger Office Files, Country Files—Middle East, Middle East HAK Trip December 1973 Miscellaneous Papers to JORDAN June 1974 The President, Box 140, Folder—NSCF: Country Files: Middle East, Sec. Kissinger's Middle East Trip Jan 11–20, 1974 (2 of 2)[1 of 2].

135. Kissinger, 937. Taken from Meir's autobiography—Golda Meir, *My Life* (New York: G. P. Putnam's Sons, 1975), 455.

136. Memorandum for Secretary Kissinger from The Situation Room, February 26, 1974, RNPL, NSCF, Henry A. Kissinger Office Files, HAK Trip Files, Box 44, Folder—HAK Trip Mid East & Europe TOHAK 1–50, Feb 25—Mar 4, 1974 (2 of 2).

137. Kissinger, p. 1,039. After finally convincing Dayan and Peres to join the cabinet, the Agranat Commission, set up to investigate the intelligence failures leading up to the 1973 Arab-Israeli War, released its first report on April 2. The report singled out Chief of Staff General David Elazar as bearing "direct responsibility," and his superior—Defense Minister Moshe Dayan—would have been the next target.

138. Kissinger, 935.

139. Spiegel, 276–77.

140. Memorandum of Conversation, Nixon, Kissinger, Scowcroft, and GOP Congressional Leadership, March 8, 1974, RNPL, NSCF, Presidential/HAK Mem-Cons, Box 1028, Folder—MemCons—HAK & Presidential, March 1–May 8, 1974 [3 of 4].

141. Diplomatic Cable, American Embassy in Jidda to Secretary of State, February 12, 1974, RNPL, NSCF, Country Files—Middle East, Box 631, Folder 1.

142. Memorandum of Conversation, Nixon, Ford, Kissinger, Scowcroft, and Congressional Leadership, April 24, 1974, RNPL, NSCF, Presidential/HAK Mem-Cons, Box 1028, Folder 4.

143. Diplomatic Cable for General Scowcroft from the Secretary, May 1, 1974, RNPL, NSCF, Henry A. Kissinger Office Files, HAK Trip Files, Box 45, Folder—HAK Trip MidEast HAKTO 1–179, Apr. 28–May 31, 1974 [2 of 4].

144. Quandt, 149.

145. Diplomatic Cable for Henry A. Kissinger from Brent Scowcroft, May 10, 1974, RNPL, NSCF, Henry A. Kissinger Office Files, HAK Trip Files, Box 46, Folder—HAK Trip MidEast; Apr. 28–May 31, 1974, HAKTO 76–160 [1 of 2].

146. Diplomatic Cable for General Scowcroft to Sec Kissinger HAKTO 87, May 14, 1974, RNPL, NSCF, Henry A. Kissinger Office Files, HAK Trip Files, Box 45, Folder—HAK Trip MidEast HAKTO 1–179, Apr. 28–May 31, 1974 [3 of 4].

147. Diplomatic Cable from Scowcroft to Bremer/Rodman for Sec. Kissinger, May 14, 1974, RNPL, NSCF, Henry A. Kissinger Office Files, HAK Trip Files, Box 47, Folder—HAK Trip MidEast HAKTO 161–245, Apr. 28–May 31, 1974 (2 of 2).

148. Scowcroft to Bremer/Rodman for Henry A. Kissinger, May 14, 1974, RNPL, NSCF, Henry A. Kissinger Office Files, HAK Trip Files, Box 47, Folder—HAK Trip MidEast HAKTO 161–245, Apr. 28–May 31, 1974 (2 of 2).

149. Scowcroft to Bremer/Rodman for Secretary Kissinger, May 13, 1974, RNPL, NSCF, Henry A. Kissinger Office Files, HAK Trip Files, Box 47, Folder—HAK Trip MidEast HAKTO 161–245, Apr. 28–May 31, 1974 (2 of 2).

150. The document was included in a letter from Mr. Norman F. Dacey to J. William Fulbright on February 16, 1977, Herman Edelsberg to Board of Governors, May 7, 1974, Tasks Confronting B'nai B'rith, Box 15, Series 2 Foreign Relations, Folder 3, MS 144-C, Middle East, 1977, J. William Fulbright Papers, University of Arkansas.

151. Fulbright to Dacey, February 21, 1977, Box 15, Series 2 Foreign Relations, Folder 3, MS 144-C, Middle East, 1977, J. William Fulbright Papers, University of Arkansas.

152. Edelsberg to Board of Governors.

153. Ibid.

154. Ibid.

155. Ibid.

156. Ibid.

157. Diplomatic Cable, from Eagleburger HAKTO 12 to General Scowcroft, January 13, 1974, RNPL, NSCF, Henry A. Kissinger Office Files, HAK Trip Files, Box 43, Folder—HAK Trip Europe & Mid East Jan 10–20, 1974, TOHAK 1–65 [1 of 2]; and Diplomatic Cable, HAKTO 015 to Scowcroft, January 14, 1974, RNPL, NSCF, Henry A. Kissinger Office Files, HAK Trip Files, Box 43, Folder—HAK Trip Europe & Mid East Jan 10–20, 1974, TOHAK 1–65 [2 of 2].

158. Kissinger, 1,091.

159. Ibid.

160. Ibid., 1,115.

161. Ibid., 1,092.

162. Spiegel, 280.

163. Kissinger, 1,116–17.

164. Ibid., 1,117.

165. Ibid., 1,120.

166. Ibid., 1,122.

167. Talking Points, Secretary Kissinger's Briefing on the President's Middle East Trip, June 20, 1974, RNPL, NSCF, Harold H. Saunders Files, Middle East Negotiations Files, Box 1189, Folder—President's Middle East Trip, June 10–19, 1974, File #2 (2 of 4).

168. Memorandum for The President from Henry A. Kissinger, "Your Talks in Israel," June 1974, RNPL, NSCF, Henry A. Kissinger Office Files, Country Files—Middle East, Box 136, Folder—Dinitz January 1–July 1, 1974 (2 of 2) [1 of 2].

169. Ibid.

170. Richard Nixon, *The Memoirs of Richard Nixon* (New York: Grosset & Dunlap, 1978), 1,007–8.

171. The American Presidency Project, "Remarks About Resumption of Diplomatic Relations Between the United States and Syria," June 16, 1974, accessed on May 7, 2015, http://www.presidency.ucsb.edu/ws/?pid=4256.

172. Memorandum of Conversation, Nixon and Bipartisan Leadership, June 20, 1974, RNPL, NSCF, Presidential/HAK MemCons, Box 1029, Folder—MEMCON'S HAK and Presidential, 1 June 1974–[Aug.8, 1974] [2 of 3].

173. The American Presidency Project, "Remarks About Resumption of Diplomatic Relations Between the United States and Syria," June 16, 1974, accessed on May 7, 2015, http://www.presidency.ucsb.edu/ws/?pid=4256.

174. Thornton, 290.

175. Diplomatic Cable, American Embassy in Tel Aviv to Kissinger, July 6, 1974, RNPL, NSCF, Harold H. Saunders Files, Middle East Negotiations Files, Box 1185, Folder—M. E. Peace Negotiations—July 1–13, 1974 [2 of 2].

176. Diplomatic Cable, American Embassy in Tel Aviv to Kissinger, July 29, 1974, RNPL, NSCF, Harold H. Saunders Files, Middle East Negotiations Files, Box 1185, Folder—M. E. Peace Negotiations—July 14–31, 1974 [1 of 2].

177. Diplomatic Cable, Kissinger to American Embassies in Jidda, Amman, Beirut, Cairo, Damascus, and Tel Aviv, and the American Consul in Jerusalem, July 13, 1974, RNPL, NSCF, Harold H. Saunders Files, Middle East Negotiations Files, Box 1185, Folder—M. E. Peace Negotiations—July 1–13, 1974 [1 of 2].

178. Diplomatic Cable, American Embassy in Tel Aviv to Kissinger, July 29, 1974, RNPL, NSCF, Harold H. Saunders Files, Middle East Negotiations Files, Box 1185, Folder—M. E. Peace Negotiations—July 14–31, 1974 [1 of 2].

179. Ibid.

180. Ibid.

4. The Spirit of the 76

1. Yanek Mieczkowski, *Gerald Ford and the Challenges of the 1970s* (Lexington: The University Press of Kentucky, 2005); and John Robert Greene, *The Presidency of Gerald R. Ford* (Lawrence: University of Kansas Press, 1995).

2. Loch K. Johnson, *America as a World Power: Foreign Policy in a Constitutional Framework,* 2nd ed. (New York: McGraw-Hill, 1991, 1995), 197. See also John A. Lawrence, *The Class of '74: Congress after Watergate and the Roots of Partisanship* (Baltimore: Johns Hopkins University Press, 2018).

3. Henry Kissinger, *Years of Renewal* (New York: Simon & Schuster, 1999), 834–35.

4. Mieczkowski, 281. Mieczkowski cites the August 21, 2003, interview with Ford in his notes (410).

5. Peter L. Hahn, *Caught in the Middle East: U. S. Policy toward the Arab-Israeli Conflict, 1945–1961* (Chapel Hill: The University of North Carolina Press, 2004). One of the first *hasbara* efforts by Israeli leaders discussed by Hahn was a "sweeping public relations campaign" to overcome Pentagon and State Department reluctance to supply Israel with arms in 1950 (73). Peter Hahn, "The View from Jerusalem: Revelations about U. S. Diplomacy from the Archives of Israel," *Diplomatic History* 22, no. 4 (Fall 1998): 509–32.

6. This chapter relies on Hebrew-language documents from the Israel State Archives. I am indebted to the excellent work of my research assistant Jonathan Matthews, who translated all of the Israeli documents discussed below. Over the course of two weeks in June and July 2015, Jonathan and I went through a series of papers from the Office of the Foreign Ministry that included extensive discussions between Jerusalem and the Israeli embassy in Washington. Jonathan carefully dictated to me the contents of the documents while I typed, and we spent a great deal of time discussing the appropriate word choice for translation. Additionally, Jonathan was a tremendous help in explaining and discussing Israeli politics during this period.

7. Steven Spiegel, *The Other Arab-Israeli Conflict: Making America's Middle East Policy, from Truman to Reagan* (Chicago: The University of Chicago Press, 1985), 297.

8. William B. Quandt, *Peace Process: American Diplomacy and the Arab-Israeli Conflict since 1967,* 3rd ed. (Washington, D.C.: Brookings Institution Press, 2005), 165.

9. Salim Yaqub, "The Weight of Conquest: Henry Kissinger and the Arab-Israeli Conflict," in *Nixon in the World: American Foreign Relations, 1969–1977,* edited by Fredrik Logevall and Andrew Preston, 227–48 (New York: Oxford University Press, 2008). See also Salim Yaqub, *Imperfect Strangers: Americans, Arabs, and U.S.-Middle East Relations in the 1970s* (Ithaca, NY: Cornell University Press, 2016), 145–82.

10. Galen Jackson, "The Showdown That Wasn't: U.S.-Israeli Relations and American Domestic Politics, 1973–1975," *International Security* 39, no. 4 (Spring 2015): 130–69.

11. Quandt, 156.

12. Quandt, 159. The League, comprised of the leading Arab states, likely endorsed the PLO to undermine Kissinger's plans to negotiate with Jordan. In

particular, Syria and Saudi Arabia put forward staunch support of the PLO. The Arab states never approved of any state separately negotiating a peace with Israel.

13. Yasser Arafat, leader of the PLO, participated in several terrorist raids against Israel while a member of Fatah. Israel cited those particular raids, along with other grievances, as its justification for war in June 1967. In addition, the United States steadfastly refused to recognize the PLO until the organization publicly acknowledged Israel's right to exist. This step was finally taken in the fall of 1988, when Arafat did recognize the State of Israel. His statement was eventually followed by U. S. diplomatic recognition of the PLO.

14. Quandt, 160.

15. Spiegel, 290.

16. Quandt, 163.

17. Summary of meeting between Thomas O'Neill and PM Rabin in Rabin's Office, written by Shalev, April 4, 1975, Ministry of Foreign Affairs—Office of the Foreign Minister [hereafter MFA-OFM], Het, Tzadik—6853/8, Israel State Archives [hereafter ISA]. O'Neill would serve as Speaker of the House between 1977 and 1987.

18. Gerald R. Ford, *A Time to Heal: The Autobiography of Gerald R. Ford* (New York: Harper & Row, Publishers), 247.

19. President/HAK Meeting with Bipartisan Leadership, March 24, 1975, GRFL, National Security Adviser: Memoranda of Conversations, 1973–1977 [hereafter NSA: MC], Box 10, March 24, 1975: Ford Kissinger, Bipartisan Congressional Leadership.

20. Ibid.

21. Ibid.

22. Ibid.

23. Memorandum of Conversation, Ford, Kissinger and Scowcroft, March 26, 1975, GRFL, NSA: MC, Box, 10, March 26, 1975—Ford, Kissinger.

24. Memorandum of Conversation, Ford, Kissinger, March 27, 1975, GRFL, NSA: MC, Box 10, March 27, 1975—Ford, Kissinger.

25. Memorandum of Conversation, Ford, Kissinger and Scowcroft, March 26, 1975, GRFL, Memcons, Box 10, March 26, 1975—Ford, Kissinger. Kissinger also cited "three million Greeks" along with Israelis for "running American foreign policy." Kissinger was referring to pro-Greek lobbying efforts in response to Turkey's invasion of Cyprus.

26. Minutes: National Security Council Meeting, March 28, 1975, GRFL, National Security Adviser: NSC Meeting File, Box 1, NSC Meeting, March 28, 1975.

27. Ibid.

28. These figures were obtained from a memorandum written by Clinton Granger and Robert Oakley sent to Scowcroft on May 6, 1975. In line with the secrecy that seems to be a staple of the U.S.-Israel relationship, Oakley recommended, "Probably it would be better not to release them [the figures] to the press

and public, but they can certainly be used to good effect with Congress and others in private." Granger and Oakley to Scowcroft, "U. S. Assistance to Israel," May 6, 1975, GRFL, Presidential Country Files for Middle East and South Asia, 1974–1977, Box 15, Israel (8).

29. Kissinger to Ford, "Discussion of Middle East Strategy," April 21, 1975, GRFL, Presidential Country Files for Middle East and South Asia, 1974–1977, Box 1, General (8).

30. Ibid.

31. Memorandum of Conversation, Ford, Kissinger, et al., Memcon, April 14, 1975, GRFL, NSA: MC, Box 10, April 14, 1975: Ford, Kissinger, U. S. Ambassadors Keating (Israel), Eilts (Egypt), Pickering (Jordan), Murphy (Syria).

32. Ibid.

33. Ibid.

34. Ibid.

35. Ibid.

36. Memorandum of Conversation, Ford, Kissinger, Jordanian King Hussein, et al., Memcon, April 29, 1975, GRFL, NSA: MC, Box 11, April 29, 1975: Ford, Kissinger, Jordanian King Hussein.

37. Ibid. At this point (though further research may prove otherwise), there is no concrete evidence to suggest Hussein had any idea that Israel had professed to Kissinger its desire to hold onto significant chunks of territory.

38. Ibid.

39. Kissinger to Ford, "Discussion of Middle East Strategy," April 21, 1975, GRFL, Presidential Country Files for Middle East and South Asia, 1974–1977, Box 1, General (8).

40. Ibid.

41. Ibid.

42. Ibid.

43. Ibid.

44. Ibid.

45. Ibid.

46. Ibid.

47. Peter Golden, *Quiet Diplomat: A Biography of Max M. Fisher* (New York: Cornwall Books, 1992), 316.

48. Transcript of interview with Zvi Rafiah, interviewed by Paul J. P. Sandal and Laura Blackburn, Stephen F. Austin State University, accessed October 9, 2015, http://www.sfasu.edu/heritagecenter/5381.asp. Although Rafiah is portrayed as a Mossad agent in the movie *Charlie Wilson's War,* as well as in the book that inspired the movie, Rafiah denied the claim in his interview.

49. Turgemon to Office of Director General; March 24, 1975, MFA-OFM, Het, Tzadik—6853/7, ISA.

50. "The Middle East," A Report by Senator Charles H. Percy to the Committee on Foreign Relations United States Senate, April 21, 1975 (Washington, D.C.:

U. S. Government Printing Office, 1975). In addition to Israel and Egypt, Percy also visited Iran, Kuwait, Bahrain, Qatar, Abu Dhabi, Dubai, Oman, Saudi Arabia, Lebanon, Syria, and Jordan.

51. "The Middle East," 18.

52. "The Middle East," 5.

53. "The Middle East," 17.

54. "Realities of the Middle East," A Report by Senator George S. McGovern to the Committee on Foreign Relations United States Senate, May 1975 (Washington, D.C.: U. S. Government Printing Office, 1975).

55. "Realities of the Middle East," 28.

56. "Realities of the Middle East," 27–28.

57. "Realities of the Middle East," 1.

58. Report to Evron and Director General from Dinitz about his meeting with fourteen members of the foreign committee, March 26, 1975, MFA-OFM, Het, Tzadik—6853/7, ISA.

59. Ibid.

60. Dinitz to Foreign Minister and Director General, March 26, 1975, MFA-OFM, Het, Tzadik—6853/7, ISA.

61. Ibid.

62. Dinitz to Director General and Evron, March 27, 1975, MFA-OFM, Het, Tzadik—6853/7, ISA.

63. Ibid.

64. Rafiah to the Ministry of Foreign Affairs, March 27, 1975, MFA-OFM, Het, Tzadik—6853/7, ISA.

65. Ibid.

66. "Interview with the President and Political Developments," written by Dinitz to Foreign Minister and Director General, March 28, 1975, MFA-OFM, Het, Tzadik—6853/7, ISA.

67. Ibid.

68. Ibid.

69. Ibid.

70. Ibid.

71. Golden, 323.

72. Dinitz to Foreign Minister and Director General, March 28, 1975, MFA-OFM, Het, Tzadik—6853/7, ISA.

73. Ibid.

74. Memorandum of Conversation, Ford, Kissinger, Scowcroft, and Max Fisher, March 27, 1975, GRFL, Memcons, Box 10, March 27, 1975—Ford, Kissinger, Max Fisher.

75. Dinitz to Director General, April 7, 1975, MFA-OFM, Het, Tzadik—6853/8, ISA.

76. Dinitz to Minister of Defense and Prime Minister and Head of IDF Intelligence, March 30, 1975, MFA-OFM, Het, Tzadik—6853/7, ISA.

77. Ibid.

78. Turgemon to the Center and Intelligence of the Foreign Office, April 1, 1975, MFA-OFM, Het, Tzadik—6853/8, ISA.

79. Ibid.

80. Evron to Dinitz, March 31, 1975, MFA-OFM, Het, Tzadik—6853/7, ISA.

81. Bentzer to Director General and Evron, April 3, 1975, MFA-OFM, Het, Tzadik—6853/8, ISA.

82. Summary of meeting between Thomas O'Neill and PM Rabin in Rabin's Office, written by Shalev, April 4, 1975, MFA-OFM, Het, Tzadik—6853/8, ISA.

83. Report of Mordechai Gazit to the Prime Minister, March 31, 1975, MFA-OFM, Het, Tzadik—6853/7, ISA.

84. Ibid.

85. Ibid.

86. Arad to Director General, Evron, and Dafney, April 1, 1975, MFA-OFM, Het, Tzadik—6853/8, ISA.

87. Arad to Director General and Intelligence of Foreign Office, April 28, 1975, MFA-OFM, Het, Tzadik—6853/9, ISA.

88. Arad to Evron, Irgov, and the Intelligence of the Foreign Office, April 2, 1975, MFA-OFM, Het, Tzadik—6853/8, ISA.

89. Dinitz to Director General, April 2, 1975, MFA-OFM, Het, Tzadik—6853/8, ISA.

90. Ibid.

91. Ibid.

92. Director General to Dinitz, April 7, 1975, MFA-OFM, Het, Tzadik—6853/8, ISA. David Ginsburg, according to the *New York Times,* successfully represented Kissinger in his battle to keep private transcripts of phone conversations while Secretary of State and National Security Advisor for Richard Nixon (William Grimes, "David Ginsburg, Longtime Washington Insider, Dies at 98," *New York Times,* May 25, 2010, accessed January 15, 2016, http://www.nytimes.com/2010/05/25/us/25ginsburg.html?_r=0). Cyrus Vance served as Deputy Defense Secretary under Lyndon Johnson and would become Jimmy Carter's Secretary of State in 1977. McGeorge Bundy served as National Security Advisor for Presidents Kennedy and Johnson. W. Averell Harriman was a longtime politician active in the presidential administrations of Franklin Roosevelt and Harry Truman; after losing the Democratic nomination for president to Adlai Stevenson in 1952 and 1956, Harriman was an important diplomat for the Johnson and Kennedy administrations. Dean Rusk served as Secretary of State for both Johnson and Kennedy. The Sonnenfeld referred to in the message was probably Helmut Sonnenfeld, a close adviser to Kissinger, whom Kissinger speaks fondly of in his third memoir, *Years of Renewal* (New York: Simon & Schuster, 1999).

93. Dinitz to Director General, April 7, 1975, MFA-OFM, Het, Tzadik—6853/8, ISA.

94. Dinitz to Director General, April 6, 1975, MFA-OFM, Het, Tzadik—6853/8, ISA.

95. Dinitz to Director General, April 8, 1975, MFA-OFM, Het, Tzadik—6853/8, ISA.

96. Dinitz to the Director General, April 9, 1975, MFA-OFM, Het, Tzadik—6853/8, ISA.

97. Rafiah to Dafney, April 10, 1975, MFA-OFM, Het, Tzadik—6853/8, ISA.

98. Dinitz to Director General and Foreign Minister, April 23, 1975, MFA-OFM, Het, Tzadik—6853/9, ISA. Rumsfeld became Secretary of Defense in the Ford administration in November 1975 and served until the end of Ford's presidency.

99. Dinitz to Director General, April 2, 1975, MFA-OFM, Het, Tzadik—6853/8, ISA.

100. Dinitz to Director General, April 7, 1975, MFA-OFM, Het, Tzadik—6853/8, ISA.

101. Rappaport to the Press and Hasbara Department of the Foreign Office, April 10, 1975, MFA-OFM, Het, Tzadik—6853/8, ISA.

102. Rafiah to the Intelligence of the Ministry, Eban meeting with Senator Bumpers, April 17, 1975, MFA-OFM, Het, Tzadik—6853/9, ISA.

103. Rafiah to the Intelligence of the Ministry, Eban meeting with Senator Griffin, April 17, 1975, MFA-OFM, Het, Tzadik—6853/9, ISA.

104. Rafiah to the Office of the Director General, Eban meeting with Stuart Symington, April 17, 1975, MFA-OFM, Het, Tzadik—6853/9, ISA.

105. Ibid.

106. Dinitz to Director General, April 23, 1975, MFA-OFM, Het, Tzadik—6853/9, ISA.

107. Ibid.

108. Shalev to Director General, April 22, 1975, MFA-OFM, Het, Tzadik—6853/9, ISA.

109. Evron to Minister of Foreign Affairs, May 2, 1975, Ministry of Foreign Affairs—Office of the CEO [hereafter MFA-CEO], Het, Tzadik—6813/11, ISA.

110. Dinitz to Evron, April 24, 1975, MFA-OFM, Het, Tzadik—6853/9, ISA.

111. Dinitz to Director General, April 24, 1975, MFA-OFM, Het, Tzadik—6853/9, ISA.

112. Dinitz to Minister of Foreign Affairs, Periodical Assessment of the Israeli Ambassador in Washington, April 28, 1975, MFA-OFM, Het, Tzadik—6853/9, ISA.

113. Ibid.

114. Ibid. The brackets are in the original document.

115. Ibid.

116. Dinitz to Director General, April 29, 1975, MFA-OFM, Het, Tzadik—6853/9, ISA.

117. Evron to Minister of Foreign Affairs, May 2, 1975, MFA-CEO, Het, Tzadik—6813/11, ISA.

118. Turgemon to the Center for Political Research and Middle East Department, May 5, 1975, MFA-CEO, Het, Tzadik—6813/11, ISA.

119. Joseph Ben-Aharon to Prime Minister, May 18, 1975, MFA-CEO, Het, Tzadik—6813/11, ISA.

120. Ibid.

121. Ibid.

122. Ibid. Although unnamed, the report likely referenced Stanley Hoffmann and someone else, perhaps Kissinger.

123. Ibid. Yaqub also discusses the rise in Arab American activism in *Imperfect Strangers*. The Hillel system refers to student-led organizations on college campuses that celebrate Jewish life and culture.

124. Bentzer to Dafney, May 19, 1975, MFA-CEO, Het, Tzadik—6813/11, ISA.

125. Dinitz to Director General and Evron, May 21, 1975, MFA-CEO, Het, Tzadik—6813/11, ISA.

126. Rafiah to Evron, May 21, 1975, MFA-CEO, Het, Tzadik—6813/11, ISA.

127. Memorandum of Conversation, Ford, Kissinger, and Scowcroft, Memcon, May 8, 1975, GRFL, NSA: MC, Box 11, May 8, 1975: Ford, Kissinger.

128. Rafiah to Evron, May 19, 1975, MFA-CEO, Het, Tzadik—6813/11, ISA; Rafiah to Evron, May 20, 1975, MFA-CEO, Het, Tzadik—6813/11, ISA.

129. Rafiah to Evron, May 21, 1975, MFA-CEO, Het, Tzadik—6813/11, ISA.

130. Ford, 287.

131. Yitzhak Rabin, *The Rabin Memoirs, Expanded Edition* (Berkeley: University of California Press, 1996), 262. George Lenczowski claims, "There were reasons to believe that the letter had been partly drafted by the pro-Israeli lobby, the American-Israel Public Affairs Committee (AIPAC)." *American Presidents and the Middle East* (Durham, NC: Duke University Press, 1990), 150. Edward Sheehan also claims, "The letter was a stunning triumph for the lobby." *The Arabs, Israelis, and Kissinger: A Secret History of American Diplomacy in the Middle East* (New York: Reader's Digest Press, 1976), 176.

132. Sheehan, 175. Sheehan includes the letter in its entirety.

133. Dinitz to Director General, May 22, 1975, MFA-CEO, Het, Tzadik—6813/11, ISA.

134. Allon to Dinitz, May 22, 1975, MFA-CEO, Het, Tzadik—6813/11, ISA.

135. Turgemon to Evron, May 30, 1975, MFA-CEO, Het, Tzadik—6813/11, ISA.

136. Richard H. Curtiss, *A Changing Image: American Perceptions of the Arab-Israeli Dispute* (Washington, D.C.: American Educational Trust, 1982), 103.

137. James Abourezk, *Advise and Dissent: Memoirs of South Dakota and the U. S. Senate* (Chicago: Chicago Review Press, 1989), 168.

138. Ibid.

139. Galen Jackson, "The Showdown That Wasn't: U.S.-Israeli Relations and American Domestic Politics, 1973–1975," *International Security* 39, no. 4 (Spring 2015): 130–69.

140. Sheehan, 175–76.

141. Terence Smith, "Israel Resisting U. S. on Sinai Pact," *New York Times,* May 27, 1975, accessed online with ProQuest, October 7, 2015.

142. Rafiah to Evron, May 27, 1975, MFA-CEO, Het, Tzadik—6813/11, ISA.

143. Dinitz to Director General, May 28, 1975, MFA-CEO, Het, Tzadik—6813/11, ISA.

144. Quandt, 168–69.

145. Henry Kissinger, *Years of Renewal* (New York: Simon & Schuster, 1999).

5. The Sinai II Agreements of 1975

1. Cecilia Albin and Harold H. Saunders, *Sinai II: The Politics of International Mediation* (*F P I Case Studies*) (Washington, D.C.: Johns Hopkins University, School of Advanced International Studies, 1993).

2. Harold H. Saunders, "The Middle East, 1973–1984: Hidden Agendas," in *The President, the Congress and Foreign Policy: A Joint Policy Project of the Association of Former Members of Congress and the Atlantic Council of the United States,* edited by Edmund S. Muskie, Kenneth Rush, and Kenneth W. Thompson, 175–205 (Lanham, MD: University Press of America, Inc., 1986); for the section about Sinai II, see 187–91.

3. William B. Quandt, *Peace Process: American Diplomacy and the Arab-Israeli Conflict since 1967,* 3rd ed. (Washington, D.C.: Brookings Institution Press, 2005); Steven Spiegel, *The Other Arab-Israeli Conflict: Making America's Middle East Policy, from Truman to Reagan* (Chicago: The University of Chicago Press, 1985); James A. Bill, *George Ball: Behind the Scenes in U. S. Foreign Policy* (New Haven, CT: Yale University Press, 1997); and Salim Yaqub, *Imperfect Strangers: Americans, Arabs, and U.S.-Middle East Relations in the 1970s* (Ithaca, NY: Cornell University Press, 2016).

4. Michael B. Oren, *Power, Faith, and Fantasy: America in the Middle East, 1776 to the Present* (New York: W. W. Norton & Co., 2007); Peter Hahn, *Crisis and Crossfire: The United States and the Middle East since 1945* (Washington, D.C.: Potomac Books, 2005).

5. Glen S. Krutz and Jeffrey S. Peake, *Treaty Politics and the Rise of Executive Agreements: International Commitments in a System of Shared Powers* (Ann Arbor: University of Michigan Press, 2009); Loch K. Johnson, *The Making of International Agreements: Congress Confronts the Executive* (New York: New York University Press, 1984).

6. Arthur Schlesinger Jr., *The Imperial Presidency* (Boston: Houghton Mifflin, 1973); Louis Fisher, *President and Congress: Power and Policy* (New York: Free Press, 1972); Arthur Schlesinger, Jr., *War and the American Presidency* (New York: W. W. Norton & Company, 2004); Andrew Rudalevige, *New Imperial Presidency: Renewing Presidential Power after Watergate* (Ann Arbor: The University of Michigan Press, 2006).

7. Schlesinger, Jr., *The Imperial Presidency*, 392.

8. Krutz and Peake, 2.

9. Marjorie Ann Brown, "Executive Agreements: A Survey of Recent Congressional Interest and Action," *Congressional Research Service: Library of Congress,* Foreign Affairs Division, September 10, 1974, Appendix A. Record Group 233: Records of the United States House of Representatives, 94th–95th Congress, Committee on Foreign Affairs, Executive Agreements (files of George R. Berdes), Box No. 2, Folder: Executive Agreements: Gen. Reference & Background Material, National Archives Building, Washington, D.C.

10. Philip A. Grant, "The Bricker Amendment Controversy," *Presidential Studies Quarterly* vol. 15, no. 3 (Summer 1985): 572–82.

11. Schlesinger, Jr., *The Imperial Presidency,* 392.

12. Ibid., 392–410.

13. U. S. Senate, Subcommittee on Separation of Powers, Hearings, *Congressional Oversight of Executive Agreements—1975,* 94th Congress, p. 1. Antonin Scalia discusses the amendment, which deleted the word "specific" within the phrase "exempting only executive agreements made pursuant to [specific] provisions of the Constitution or laws" (171).

14. S. 632, S. 1251, H. R. 1268, H. R. 1273, H. R. 4438, and H. R. 4439.

15. "Remarks by the Honorable Thomas E. Morgan, Upon Introduction of the Executive Agreements Review Act," page 1, Record Group 233: Records of the United States House of Representatives, 94th–95th Congress: Committee on Foreign Affairs, Executive Agreements (files of George R. Berdes), Box #2, Folder: Executive Agreements—Legislation, National Archives Building, Washington, D.C.

16. "Remarks of Hon. Clement J. Zablocki, March 6, 1975," page 1, Record Group 233: Records of the United States House of Representatives, 94th–95th Congress: Committee on Foreign Affairs, Executive Agreements (files of George R. Berdes), Box #2, Folder: Executive Agreements—Legislation, National Archives Building, Washington, D.C.

17. U. S. Senate, Subcommittee on Separation of Powers, *Hearings, Congressional Oversight of Executive Agreements—1975,* 94th Congress, p. 1–4.

18. Ibid., 322.

19. Ibid.

20. Ibid.

21. "To Implement the United States Proposal for the Early-Warning System in Sinai," *Report of the Committee on International Relations together with Supplemental and Additional Views on House Joint Resolution 683,* October 6, 1975 (Washington, D.C.: U. S. Government Printing Office), 31–38.

22. The details of the agreement are taken from Spiegel, 301–2, and Quandt, 242–43.

23. Author Interview with Amos Eiran, Dan Accadia Herzliya Hotel, Herzliya, Israel, May 6, 2019.

24. "Israelis Say U. S. Ends Ban on Sale of Arms," *New York Times,* September 7, 1975, University of South Dakota, University Libraries, Archives and Special Collections, James G. Abourezk Papers [hereafter JGAP], Box 837, Sinai Amendments.

25. William J. Drummond, "Secret Accord Lets Israelis Control Next Mideast Step," *Washington Post* [originally, *Los Angeles Times*], September 6, 1975, JGAP, Box 837, Sinai Amendments.

26. "The Escalating Cost of Peace," *Chicago Tribune,* September 7, 1975, JGAP, Box 837, Sinai Amendments.

27. "The Middle East Agreement: An Assessment of Potential Costs," Prepared by Allen Merrill, National Security and International Affairs Division, Congressional Budget Office, October 8, 1975, JGAP, Box 837, Mideast Peace Settlement 1975.

28. Seth Tillman to James Abourezk, September 12, 1975, "Public Opposes Military, Economic Aid to Israel," *Gannett News Service,* JGAP, Box 837, Mideast Peace Settlement 1975.

29. Statement by Senator Clifford P. Case on Congressional Approval of U. S. Personnel in the Sinai Area and Approval of United States Commitments To Israel and To Egypt, From the Office of Senator Clifford P. Case (R-NJ), September 4, 1975, Gerald R. Ford Library [hereafter GRFL], Max L. Friedersdorf, Box 14, Middle East.

30. Timetable for House Action on Sinai Agreement, Memorandum for Jack Marsh, September 12, 1975, GRFL, Max L. Friedersdorf, Box 14, Middle East.

31. United States Senate Committee on Foreign Relations—For Immediate Release, October 3, 1975, GRFL, Max L. Friedersdorf, Box 14, Middle East.

32. National Security Council Meeting with Bipartisan Congressional Leadership, Memorandum for the Record, September 4, 1975, National Security Advisor, NSC Press and Congressional Liaison Staff: Files, 1973–1976, GRFL, Box 8, September 4, 1975—Bipartisan Leaders (MEMCON—Middle East Agreement).

33. Ibid.

34. Ibid.

35. "Middle East Agreements and the Early Warning System in the Sinai," *Hearings of the Committee on International Relations, House of Representatives, Ninety-Fourth Congress,* First Session on the Middle East Agreements and Legislation to Implement the United States Proposal for the Early-Warning System in Sinai, September 8, 11, 18, and 25, 1975 (Washington, D.C.: U. S. Government Printing Office, 1975), 8.

36. Ibid.

37. Ibid.

38. Ibid.

39. "Middle East Agreements and the Early Warning System in the Sinai," 29.

40. "U. S. Documents Accompanying the Sinai Accord," *New York Times,* September 16, 1975, JGAP, Box 837, Sinai Amendments.

41. "Middle East Agreements and the Early Warning System in the Sinai," 18.

42. Roland Evans and Robert Novak, "Standstill in the Mideast," *Washington Post,* September 29, 1975, JGAP, Box 837, Sinai Amendments.

43. Ibid.

44. "To Implement the United States Proposal for the Early-Warning System in Sinai," *Report of the Committee on International Relations together with Supplemental and Additional Views on House Joint Resolution 683,* October 6, 1975 (Washington, D.C.: U. S. Government Printing Office, 1975), 2.

45. *Near East Report,* published by AIPAC, referred to him as one of the "Spokesmen for the Arab Cause." JGAP, Box 838, Middle East Statements.

46. "Abourezk Asks Moratorium on U. S. Arms Aid to All Sides in Middle East Conflict," January 17, 1975, JGAP, Box 838, Middle East Statements.

47. "Negotiating with the PLO," January 28, 1975, *Congressional Record,* 94th Congress, 1st Session, JGAP, Box 109, Speeches, Reprints.

48. Paul Chamberlin, *The Global Offensive: The United States, the Palestine Liberation Organization, and the Making of the Post-Cold War Order* (Oxford, UK: Oxford University Press, 2012).

49. "Negotiating with the PLO," January 28, 1975, *Congressional Record,* 94th Congress, 1st Session, JGAP, Box 109, Speeches, Reprints.

50. "The Sinai Agreement: A Giant Step Backward," September 23, 1975, *Congressional Record,* 94th Congress, 1st Session, JGAP, Box 31, Sinai Agreement Position.

51. "Early Warning System in Sinai," *Hearings before the Committee on Foreign Relations, United States Senate, Ninety-Fourth Congress,* First Session on Memoranda of Agreements between the Governments of Israel and the United States, October 6 and 7, 1975 (Washington, D.C.: U. S. Government Printing Office, 1975), 3.

52. Ibid., 5.

53. Ibid., 1–17.

54. Dana Adams Schmidt, "Fulbright Calls Sinai Accord Too Costly for U.S.," *Christian Science Monitor,* September 23, 1975, JGAP, Box 1156, 1975 Sinai Agreement 2 of 2.

55. "Early Warning System in Sinai," 198.

56. Ibid.

57. Ibid., 198–99.

58. Ibid., 200.

59. Ibid., 233.

60. U. S. Senate, Subcommittee on Separation of Powers, *Hearings, Congressional Oversight of Executive Agreements—1975,* 94th Congress, p. 396.

61. 121 CR, 94th Congress, 1st Session, 32342 (October 8, 1975); George McGovern letter and amendment, October 8, 1975, JGAP, Box 837, Sinai Amendments.

62. "Statement by Senator McGovern, Toward Final Peace Agreement," undated, George McGovern Papers, Princeton University, Seeley G. Mudd Manuscript Library, Box 1890, Folder Near East Subcommittee (5) FRC.

63. Text of joint resolution accessed on March 26, 2020. http://www.gpo.gov/fdsys/pkg/STATUTE-89/pdf/STATUTE-89-Pg572.pdf.

64. 121 *CR,* 94th Congress, 1st Session, 32022 (October 7, 1975).
65. 121 *CR,* 94th Congress, 1st Session, 32327 (October 8, 1975).
66. 121 *CR,* 94th Congress, 1st Session, 32332 (October 8, 1975).
67. 121 *CR,* 94th Congress, 1st Session, 32327 (October 8, 1975).
68. Ibid.
69. Ibid.
70. 121 *CR,* 94th Congress, 1st Session, 32332 (October 8, 1975).
71. 121 *CR,* 94th Congress, 1st Session, 32335 (October 8, 1975).
72. 121 *CR,* 94th Congress, 1st Session, 32332–2335 (October 8, 1975).
73. 121 *CR,* 94th Congress, 1st Session, 32335–2336 (October 8, 1975).
74. 121 *CR,* 94th Congress, 1st Session, 32336 (October 8, 1975).
75. 121 *CR,* 94th Congress, 1st Session, 32339–2340 (October 8, 1975).
76. 121 *CR,* 94th Congress, 1st Session, 32384 (October 8, 1975).
77. 121 *CR,* 94th Congress, 1st Session, 32388–2389 (October 8, 1975).
78. 121 *CR,* 94th Congress, 1st Session, 32391 (October 8, 1975); 121 CR, 94th Congress, 1st Session, 32718 (October 9, 1975). Section 10 states, "In view of the long-standing United States commitment to the survival and security of Israel, the United States Government will view with particular gravity threats to Israel's security or sovereignty by a world power. In support of this objective, the United States Government will in the event of such threat consult promptly with the Government of Israel with respect to what support, diplomatic or otherwise, or assistance it can lend to Israel in accordance with its constitutional practices."
79. 121 *CR,* 94th Congress, 1st Session, 32405 (October 8, 1975).
80. 121 *CR,* 94th Congress, 1st Session, 32406 (October 8, 1975).
81. 121 *CR,* 94th Congress, 1st Session, 32404 (October 8, 1975).
82. 121 *CR,* 94th Congress, 1st Session, 32404 (October 8, 1975).
83. 121 *CR,* 94th Congress, 1st Session, 32398 (October 8, 1975).
84. 121 *CR,* 94th Congress, 1st Session, 32410 (October 8, 1975).
85. 121 *CR,* 94th Congress, 1st Session, 32409–32410 (October 8, 1975).
86. 121 *CR,* 94th Congress, 1st Session, 32049 (October 7, 1975).
87. 121 *CR,* 94th Congress, 1st Session, 32393 (October 8, 1975).
88. 121 *CR,* 94th Congress, 1st Session, 32395 (October 8, 1975).
89. 121 *CR,* 94th Congress, 1st Session, 32399, 32401 (October 8, 1975).
90. 121 *CR,* 94th Congress, 1st Session, 32413–32414 (October 8, 1975).
91. 121 *CR,* 94th Congress, 1st Session, 32415 (October 8, 1975).
92. 121 *CR,* 94th Congress, 1st Session, 32394 (October 8, 1975).
93. 121 *CR,* 94th Congress, 1st Session, 32418–32420 (October 8, 1975).
94. 121 *CR,* 94th Congress, 1st Session, 32419–32426 (October 8, 1975).
95. 121 *CR,* 94th Congress, 1st Session, 32434 (October 8, 1975).
96. 121 *CR,* 94th Congress, 1st Session, 32680–32682 (October 9, 1975).
97. 121 *CR,* 94th Congress, 1st Session, 32682–32683 (October 9, 1975).
98. 121 *CR,* 94th Congress, 1st Session, 32687 (October 9, 1975).
99. 121 *CR,* 94th Congress, 1st Session, 32688–32690 (October 9, 1975).

100. 121 *CR,* 94th Congress, 1st Session, 32717 (October 9, 1975).

101. Joe Biden letter discussing his amendment, October 8, 1975, JGAP, Box 837, Sinai Amendments.

102. 121 *CR,* 94th Congress, 1st Session, 32733 (October 9, 1975).

103. 121 *CR,* 94th Congress, 1st Session, 32733–32737 (October 9, 1975).

104. 121 *CR,* 94th Congress, 1st Session, 32737–32740 (October 9, 1975).

105. 121 *CR,* 94th Congress, 1st Session, 32740–32741 (October 9, 1975).

106. 121 *CR,* 94th Congress, 1st Session, 32704, 32732 (October 9, 1975).

107. 121 *CR,* 94th Congress, 1st Session, 32742–32743 (October 9, 1975).

108. Ibid.

109. 121 *CR,* 94th Congress, 1st Session, 32749 (October 9, 1975).

110. 121 *CR,* 94th Congress, 1st Session, 32743–32744, (October 9, 1975).

111. 121 *CR,* 94th Congress, 1st Session, 32747 (October 9, 1975).

112. 121 *CR,* 94th Congress, 1st Session, 32748 (October 9, 1975).

113. 121 *CR,* 94th Congress, 1st Session, 32755–32756 (October 9, 1975).

114. 121 *CR,* 94th Congress, 1st Session, 32752–32753 (October 9, 1975).

115. 121 *CR,* 94th Congress, 1st Session, 32744 (October 9, 1975).

116. "Peace Efforts in the Middle East Area," Report of a Study Mission to the Middle East, January 3–16, 1976 (Washington, D.C.: U. S. Government Printing Office, 1976), 9. Morgan was unable to join the group in Egypt and Israel due to "a mishap in Naples, requiring medical attention" (2).

117. Marvin Feuerwerger, *Congress and Israel: Foreign Aid Decision-Making in the House of Representatives, 1969–1976* (Westport, CT: Greenwood Press, 1979), 128–33.

118. Ibid., 137.

119. "There Are Plenty of Risks in that Mideast Accord," *Philadelphia Inquirer,* September 3, 1975, JGAP, Box 837, Sinai Amendments.

120. Memorandum of Conversation, President Gerald Ford, Henry Kissinger, and Brent Scowcroft, September 26, 1975, Memcons, GRFL, Box 15, September 26, 1975—Ford, Kissinger.

Conclusion

1. Salim Yaqub, *Imperfect Strangers: Americans, Arabs, and U.S.-Middle East Relations in the 1970s* (Ithaca, NY: Cornell University Press, 2016), 239–75; Daniel Strieff, "Arms Wrestle: Capitol Hill Fight Over Carter's 1978 Middle East 'Package' Airplane Sale," *Diplomatic History* vol. 40, no. 3 (2016): 475–99; Craig Daigle, "Beyond Camp David: Jimmy Carter, Palestinian Self-Determination, and Human Rights," *Diplomatic History* vol. 42, no. 5 (2018): 802–30; William Quandt, *Camp David: Peacekeeping and Politics* (Washington, D.C.: The Brookings Institution, 1986); and Zahid Mahmood, "Sadat and Camp David Reappraised," *Journal of Palestine Studies* vol. 15, no. 1 (Autumn 1985): 62–87.

2. Memorandum of Conversation, Washington, September 21, 1977, *Foreign Relations of the United States* [hereafter FRUS], 1977–1980 Vol. VIII, Arab-Israeli Dispute, January 1977–August 1978, Document 107.

3. Carter-Mondale Transition Planning Group, Jack Watson, David Aaron, and Tony Lake to The President-elect, November 1976, page 7, and Memorandum for the President-elect, November 1976, page 5, Jimmy Carter President Library [hereafter JCPL], Office of Staff Secretary, 1976 Campaign Transition File, Congressional Relations, 11/76–12/76, Container 1, accessed online January 30, 2018, https://www.jimmycarterlibrary.gov/digital_library/sso/148838/1/SSO_148838_001_10.pdf.

4. Memorandum from William B. Quandt of the National Security Council Staff to the President's Assistant for National Security Affairs (Brzezinski), March 20, 1979, FRUS, 1977–1980 Vol. IX, Arab-Israeli Dispute, August 1978–December 1980, Document 220.

5. William B. Quandt, *Peace Process: American Diplomacy and the Arab-Israeli Conflict Since 1967,* 3rd ed. (Washington, D.C.: Brookings Institution, 2005), 281.

6. Yaqub, 267.

7. *Peace Process,* 279.

8. Strieff, "Arms Wrestle."

9. Spiegel, 349.

10. Yaqub, 268.

11. Ibid.

12. Spiegel, 366.

13. Ibid.; Daigle, 827.

14. Spiegel, 362.

15. Ibid., 368.

16. Ibid., 367.

17. Ibid., 369.

18. Memorandum from Edward Sanders for Hamilton Jordan, "Future Political Plans Relating to the Jewish Community," February 8, 1979, Sr. Advisor to the Pres.—Sanders, Box 1, JCPL.

19. *Camp David,* 296; Yaqub, 269.

20. Spiegel, 373.

21. Anwar el-Sadat, *In Search of Identity: An Autobiography* (New York: Harper & Row, Publishers, 1977), 213.

22. Sadat, 215.

23. "Cyrus Vance Dies at 84," *Jewish Telegraphic Agency,* January 14, 2002, accessed January 16, 2016, http://www.jta.org/2002/01/14/life-religion/features/cyrus-vance-dies-at-84.

24. James Siekmeier, *The Bolivian Revolution and the United States, 1952 to the Present* (University Park, PA: Penn State University Press, 2011); Eric Paul Roorda, *The Dictator Next Door: The Good Neighbor Policy and the Trujillo Regime in the Dominican Republic, 1930–1945* (Durham, NC: Duke University Press, 1998); Kyle

Longley, *The Sparrow and the Hawk: Costa Rica and the United States during the Rise of Jose Figueres* (Tuscaloosa: University of Alabama Press, 1997); Seth Jacobs, *America's Miracle Man in Vietnam: Ngo Dinh Diem, Religion, Race, and U. S. Intervention in Southeast Asia, 1950–1957* (Durham, NC: Duke University Press, 2004); Sayuri Shimizu, *Creating People of Plenty: The United States and Japan's Economic Alternatives, 1950–1960* (Kent, OH: Kent State University Press, 2001); and Zachary Karabell, *Architects of Intervention: The United States, the Third World, and the Cold War, 1946–1962* (Baton Rouge: Louisiana State Press, 1999).

25. Letter from Social Studies Class 7A, Trinity Lutheran School to Senator Hiram Fong, March 10, 1975, National Archives II, Record Group 59, Container #58C, Folder—P750058–1499 through P750058–1596, Document 1557.

Bibliography

Primary Sources

Lyndon Johnson Presidential Library

National Security Files, National Security Council History, Papers of LBJ

Richard Nixon Presidential Library

National Security Council Files, Harold H. Saunders Files/Middle East Negotiation Files

National Security Council Files, Henry A. Kissinger Office Files, Country Files—Middle East

National Security Council Files, Henry A. Kissinger Office Files, HAK Trip Files

National Security Council Files, Presidential/HAK MEMCONS

Gerald Ford Presidential Library

Max L. Friedersdorf Papers

Memcons

National Security Adviser: Memoranda of Conversations, 1973–1977

National Security Adviser: NSC Meeting File

NSC Press and Congressional Liaison Staff: Files, 1973–1976

Presidential Country Files for Middle East and South Asia, 1974–1977

Jimmy Carter Presidential Library

Office of Staff Secretary, 1976 Campaign Transition File

Senior Advisor to the President, Ed Sanders

Princeton University

George McGovern Papers

University of Arkansas

J. William Fulbright Papers

University of South Dakota

James Abourezk Papers

University of Washington

Henry "Scoop" Jackson Papers

National Archives I and II

Records of the U.S. Senate (Record Group 46)
Records of the Department of State (Record Group 59)
Records of the United States House of Representatives (Record Group 233)

Israel State Archives

Ministry of Foreign Affairs—Office of the Chief Executive Officer
Ministry of Foreign Affairs—Office of the Foreign Minister

Government Publications

"Aid to Israel Legislation Sails Through Congress." CQ Almanac 1973, 29th Edition. Washington, D.C.: Congressional Quarterly, 1974.

"Early Warning System in Sinai." Hearings before the Committee on Foreign Relations, United States Senate, Ninety-Fourth Congress, First Session on Memoranda of Agreements between the Governments of Israel and the United States, October 6 and 7, 1975. Washington, D.C.: U.S. Government Printing Office, 1975.

"The Middle East." A Report by Senator Charles H. Percy to the Committee on Foreign Relations United States Senate, April 21, 1975. Washington, D.C.: U.S. Government Printing Office, 1975.

"Middle East Agreements and the Early Warning System in Sinai." Hearings of the Committee on International Relations for the House of Representatives, Ninety-Fourth Congress, First Session on The Middle East Agreements and Legislation to Implement the United States Proposal for the Early-Warning System in Sinai. Washington, D.C.: U.S. Government Printing Office, 1975.

"Peace Efforts in the Middle East Area." Report of a Study Mission to the Middle East, January 3–16, 1976. Washington, D.C.: U.S. Government Printing Office, 1976.

"Priorities for Peace in the Middle East." Hearings Before the Subcommittee on Near Eastern and South Asian Affairs of the Committee on Foreign Relations, United

States Senate, Ninety-Fourth Congress, First Session on the Arab Israeli Dispute: Priorities for Peace, July 23 and 24, 1975. Washington, D.C.: U.S. Government Printing Office, 1975.

"Realities of the Middle East." A Report by Senator George S. McGovern to the Committee on Foreign Relations United States Senate, May 1975. Washington, D.C.: U.S. Government Printing Office, 1975.

"To Implement the United States Proposal for the Early-Warning System in Sinai." Report of the Committee on International Relations together with Supplemental and Additional Views on House Joint Resolution 683, October 6, 1975. Washington, D.C.: U.S. Government Printing Office.

U.S. Senate, Subcommittee on Separation of Powers, Hearings, Congressional Oversight of Executive Agreements—1972, 92nd Congress. Washington, D.C.: U.S. Government Printing Office, 1972.

U.S. Senate, Subcommittee on Separation of Powers, Hearings, Congressional Oversight of Executive Agreements—1975, 94th Congress. Washington, D.C.: U.S. Government Printing Office, 1975.

Congressional Record

U.S. Congress, *Congressional Record,* 89th Congress, 2nd Session, 1966.

U.S. Congress, *Congressional Record,* 90th Congress, 1st Session, 1967.

U.S. Congress, *Congressional Record,* 90th Congress, 2nd Session, 1968.

U.S. Congress, *Congressional Record,* 91st Congress, 2nd Session, 1970.

U.S. Congress, *Congressional Record,* 92nd Congress, 1st Session, 1971.

U.S. Congress, *Congressional Record,* 92nd Congress, 2nd Session, 1972.

U.S. Congress, *Congressional Record,* 93rd Congress, 1st Session, 1973.

U.S. Congress, *Congressional Record,* 94th Congress, 1st Session, 1975.

Foreign Relations of the United States

Foreign Relations of the United States, 1964–1968, Vol. XVIII, Arab-Israeli Dispute, 1964–1967.

Foreign Relations of the United States, 1964–1968, Vol. XIX, Arab-Israeli Crisis and War, 1967.

Foreign Relations of the United States, 1964–1968, Vol. XX, Arab-Israeli Dispute, 1967–1968.

Foreign Relations of the United States, 1969–1976, Vol. XXIV, Middle East Region and Arabian Peninsula, 1969–1972; Jordan, September 1970.

Foreign Relations of the United States, 1969–1976, Vol. XXIII, Arab-Israeli Dispute, 1969–1972.

Foreign Relations of the United States, 1977–1980, Vol. VIII, Arab-Israeli Dispute, January 1977–August 1978.

Foreign Relations of the United States, 1977–1980, Vol. IX, Arab-Israeli Dispute, August 1978–December 1980.

Memoirs

Abourezk, James. *Advise and Dissent: Memoirs of South Dakota and the U.S. Senate.* Chicago: Chicago Review Press, 1989.

Ford, Gerald R. *A Time to Heal: The Autobiography of Gerald R. Ford.* New York: Harper & Row, Publishers, 1979.

Kissinger, Henry. *White House Years.* Boston: Little, Brown and Company, 1979.

———. *Years of Upheaval.* Boston: Little, Brown and Company, 1982.

———. *Years of Renewal.* New York: Simon & Schuster, 1999.

Meir, Golda. *My Life.* New York: G. P. Putnam's Sons, 1975.

Nixon, Richard. *The Memoirs of Richard Nixon.* New York: Grosset & Dunlap, 1978.

Rabin, Yitzhak. *The Rabin Memoirs,* Expanded Edition. Berkeley: University of California Press, 1996.

el-Sadat, Anwar. *In Search of Identity: An Autobiography.* New York: Harper & Row, Publishers, 1977.

Interviews

Author interview with Eiran, Amos. Dan Accadia Herzliya Hotel, Herzliya, Israel. May 6, 2019.

Transcript of interview with Rafiah, Zvi. Interviewed by Paul J. P. Sandal and Laura Blackburn. Stephen F. Austin State University, accessed October 9, 2015, http://www.sfasu.edu/heritagecenter/5381.asp.

Newspapers

Aberdeen American News (Aberdeen, SD)
Appeal-Democrat (Marysville, CA)
Boston Globe
Chicago Tribune
The Detroit News
Evening Journal (Wilmington, DE)
The Evening Star (Washington, D.C.)
Hebrew Watchman (Memphis, TN)
Herald (Everett, WA)
Houston Chronicle
Intermountain Jewish News (Denver, CO)
Jewish Chronicle (Dayton, OH)
Jewish Chronicle (Kansas City, MO)
Jewish Week and American Examiner (New York, NY)
Jewish World (Albany, NY)
The Light (San Antonio, TX)
News Miner (Fairbanks, AK)

The Pittsburgh Press
Philadelphia Inquirer
The Providence Journal
New York Times
The Salt Lake City Tribune
Scranton Tribune
Tulsa World
Washington Post

Books and Articles

Abu-Jabir, Faiz S. *American-Arab Relations from Wilson to Nixon*. Washington, D.C.: University Press of America, Inc., 1979.

Adamsky, Dima P. "Disregarding the Bear: How U.S. Intelligence Failed to Estimate the Soviet Intervention in the Egyptian-Israeli War of Attrition." *Journal of Strategic Studies* vol. 28, issue 5 (2005): 803–31.

———. "'Zero-Hour for the Bears': Inquiring into the Soviet Decision to Intervene in the Egyptian-Israeli War of Attrition, 1969–70." *Cold War History* vol. 6, no. 1 (February 2006): 113–36.

Albin, Cecilia, and Harold H. Saunders. *Sinai II: The Politics of International Mediation (F P I Case Studies)*. Washington, D.C.: Johns Hopkins University, School of Advanced International Studies, 1993.

Alvandi, Roham. *Nixon, Kissinger, and the Shah: The United States and Iran in the Cold War*. Oxford, UK: Oxford University Press, 2014.

Aronson, Shlomo. *Conflict & Bargaining in the Middle East: An Israeli Perspective*. Baltimore: The Johns Hopkins University Press, 1978.

el Azhary, M. S. *Political Cohesion of American Jews in American Politics*. Lanham, MD: University Press of America, 1980.

Ball, George W., and Douglas B. Ball. *The Passionate Attachment: America's Involvement with Israel, 1947 to the Present*. New York: W. W. Norton & Company, 1992.

Bar-Siman-Tov, Yaacov. "The United States and Israel since 1948: A 'Special Relationship'?" *Diplomatic History* vol. 22, issue 2 (Spring 1998): 231–62.

Bard, Mitchell Geoffrey. *The Water's Edge and Beyond: Defining the Limits to Domestic Influence on United States Middle East Policy*. New Brunswick, NJ: Transaction Publishers, 1991.

Bass, Warren. *Support Any Friend: Kennedy's Middle East and the Making of the U.S.-Israel Alliance*. Oxford, UK: Oxford University Press, 2003.

Ben-Zvi, Abraham. *The United States and Israel: The Limits of the Special Relationship*. New York: Columbia University Press, 1993.

———. *The Origins of the American-Israeli Alliance: The Jordanian Factor*. New York: Routledge, 2007.

Blanga, Yehuda. "'The Russians Are Coming, the Russians Are Coming': American Management of the Crisis Associated with Ending the October 1973 War." *Middle Eastern Studies* vol. 49, issue 4 (2013): 563–89.

Brown, Seyom. *The Crises of Power: An Interpretation of United States Foreign Policy during the Kissinger Years*. New York: Columbia University Press, 1979.

Buheiry, Marwan R. *U.S. Threats of Intervention Against Arab Oil: 1973–1979*. Beirut: Institute for Palestine Studies, 1980.

Bunch, Clea Lutz. "Strike at Samu: Jordan, Israel, the United States, and the Origins of the Six-Day War." *Diplomatic History* vol. 32, issue 1 (January 2008): 55–76.

Chamberlin, Paul. *The Global Offensive: The United States, the Palestine Liberation Organization, and the Making of the Post-Cold War Order*. Oxford, UK: Oxford University Press, 2012.

Chomsky, Noam. *Fateful Triangle: The United States, Israel & The Palestinians*, Updated Edition. Cambridge, UK: South End Press, 1999.

Clark, Victoria. *Allies for Armageddon: The Rise of Christian Zionism*. New Haven, CT: Yale University Press, 2007.

Curtiss, Richard H. *A Changing Image: American Perceptions of the Arab-Israeli Dispute*. Washington, D.C.: American Educational Trust, 1982.

Daigle, Craig. *The Limits of Détente: The United States, the Soviet Union, and the Arab-Israeli Conflict, 1969–1973*. New Haven, CT: Yale University Press, 2012.

———. "Beyond Camp David: Jimmy Carter, Palestinian Self-Determination, and Human Rights." *Diplomatic History* vol. 42, no. 5 (2018): 802–30.

Dickson, Peter W. *Kissinger and the Meaning of History*. Cambridge, UK: Cambridge University Press, 1978.

Feuerwerger, Marvin C. *Congress and Israel: Foreign Aid Decision-Making in the House of Representatives, 1969–1976*. Westport, CT: Praeger, 1979.

Findley, Paul. *They Dare to Speak Out: People and Institutions Confront Israel's Lobby*. Chicago: Lawrence Hill Books, 2003.

———. *Deliberate Deceptions: Facing the Facts about the U.S.-Israeli Relationship*. New York: Lawrence Hill, 1993.

Fisher, Louis. *President and Congress: Power and Policy*. New York: The Free Press, 1972.

Franck, Thomas M., and Edward Weisband. *Foreign Policy by Congress*. Oxford, UK: Oxford University Press, 1979.

Fulbright, J. William. *The Arrogance of Power*. New York: Random House, 1966.

———. *The Crippled Giant: American Foreign Policy and Its Domestic Consequences*. New York: Vintage Books, 1972.

Gat, Moshe. *In Search of a Peace Settlement: Egypt and Israel Between the War, 1967–1973*. New York: Palgrave Macmillan, 2012.

Ghanayem, Ishaq I., and Alden H. Voth. *The Kissinger Legacy: American-Middle East Policy*. New York: Praeger, 1984.

Golan, Galia. "The Soviet Union and the Outbreak of the June 1967 Six-Day War." *Journal of Cold War Studies* vol. 8, no. 1 (Winter 2006): 3–19.

Golan, Matti. *The Secret Conversations of Henry Kissinger*. New York: Quadrangle, 1976.

Goldberg, Arthur J. "What Resolution 242 Really Said." *American Foreign Policy Interests* vol. 33, issue 1 (2011): 41–46.

Golden, Peter. *Quiet Diplomat: A Biography of Max M. Fisher*. New York: Cornwall Books, 1992.

Govrin, Yosef. *Israeli-Soviet Relations 1953–1967: From Confrontation to Disruption.* Portland, OR: Frank Cass, 1998.

Graf, Rudiger. "Making Use of the 'Oil Weapon': Western Industrialized Countries and Arab Petropolitics in 1973–1974." *Diplomatic History* vol. 36, issue 1 (January 2012): 185–208.

Grant, Philip A. "The Bricker Amendment Controversy." *Presidential Studies Quarterly* vol. 15, no. 3 (Summer 1985): 572–82.

Greene, John Robert. *The Presidency of Gerald R. Ford*. Lawrence: University of Kansas Press, 1995.

Hahn, Peter L. *Caught in the Middle East: U.S. Policy toward the Arab-Israeli Conflict, 1945–1961*. Chapel Hill: University of North Carolina Press, 2004.

———. *Crisis and Crossfire: The United States and the Middle East since 1945*. Washington, D.C.: Potomac Books, 2005.

———. "The View from Jerusalem: Revelations about U.S. Diplomacy from the Archives of Israel." *Diplomatic History* vol. 22, issue 4 (Fall 1998): 509–32.

Hanhimaki, Jussi. *The Flawed Architect: Henry Kissinger and American Foreign Policy*. Oxford, UK: Oxford University Press, 2004.

Heimann, Gadi. "From Friendship to Patronage: France-Israel Relations, 1958–1967." *Diplomacy & Statecraft* vol. 21, issue 2 (June 2010): 240–58.

———. "From 'Irresponsible' to 'Immoral': The Shifts in de Gaulle's Perception of Israel and the Jews." *Journal of Contemporary History* vol. 46, no. 4 (October 2011): 897–919.

Hersh, Seymour M. *The Price of Power: Kissinger in the Nixon White House*. New York: Summit Books, 1983.

Hixson, Walter. *Israel's Armor: The Israel Lobby and the First Generation of the Palestine Conflict*. New York: Cambridge University Press, 2019.

Hummel, Daniel G. *Covenant Brothers: Evangelicals, Jews, and U.S.-Israeli Relations*. Philadelphia: University of Pennsylvania Press, 2019.

Irons, Peter. *War Powers: How the Imperial Presidency Hijacked the Constitution*. New York: Metropolitan Books, 2005.

Isaacson, Walter. *Kissinger: A Biography*. New York: Simon & Schuster, 1992.

Jackson, Galen. "The Showdown That Wasn't: U.S.-Israeli Relations and American Domestic Politics, 1973–1975." *International Security* vol. 39, no. 4 (Spring 2015): 130–69.

Jacobs, Seth. *America's Miracle Man in Vietnam: Ngo Dinh Diem, Religion, Race, and U.S. Intervention in Southeast Asia, 1950–1957*. Durham. NC: Duke University Press, 2004.

Johnson, Loch K. *The Making of International Agreements: Congress Confronts the Executive*. New York: New York University Press, 1984.

———. *America as a World Power: Foreign Policy in a Constitutional Framework,* 2nd ed. New York: McGraw-Hill, 1995.

Johnson, Robert David. *Congress and the Cold War*. Cambridge, UK: Cambridge University Press, 2006.

———. *Lyndon Johnson and Israel: The Secret Presidential Recordings*. Tel Aviv: Tel Aviv University, 2008.

Kaplan, Amy. *Our American Israel: The Story of an Entangled Alliance*. Cambridge, MA: Harvard University Press, 2018.

Karabell, Zachary. *Architects of Intervention: The United States, the Third World, and the Cold War, 1946–1962*. Baton Rouge: Louisiana State Press, 1999.

Kaufman, Burton I. *The Arab Middle East and the United States: Inter-Arab Rivalry and Superpower Diplomacy*. New York: Twayne Publishers, 1996.

Kaufman, Robert Gordon. *Henry M. Jackson: A Life in Politics*. Seattle: University of Washington Press, 2000.

Kochavi, Noam. *Nixon and Israel: Forging a Conservative Partnership*. Albany: State University of New York Press, 2009.

Korn, David. *Stalemate: The War of Attrition and Great Power Diplomacy in the Middle East, 1967–1970*. Boulder, CO: Westview Press, 1992.

Krutz, Glen S., and Jeffrey S. Peake. *Treaty Politics and the Rise of Executive Agreements: International Commitments in a System of Shared Powers*. Ann Arbor: The University of Michigan Press, 2009.

Labelle, Maurice, Jr. "The Only Thorn: Early Saudi-American Relations and the Question of Palestine, 1945–1949." *Diplomatic History* vol. 35, issue 2 (April 2011): 257–81.

LaFeber, Walter, Richard Polenberg, and Nancy Woloch. *The American Century: A History of the United States since the 1890s,* 7th ed. Armonk, NY: M. E. Sharpe, 2013.

Lahr, Angela M. *Millennial Dreams and Apocalyptic Nightmares: The Cold War Origins of Political Evangelicalism*. Oxford, UK: Oxford University Press, 2007.

Lawrence, John A. *The Class of '74: Congress after Watergate and the Roots of Partisanship*. Baltimore: Johns Hopkins University Press, 2018.

Lehman, John. *The Executive, Congress, and Foreign Policy: Studies of the Nixon Administration*. New York: Praeger, 1974.

Lenczowski, George. *American Presidents and the Middle East*. Durham, NC: Duke University Press, 1990.

Levey, Zach. "Anatomy of an Airlift: United States Military Assistance to Israel during the 1973 War." *Cold War History* vol. 8, no. 4 (November 2008): 481–501.

———. "The United States' Skyhawk Sale to Israel, 1966: Strategic Exigencies of an Arms Deal." *Diplomatic History* vol. 28, issue 2 (April 2004): 255–76.

Little, Douglas. *American Orientalism: The United States and the Middle East since 1945*. Chapel Hill: The University of North Carolina Press, 2002.

———. "The Making of a Special Relationship: The United States and Israel, 1957–68." *International Journal of Middle East Studies* vol. 25, no. 4 (November 1993): 563–85.

Logevall, Fredrik, and Andrew Preston, eds. *Nixon in the World: American Foreign Relations, 1969–1977*. New York: Oxford University Press, 2008.

Longley, Kyle. *The Sparrow and the Hawk: Costa Rica and the United States during the Rise of Jose Figueres*. Tuscaloosa: University of Alabama Press, 1997.

Louis, William Roger, and Avi Shlaim, eds. *The 1967 Arab-Israeli War: Origins and Consequences*. New York: Cambridge University Press, 2012.

Mahmood, Zahid. "Sadat and Camp David Reappraised." *Journal of Palestine Studies* vol. 15, no. 1 (Autumn 1985): 62–87.

Mann, Thomas E., ed. *A Question of Balance: The President, the Congress, and Foreign Policy*. Washington, D.C.: The Brookings Institution, 1990.

Mansour, Camille. *Beyond Alliance: Israel in U.S. Foreign Policy*. Translated by James A. Cohen. New York: Columbia University Press, 1994.

Margolis, Lawrence. *Executive Agreements and Presidential Power in Foreign Policy*. New York: Praeger Publishers, 1986.

Mart, Michelle. *Eye on Israel: How America Came to View Israel as an Ally*. Albany: State University of New York Press, 2006.

McAlister, Melani. *Epic Encounters: Culture, Media, and U.S. Interests in the Middle East, 1945–2000*. Berkeley: University of California Press, 2001.

McLaurin, R. D. *The Middle East in Soviet Policy*. Lexington, KY: D. C. Heath and Company, 1976.

McLaurin, R. D., Mohammed Mughisuddin, and Abraham R. Wagner. *Foreign Policy Making in the Middle East: Domestic Influences on Policy in Egypt, Iraq, Israel, and Syria*. New York: Praeger, 1977.

Mearshimer, John J., and Stephen M. Walt. *The Israel Lobby and U.S. Foreign Policy*. New York: Farrar, Straus and Giroux, 2007.

Mieczkowski, Yanek. *Gerald Ford and the Challenges of the 1970s*. Lexington: University Press of Kentucky, 2005.

Morris, Roger. *Uncertain Greatness: Henry Kissinger and American Foreign Policy*. New York: Harper & Row, 1977.

Muskie, Edmund S., Kenneth Rush, and Kenneth W. Thompson, eds. *The President, the Congress, and Foreign Policy: A Joint Policy Project of the Association of Former Members of Congress and the Atlantic Council of the United States*. Lanham, MD: University Press of America, Inc., 1986.

Novik, Nimrod. *The United States and Israel: Domestic Determinants of a Changing U.S. Commitment*. Boulder, CO: Westview Press, 1986.

Oren, Michael B. *Power, Faith, and Fantasy: America in the Middle East, 1776 to the Present*. New York: W. W. Norton & Company, 2007.

———. *Six Days of War: June 1967 and the Making of the Modern Middle East*. Oxford, UK: Oxford University Press, 2002.

Parker, Richard. *The Politics of Miscalculation in the Middle East*. Bloomington: Indiana University Press, 1993.

———. *The Six Day War: A Retrospective*. Gainesville: University Press of Florida, 1996.

Paterson, Thomas G., et al. *American Foreign Relations, Volume Two,* 7th ed. Boston: Wadsworth, 2010.

Pollock, David. *The Politics of Pressure: American Arms and Israeli Policy since the Six Day War*. Westport, CT: Greenwood Press, 1982.

Quandt, William B. *Camp David: Peacekeeping and Politics*. Washington, D.C.: The Brookings Institution, 1986.

———. *Peace Process: American Diplomacy and the Arab-Israeli Conflict Since 1967,* 3rd ed. Washington, D.C.: Brookings Institution, 2005.

Rabie, Mohamed. *The Politics of Foreign Aid: U.S. Foreign Assistance and Aid to Israel*. New York: Praeger, 1988.

Reich, Bernard. *Quest for Peace: United States-Israel Relations and the Arab-Israeli Conflict*. New Brunswick, NJ: Transaction Books, 1977.

———. *The United States and Israel: Influence in the Special Relationship*. New York: Praeger, 1984.

Ro'i, Yaacov, and Boris Morozov, eds. *The Soviet Union and the June 1967 Six Day War*. Stanford, CA: Stanford University Press, 2008.

Rock, Stephen R. *Faith and Foreign Policy: The Views and Influence of U.S. Christians and Christian Organizations*. New York: The Continuum International Publishing Group, 2011.

Rodman, David. "Phantom Fracas: The 1968 American Sale of F-4 Aircraft to Israel." *Middle Eastern Studies* vol. 40, no. 6 (November 2004): 130–44.

Roorda, Paul. *The Dictator Next Door: The Good Neighbor Policy and the Trujillo Regime in the Dominican Republic, 1930–1945*. Durham, NC: Duke University Press, 1998.

Ross, Dennis. *Doomed to Succeed: The U.S.-Israel Relationship from Truman to Obama*. New York: Farrar, Straus and Giroux, 2015.

Rostow, Eugene V., ed. *The Middle East: Critical Choices for the United States*. Boulder, CO: Westview Press, 1976.

Rubenberg, Cheryl A. *Israel and the American National Interest: A Critical Examination*. Urbana: University of Illinois Press, 1986.

Rudalevige, Andrew. *New Imperial Presidency: Renewing Presidential Power after Watergate*. Ann Arbor: University of Michigan Press, 2006.

Said, Edward. *Orientalism*. New York: Pantheon Books, 1978.

Sargent, Daniel J. *A Superpower Transformed: The Remaking of American Foreign Relations in the 1970s*. New York: Oxford University Press, 2015.

Saunders, Harold H. "The Middle East, 1973–1984: Hidden Agendas." In *The President, the Congress, and Foreign Policy: A Joint Policy Project of the Association of Former Members of Congress and the Atlantic Council of the United States*, edited by Edmund S. Muskie, Kenneth Rush, and Kenneth W. Thompson, 175–205. Lanham, MD: University Press of America, Inc., 1986.

———. *The Other Walls: The Arab-Israeli Peace Process in a Global Perspective.* Rev. ed. Princeton, NJ: Princeton University Press, 1991.

Savage, Charlie. *Takeover: The Return of the Imperial Presidency and the Subversion of American Democracy.* New York: Back Bay Books, 2007.

Schlesinger, Arthur, Jr. *The Imperial Presidency.* Boston: Houghton Mifflin, 1973.

———. *War and the American Presidency.* New York: W. W. Norton, 2004.

Schoenbaum, David. *The United States and the State of Israel.* Oxford, UK: Oxford University Press, 1993.

Schulman, Bruce J. *The Seventies: The Great Shift in American Culture, Society, and Politics.* New York: Free Press, 2001.

Schulzinger, Robert D. *Henry Kissinger: Doctor of Diplomacy.* New York: Columbia University Press, 1989.

Schwartz, Thomas Alan. "Henry, . . . Winning an Election Is Terribly Important': Partisan Politics in the History of U.S. Foreign Relations." *Diplomatic History* vol. 33, issue 2 (April 2009): 173–90.

Sheehan, Edward R. F. *The Arabs, Israelis, and Kissinger: A Secret History of American Diplomacy in the Middle East.* New York: Reader's Digest Press, 1976.

Shimizu, Sayuri. *Creating People of Plenty: The United States and Japan's Economic Alternatives, 1950–1960.* Kent, OH: Kent State University Press, 2001.

Shlaim, Avi. *The Iron Wall: Israel and the Arab World.* New York: W. W. Norton & Company, 2000.

———. *War and Peace in the Middle East: A Critique of American Policy.* New York: Penguin Group, 1994.

Siekmeier, James. *The Bolivian Revolution and the United States, 1952 to the Present.* University Park, PA: Penn State University Press, 2011.

Small, Melvin. *Democracy and Diplomacy: The Impact of Domestic Politics on U.S. Foreign Policy, 1789–1994.* Baltimore: The Johns Hopkins University Press, 1996.

Sohns, Olivia. "The Future Foretold: Lyndon Baines Johnson's Congressional Support for Israel." *Diplomacy & Statecraft* 28:1, 57–84.

Sosland, Jeffrey K. *Cooperating Rivals: The Riparian Politics of the Jordan River Basin.* Albany: State University of New York Press, 2007.

Spanier, John, and Joseph Nogee, eds. *Congress, the Presidency and American Foreign Policy.* New York: Pergamon Press Inc., 1981.

Spector, Stephen. *Evangelicals and Israel: The Story of American Christian Zionism.* Oxford, UK: Oxford University Press, 2008.

Spiegel, Steven L. *The Other Arab-Israeli Conflict: Making America's Middle East Policy, from Truman to Reagan.* Chicago: University of Chicago Press, 1985.

Stivers, William. *America's Confrontation with Revolutionary Change in the Middle East, 1948–1983.* New York: St. Martin's Press, 1986.

Strieff, Daniel. "Arms Wrestle: Capitol Hill Fight Over Carter's 1978 Middle East 'Package' Airplane Sale." *Diplomatic History* vol. 40, no. 3 (2016): 475–99.

Sundquist, James L. *The Decline and Resurgence of Congress*. Washington, D.C.: Brookings Institution Press, 1981.

Thornton, Richard C. *The Nixon-Kissinger Years: Reshaping America's Foreign Policy*, 2nd ed. St. Paul, MN: Paragon House, 2001.

Tillman, Seth P. *The United States in the Middle East: Interests and Obstacles*. Bloomington: Indiana University Press, 1982.

Tivnan, Edward. *The Lobby: Jewish Political Power and American Foreign Policy*. New York: Simon & Schuster, 1987.

Trice, Robert H. "Interest Groups and the Foreign Policy Process: U.S. Policy in the Middle East." *Sage Professional Papers: International Studies Series, Volume 4*. Beverly Hills: Sage Publications, Inc., 1976.

Urofsky, Melvin I. *We Are One! American Jewry and Israel*. Garden City, NY: Anchor Press, 1978.

Vanetik, Boaz, and Zaki Shalom. *The Nixon Administration and the Middle East Peace Process, 1969–1973*. Chicago: Sussex Academic Press, 2013.

Wagner, Donald. "Evangelicals and Israel: Theological Roots of a Political Alliance." *Christian Century*, November 4, 1998, vol. 115, issue 30.

Weber, Timothy P. *On the Road to Armageddon: How Evangelicals Became Israel's Best Friend*. Grand Rapids, MI: Baker Academic, 2004.

Westad, Odd Arne. *The Global Cold War: Third World Interventions and the Making of Our Times*. Cambridge, UK: Cambridge University Press, 2007.

Woods, Randall Bennett. *Fulbright: A Biography*. Cambridge, UK: Cambridge University Press, 1995.

Yaqub, Salim. *Containing Arab Nationalism: The Eisenhower Doctrine and the Middle East*. Chapel Hill: The University of North Carolina Press, 2004.

———. *Imperfect Strangers: Americans, Arabs, and U.S.-Middle East Relations in the 1970s*. Ithaca, NY: Cornell University Press, 2016.

———. "The Weight of Conquest: Henry Kissinger and the Arab-Israeli Conflict." In *Nixon in the World: American Foreign Relations, 1969–1977*, edited by Fredrik Logevall and Andrew Preston, 227–48. Oxford, UK: Oxford University Press, 2008.

Yergin, Daniel. *The Prize: The Epic Quest for Oil, Money & Power*. New York: The Free Press, 1991.

Zernichow, Simen, and Hilde Henriksen Waage. "The Palestine Option: Nixon, the National Security Council, and the Search for a New Policy, 1970." *Diplomatic History* vol. 38, issue 1 (January 2014): 182–209.

Index

Abourezk, James, 92, 96–97, 103, 146, 154, 161–65, 171–72
Abzug, Bella, 85, 90
Addabbo, Joseph, 35
Agnew, Spiro, 90
Aiken, George, 60, 77
Akins, James, 104
al-Assad, Bashar, 112
al-Assad, Hafez, 100, 133
Albert, Carl, 158
Algeria, 27
Algiers, 100
Allon, Yigal, 92, 104, 112–13, 118, 127, 130–32, 136, 139–41, 146, 189
American Jewish Congress, 102
American Jewish Zionists, 34, 79, 91, 101–2, 105–6, 114, 127, 134, 137, 148, 184, 188–89, 205
American Israel Public Affairs Committee (AIPAC), 11, 18, 50–51, 76, 86, 141, 188, 201, 209, 231, 235
American Palestine Committee, 13, 108
American Zionist Federation, 76
Amitay, Morris, 141, 146, 188
Angola, 6, 174
anti-communist, 13–14, 54
anti-Semitism, 1, 13, 16, 77, 118, 134
anti-Westernism, 1
appeasement, 39, 134. *See also* Munich
Arab League, 120, 178–80, 182
Arab lobby, 18
Arab-Israeli conflict, 19, 25, 27, 55–56, 60–63, 72, 83, 89, 100, 178, 182; war of 1948–49 (War for Independence; *nakba*), 25, 118; war of 1956 (Suez Crisis), 4, 21, 31, 37, 40, 42, 61, 88, 118; war of 1967 (Six-Day War), 1–2, 4–5, 10, 14, 16–19, 21, 23–26, 30–48, 51, 53–55, 62, 66, 74, 77, 99–100, 102, 118, 124–25, 128, 182, 226; war of 1973 (Yom Kippur War; October War), 5–6, 18, 21, 71, 80–102, 110, 114, 118, 120, 122–23, 126, 144, 182, 186–87, 221–22
Arab-Israeli peace process, 3, 5, 10, 18, 20–21, 31, 48, 53, 56–58, 63, 73, 75, 78–80, 82, 84, 92, 99, 101, 105–6, 111, 115, 119–21, 124, 127, 140, 147, 150, 155–56, 163, 175, 180–82, 184–89, 191–92
Arafat, Yasser, 26, 100, 162, 180, 226
Armed Services Committee, Senate, 64–65, 67, 69–70, 72, 130
armistice agreements, 1949, 40, 46, 111
armored personnel carrier (APC), 31
arms race, 6, 24, 28, 39–42, 49, 53, 78
Auschwitz, 134
Austria, 147

Badillo, Herman, 85, 90
Baker, Howard, 173
Balfour Declaration, 13

Ball, George, 135, 163
Bar-Lev, Haim, 71
Battle, Lucius, 43–44
Bayh, Birch, 68, 75, 89, 147
Begin, Menachem, 104, 177–80
Bell, Alphonzo, 37, 52
Bellmon, Henry, 68
Ben-Aharon, Joseph, 143
Biaggi, Mario, 86, 95
Biden, Joe, 21, 151, 164–66, 171–72s
Biester, Edward, 171
Bingham, Jonathan, 32–33, 42, 47, 85, 171
Blackburn, Benjamin, 35, 52
Black Power movement, 14
Bloomberg, Daniel, 102
B'nai B'rith, 26, 46, 51, 72, 95, 102, 107–9, 115
Boeing, 15, 41, 60
Brasco, Frank, 84, 90
Bretton Woods Agreement, 88–89
Brewster, Daniel, 41
Brinkley, Jack, 32
Britain, 17, 27, 32, 36
Brooke, Edward, 39
Broomfield, William, 129, 161
Broyhill, Joel, 46
Brzezinski, Zbigniew, 35, 177–78
Buckley, James L., 76
Bumpers, Dale, 59, 108, 138
Bundy, McGeorge, 29, 35, 135–36, 229
Burdick, Quentin, 97
Bush, George H. W., 139
Bush, George W., 45, 130
Byrd, Robert, 38
Byrd, Harry, Jr., 172

Califano, Joseph, 34
Cambodia, 63, 65, 67, 88–89
Camp David Accords, 4, 9, 150, 157, 175–82, 186, 189
Carter, Jimmy, 4, 33, 35, 176–80, 182, 184–85, 188–89, 196, 229
capitalism, 14
Case, Clifford, 52, 147, 153–54, 157–58
Celler, Emmanuel, 42
Centurion tanks, 27
China, 175, 192
Chisholm, Shirley, 95
Christian Zionism, 16
Church, Frank, 35, 39, 51, 65, 67, 85
civil liberties, 14
Civil Rights Movement, 14, 16, 26, 54
Clark, Dick, 171–72
Clark, Joseph, 32, 34
Class of 1974, 116
Clausen, Donald, 37
Cold War, 1–2, 5–6, 10, 13–17, 19, 27–29, 47–48, 54–57, 60, 62, 64, 66, 72, 96, 114–15, 151–52, 178, 181, 183, 185, 188, 190–92, 200
Cold War consensus, 13–14
Committee on International Relations, House, 129, 153, 159, 176
communism, 2, 6, 14–16, 30, 42, 57, 60–61, 182, 185
comprehensive peace, 20, 43, 56, 61, 82, 97, 101, 104, 111, 113, 118, 120, 122–24, 128, 135, 148, 164, 175, 178, 184, 186
Conference of Presidents of Major American Jewish Organizations, 10, 92, 134–35
Congressional Budget Office, 157
Conte, Silvio, 33
Conyers, John, 33
Cooper, John Sherman, 65, 67, 77
Corman, James, 37, 90
Cotter, William, 95
Coughlin, Lawrence, 84
Cox, Archibald, 90
Cranston, Alan, 79
Cuban Missile Crisis, 63
Cunningham, Glenn, 30
Cyprus, 6, 226

Dacey, Norman, 108
Dayan, Moshe, 71, 105, 113, 222
defense contracts, 15, 41, 60, 95
defense spending, 14–15, 17, 57, 60, 92, 182
de Gaulle, Charles, 40
Dellums, Ronald, 94
Dennis, David, 94
Dent, John, 169
Department of Defense, 11, 27, 39, 48, 127
Department of State, 5, 11, 21, 27, 34–35, 37–38, 43, 48, 52, 69, 72, 77–79, 108, 127, 130, 132–33, 139, 143, 225
Derwinski, Edward, 170
détente, 14, 56–57, 59–60, 84–86, 95–96, 190
Dinitz, Simcha, 104, 118–19, 127, 129–33, 135–42, 144–47, 156, 189
Dole, Robert, 68, 172
doves, 32, 70, 87, 89, 95
Dow, John, 42
Drinan, Robert, 89, 96
Dulles, John Foster, 32, 158

Eagleburger, Lawrence, 139, 142
Eagle fighter jets, 138
Eagleton, Thomas, 163
Eban, Abba, 38, 46, 75, 92, 100, 104, 138–39
Edelsberg, Herman, 107–9
Egypt, 2–4, 10, 19, 21–23, 27, 30–39, 44, 47, 50, 53, 55–58, 61, 63, 66, 68, 70, 73–74, 78–87, 99–101, 103, 112–13, 117, 119–21, 125, 128–31, 135, 137, 140–42, 148, 150, 152, 155–56, 162–66, 171–82, 185–87, 193, 207, 220; relations with United States, 3, 10, 12, 22, 35, 41, 63, 70, 73, 75, 79–80, 99–100, 103, 106, 112, 119, 124, 150, 155–59, 163, 171–74, 176–78, 180–82, 186, 220, 228, 237. *See also* Soviet Union relations with Egypt
Egyptian Islamic Jihad, 182
Eilat, 47
Eilberg, Joshua, 41
Eilts, Hermann, 124
Eiran, Amos, 64–66, 96, 156, 187, 195, 199
Eisenhower, Dwight, 4, 16, 55, 61, 88, 117; and Eisenhower Doctrine, 61; and Suez Crisis, 40, 94
Energy crisis, 88
Ervin, Sam, Jr., 153–54, 172
Eshkol, Levi, 49
evenhanded policy, 4, 24, 28, 34–35, 55, 61–62, 67, 75, 85, 87, 93, 97, 114, 161, 176, 184–86, 189
Evron, Ephraim, 45–46, 133, 142, 187
executive agreements, 151–55, 158, 174, 188; Bricker Amendment, 153; Case-Zablocki Act, 153; Ervin Bill of 1972, 153; Executive Agreements Review Act of 1975, 151, 153, 157, 161, 163; and Sinai II, 2, 8–10, 21–22, 148, 150–52, 155, 157, 159–65, 169, 173–74, 186–89
Export-Import Bank, 7, 41

F-104 jets, 28
Falwell, Jerry, 16
Fahmy, Ismail, 176
Farbstein, Leonard, 33, 47, 50, 52
Fascell, Dante, 171
Fatah (Palestine National Liberation Movement), 26, 30, 203, 226
Findley, Paul, 87, 93–94, 168–71, 217
Fino, Paul, 39
Fish, Hamilton, 85
Fisher, Max, 102, 131–32, 134–38
Fisher, Ovie Clark "O. C.," 52
Fong, Hiram, 191
Ford, Betty, 140

Ford, Gerald, 116; as president, 2–4, 20–21, 29, 45, 83, 106, 114–27, 129–32, 135, 137–40, 142–48, 150–51, 155–56, 158–62, 165–66, 169–70, 173–75, 184–86, 188–89; as representative, 76–77, 89–90, 116; and as vice president, 90–91, 109
Foreign Relations Committee, Senate, 11, 29–30, 51, 56, 60–61, 65, 67, 72, 97–98, 109, 111, 129, 138, 151, 158–59, 161, 163–67, 176; Subcommittee on Near Eastern Affairs, 128–29
Fortis, Dave, 136
Fosdick, Dorothy, 65
France, 17, 27, 32, 41, 45, 57
Frelinghuysen, Peter, 95
Frenzel, Bill, 74
Fulbright, J. William, 11, 20, 54–56, 59–61, 129, 138, 161; and U.S.-Israel policies, 11, 20, 54, 56, 59–65, 67, 69–70, 72–74, 76–77, 81, 92–93, 96–98, 101, 107–8, 114, 163; and Vietnam War, 29, 60
Fulton, James, 47

Gannett News Service, 157
Garment, Leonard, 136–37
Gaza Strip, 23–24, 40, 128, 177–79
Gazit, Mordechai, 134
Geneva Conference, 82, 95, 97–98, 101–2, 114; and potential venue for comprehensive peace talks, 118, 122–23, 132, 136, 140, 148, 159, 162
Gilbert, Jacob, 35, 52
Gilman, Benjamin, 95, 171
Ginsburg, David, 34, 229
Glennon, Michael J., 164
Golan Heights, 23–24, 38, 71, 83, 110–11, 119, 125, 177
Goldberg, Arthur, 43, 49, 135–36
Goldberg, Samuel H., 143–44
Goldmann, Nahum, 135
Goldwater, Barry, 76
Grassley, Charles, 169
Great Society, 26, 89
Griffin, Robert, 138
Gross, Harold Royce, 36, 93–94
Grover, James, 89
Gruening, Ernest, 31–32, 39, 42
Gurney, Edward, 47

Haig, Alexander, 106–7
Haldeman, H. R., 70
Halpern, Seymour, 30, 32, 37, 46
Hamas, 181, 193
Hamilton, Lee, 94–95, 97, 170
Harman, Abraham, 43–44, 46
Harriman, W. Averell, 28, 136, 229
Harrington, Michael, 68
hasbara, 117, 119, 126, 129–31, 134, 136–40, 145, 147–48, 225
Haskell, Floyd, 171
Hatfield, Mark, 91, 97
HAWK (Homing All the Way Killer) antiaircraft missile system, 27
hawks, 14, 32, 57, 59, 70, 76, 87, 93, 112
Hayes, Wayne, 32, 38
Heckler, Margaret, 35, 170
Helms, Jesse, 172
Helms, Richard, 74
Hertzberg, Arthur, 102
Hezbollah, 181, 193
Hicks, Floyd, 37
Hollings, Fritz, 164, 166–68
Holocaust, 1, 23, 32
Holtzman, Elizabeth, 86, 170
Horton, Arthur, 127–28
Howe, Allan, 170
human rights, 14, 57
Humphrey, Hubert: as senator, 74, 87, 89, 97, 114, 129, 165, 168, 171–72, 190; and as vice president, 34, 51, 53

Ichord, Richard, 94, 169
Imperial Presidency, 5, 29, 151, 191
Inouye, Daniel, 128–29
Interior Committee, Senate, 103
Intifada: first, 181–82; and second, 182
Iraq, 2, 27, 35, 43, 103, 151, 181
Iran, 133, 179–80, 188, 193
Iran-Contra, 185
Iran Nuclear Agreement Act, 174, 188
Ismail, Hafiz, 79
Israel Defense Forces (IDF), 36,
Israel lobby, 3–5, 10–13, 17–20, 25, 28, 33, 50, 56, 61–62, 64, 83, 102, 108, 115, 118–19, 142, 146, 148, 183–84, 189
Israel-Syria disengagement agreement, 83, 100, 105–7, 110–11, 113
Israeli embassy, Washington, D.C., 20, 61, 102, 116–19, 127, 130, 132, 138, 140, 142, 146–48, 189, 225
Israeli Knesset, 71, 103
Israeli political parties: Alignment, 14, 103; Labor, 14, 92, 104; Likud, 103–4, 221; and National Religious, 104
Israeli settlement construction, 38, 44, 54, 71, 179

Jackson, Henry "Scoop," 19–20, 41, 54–57, 59–63, 71–76, 85, 95–96, 108, 130, 144, 147, 189–90; and Jackson Amendment, or Section 501 of Defense Procurement Act of 1970, 8, 63–67, 69–72, 77–78, 80, 86; and Jackson-Vanik Amendment, 47, 95–96, 105, 190
Japan, 83, 88, 102, 123, 172
Jarring, Gunnar, 48–49, 52–53, 57, 59, 72–74, 79, 142
Javits, Jacob, 32–33, 36, 38, 51–52, 68, 74–75, 91, 98, 102, 113, 123, 137, 144, 147, 168, 190
Jerusalem, 16, 20, 23–24, 82, 103, 105, 111, 113, 117, 124–25, 129, 134, 136, 139, 141, 159, 177, 179, 189, 192, 225
Johnson, Jim, 87, 169
Johnson, Lyndon, 4, 19, 23–34, 39–40, 43–45, 55, 57, 59–60, 62, 128, 184–85, 187, 192–93, 209, 229; and affinity for Israel, 24, 26–27, 53, 184; and arms embargo to Middle East, 40, 45–47; and Five Principles, June 1967, 40; and weapons sales to Israel, 25, 27–31, 39, 48–53, 55
Joint Chiefs of Staff, 30, 48, 108
Jordan, 12, 27–30, 33, 39, 41–44, 50, 100–101, 105–6, 112–13, 120, 124–25, 128, 177, 179–80, 192–93, 225; and Black September, 1970, 2, 73, 101, 113
Jordan River, 26

Kamel, M., 73
Kampelman, Max, 134
Kastenmeier, Robert, 94, 169
Katzenbach, Nicholas, 31
Keating, Kenneth, 124
Kemp, Jack, 85
Kenen, I. L. "Si," 11, 51, 201
Kennedy, Edward "Ted," 32, 146, 173
Kennedy, John F., Jr., 4, 27, 55, 61, 229
Kennedy, Robert, 36
Kent State shootings, 67
Khartoum Declaration, 42–44
Kilometer 101 agreement, 99, 220
King Faisal, 43, 99, 104
King Hussein, 2, 12, 27, 30, 43–44, 101, 113, 125–26, 192
Kissinger, Henry, 5, 20, 58, 63, 70, 74, 76–77, 79–80, 82, 84, 86, 90–91, 93–94, 97–111, 113–21, 182, 191, 216, 220, 225–27, 229, 231; and reassessment period, 122–42, 144,

146–49; and shuttle diplomacy, 4, 103–7, 109–10, 121, 221; and Sinai II agreement, 152, 156, 158–60, 162–63, 167–68, 171, 173–75; and step-by-step diplomacy, 18–19, 22, 82–83, 98–100, 102–4, 109, 112–14, 117–22, 129, 136, 140, 185, 216, 221; and Watergate, 109–11
Kissinger, Nancy, 142
Koch, Ed, 89
Komer, Robert, 28–29
Kristol, Irving, 15

Laird, Melvin, 74
land-for-peace diplomacy, 24, 40, 48, 124, 182
Laos, 65
League of Nations mandate system, 17
Lebanon, 161, 179, 181, 228
Lehman, William, 85, 89
Leigh, Monroe, 163–64, 171
Levitas, Elliot, 144
Lloyd, Marilyn, 170
Long, Clarence, 85

M-4 Sherman tanks, 27
Madden, Ray, 38
Mansfield, Mike, 68, 77, 122, 158, 165, 171
Maraziti, Joseph, 91
Mathias, Charles, 87, 172
May 1975 Senate letter, 20, 21, 118–19, 141–42, 144 147–50, 152, 159, 168, 170, 184, 191, 231
McCarthy, Richard, 52
McCloskey, Robert, 34, 45
McClure, James, 87, 92, 96–97, 168–69
McCormack, John, 47
McDonnell Douglas, 15, 65, 138
McGovern, George, 84, 116, 128–29, 146–47, 163–64, 191
McIntyre, Thomas, 172
McNamara, Robert, 29–30, 46, 60, 136, 204, 208
Meany, George, 90
Mediterranean, 36, 58
Meir, Golda, 67–68, 71, 73, 77–78, 80, 90, 92, 101, 103–7, 115, 127, 131, 184
military-industrial complex, 16, 59
Miller, Israel, 102, 134–35
Moakley, Joe, 85
Mondale, Walter, 32, 37, 39, 85, 89–90
Montoya, Joseph, 32, 74, 173
Morgan, Robert, 172,
Morgan, Thomas, 94, 153–54, 161, 168, 173, 237
Morgenthau, Hans, 134
Morocco, 99, 120
Morris, Thomas, 37
Morse, Wayne, 32
Mossad, 2, 227
Munich, 32, 39
Murphy, Richard, 124
Muskie, Edmund, 76

Nasser, Gamal Abdel, 19, 23, 27, 30–33, 35, 39, 41, 43, 57, 63, 73, 181, 207
National Association of Arab Americans (NAAA), 18
National Security Council, 28, 33, 76, 123, 177
Nation of Islam, 14
neoconservatism, 15
Nes, David, 73
New Deal, 16, 26
New Left, 14–15, 54, 60, 77
New York Times, 75, 81, 88, 109–10, 129, 135, 138, 147, 154, 156, 162, 229
Nixon, Richard, 2, 4, 16–17, 20, 29, 33, 51, 53–55, 57–59, 62–64, 68–71, 74–80, 83–85, 99, 112,

114–15, 119, 129, 136, 153–54, 184, 188, 190, 210, 220, 229; and Arab-Israeli diplomacy, 5, 20, 56, 58, 63, 67, 73–81, 101–15; and concerns about American Jewish Zionists, 105–6, 112, 114; and military aid to Israel, 6, 20, 55, 58–59, 66–67, 70–72, 78, 80; and Nixon Doctrine, 55–56, 69, 85; and resignation, 20, 109, 113, 115–16, 143, 185; and response to 1973 war, 6, 20, 81–98; and threats to cut off aid to Israel, 20, 82, 106–7, 184
North Vietnam, 154
North Yemen, 179
Nuclear Nonproliferation Treaty (NPT), 49, 52, 57
nuclear weapons, 27, 40, 48, 50, 56, 59, 66, 155, 159, 193
Nunn, Sam, 144

Oakley, Robert, 127, 142, 226
Obama, Barack, 188
Obey, David, 169
occupied territories, 3, 6, 10, 14, 18–19, 23, 34, 37–38, 40, 43, 48, 54, 62, 69, 74–75, 88, 96, 99, 103, 113–14, 117–18, 123, 125, 147, 167, 176, 184–85, 187, 190–93
oil embargo: 1967, 36; 1973–1974, 5–6, 18, 82–83, 88–90, 98–99, 103–5, 114; and fears of, 21–22, 118, 123, 131, 162, 164, 186
O'Neill, Thomas "Tip," 86, 95, 121, 133–34, 139, 174, 190, 226
Organization of Petroleum Exporting Countries (OPEC), 83, 88, 90, 99, 105, 156, 179
Orientalism, 17

Pachachi, Adan, 43
Palestine, 61, 105
Palestine Liberation Organization (PLO), 3, 26, 30 100–101, 103, 120, 123, 148, 155, 159, 162, 180–81, 188, 192, 225–26
Palestinians, 2–3, 14, 25, 30, 92–93, 97, 99, 100–101, 113, 120, 123, 128, 147, 162, 176–77, 179–82, 191–93; refugee crisis of, 25, 38–39, 100, 103, 111, 113, 164; and state for, 3, 100–101, 105, 128, 141, 181, 183, 188, 192–93
Pearson, James, 172
Pell, Claiborne, 39
Pelly, Thomas, 31, 52
Peres, Shimon, 105, 112–13, 125, 127–28, 131, 136, 189, 222
Pepper, Claude, 32,
Percy, Charles, 68, 128–29, 144, 173, 228
Perle, Richard, 130, 147
Petrodollars, 18
Phantom jets, 48, 52–53, 55, 59, 63–65, 68, 73, 77–78, 87
Pickering, Thomas, 124,
Podell, Bertram, 50, 52, 85, 90
Podhoretz, Norman, 15
Portugal, 86
Prince Fahd, 179
Pucinski, Roman, 36–38
Purcell, Graham, 68

Quandt, William, 33, 42, 49, 58, 84, 118, 177–78, 180

Rabin, Yitzhak: as ambassador to United States, 50, 63, 74; and as Israeli prime minister, 110, 112–13, 121, 127, 131, 134, 136, 142–43, 145, 147, 156, 189, 199
Rafiah, Zvi, 127, 130, 141, 144, 147, 227
Rarick, John, 93
Read, Benjamin, 35

Reagan, Ronald, 8, 16, 130, 185
Reassessment, 1975, 20, 116–19, 121–22, 124, 126–27, 131–33, 137–38, 145–47, 149, 156, 189
Redfa, Munir, 2
Reid, Ogden, 37
Riad, Mahmoud, 44
Ribicoff, Abraham, 64, 68, 74–75, 84, 89, 123, 190
Richardson, Elliot, 90
Rinaldo, Matthew, 95
Robertson, Pat, 16
Rockefeller, Nelson, 142
Rogers, William, 5, 58–59, 62, 64, 68, 70, 72–75, 77–78, 142; and Rogers Plan, 57–58, 62, 79; and "second" Rogers Plan, 63, 67
Roncallo, Angelo, 85, 89
Rostow, Eugene, 44
Rostow, Walt, 44, 46
Roth, Bill, 52
Ruckelshaus, William, 90
Rules Committee, House, 153
Ruppe, Philip, 90
Rusk, Dean, 29, 34–35, 44, 52, 64, 136
Rumsfeld, Donald, 45–46, 137, 230
Runnels, Harold, 92, 94
Russia, 47, 192
Ryan, William, 33, 35, 39, 41–42

Sadat, Anwar, 12, 73–75, 79, 84, 99–101, 106, 112, 119–21, 125, 129, 133, 147–48, 165–67, 177–82, 220
Said, Edward, 17
Samu, 23, 30; and U.S. censure of Israel in U. N. Security Council, 30
Saturday Night Massacre, 90–91
Saudi Arabia, 43, 99, 133, 178–80, 182, 189, 226, 228
Saunders, Harold, 5, 44–45, 130, 150
Scalia, Antonin, 154, 233
Scheuer, James, 31
Schlesinger, Arthur, Jr., 153
Schlesinger, James, 98, 107–8, 123
Schweiker, Richard, 69, 84, 144
Scott, Hugh, 51, 68, 74, 76–77, 101, 129
Scott, William, 34
Scowcroft, Brent, 96, 98, 102, 106–7, 110, 127, 132, 142
Sharaf, Abdul-Hamid, 44
Sharm El-Sheikh, 75, 166
Shuster, Elmer, 169
Sikes, Robert, 37, 41–42
Sinai I disengagement agreement, 83, 99, 103, 111, 113
Sinai II disengagement agreement, 2, 5, 8–10, 21, 117–19, 139, 146, 148–52, 155–60, 162–70, 173–76, 184, 186–89, 232
Sinai Peninsula, 23–24, 31, 37–38, 40, 75, 83, 119, 121, 124–25, 131, 150, 155, 159, 182; Abu Rudeis and Ras Sudr oil fields, 120, 125; early warning station, 21, 150, 152, 158–59, 161, 163–65, 170, 175; and Mitla and Gidi passes, 120, 155
Sisco, Joseph, 63, 76, 129–30, 133, 135, 139, 142, 160–61
Skubitz, Joe, 169
Skyhawk jets, 29–30, 45–48, 58, 68, 70–71, 79–80
Smith, Henry, 94
Smith, Terence, 147
Sober, Sidney, 146
Sonnenfeld, Ted, 136, 229
South Vietnam, 154, 174, 180, 188
South Yemen (People's Democratic Republic), 27, 179
Soviet Union, 2, 13–14, 20, 24, 27, 29, 31–32, 38–42, 45, 47–52, 56–64, 60, 63, 69, 72, 74, 78–79, 81, 83–87, 90, 98, 101–2, 105–6, 114, 117–18, 122–23, 137, 175, 178, 188,

193; and invasion of Czechoslovakia, 52; and Operation *Kavkas,* 58, 63; relations with Egypt, 3, 10, 22, 27–28, 33, 41, 47, 50, 53, 56–58, 61, 63, 66, 68, 70–71, 82–85, 99–100, 106, 181–82; relations with Syria, 26–28, 33, 66, 82–83, 85, 100; and restrictions on Jewish emigration, 47, 95–96, 105, 190. *See also* Jackson-Vanik Amendment
Stagflation, 89
Stein, Jacob, 102
Stennis, John C., 67, 70
Stevenson, Adlai II, 229
Stevenson, Adlai III, 89, 171–72
Stoddard, Phillip, 132–33
Stoessinger, John, 134
Stone, Richard, 129, 139–40
Straits of Tiran, 31, 33, 74
Strategic Arms Limitation Treaty (SALT), 79, 95
Stratton, Samuel, 93, 171
Suez Canal, 44, 56–58, 61, 68, 71, 73–74, 78–79, 83, 103, 166
Symington, Stuart, 50–51, 65–66, 138–39, 190
Symms, Steve, 87
Syria, 2, 23, 26–27, 30–31, 33, 36, 38, 44, 66, 82–83, 85–86, 100–101, 104–7, 109–11, 119, 127, 156, 177, 180–81, 207, 221, 226; relations with United States, 35, 87, 100, 105–6, 112–13, 124, 133, 228. *See also* Soviet Union relations with Syria

Talcott, Burt, 95
terrorism, 18, 26, 30, 120, 182, 193, 200, 226
Thant, U, 31
Thompson, S. Fletcher, 50
Tonkin Gulf Resolution, 60, 67, 166, 169, 171
Tower, John, 36, 41, 69, 130, 207
Tripartite Declaration, 1950, 32, 40
Truman, Harry, 13, 32, 55, 117, 229; and arms embargo to Middle East, 4; and recognition of Israel, 4, 61
Trump, Donald J., 188, 193
Tunisia, 99, 180
Tunney, John, 84–85
Turgemon, David, 127, 132–33, 142, 146
Turkey, 174, 226
Tydings, Joseph, 68

United Nations (U.N.), 37–38, 43, 56, 60, 62, 84, 124, 128, 135, 172; Emergency Force (UNEF), 31; General Assembly, 25; Resolution 242, 21, 47–48, 59, 67–68, 82, 87–88, 93–94, 97, 100, 111, 124, 133–35, 148, 155, 164, 166, 168, 180; Security Council, 30, 47
U.S. airlift to Israel, 1973, 71, 86–98
U.S.-Israel special relationship, 1–3, 12, 16–17, 19–20, 25, 32, 35, 40, 45, 53, 82, 96, 181, 190, 192
U.S.-Israel strategic alliance, 1–2, 10, 13, 20, 25, 45–46, 48–49, 53, 55, 57–58, 60, 66, 69, 79, 82, 96, 114, 120, 152, 159, 184–85, 190, 192
USS *Liberty,* 36, 47

Van Thieu, Nguyen, 154
Vance, Cyrus, 135–36, 188, 229
Vanik, Charles, 47, 95–96, 190
Vietnam War (Southeast Asia; East Asia), 2, 4–6, 10, 14–16, 20, 25–26, 29–30, 32, 38, 49–50, 53–57, 60, 62–63, 67, 70, 76, 85–87, 89, 91, 93, 95, 119, 126, 129, 139–40, 142–45, 151, 156, 158, 160, 166, 171, 183–86, 188, 191–92

Waldi, Jerome, 85
War of Attrition, 21, 55, 57–58, 63, 67–68, 118
War Powers Act, 5, 91, 154, 164, 174–75
Warnke, Paul, 53
Washington Post, 73, 75, 110, 156, 160, 162, 168–69
Watergate, 6, 10, 20, 54–55, 81, 90–91, 109–11, 113, 115, 142–44, 153, 157, 185
Watergate Committee, Senate, 153
Weisman, Herman, 102
West Bank, 23–24, 37, 44, 113, 119–20, 124–25, 128, 159, 176–79, 181, 185, 188, 192
Western Europe, 27–28, 83, 86, 88, 172
West Germany, 27–28, 203
Widnall, William, 37, 50
Wiesel, Elie, 134,
Wilson, Bob, 47
Wilson, Charles H., 45
Wolff, Lester, 30, 51, 85, 94
World Jewish Congress, 135
Wright, Jim, 38–39
Wydler, John, 89
Wylie, Chalmers, 94
Wyman, Louis, 34

Yariv, Aharon, 71
Yates, Sidney, 32

Zablocki, Clement, 94, 153–54, 168–69, 171
Zemer, Hannah, 71
Zionism, 13–14, 16, 62, 73
Zionist Federation of America, 102
Zionist Organization of America, 102

Studies in Conflict, Diplomacy, and Peace

Series Editors: George C. Herring, Andrew L. Johns, and Kathryn C. Statler

This series focuses on key moments of conflict, diplomacy, and peace from the eighteenth century to the present to explore their wider significance in the development of U.S. foreign relations. The series editors welcome new research in the form of original monographs, interpretive studies, biographies, and anthologies from historians, political scientists, journalists, and policymakers. A primary goal of the series is to examine the United States' engagement with the world, its evolving role in the international arena, and the ways in which the state, nonstate actors, individuals, and ideas have shaped and continue to influence history, both at home and abroad.

Advisory Board Members

Books in the Series

Truman, Congress, and Korea: The Politics of America's First Undeclared War
Larry Blomstedt

The Legacy of J. William Fulbright: Policy, Power, and Ideology
Edited by Alessandro Brogi, Giles Scott-Smith, and David J. Snyder

The Gulf: The Bush Presidencies and the Middle East
Michael F. Cairo

Reagan and the World: Leadership and National Security, 1981–1989
Edited by Bradley Lynn Coleman and Kyle Longley

A Diplomatic Meeting: Reagan, Thatcher, and the Art of Summitry
James Cooper

American Justice in Taiwan: The 1957 Riots and Cold War Foreign Policy
Stephen G. Craft

Soccer Diplomacy: International Relations and Football since 1914
Edited by Heather L. Dichter

Diplomatic Games: Sport, Statecraft, and International Relations since 1945
Edited by Heather L. Dichter and Andrew L. Johns

Nothing Less Than War: A New History of America's Entry into World War I
Justus D. Doenecke

Aid under Fire: Nation Building and the Vietnam War
Jessica Elkind

Enemies to Allies: Cold War Germany and American Memory
Brian C. Etheridge

Grounded: The Case for Abolishing the United States Air Force
Robert M. Farley

Foreign Friends: Syngman Rhee, American Exceptionalism, and the Division of Korea
David P. Fields

The Myth of Triumphalism: Rethinking President Reagan's Cold War Legacy
Beth A. Fischer

The American South and the Vietnam War: Belligerence, Protest, and Agony in Dixie
Joseph A. Fry

Lincoln, Seward, and US Foreign Relations in the Civil War Era
Joseph A. Fry

The Turkish Arms Embargo: Drugs, Ethnic Lobbies, and US Domestic Politics
James F. Goode

Obama at War: Congress and the Imperial Presidency
Ryan C. Hendrickson

Fourteen Points for the Twenty-First Century: A Renewed Appeal for Cooperative Internationalism
Edited by Richard H. Immerman and Jeffrey A. Engel

The Cold War at Home and Abroad: Domestic Politics and US Foreign Policy since 1945
Edited by Andrew L. Johns and Mitchell B. Lerner

US Presidential Elections and Foreign Policy: Candidates, Campaigns, and Global Politics from FDR to Bill Clinton
Edited by Andrew Johnstone and Andrew Priest

Paving the Way for Reagan: The Influence of Conservative Media on US Foreign Policy
Laurence R. Jurdem

The Conversion of Senator Arthur H. Vandenberg: From Isolation to International Engagement
Lawrence S. Kaplan

Harold Stassen: Eisenhower, the Cold War, and the Pursuit of Nuclear Disarmament
Lawrence S. Kaplan

JFK and de Gaulle: How America and France Failed in Vietnam, 1961–1963
Sean J. McLaughlin

Nixon's Back Channel to Moscow: Confidential Diplomacy and Détente
Richard A. Moss

Breaking Protocol: America's First Female Ambassadors, 1933–1964
Philip Nash

Peacemakers: American Leadership and the End of Genocide in the Balkans
James W. Pardew

The Currents of War: A New History of American-Japanese Relations, 1899–1941
Sidney Pash

Eisenhower and Cambodia: Diplomacy, Covert Action, and the Origins of the Second Indochina War
William J. Rust

So Much to Lose: John F. Kennedy and American Policy in Laos
William J. Rust

The Sailor: Franklin D. Roosevelt and the Transformation of American Foreign Policy
David F. Schmitz

Foreign Policy at the Periphery: The Shifting Margins of US International Relations since World War II
Edited by Bevan Sewell and Maria Ryan

Lincoln Gordon: Architect of Cold War Foreign Policy
Bruce L. R. Smith

Thomas C. Mann: President Johnson, the Cold War, and the Restructuring of Latin American Foreign Policy
Thomas Tunstall Allcock